DAROJI VALLEY

VIJAYNAGARA RESERACH PROJECT MONOGRAPH SERIES

General Editors
JOHN M. FRITZ, University of Pennsylvania
GEORGE MICHELL, London
R. GOPAL, Karnataka Department of Archaeology and Museums

Vol. 1 *Pots and Palaces* by Carla M. Sinopoli

Vol. 2 *The Ramachandra Temple at Vijayanagara* by Anna L. Dallapiccola, John M. Fritz, George Michell and S. Rajasekhara

Vol. 3 *The Vijayanagara Courtly Style* by George Michell

Vol. 4 *Religious Traditions at Vijayanagara as Revealed through its Monuments* by Anila Verghese

Vol. 5 *The Irrigation and Water Supply Systems of Vijayanagara* by Dominic J. Davison-Jenkins

Vol. 6 *Sculpture at Vijayanagara: Iconography and Style* by Anna L. Dallapiccola and Anila Verghese

Vol. 7 *Anegondi: Architectural Ethnography of a Royal Village* by Natalie Tobert

Vol. 8 *Vijayanagara: Architectural Inventory of the Sacred Centre* (in 3 volumes) by George Michell and Phillip B. Wagoner

Vol. 9 *King, Court and Capital: An Anthology of Kannada Literary Sources from the Vijayanagara Period* translated by C.T.M. Kotraiah and edited by Anna L. Dallapiccola

Vol. 10 *Vijayanagara: Archaeological Exploration, 1990-2000, Papers in Memory of Channabasappa S. Patil* (in 2 parts) by John M. Fritz, Robert P. Brubaker and Teresa P. Raczek with the assistance of George Michell

Vol. 11 *Daroji Valley: Landscape History, Place, and the Making of a Dryland Reservoir System* by Kathleen D. Morrison

Jacket Illustration: Topographic map of the eastern part of Daroji Valley.

DAROJI VALLEY

Landscape History, Place, and the Making of a Dryland Reservoir System

Kathleen D. Morrison

MANOHAR

AMERICAN INSTITUTE OF INDIAN STUDIES

2009

First published 2009

ISBN 978-81-7304-779-4

Published by
Ajay Kumar Jain *for*
Manohar Publishers & Distributors
4753/23 Ansari Road, Daryaganj
New Delhi 110 002

Printed at
Salasar Imaging Systems
Delhi 110 035

CONTENTS

ACKNOWLEDGEMENTS

This book traveled an unduly long and tortuous path to existence, a fact which makes the expression of debts even more onerous than usual. The fieldwork on which this work is based took place over the period between 1986 and 2001, much of it on Mondays, the market day in the nearby village of Kamalapura and hence the "free" day from the ordinary work of the Vijayanagara Metropolitan Survey (VMS), a project I co-directed with Carla Sinopoli between 1987 and 1997. For most of the time, my sole fieldwork companion was Mark Lycett who visited innumerable reservoirs, temples, villages, and other places with me and also supplied most of the best ideas incorporated into the text. His contribution to this work is immense. Near the end, students and colleagues from the VMS pitched in to finish the Daroji site descriptions, for which I am very grateful. In 2000, Peter Johansen and Sandra Morrison assisted me for about a week of fieldwork in and around Kurekuppa. Robert Brubaker and Michael Dega worked on a description of VMS-6 from which I drew some material. Inspired, perhaps, by that small fort, Rob completed a dissertation on Vijayanagara fortifications in which he made detailed observations of some of the long walls at the eastern end of the Daroji Valley that I first noticed in 1987. Special mention should be made to the efforts of U.V. Sriniwas, whose trusty Ambassador took me to the furthest corners of the region and who came to know the area almost as well as I did. We shared a personal set of spatial referents for particular locations, most notably, "the place where the car caught on fire", and, I should add, where he refused to go for medical help because I was several kilometers away down a reservoir embankment.

Permission for the research was facilitated by the American Institute of Indian Studies (AIIS), in particular through the efforts of Dr. Pradeep Mehendiratta, who worked tirelessly on our behalf. Research permissions were generously granted by the Government of India and the Archaeological Survey of India; I thank them for the opportunity to work with such an amazing corpus of materials. To my close colleagues in the Karnataka State Directorate of Archaeology and Museums (DAM), my official collaborators for the past twenty-plus years, I extend my sincere thanks. DAM personnel were always helpful when it came to recording inscriptions and hero stones and generously shared their field camp with us for many years. We are all saddened by loss of C.S. Patil and Balasubrahmanya, two valued colleagues and friends from the DAM (Bala having joined the faculty of Kaṇnada University in the interim). I am deeply indebted to Patil's careful research on the immediate pre-Vijayanagara periods in this area and in particular to his work on the Daroji fort and the area around it and on the temples of the Sandur Hills. We discussed the fine points of this analysis at length, usually to the chagrin of waiters who wanted to clear the table. He was perhaps the only person on earth who was as enthralled as I was about reconstructing the details of Daroji Valley history and I sorely miss his comments on the final version of the text.

Phillip Wagoner generously made a translation of the Dharmasagara reservoir inscription; this is to date the only published version of this text and I apologize to him for omitting the diacritics he carefully supplied. Thanks to Phil also for helping me with some icono-graphic issues. Purushothama Billemale shared some unpublished papers on local folklore with me and directed me to some very useful articles about the local hero Kumara Rama. Jim Nye and Bronwen Bledsoe facilitated my work on Colonial-era land records and census data, generously scanning page after page of material from Chicago's special South Asia collection.

In addition to the rather extended fieldwork history behind this book, there is also the long and rather tedious saga of its writing. First one large book, then two, then one again, and finally back to two, this volume has a sibling, *Oceans of Dharma*, which should soon be in press and which addresses some of the issues of power and agricultural production in the Vijayanagara period more specifically. Although *Oceans* relies on the empirical analysis presented on these pages, its point has more to do with the inscription of power on the landscape over a short period of time and somewhat less to do with the long-term landscape histories and place-making processes that concern us here. For all my students, colleagues, and friends who read draft after draft of both expanded and compressed versions, my apologies and thanks.

Funding for the research came from the National Science Foundation, the Wenner-Gren Foundation for Anthropological Research, the National Geographic Society, the Smithsonian Institution, and the University of Chicago. Two research leaves, one from the American Association of University Women and the other in the idyllic setting of the Center for Advanced Studies in the Behavioral Sciences (CASBS) at Stanford, allowed me to write both this book and most of its companion. At CASBS, access to library runners almost certainly slowed down the writing but no doubt enhanced the research as literally everything I read seemed somehow relevant to the argument of the magically expanding and shrinking book project. If nothing else, the shifting contours of this book have taught me a lesson in how not to structure time that I try to pass on to my students.

Pieces of this book were presented as talks at the Netherlands Institute for Advanced Study (NIAS), the University of Pennsylvania Ethnohistory Workshop, the University of California, Berkeley, Stanford University, Northwestern University, the University of New Mexico, the Shanghai meeting of the International Association of Asian Studies, the University of Chicago Workshop on the Global Environment, the University of Wisconsin, Madison, and Daud Ali and Emma Flatt's Hyderabad conference on Deccani gardens. The manuscript has been greatly enriched by the comments of these audiences. Thanks also to the several readers of (and commentators on) the manuscript, in its various guises, including Mark Lycett, Andrew Bauer, Namita Sugandhi, Peter Johansen, Sandra Morrison, C.S. Patil, George Michell, Vernon Scarborough, and Steven Kosiba. Many of the figures were prepared by Peter Johansen and Andrew Bauer, with the labor-intensive initial preparation and inking of the topographic maps done by Oona Paredes longer ago than we care to recall. Anwen Tormey helped with the conversion from the VRP to VMS numbering system. Many, many volunteers in the Paleoecology Lab at Chicago helped with scanning of site plans and typing of site descriptions.

Much credit is also due to John Fritz and George Michell, not only for bringing me to India in the first place, but also for their leadership in establishing this publication series. George, in particular, has been the consummate editor, precise, detail-oriented, and firm, both gently persistent and yet also understanding of the many time constraints that slowed down production.

It would probably not be possible to start on the fieldwork for this book today, as so much has changed in the Daroji Valley with the expansion of Sandur Hills mining and the opening of a huge steel plant near Toranagallu. The volume of traffic through the valley has greatly increased and erosion of red, iron-rich earth from the Sandur Hills has made a substantial impact on the western valley. Neolithic ashmounds are everywhere under attack, mined for their lime content by local people who, trying to make a living, are unaware of their deep antiquity. The expansion of electric pump-sets and deep bore wells has transformed agricultural production in the valley, making some farmers much better off but also creating serious pressure on the already-low water table. Thus, we can see both continuity and change in the multiple constitutions of place, a process which, as we know, will never end. I end, then, with thanks to the people of the Daroji Valley and its environs, people who attended my research with immense curiosity and almost boundless good will, inheritors of the long and fascinating history of this place.

KATHLEEN D. MORRISON

Chapter One

MAKING SOUTH INDIA: LANDSCAPE HISTORIES

> [The king should] bear on his sturdy shoulders the entire circle of the earth, which is surrounded by the seven oceans of salt, sugar, alcohol, ghee, curds, milk, and pure water. (Wagoner 1992: 90, from *Rayavacakamu*, a seventeenth-century Telugu text referring to the Vijayanagara king Krishnadeva Raya)

If you were to walk across the fields, around the bases of rocky hills, and along the colluvial valleys of northern Karnataka in the area around the once-populous but now ruined city of Vijayanagara, you might come across some curious features (Figures 1, 2, and 3). These features look a great deal like the doorways of temples, made of quarried granite slabs and often decorated with formal mouldings and even sculptures. Despite their differences with contemporary sluice gates, it would also be clear from the carefully-constructed tunnels that run from these features and under the embankments of associated runoff-fed reservoirs that these are indeed older sluice gates, elaborately contrived and, for the most part, no longer in active use. Reservoir embankments themselves often preserve histories of violent destruction – powerful floods that breached the dam; of gradual decline – the steady accumulation of silt, of active deconstruction – the mining of sediment or masonry from the dam; or simply years of neglect. Sluices, however, are often painted with red and white stripes. There may be nearby oil lamps, freshly-cut banana fronds, bangles, flowers, and other evidence of offering and worship. These features, five to seven hundred year old abandoned sluices, are also contemporary shrines, living parts of a rural landscape. Even if our goal were only to better understand the present, the long-term histories of these features are still salient, with the specific and varied meaning associated with these features tracking – but never precisely – the changing contexts of human history in the region. For the development of any historical understanding, however, these long-term records are essential and, as this book demonstrates, such records have powerfully shaped both the "natural" and "built" forms of the south Indian landscape, as well as the possibilities for past and present residents of the area.

This is a study of long-term landscape history and an attempt to track the specific trajectory of change in one large valley in southern India, the Daroji Valley, a place that moved in and out of different regimes of land use, politics, and economic organization. I focus on a single region in order to make clear that the contemporary landscape is itself a complex, accretional product that cannot be fully understood without reference to longer term human and environmental history. The concept of *landscape history*, as I use it here, embraces a fundamental contradiction and grows, quite explicitly, from my own experience of working more than a decade and a half on a specific *place*, research that is spatially rooted, on the one hand, and temporally inferential on the other. Although scholars and residents alike experience the world only in terms of contemporary places, we all assign, in different ways, historicity to these places and construct historical sequences and accounts from present features and their distribution.[1] This is accomplished in varying ways – though forms of oral and written memory or through the techniques of archaeology and paleoecology – but however this history is made, it builds from (and thus also may change) the physical world itself and our understandings of it.

Figure 1. VMS-417, Vijayanagara period sluice gate, in worship.

Figure 2. VMS-4, Malapannagudi reservoir sluice with donor portraits.

Figure 3. Vijayanagara period sluice gate and tunnel in worship.

Because no single work can encompass everything, I focus here on human land use and agricultural production, tracking the creation, use, recreation, and reconstruction of a particular agricultural landscape through time. In this I make the point that agricultural landscapes, as such, are not necessarily solely or even primarily "economic" or "mundane" (cf. Barrett 1994: 132) as opposed to some separate, isolable landscape we may term "sacred". Instead, places where food was produced were *both* economically important *and* sacred, imbued with reference to the actions of gods and heroes, both of whom often resided in and around the fields and other places where south Indian women and men labored on a daily basis. Most clearly, Vijayanagara reservoirs were meant to both invoke and to *be* monuments, (eternal) oceans, and even temples, as well as technological devices and physical manifestations of elite power, influence, just rule, and right action.

At the center of this book is a rural region, albeit one that was once near a large city, and although I do consider the landscapes of surrounding cities as well as the demands of their inhabitants, the majority of this work deals with what were largely agrarian worlds. In these worlds we can see both continuity and change, both in ways in which places were configured and reconfigured, and in their interrelations with the larger world. Although the temporal scope of this volume is extensive – nearly five millennia – a great deal of the work focuses on the period between about AD 1300 and 1700, when the transformation of the Daroji Valley was most extensive, and when it became the locus of a complex of interconnected reservoirs, an expansion that changed the very shape of the land as well as the conditions of life for most, if not all, of its inhabitants.

Although the life-histories of specific places might hold some interest in their own right, my intention in detailing some of the landscapes of southern India and their transformations is directed toward a larger objective, and that is to begin to understand the implications for local residents of being rooted (placed) in a specific locality. The power relations that enmeshed people in this area at different times were themselves profoundly structured, though never fully determined, by local landscape histories, by the specifics of place. Here I am concerned, not only with past agency but with the structures in place and in flux at different times which constituted possible fields of action.[2] To follow the sociopolitical history of southern India, one must attend to its geographic and architectural dimensions – decisions about regional settlement distributions, temple styles, investments in different types and forms of agricultural facilities, road construction, and many other actions worked together with local environmental variation, tax policy, cultural values of foodstuffs, ritual practice, social organization, and economic forms, to create a complex, temporally-contingent and spatially-situated field of power relations.[3] Thus, it seems impossible to separate place, as an historically-constructed product, from relations of power and prestige. It is this nexus which I explore in this volume.

More specifically, this work examines the long-term landscape history of one peripheral place – the Daroji Valley – building toward a comparison with both the urban center it once served as well as other locations around the city. These disparate places, built over millennia of human action, were associated with different forms of agricultural production and residents of each place were thus differentially integrated into past political economies in ways they could not fully control. The contrast between the ecological, economic, social, and ritual possibilities of dry farming *versus* permanent irrigated agriculture is especially salient here, as are the human consequences of agricultural expansion and intensification in both urban and rural areas. It is this human dimension, and especially past power relations, that I seek to elucidate here and, critically, to link with the landscapes they are a part of.

THE TIME AND SPACE OF LANDSCAPE HISTORY

My account in this volume incorporates two kind of narrative strands. These are, on the one hand, a reconstructed historical sequence built around the inferential dimension of time and, on the other, the untidy space of the archaeological landscape where structures, features, and places "out of time" constantly impinge on one another in ways that standard field practices tend to elide or fail to acknowledge altogether. Like many progressive schemes of cultural evolution which order contemporaneous variability into pseudo-historical sequences of change (see Morrison 1996 for a more complete discussion), the temporal dissection of unified material landscapes similarly creates time out of space, or better yet, *out of place.* In archaeology, then, reporting practices of the discipline thus tend to erase practitioners' own lived experiences of the landscape, as well as those of past and present others.

The first narrative that structures my paper – the chronologically-ordered, historical reconstruction of some aspects of life in southern India between about 3000 BC and AD 1700 – is, then, actually the second one created. This sequence is outlined in Chapter 2. In this Chapter I mention many kinds of features that we will meet out on the landscape of the Daroji Valley; here I place them chronologically by time period, an archaeological convenience whose conventional character is immediately evident. That is, if we are now able to locate and record these features and structures, then they "belong" as much to the present (and thus to all the "periods" after their creation) as they do the time of their initial construction. The perhaps necessary violence that the creation of distinct phases does to actual lived landscapes, past and present, must therefore, be kept in mind.

Throughout this study, I try to balance chronological diagnosis with a more place-based perspective where features and structures built at different times, all with complex life histories, sit side by side on the landscape. Although a good part of this volume is dedicated to an analysis of reservoirs (of which more below), a case could also be made that this landscape – and indeed all landscapes in their own context – consists of a wide variety of what we might call "south Indian places", specific kinds of features and places such as ashmounds, megaliths, forests, temples, and hero stones, features and places that, while they might be found elsewhere, often have distinctive local meanings and histories.

Perhaps the central example of this is the reservoir, a type of agricultural facility of great importance in the dry regions of southern India and Sri Lanka. Reservoirs, or tanks, as they are commonly called, have not received much systematic study. This lack of attention may be due in part because they occur in relatively late contexts and thus fall more often into the academic realm of art history than archaeology, as these fields tend to be defined in South Asia, and, as such, may seem a bit too utilitarian to merit much analysis. Further, what archaeology is carried out on later time periods has tended to focus on monumental architecture and on urban locations at the expense of more modest scale or rural remains. Reservoirs can, however, be both monumental and urban – as well as architecturally elaborated – although they are more often small, remote, and only minimally decorated, if at all. Not since Brohier (1934), perhaps, has there been a full-length study of a specific corpus of reservoirs.[4] All across southern India and Sri Lanka are tens of thousands of reservoirs that channeled and controlled runoff and soil, that collected the monsoon rains or water from perennial rivers, that allowed the production of crops and watered animals and humans in a thirsty landscape. Reservoirs shaped the very ways in which people could move across the region, either creating barriers of water, mud, and masonry or carrying paths high and dry above the fields. The Daroji system of interconnected reservoirs is, further, an example of a broader pattern of interlinked agricultural facilities found across large parts of southern India (Morrison 1994a) and is thus in some sense exemplary rather than unique.

Reservoirs have a long history in South Asia. In southern India, Iron Age sites have the earliest known examples. The Iron Age dates to between approximately 1000 and 500 BC. Iron Age reservoirs differ morphologically from Vijayanagara reservoirs in that they lack both masonry facing and, apparently, sluice arrangements. In and near the Vijayanagara survey area, pre-Vijayanagara reservoirs (Iron Age/Early Historic; the Early Historic may be taken to include the period between 500 BC and AD 500) include both upland reservoirs in mortuary contexts and reservoirs near settlements that may have also served some agricultural purpose. No isolated (that is, not associated with either settlements or mortuary sites) reservoirs from the Iron Age/Early Historic are known to exist in the Vijayanagara study area. However, there has never been any systematic study of Iron Age reservoirs beyond this small region and this lack may be more apparent than real. Thus, the potential role of reservoir irrigation in south Indian agriculture before about AD 500 is still far from clear.

Following the Early Historic, reservoirs played an important role in the so-called Early Medieval (AD 500-1300) or Early Middle period, as numerous textual sources make clear. However, Early Middle period settlement in the survey area was relatively sparse and we have no archaeological indications of reservoirs dating to this period.[5] In the larger region surrounding our survey area there are, however, many Early Middle period settlements and temples but very few reservoirs. Thus, although reservoirs were certainly in use in prior to the Vijayanagara period, they appear not to have been a major component of Early Middle agricultural strategies in this part of northern Karnataka.

With the founding of the city of Vijayanagara in the early 1300s and the subsequent expansion of settlement and explosion in population in the region, reservoirs became an increasingly important component of larger agrarian and political strategies. Important from the start of the Vijayanagara period, reservoirs also constituted a key form of agricultural intensification in the sixteenth century or Late Vijayanagara period, especially in regions such as the Daroji Valley where canal irrigation was not feasible. Although the Daroji Valley has evidence of a long history of human habitation and use, it was during the sixteenth century that the system of interlinked reservoirs described in this book really took shape; this was also the century prior to the twentieth in which the occupation of the valley was the densest.

Reservoirs played variable roles in the processes of Vijayanagara agricultural intensification and collapse. The situation in the Daroji Valley differed significantly from, for example, the area north of the city of Vijayanagara and just north of the Tungabhadra river where reservoirs from the Early and Middle Vijayanagara periods were superseded by canals and never regained their importance. In this sense, then, this study of the Daroji Valley cannot be made to stand for the agrarian history of the entire region. What is common to most parts of the study area, however, is the way in which the vast majority of reservoirs fell out of use after (or in some cases, during) the Vijayanagara period, a collapse that has, in some ways, facilitated archaeological research. Very few of the reservoirs from the original system still effectively function. The most notable "living" reservoir is the Daroji reservoir itself, a facility with a long and complex history of maintenance and reconstruction.

Reservoirs, as I discuss in more detail in Chapter 4, were one, if not *the* premier form of water collection and storage in the dry regions of southern India and Sri Lanka. Although many reservoirs, even ones first built as long as a thousand years ago, continue to be used and to be important, new forms of irrigation, particularly the electric pump-set (a well with an electric pump), are gradually moving into areas formerly dominated by reservoir irrigation. Further, as we shall see, reservoirs of a certain scale require coordinated labor and resources for their continued maintenance (to say nothing of their initial construction); new forms of economic organization often mitigate against the continuing effective use of reservoir irrigation. The availability of electricity and deep bore wells has also modified the relationships between nucleated settlements and reservoirs. While once all rural villages in this region were located next to a reservoir, now towns and villages can survive some distance from their reservoirs as most now have wells with pumps (hand-pumped, for the most part) within the settlement itself and residents need not rely on reservoir water for drinking and cooking. In spite of these changes in the roles of reservoirs, they remain extremely important facilities for agricultural irrigation, stock watering, washing clothes, and gathering aquatic products such as fish. In the past, reservoirs were also important sources of water for domestic uses. If we are to understand Vijayanagara reservoirs in general, it will be necessary to consider them within the larger contexts of agricultural organization and land use history in the Vijayanagara period and beyond; if we are to understand the Daroji Valley in particular, we must pay attention to the special role played by reservoirs in humanizing and making fertile the dry zones of southern India.

THE MAKING OF SOUTH INDIA

In the simplest possible terms, two of the key questions that lie behind my adoption of a long-term perspective are these: How have south Indian society and the south Indian landscape come to be the way they are now? What are the salient processes of change through which we might understand this history? My concern, then, is both with process and with the substantive trajectory of change and stability in this remarkable region. South India today is multilingual; there are four major south Indian languages all belonging to the Dravidian language family, many minor ones, and a significant admixture of non-Dravidian languages including Urdu, English, Hindi, Marwari and others. This is a powerfully hierarchical society in which distinctions of class, caste, ethnicity, and gender are marked and institutionalized in a number of ways including marriage patterns, cuisine, dress, and occupation, among others. It is a religiously diverse region, with Shaivite, Vaishnavite, and Goddess-worshipers, Jains, Muslims, Christians, and others.

There is a complex agro-pastoral economy which includes both intensive irrigation agriculture and extensive dry farming; patterns of social, class, and community distinction also follow this divide, with rice the preferred food of those wealthy enough to afford it and Sorghum and other millets the staples of the poor. Regional vegetation patterns and even some landforms have been radically transformed by human action; forests have been denuded and transformed, weed floras include aggressive New World taxa, and drainage patterns have been radically altered. Settlement patterns are strongly aggregated with agglutinated villages, towns and cities; political power resides at a number of levels from the locality to the nation and, in spite of significant political centralization, power relations are often shifting and contested.

This is, of course, a very simple picture of a complex world, but one that is already quite familiar by around the fourteenth century AD, the beginning of what historians often call the "Late Middle" period. In my first major field project, the Vijayanagara Metropolitan Survey (VMS), my colleagues and I sought to understand the structures of and changes in this important era (fourteenth to sixteenth centuries), when forms of production, social organization, and politics changed significantly and when many of the features of south Indian society that would be so energetically recorded and represented by British colonial observers from the seventeenth century onward came into being. So, while there were quite a number of significant differences between, for example, sixteenth- and nineteenth-century southern India, it would not be right to say that these were entirely different and incommensurate worlds. This is an important point, since a great deal of the historical and ethnographic information we have available to us comes filtered through this colonial lense.

If we take a longer-term view, we can see that some features long thought to be "natural" parts of the south Indian world have instead a complex history – here I mention deforestation, hierarchy, social differentiation, settlement aggregation, occupational differentiation, the economic and symbolic importance of rice agriculture, the dominance of Hinduism and of temple-based forms of worship as just a few examples. Tracing out any of these issues shows us first of all that historically and ethnographically documented states of affairs are profoundly historically constituted, far from inevitable, and perhaps most intriguing, shows us that much of the past of any given place was radically different from any historically or ethnographically described situation.

When I started my analysis of the system of interlinked Vijayanagara reservoirs in the Daroji Valley, I had no idea that the project would last for so many years and lead me down so many different roads. In the beginning I conceived of the Daroji Valley study as one case in an analysis of reservoirs that would take into account all reservoirs in our survey area. Reservoirs not only directly facilitate changes in the structure and content of agricultural production, but they also operate in a realm of ritual politics and economics, as discussed below. Thus, a focus on the facilities themselves seemed to be a reasonable way to approach problems of both landscape history and its political/ritual constitution while contributing to the substantive record of south Indian archaeology. However, a reservoir-focused approach began to appear increasingly problematic in light of the complex internal differentiation of Vijayanagara agricultural systems and the importance of *all* kinds of facilities and strategies of production for understanding any other (cf. Morrison 1995a). Further, it is clear that agricultural production is itself profoundly implicated in political, social and ritual practice and as such, my consideration of the salient features of this agrarian landscape continued to grow and I soon realized that reservoirs, however important they were to agricultural production and stock grazing, must always be situated within larger cultural landscapes. Consequently, I changed my focus to constructing an agricultural history of the Daroji Valley, part of a larger study of the region. Although I still plan to carry out that larger study, it is clear that our understanding of the agricultural history of the Daroji Valley is still far from complete. In addition to data from excavation and additional paleoecological work, very close survey of the sort that took us ten years to complete for the region to the north of the valley would be required to really map out all the small-scale agricultural features and to make sure that settlements, roads, temples, and other features of importance to understanding changing patterns of land use were sufficiently well understood. Nevertheless, I have amassed a great deal of spatial information on archaeological features in and around the valley, information that moves us quite a bit beyond a simple study of reservoirs, and at least the major contours of land use patterns and settlement are clear.

In the end, I have returned to a version of my original plan. In this volume, I focus closely on reservoirs – which, after all, were the primary form of agricultural feature in this valley – moving from a more general discussion of Vijayanagara reservoirs to closer descriptions of those in the Daroji system. Beyond this, however, I also present the beginnings of a broader landscape history of the Daroji Valley, a history that cannot be understood in any case without a close study of reservoirs. This dual focus, on reservoirs as objects of human manufacture and of institutional investment on the one hand, and on the specific trajectory of human land use and landscape transformation in one valley, on the other hand, moves us rather quickly between the general and the very specific, between institutional analysis and generalization and close description of material features.

I see this study, then, as a kind of experiment in landscape history, an exercise which, I argue, is intimately connected with the local and with changing contexts of places in time and space. If this is correct, then landscape histories, at least ones that are concerned with a human scale (which is to say all anthropological landscape histories), must *necessarily* attend to locality while still working toward a broader view. In an attempt to create this kind of close reading of a particular landscape, I have situated this study in a relatively small space and in a place that can be argued to have had its own distinct culturally-assigned identity for at least some periods of time. How we might move between localities and larger contexts is an important question, as is the transition from particularities to generalities. I claim no solution to these issues. Instead I present a trial effort that focuses on selected landscape elements – especially those having to do with agricultural production, settlement, and ritual – in a very particular place. This study, however, also moves out from that place to consider it in the contexts of its larger world and, importantly, to move beyond place itself to consider some of the implications of these histories for the people who lived and worked there.

RESEARCH METHODS

My approach to this project has been to make use of multiple forms of evidence, not all of which tell us about the same kinds of things. Because few people are specialists in all these fields, I have attempted to explain each clearly and avoid jargon. Three main forms of information shape my account. The first is the material record; archaeological, architectural, and artifactual patterns (objects that are overtly cultural) as well as anthropogenic landforms, soil and sediment patterns, and drainage routes (objects acted on but not solely of human manufacture). The second is the textual record. This includes, importantly, Middle Period (see Chapter 2) inscriptions in stone and on copper plates as well as religious and literary texts and accounts of visitors to the region. More information is presented on these sources below (see Morrison 1995b; Morrison and Lycett 1994, 1997 for a more complete discussion). Thirdly, my interpretations of vegetation history derive from paleoenvironmental analysis I carried out in a number of contexts both near the city and in the Daroji Valley (see Morrison 1995a for more information). Here I limit my explanation to research on the material record.

Most of the archaeological and architectural information presented in this volume is based on original fieldwork (Figure 4). The systematic, intensive surface survey project known as the VMS (1987-97, co-directed by Morrison and Sinopoli) was devoted to documenting the area around the great city of Vijayanagara, in order to place the city into its regional context.[6] In that project, we surveyed a 50 per cent sample of 8 *c.* 20 square kilometers blocks of land around the city, covering the ground very closely (20 meters crew spacing) and systematically. In practice, our ground coverage was always more than 50 per cent as we documented all archaeological remains we encountered, whether or not they fell in the sample transects. We located, recorded, mapped, photographed, and described all archaeological sites we encountered and collected and analyzed artifacts from most of them. In this area, then, we can be confident that we have recorded most large sites in the 8 blocks and most sites of all size in the sampled transects. My discussion of the city and the irrigated zone around it (and see Morrison in press b) is largely based on this work though I also rely on my own and others' work within the city as well.[7]

One component of the VMS was a more extensive program of documentation within a much larger area around the city, an area that includes all of the Daroji and Avinamodugu Valleys. Here survey was less intensive and systematic, using ground-checking of features noted on Survey of India maps, visits to villages and temples, and exploration on foot. I conducted most of this work alone or with Mark Lycett; near the end of the more than ten years I studied the Daroji Valley, I did divert some VMS survey teams to assist me. As noted in Chapter 8, coverage of the Avinamodugu Valley was selective; within the Daroji Valley, however, I have visited each known reservoir, village, and temple and have discovered and recorded many, many more of these and other cultural remains. With the exception of VMS-110, discussed in Chapter 5, we did not excavate any of these sites.

ORGANIZATION OF THE WORK

The theoretical concerns of this project sketched out in this Chapter are more fully explored in Morrison (in press b). There I discuss in some detail my approach to political ecology, linking this notion more explicitly with that of landscape history. In Chapter 2, I relate, out of order in some sense, an historical, narrative account of the history of the Daroji region, including some discussion of the basic forms and tempos of south Indian agriculture as well as of the kinds of landscape modification entailed by different productive forms.[8] Agricultural production in the Vijayanagara period was intimately connected with forms of prestation and investment involving both

Figure 4. The Greater Metropolitan Region, with inset map of India.

temples and local politics. These connections, known primarily from texts, resonate in the physical forms of reservoirs and of the landscape.

Chapters 3 and 4 focus on various kinds of "south Indian places" such as ashmounds, megaliths, temples, and reservoirs, taking the features themselves rather than their dates of construction as the basic frame of reference. Because of their importance to this analysis, Chapter 4 is dedicated to the morphology, meaning, and functioning of Middle Period reservoirs. Some of the variability in reservoir form, scale, and operation is considered, as are the relationships between reservoirs and other kinds of soil and water control devices. In this Chapter I also discuss the problems of dating individual facilities and consider some of the formal links between reservoirs and other kinds of architecture.

Chapter 5, a discussion of the western Daroji Valley, begins the actual study of the Daroji valley and its material landscape. I have divided the Daroji Valley into three major sections; the western valley, the western part of the main valley, and the eastern part of the main valley, the two primary divisions differentiated by the direction of runoff flow and hence drainage into reservoirs and fields. Chapters 6 and 7 describe the main valley, which culminates in the massive Daroji reservoir. The main valley has several isolable clusters of reservoirs and settlements and bears the scars of several episodes of construction and reconstruction.

Chapter 8 moves us out of the Daroji Valley proper, to consider the Avinamodugu Valley, a more remote appendage of the Daroji Valley where trajectories of change and patterns of continuity differed from the Daroji Valley pattern. Finally, in Chapter 9, I present a broad overview of what this analysis has revealed about the Daroji valley, providing some synthesis of the more detailed descriptions found in Chapters 5 through 8. I then take up some of the themes discussed in this Chapter, including the possible roles of reservoirs and other landscape features in agricultural as well as social and political change. Here I will suggest that these processes are profoundly anchored to local politics, ecology, and landscape history – the reason this book spends so much energy on local detail. If such processes have very localized contents, at the same time they certainly have some generalizable contours. I conclude by considering some possible shapes of these contours and how we might navigate the difficult terrain between local histories and larger questions.

NOTES

1. Compare Binford's discussion of the central dilemma of archaeology; that we experience the archaeological record only as a contemporary phenomenon and that any statements about past action are, necessarily, inferential (1983, and see Binford 1982). I also thank Mark Lycett (1995) for his constant insistence that archaeological excavation and survey are, fundamentally, studies of particular locations, of *places* rather than, for example, people, problems, or time periods.
2. Here I use the term metaphorically, but of course many of these fields were literally fields. As I will demonstrate, localized possibilities for agricultural production counted as among the most important factors in the range of responses to cultural-political opportunities and constraints.
3. Using the notion of architecture in its broadest sense, to include the built environment more broadly; generally I will refer to this material world, especially as modified by human action, as the archaeological record.
4. As this volume was being completed, Mosse (2003) published an excellent ethnographic study of a reservoir system in Tamil Nadu.
5. The term Middle here replaces Medieval. There is generally a division between the early (*c.* AD 500-1300) and late Middle periods (AD 1300-1700, when the Early Modern period begins). These divisions are by no means universally agreed upon. Obviously, "middle" is only a scant improvement over "medieval", but, I would say, represents an important step toward breaking South Asian history away from implicit European parallels and their presumed developmental comparisons.
6. Some publications from the survey include Morrison 1995; Morrison and Sinopoli 1992; Sinopoli and Morrison 1995; and various papers in Fritz, Brubaker, and Raczek 2006.
7. Generally, speaking research inside the city comes from one of three institutional contexts: (1) the Archaeological Survey of India; (2) the Karnataka

State Directorate of Archaeology and Museums; or (3) the Vijayanagara Research Project directed by Fritz and Michell. I have also used a few older descriptions of the city by scholars and visitors.

8. Out of order in the sense that, as I have argued, physical things, places, and memories take inferential priority to (reconstructed) histories, whether the latter come from oral histories, written texts, archaeology, or paleoecology. I practice this inversion deliberately, in order to make later chapters more understandable.

Chapter Two

BEYOND THE LOCAL: THE DAROJI VALLEY IN TIME

> It is not just that "places" serve to remind us of stories that are associated with them; in certain respects, the places only exist (in the sense that they are identified by name) because they have stories identified with them. But once they acquire this story-based existence, the landscape acquires the power of "telling the story". (Leach 1985: 356)

One paradox of place may be the way in which places, as such, appear and disappear at different analytical scales.[1] Linked to this is the recursive nature of understanding involved in the study of any particular place; the "larger picture" is one abstracted from many localities, each with its own story and salience, but the history of any locality is difficult, if not impossible to understand without recourse to that larger picture. In examining the Daroji Valley, while looking closely at the valley itself and its transformations through time, we will have to ask when and how the world outside came to the valley and, reciprocally, how the valley itself contributed to that larger world. How did people living in and using this region relate to people and places outside – how were structures of meaning, power relations, material flows, networks of affect and knowledge spun across the valley's places and how did these involve the valley's residents? Clearly, these kinds of questions open enormous areas of inquiry and even a detailed landscape history such as the one I present here can only begin to touch on this history, a history as large as the time and space of the valley itself, something like Borges' map that precisely matches, at the same scale, the physical world it (tries to) represent.

My treatment of these connections is, then, highly selective, partly because of the impossibility of addressing them all, but also because of the differential impact of the actions of people in different eras on our region and the differential nature of the evidence about those actions. To a large extent, my discussion follows the land use history of the valley itself, taking its cues from the material and textual records of change. However, within this framework, I focus on several periods of radical change and – what must be equally noted and problemetized – what we might call *radical continuity*. The Southern Neolithic, the earliest period for which we have substantial evidence of human presence in the Daroji Valley, involved very different patterns of residence, land use, mobility, and landscape marking than did later periods.[2] The Iron Age and Early Historic, both poorly understood as yet, were also times of significant transformation but eras which left somewhat more modest marks on the valley landscape, a pattern which contrasts sharply with that of the Tungabhadra basin just a few kilometers to the north. In this study I focus particularly on the Middle periods, the centuries between about AD 1000 and 1600, centuries during which the valley landscape was significantly transformed and many of basic patterns established that continue to structure all subsequent experiences of the region. In the Early Middle period, in particular, we can see for the first time the valley and its environs *as* a particular, named locality, a place integrated into supraregional political formations in specific ways, perhaps the very reason that this particular local identity can be seen to emerge. This identity continued, and was to a certain extent transformed with the Late Middle period or Vijayanagara-era transformation of the valley, a reworking of the topography, economy, settlement, and ritual structure of the valley

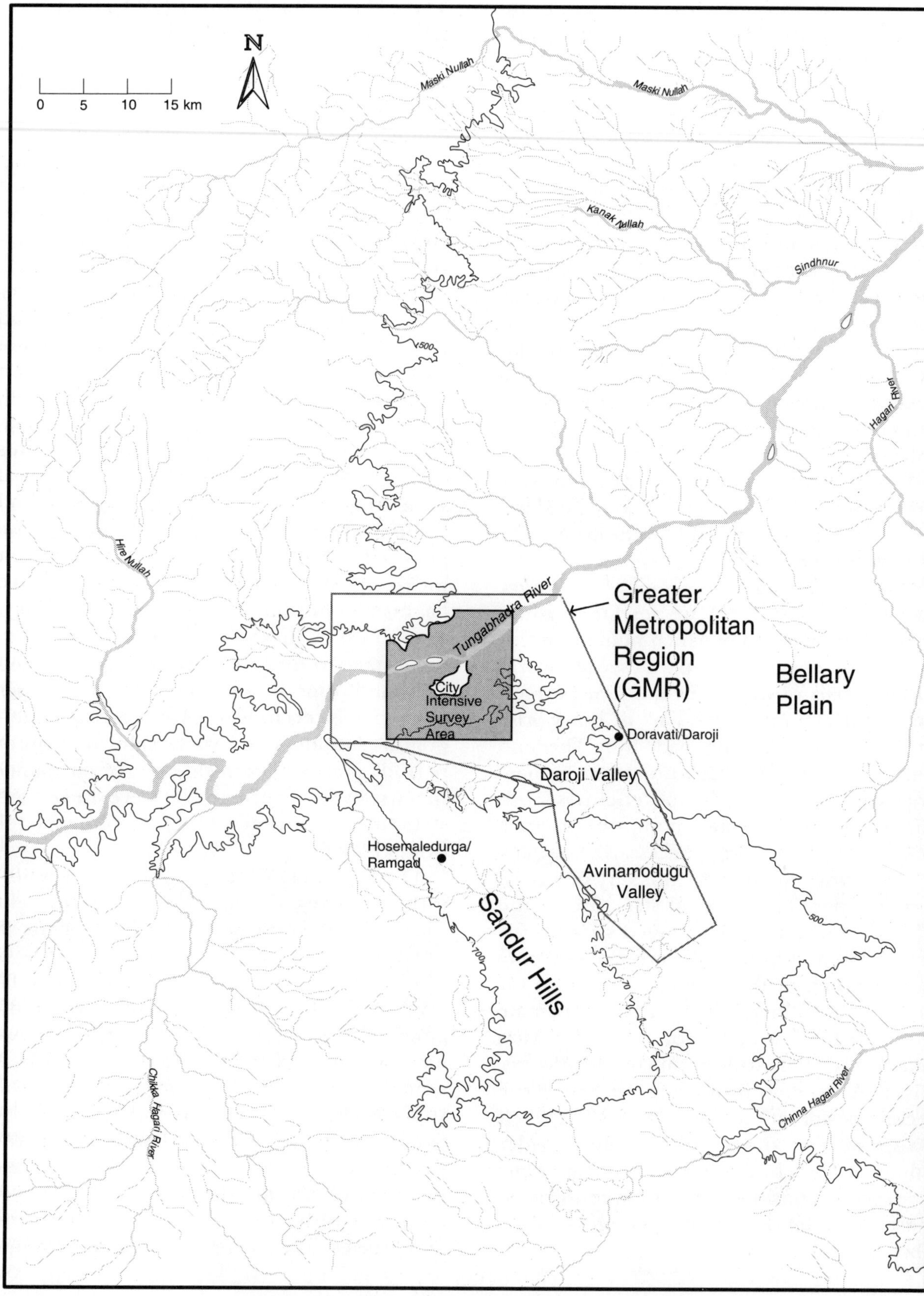

Figure 5. Daroji Valley, in the context of the larger region.

that was more thoroughgoing and profound than that of any time before or after. The Vijayanagara period, a time of radical change in the valley, is then, of necessity, by its sheer physical presence, the primary focus of this book (Figure 5). Although this discussion the Daroji region touches on information from later periods, it is systematic only until around the beginning of the seventeenth century. Of course, this re-constructed time line should not obscure the fact that my enquiry took place much later, between AD 1987 and 2002, and my observations on the valley landscape are thus themselves temporally situated in a particular way. I take this to be not a weakness but a strength, a chance to view some of the long-term consequences of the periods of greatest analytical interest here, consequences evident in, for example, patterns of contemporary worship and agricultural production, the placement of roads, and the distribution of soils, just to name a few.

Before discussing some issues of the larger history of southern India, we need to consider the biophysical world of which humans in this region were (and are) one part. I see this world as itself a part of the landscape – or perhaps more clearly, humans are part of this world, both making it and being made by it. The land itself, then, is not mere backdrop to the human-centered "scape"; landscape encloses both human and non-human components in a dynamic, often confusing, necessarily complex set of relations we encode, not very precisely, as landscapes. The physical structure of the valley and its biota have changed significantly over the last four thousand years, making some understanding of these changes essential for any study of human history across this same time. In the following sections I briefly review some of the evidence on climate, landforms, soils, and vegetation, moving on to a more specific consideration of the Daroji Valley itself as a spatial unit and to some of the broader outlines of south Indian history that help frame more specific considerations of the constructed landscape of the valley that follow in Chapters 5 through 8.

THE STRUCTURE OF THE LONG RUN: LAND AND CLIMATE

The region considered here is part of the semi-arid uplands of the Karnatak plateau, immediately south of the much larger Deccan Plateau, whose southern border is the Tungabhadra River. In contrast to the Deccan shield, the basal geology of the Karnatak Plateau consists largely of a gneissic complex (Krishnamurthy 1978; Naqvi and Rogers 1987). This material, more commonly known as granite, forms the raw material of the Hampi-Daroji Hills, a series of low, northwest-southeast trending outcrops that run both north and south of the Tungabhadra River and shape the dominant physical impression of the landscape today. These granitic hills have weathered into what look like large heaps of rounded boulders, some huge, some smaller (Figures 6 and 7), features which provide a visual framework that powerfully shapes one's overall impression of the region. As discussed below, however, there has been significant regional deforestation and erosion off of these hills. It would, therefore, be mistake to directly map the stark, striking, hilly landforms of today onto past landscapes. Even so, it is certainly true that particular large granitic boulders and rocky hills were, in all periods places of significance, often named places, even where there were never any structures or other obtrusive remains (cf. Bradley 2000).

The Deccan Plateau is a vast volcanic shield formed during the late Cretaceous to early Tertiary. It contains valuable deposits of precious and semi-precious stones, some of which occur in river gravels, occasionally as far south as the Tungabhadra. Striking across the granitic base of the Karnatak plateau are two narrow bands of metamorphic schist which sandwich our region. Of importance to this study is the southern band that forms the Sandur Hills, the highest landforms in the region (600 to 900 meters, above a base elevation of 300 to 600 meters). The Sandur Hills not only support a more stable and developed soil and vegetation than the Hampi-

Figure 6. Regional landscape with granitic hills and irrigated fields.

Figure 7. Regional landscape, Hampi-Daroji granitic hills.

Daroji Hills, but they also contain rich deposits of ores, including manganese and iron. For this reason, they are currently under intense pressure from strip mining and are literally being blown away each day by mine blasting (Morrison 2007). Sandur Hills iron ore was subject to intensive human exploitation by the Early Historic period and perhaps as early as the Iron Age. Archaeological evidence of intensive iron-working at VMS-110 in the Daroji Valley begins in the Early Historic (Chapter 5); chemical analyses of slags and ores from smelting locations throughout the region indicate that Sandur ores continued to be employed through the Vijayanagara period. As discussed below, the Sandur Hills make up the southern edge of the Daroji Valley and the southern and western edges of the Avinamodugu Valley, and are extremely important watersheds for monsoon runoff.

The dry and warm south Indian climate is dominated by the tempo and intensity of the summer monsoons. This region experiences one major rainy season each year, at the time of the southwest or advancing monsoon, approximately between June and September. Within this period, there is a bimodal pattern of precipitation, rainfall exhibiting a minor peak in early summer, around June, followed by a larger peak in late September or early October. However, these patterns may vary so that in any given year the expected rains may fail to come at the right moment in the growing season, or fail to come at all. Although there is a minor contribution made by winter rainfall (the so-called northeast or retreating monsoon), in practice this rainfall is erratic and is of less importance than elsewhere in the south. Average annual rainfall hovers around 500 millimeters year, but this figure is highly variable and rainfall in any particular year may vary markedly from the mean, a dilemma common to many semi-arid regions. Also like other dry regions, rain showers may be very localized and thus coverage can be quite uneven. Partly because of the region's aridity, the Tungabhadra river and its tributaries formed the major foci of settlement in the region until the thirteenth century and, until the middle of the twentieth century, the Tungabhadra was the only source of water for perennial irrigation. The twentieth-century Tungabhadra dam project, begun prior to Indian independence in 1947 and completed afterward, has had a significant effect on the river regime, controlling and regulating the flow of this once-turbulent river, although it has not completely eliminated summer floods.

Frost is unknown in this part of the world and temperatures are generally warm so that water and, secondarily, soil, form the major non-human factors structuring opportunities for agricultural production. As discussed below, however, it is in fact hardly possible to separate such "natural" factors as edaphic conditions (soil depth, pH, grain size, texture, color, organic content, and nutrient levels, for example), water availability, and slope, from "cultural" factors such as access to land, labor, seeds, traction, manure, and outlets for produce in the context of the highly transformed, complex anthropogenic environment of pre-colonial south India. All these natural conditions were, in fact, susceptible to manipulation and the face of the land had already assumed a much modified form even before the Late Vijayanagara period, the time of major expansion into and transformation of the Daroji Valley.

Change Through Time: The Monsoons

Although soils, slopes, and vegetation are often viewed as essentially unchanging components of the natural environment, this cannot be assumed but must instead be demonstrated. Some changes in vegetation, particularly, as well as possibilities for agriculture, depended on the intensity and timing of the monsoon rains, patterns which appear to have changed through time. Paleoclimate data for southern India are scarce and in many cases we must extrapolate from north Indian or even global patterns. This is not as problematic as one might think since South Asian climates are strongly determined by the monsoon, especially the southwest or summer monsoon. These rains are influenced by jet streams which operate on a sub-global scale so that, for example, the East Tropical jet that links north India and Tibet with northern tropical and subtropical Africa (van Campo and Gasse 1993) powerfully influences rainfall on both continents. Thus, at a general level, paleoclimate studies from one continent may be quite relevant to the other. However, it is also the case that even well-established large-scale climate changes may vary locally in their severity, effect, and timing, so that the need for additional regional studies, especially in the south and in lower elevation areas, remains critical.

It is now possible to sketch the broad outlines of Holocene change in climate and rainfall on the subcontinent. Data sources include analysis of pollen and diatoms, oxygen and carbon isotopes, and speleothem (stalactites and stalagmites) formation, among others. Because of sampling requirements for these proxy climatic indicators, lakes, bogs, peat deposits, caves, and the ocean floor have been the most important study locales. With the exception of marine deposits, southern India is generally lacking in these kinds of contexts and only in the high-elevation zones of the Nilgiri Hills, in the Western Ghats, are suitable deposits of peat to be found. This explains, in part, the paucity of information from the south, though the relative difficulty of studying tropical and subtropical climates has probably also encouraged the focus on more temperate regions in north India and Tibet.

Considering only the Holocene, we may begin with Phadtare's pollen analysis of a 7,800 year-long Himalayan peat deposit. Phadtare found (2000: 127) that beginning around 5800 BC, there was an overall warming of the climate, with monsoon strength increasing from about 5200 BC and reaching its maximum about 3000 BC. Following a gradual decrease from 2500 to 2000 BC, monsoon strength quickly diminished to a minimum at 1500 BC. From this time to about the AD/BC boundary, the monsoon was highly unstable, but in general showed a gradual strengthening. Thereafter, rainfall steadily increased until about AD 1000, when it again decreased for about two hundred years, or up until AD 1200. Since then, it has gradually strengthened toward the present. He thus isolated two dry intervals, one between 2000 and 1500 BC and one between AD 1000 and 1200, with the period of minimum rainfall occurring around 1500 BC (Phadtare 2000).

If we compare these results with pollen studies from lakes in northwestern India (Singh et al. 1974, 1990; Bryson and Swain 1981), it is clear that there is both broad agreement with Phadtare's findings. Singh et al. (1974, 1990) located the onset of arid conditions at around 2000 BC, a pattern also isolated by Naidu (1996) from analysis of foraminifera in the Arabian Ocean. More recent analyses of lake Lunkaransar (Enzel et al. 1999), one of the same lakes analyzed by Singh et al., present a slightly different picture. Enzel at al. (1999) obtained a new series of 15 radiocarbon dates from the beginning of the Holocene to between the fifth and first century BC, a significant improvement over the temporal resolution of earlier studies. Using stable carbon isotope data from both carbonates and organic matter, they found the Lunkaransar record to be in broad agreement with studies from the Arabian Sea (Kutzbach 1987; Prell and Kutzbach 1992; Overpeck et al. 1996; Sirocko et al. 1993) showing both monsoon weakening around 5500 BP (roughly 3500 BC) as well as a basic difference between early and later Holocene conditions (Enzel et al. 1999: 127). Although some of the same broad patterns are seen, the timing of the trends discussed by Enzel et al. (1999) differ from those of Phadtare, Singh et al., and Bryson and Swain (1981), suggesting the need for additional work and especially more well-dated sequences.

From southern India itself, pollen data from a near-shore marine core near Karwar (Caratini et al. 1991, 1994) indicate decreased monsoon strength from about 3500 years ago (2500 BC), but no significant directed variation in precipitation since then. This study is extremely important as it establishes the relevance of established patterns of change for the south, although as discussed below, there do appear to have been some additional though less dramatic changes in precipitation and temperature since the onset of major dessication at 2500 BC.[3]

Beyond this now well-established (if not well-dated) pattern of monsoon weakening somewhere around 2500 BC, there are also indications of lower-intensity but still important rainfall variations.[4] As noted, Phadtare isolated a minor dry period between AD 1000 and 1200. In their studies of well-dated speleothems from central Nepal, Denniston et al. (2000) found strong evidence of increased aridity between 300 BC and AD 500 and increased humidity after AD 500. Pollen analyses from northeastern India (Mazari et al. 1996) indicated cool and dry conditions for the first thousand years AD and a warmer, wetter interval between AD 1000 and 1600. Denniston et al. also found that between AD 1550 and 1640 (the uncertainty on these dates is between 5 and 20 years), dense calcite layers formed on the speleothems, indicating moister and cooler conditions the authors suggest relate to Little Ice Age effects.[5] Pollen evidence from the Dunde ice cap (Liu et al. 1998) also suggests a wetter interval between AD 1400 and 1920 which again could relate to the Little Ice Age; Denniston et al. note (2000: 200) that the onset of Little Ice Age conditions seems to have started some 100 years sooner in the Pokhara Valley, Nepal, than at the Dunde ice cap. It will be critical to be able to match these Little Ice Age indicators from the north and northeast with data from the south; this has not yet been done systematically. However, Sukumar et al.'s (1993: 705) carbon isotope work on Nilgiri peat deposits in southern India indicates a brief, two-hundred year (AD 1200-1400) shift to C3 vegetation, indicating an increase in soil moisture they correlate with the Medieval Warm Period (AD 1100-1300) of Europe.[6]

What all this indicates, then, is some evidence for a major dry period that in our region coincides largely with the Southern Neolithic. The Early Historic saw a number of climate fluctuations, though these patterns are less clear and perhaps were more locally variable than the pan-Asian monsoon weakening that falls between 3500/2000 and 1500/1000 BC. Later climate fluctuations are also difficult to isolate for the south, but it now seems likely that there were some climate shifts that coincided largely with the Vijayanagara and the following Nayaka periods, an effect that was probably favorable to agriculture. Prior to this, there may have been a dry period between about AD 1000 and 1200 and a wetter period from 1200 to 1400, the first falling in the Early Middle Period and the second before and during the transition to Vijayanagara rule. These rainfall variations may have had a significant effect on the relative success of rainfed agriculture, already a marginal strategy in this dry region, and may also have helped influence whether or not runoff-fed facilities would repay the labor of their construction and maintenance.

Change Through Time: Vegetation and Soil

Although vegetation patterns are certainly influenced by climate change, it is probable that only large-scale changes in rainfall patterns would have significantly modified vegetation in the study area. Most marked, perhaps, during the Neolithic dry period would have been the retreat of the distinct vegetation of the Sandur Hills upslope and perhaps even its replacement by a more xeric group of plants. Further, there would have been significantly less surface runoff in these centuries and it may be no coincidence that runoff-harvesting strategies did not become important until after 1000 BC.

It is difficult to say precisely what the nature of later Little Ice Age effects may have been (if any), though certainly rainfall changes would always have been more significant than changes in temperature and it would never have been the case that growing seasons would be affected by frost or severe cold. Although I do not discount the potential importance of changes in rainfall – indeed, I think they were probably crucial for dry farmers in particular – it is probably the case that the most significant factor restructuring regional vegetation was human action and not climate change in itself. For our purposes here, vegetation change must be studied at a local scale, one congruent with human action in the region, and to date only a very few studies address change at this spatial and temporal scale. It is certainly possible that deforestation has itself caused micro-scale climatic changes, so that vegetation change and climate are not entirely separate considerations.[7] Whatever the relationship between changes in rainfall and changes in vegetation, it is clear that first of all, there has been massive deforestation of the Sandur Hills throughout the twentieth century. Documentary evidence, historical photographs, and oral histories recall dense forests on these hills which are now vegetated primarily by grasses, thorny scrub, and remnant stands of the *Anogeissus-Terminalia-Tectona* series, a relatively moist forest association also found in the Ghat foothills that creates a small island in the dry vegetation types (Gaussen et al. 1960; N.P. Singh 1988) of the Karnataka *maidan*, or plain, a term used to contrast dry, relatively level eastern Karnataka with the hilly, wet, western *malnad* region. The *raja* of Sandur, a small, nominally independent princely state during the British colonial period (eighteenth century to AD 1947) hunted leopards and other large animals in the Sandur Hills, which now support almost no large mammals. The present treeless condition of the Sandur Hills appears to have been duplicated during the Vijayanagara period, as indicated by pollen evidence (Morrison 1995a). At this time, then, erosion off of these steep hills must have created both serious problems (reservoir siltation, for example) and perhaps potentials (renewal of fertile soil on the valley floor) for local agriculturalists, consequences also apparent from the archaeological record.

In the Daroji-Vijayanagara region, the best evidence for past vegetation comes from a series of pollen cores taken from Vijayanagara reservoirs. Reservoirs, like natural lakes and bogs, act as traps for pollen produced by the surrounding vegetation. Airborne pollen settles onto the surface of the water, some of it eventually settling to the bottom. Inwashed sediments may also carry pollen; together these aggrading materials create a complex stratified record that carries information about past vegetation. The analysis of sediment and pollen profiles from these reservoirs affords a uniquely detailed view of land use patterns and of human impact on the south Indian countryside from the onset of reservoir infilling to the present. Charcoal particles from local and regional fires – caused by, among other things, agricultural clearing, sugar cane burning, charcoal production, and domestic burning – also settle into reservoir settlements, leaving a proxy record of the intensity of past burning (Clark 1988; MacDonald et al. 1991; Morrison 1994; Patterson et al. 1987). Such pollen records can be dated by radiometric methods as well as by internal evidence such as botanical evidence for introduced New World species or correlation with reservoir construction dates.

The most continuous pollen record for the region comes from the Kamalapuram reservoir (VMS-231), one of the few canal-fed reservoirs in the study area. This artificial lake lies 5 kilometers north of the Daroji Valley and has a water-spread of some 200 hectares. A large body of water that also takes in significant quantities of pollen from a river-fed canal (the Raya canal) as well as from runoff, the pollen record from the Kamalapuram *kere* should be broadly representative of the regional vegetation record (cf. Bonny 1976; Faegri et al. 1989). Further, the watershed of the Kamalapuram reservoir draws from both the granitic Hampi-Daroji Hills that border the north side of the Daroji Valley and, in part, from the Sandur Hills themselves, where the Hampi-Daroji Hills recede on the extreme west end of the Daroji Valley. This contribution from the iron and manganese-rich Sandur Hills can be seen quite clearly in the red, iron-rich water of the Kamalapuram reservoir; water redder than that found in any Daroji Valley reservoir, a pattern exacerbated by recent open mining in the Sandur Hills.

Beginning in the fourteenth century, the Kamalapuram pollen sequence (Morrison 1995a, 1996) shows a pattern of open vegetation, dominated by grasses and probably cultivated fields. Weedy flora and charcoal data are consistent with the production of wet rice under the reservoir, in contrast to the current focus on commercial sugar cane production. The Vijayanagara period witnessed significant and sustained pressure on woody plants – trees and shrubs declined throughout the period, virtually disappearing at the height of the city's occupation, rebounding only after the abandonment of the city. This pattern also corresponds with the evidence of microscopic charcoal, which suggests intense regional burning during the Vijayanagara period (Morrison 1994). Coconut (*Cocos nucifera*) trees, which require irrigation or supplemental watering in this dry region, show up in significant numbers during both the Vijayanagara period and the twentieth century, but not in large numbers in the centuries between. Other non-grain cultivated plants from the Vijayanagara period include *Ricinus* (castor oil bean) and *Arenga* (an edible palm).

The pattern of aquatic vegetation is particularly interesting, indicating maintenance of this reservoir during its early history, a long period of post-Vijayanagara invasion of the facility by aquatic plants, and a later renewal of maintenance during what seems to be the colonial period. This latter supposition is also supported by the records of the British irrigation department. Some New World taxa – all weedy plants – may have been introduced before the fall of the city, but the full establishment of alien weed assemblages took much longer and, importantly, the contemporary weedy flora looks quite different from that of the sixteenth century. Importantly, the initial picture of vegetation we see from the Kamalapuram cores, a pattern dating to the early Vijayanagara period, is one of extensive fields and open areas with grasses and weeds. The agricultural expansion and intensification associated with the expansion of the city in the fourteenth century was very rapid; it did not begin from a point of "untouched" natural vegetation, but built on a long history of anthropogenic transformation of the local flora.

Post-Vijayanagara vegetation changes are also marked and are particularly interesting between about the nineteenth and twentieth centuries. Just to summarize these patterns, the colonial and post-colonial palaeobotanical record shows a renewed focus on burning and changes in charcoal particle sizes, this time possibly a result of large-scale commercial sugar cane production (Morrison 1994). We also see the introduction of new weed taxa, including New World taxa, and a shift within the irrigated zones away from wet rice and toward large-scale cultivation of coconuts and sugarcane (bananas are also important now, but they do not produce pollen and hence their past importance is difficult to assess). Forests, as limited as they now are, are presently more developed than they were during the Vijayanagara period.

Like vegetation, soil is also a somewhat vulnerable landscape element in this semi-arid setting. There is good evidence for quite severe erosion in the study area, especially in the more densely settled areas. Although it is not now clear precisely how much soil cover the Hampi-Daroji Hills may have had before the fourteenth century, and earlier, it was certainly more than the present. In the northeast valley of the urban core (Morrison 1990), a combination of cultural debris and colluvial inwash from similar rocky hills has buried several small temples right up to the tops of their doors.[8] As should become clear through this study, erosion and colluviation were serious concerns wherever reservoirs or terraces were built, and there is evidence for locally variable, but often very severe erosion and redeposition of soil cover. Much of this erosion is no doubt related to the large-scale destabilization and degradation of the local vegetation cover, especially the loss of woody taxa. Local responses to such sedimentary processes are evident from the many archaeological features designed to retard erosion and protect downstream facilities as well as, more immediately, to channel, slow, and/or collect runoff for agriculture, livestock, or people. Given the changes in vegetation cover and sediment regimes, we may also expect some transformations in micro-scale hydrology, landforms, and aspects of soil structure and fertility.

Soils in the region are primarily thin, rocky, and sandy; most common are red sandy soils (*masab*) and what are usually called "mixed black and red" soils. Although there are limited alluvial deposits along the banks of the Tungabhadra River, these do not extend into the Daroji Valley, nor are there any deposits of southern India's famous "black cotton soil" or *regur* in the valley itself. The nutrient- and clay-rich *regur* soils hold water extremely well and are famed both for their productivity and for the difficulty of working them. Heavy black cotton soils may require as many as four bullocks per plow (two being the usual number) to till, though these soils are not always plowed annually.[9] Such soils typically occur on broad, level plains – their association with extensive cotton cultivation is clear from the name. Here it is important to note that dry farming on this clay-rich substrate was quite different from farming the sandy soils of the Daroji Valley and the Vijayanagara region more generally. The broad plains to the east of the Daroji reservoir, toward Bellary, have black soils (somewhat sandy) which change abruptly to the red *masab* at the edge of the Daroji Valley.

REGIONAL SETTLEMENT DYNAMICS: AN OVERVIEW

Human action in South Asia has a history nearly as long as humanity itself, and southern India is no exception to this, containing abundant remains of the Palaeolithic periods. Both the Palaeolithic and the following Mesolithic are still relatively poorly-understood in this area, though it is certain that mobile gatherer-hunters lived in and moved across this region for many, many thousands of years before the herders and farmers of the so-called Southern Neolithic began to leave their mark on the landscape. In this section, I briefly review the longer-term and larger-scale history of the area surrounding the Daroji Valley in order to provide some context for the more specific discussion of the valley itself. In the next Chapter, I consider this history again, but from a somewhat different perspective, thinking about some of the specific kinds of places that emerge from this historical trajectory. Some of these places – villages, temples, ashmounds, megaliths, and reservoirs, for example, appear in the following discussion, but they appear not so much as landscape elements, as they will in Chapter 3, but as components of economic, social, and cultural systems. Clearly, both kinds of views are necessary and relevant, especially as older features and places continue to play a role in later periods, those roles being multiply determined by, among other things, the original function and significance of that feature or place, as well as its potential for the contemporary situation. Older temples, for example, still generally function as temples in some way while Neolithic ashmounds now have entirely different roles and meanings than they presumably once did. Meaning and function are clearly time- and place-dependent. This landscape history, then, ranges analytically through time and physically across space, switching between consideration of places in their "own" time and as more or less enduring landscape elements.

Early Settlement Dynamics: The Southern Neolithic

Although, as noted, there must have been Palaeolithic and Mesolithic use of this region, the earliest well-dated evidence of occupation in and use of the Daroji Valley and its environs is about 2400 BC, in the middle of the Southern Neolithic (Figure 8). Existing analyses of the Southern Neolithic (*c.* 3000 to 1000 BC, Possehl and Rissman 1992; Korisettar et al. 2001) give a picture of small-scale, primarily pastoral economies with some farming of millets. As discussed above, the earlier part of the Southern Neolithic appears to have been a period of relative aridity in this already-dry region, thus making dry farming somewhat more problematic than it is at present. This dryness may, however, have been offset to some extent by the presumably greater fertility of land that had only just come under cultivation for the first time. In any event, it is clear that, relative to later periods, the Southern Neolithic was marked by low population densities and high mobility. Although the nature of that mobility is not entirely clear, it seems to have included both rarer residential mobility and a more tethered, logistic mobility around places used often or for longer periods of time, patterns it is tempting, if probably too simplistic, to match with the differential tempo of field movement on the one hand, and herd movement on the other. Ongoing research by Korisettar and Fuller (Korisettar et al. 2001) promises to document changes in these patterns within the Neolithic era; preliminary work suggests a decrease in residential mobility through time, but much more remains to be done to clarify these patterns.

Recent excavations by Paddayya (1993a, 1993b,1998; Paddayya et al. 1995) at Budihal, in the Gulbarga district of Karnataka, some 150 kilometers north of the Daroji Valley, have significantly improved our knowledge of Neolithic economies, with well-documented

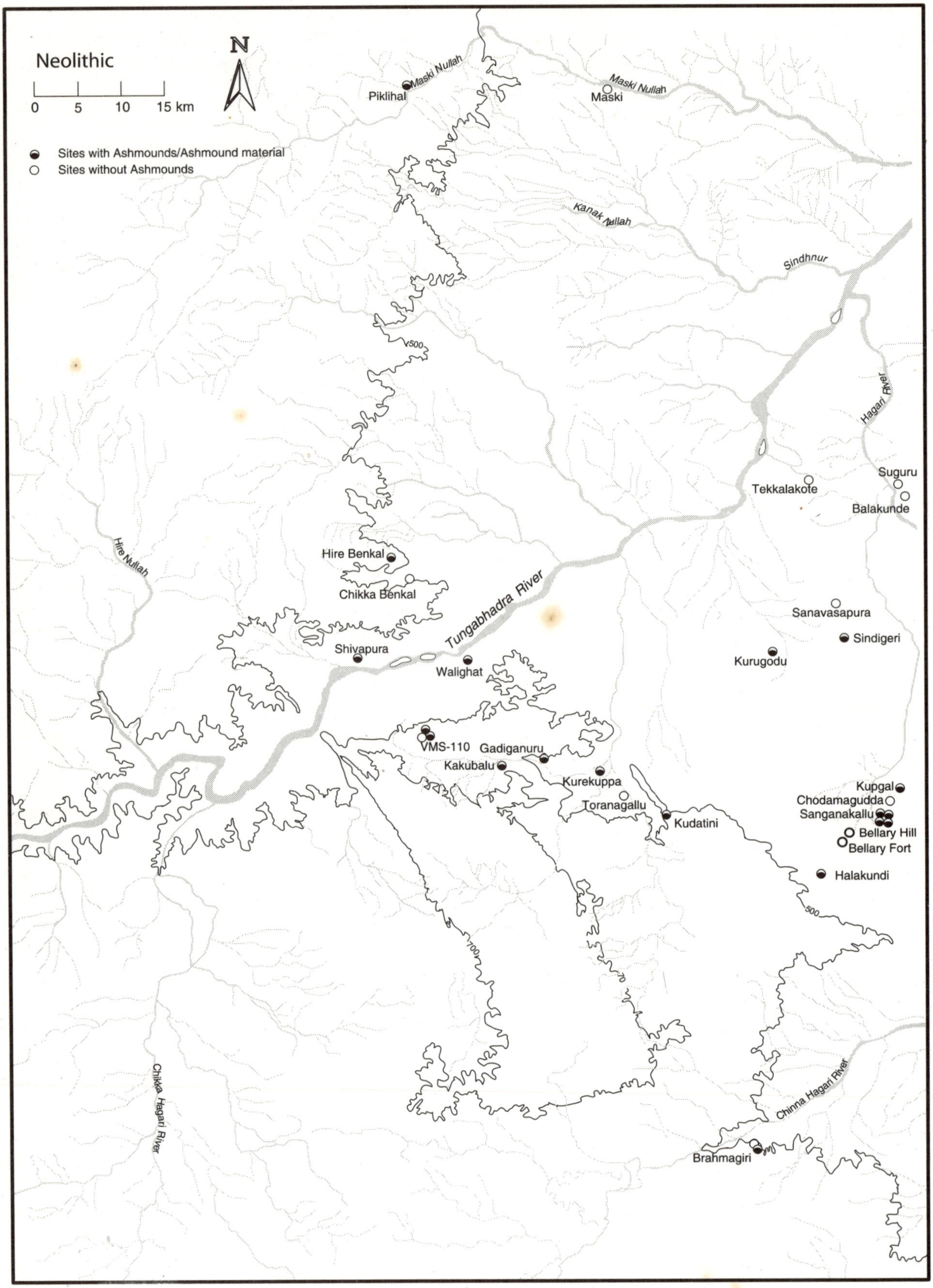

Figure 8. Distribution of Neolithic sites in the study area.

evidence for a mixed subsistence regime including rain-fed agriculture of millets, livestock husbandry focused on cattle, and gathering and hunting. Paddayya and his colleagues have documented a large (*c.* 250 m^2) butchering area with roasting pits and huge quantities of domestic cattle (*Bos indicus*) bone at Budihal, as well as several ashmounds, habitation areas, and areas of specialized lithic production.[10] Ashmounds, not made of ash at all, are actually hills or mounds of fired cattle dung in a vitrified, slaggy state and are typical features of the Southern Neolithic in the Bellary and Raichur Districts of Karnataka.[11] Rarely found outside this delimited region, these "cinder mounds" (Foote 1887a, 1914, 1916) and their associated settlements have long attracted archaeological and popular attention. Many ashmounds have now been excavated and well-studied locations indicate that although there is certainly evidence for large-scale burning episodes, in most cases construction was at least partially accretional. There is little doubt that ashmounds were meant for public display, but beyond that there is little concrete evidence of their uses (Paddayya 1993a, 1998; Johansen 2004). Certainly ashmounds have proven to be enduring features of the landscape; although they are valued as sources of raw material for lime kilns and thus are always under threat, many still remain throughout the region. Although popular accounts tend to assign them varying degrees of antiquity, they are generally not recognized as dung accumulations nor are they imagined to be nearly as old as they actually are (see Morrison 1995a: 32-3 and the next Chapter for more details).

Even given the massive destruction of ashmounds in recent centuries and uneven research coverage, Neolithic ashmounds and habitations (all ashmounds seem to have a least a modest artifact scatter in association, though apparently not all habitation locales have ashmounds) are widely distributed across this area, which seems to have been a particular focus of regional land use at this time. Residential locations cluster in specific topographic contexts, particularly in places where there was access to the bases of granitic hills where runoff could be harvested for production of millets and other crops. On a regional scale, many Neolithic sites are strung out along or near the 500 meter contour (Figure 5) which in this area is often an important topographic break between the rocky hills and adjoining colluvial valleys. Neolithic sites are not, in general, associated with the banks of major rivers such as the Tungabhadra though they may be located near (but not on) minor streams. Examples of this pattern include Brahmagiri which is near the Chinna Hagari and Suguru and Kanchagara Bellagallu on the Hagari. Settlements off the 500 meter contour such as Tekkalakota, Kupgal (Kappagalu), Sanganakallu, Halekundi, Toranagallu, Kurekuppa, and Maski, are all associated with high granitic inselbergs as indeed are some of those near the 500 meter contour. In many cases, the actual residential areas and sometimes the ashmounds are situated high atop these hills in quite imposing locations, as discussed in the following Chapter. Neolithic settlement locations, while clearly selected (in part) for the availability of both forage for cattle and other animals and of land suitable for dry-farming of millets, were significant, marked places on the landscape as were the widespread ashmounds. Less visible, but no less important, were the many locations of ceramic raw material, lithic sources, and other valued resources, places little-studied, marked by small scatters of artifacts and other subtle traces but by no means invisible to us or, presumably, to Neolithic and later residents of and visitors to the area.

Because Neolithic people were certainly at least occasionally mobile, perhaps moving out from more tethered locations for grazing and raw material procurement as well as for visits to other settlements and ashmound locations, and because few of the settlements in this area have been excavated or studied in any detail, it is impossible at this point to know the scale of regional population though clearly it was much larger than that of preceding periods. Many of the excavated sites, including Tekkalakota (Nagaraja Rao and Malhotra 1965) and Brahmagiri (Wheeler 1947), have very deep and substantial Neolithic deposits so if these represent periodic reoccupations by mobile people, these must have been very regular re-occupations by large groups over a substantial period of time. Not all Neolithic sites are large and deeply stratified, however, and we have as yet only a very superficial understanding of how these smaller locations fit into the overall pattern of land use and the use of space on a regional and supra-regional scale.

We may, however, be more certain that the Neolithic was the beginning of the long trajectory of agricultural history in this area and, while we know very little at present about what went before it, the Neolithic does seem to represent both rupture and continuity. Continuity in that some excavated sites show stratified deposits of the Paleolithic and/or Mesolithic under Neolithic levels, rupture in that the herding and farming carried out in this period stand in stark contrast to the economic strategies of those preceding it and in the way in which places were marked and modified on the landscape. The area to the east of the Daroji Valley was an important locus of land use and settlement in the Neolithic, and the valley itself appears to have been a major route of movement at this time, as discussed in the following Chapters.

The Iron Age

The transition from the late Neolithic to the Iron Age is, again, a poorly-studied one. The Iron Age is sometimes referred to as the Megalithic period because of its presumed temporal association with the megalithic monuments that are widespread in southern India. The notion of a Megalithic *period* is problematic in the extreme, and I do not use it here, mentioning it only for comparison with the published literature. If we provisionally define the Iron Age as that period after the Neolithic (this is also problematic, as variably proposed dates for the two periods, even using an intermediate "Neolithic/Chalcolithic" period as some have suggested, may still leave us with something of a gap), then we have some sort of delineation of a time period but are far short of a clear understanding of regional dynamics. The Iron Age, then, is provisionally dated here to between *c.* 1000 BC and 500 BC, and is followed by the Early Historic period (500 BC to AD 500).[12]

South Indian megaliths, like Neolithic ash-mounds, are restricted in their distribution though megaliths are found across a somewhat larger region than ashmounds. Northern Karnataka contains many isolated megalithic features as well as huge megalithic complexes containing hundreds, and even thousands of features. In our intensively surveyed area, megalithic complexes are often found in association with settlements which we presume to have been occupied during both the Iron Age and the Early Historic. Again, like ash-mounds, megaliths have attracted antiquarian and archaeological attention for over a hundred years (see reviews by Krishnaswami 1949; Leshnik 1973). In spite of all this attention, controlled excavations have been relatively few and there are a limited number of megaliths associated with chronometric dates. Based on information from our intensive survey as well as from the published literature, it seems, however, that megaliths were constructed over a very long period and that they do not necessarily track the Iron Age precisely. As Lycett and I have suggested (1998, and see the next Chapter), it may be most useful to think of megaliths not as chronological markers but as sets of *features and practices* that were popular at different times in different places, and that were used and reused over long periods of time. The potential time-scale for megalith use is broad indeed. From our survey work, we suspect that megaliths may have been used (if perhaps not built) well into the Early Historic or even later; Wagoner (1995) also speculates about a connection between megaliths and Early Middle period temples in Andhra Pradesh. Recent re-analysis of the collections from Brahmagiri, the type-site for the "Megalithic" in southern India (Wheeler 1947), has produced a somewhat surprising radiocarbon date of *c.* 2000 BC for an excavated cist-circle megalith (Morrison 2005); tantalizing evidence for connections between the Neolithic and subsequent Iron Age (and see the following Chapter).

If we dissociate megaliths from the definition of the Iron Age (although there is no doubt that Iron Age peoples built and used megalithic features), we are left with, at the moment, radiometric dates and ceramic typology as temporal indicators. In the absence of excavation, then, places used during the Iron Age can be recognized, at present, only by ceramics. Unfortunately, the "archetypical" Iron Age ceramic type, Black-and-Red Ware (BRW), is also common in the Early Historic (and see Morrison 2005 on the problems of distinguishing so-called "Megalithic BRW" from "Early Historic BRW") and a variety of BRW was made as early as the Neolithic. The Iron Age, then, is in the curious position of being defined by the *absence* of ceramic types such as the later Russet-Coated Painted Ware (RCPW, Early Historic) or earlier Micaceous Ware (Neolithic). Even this distinction is problematic, however, as several excavated sites, including both Brahmagiri (Wheeler 1947; Morrison 2005) and the more recently-excavated site of Watgal (Devaraj et al. 1995) in Raichur district, show a clear pattern of overlap between these ceramic types, suggesting that the simple correlation between ceramic ware and chrono-cultural period is seriously misinformed (Morrison 2005).

Further, in several key excavations, there seems to be a lack of any clear or substantial gap between deposits containing Neolithic ceramics and deposits containing Early Historic ceramic types. For example, there were pronounced stratigraphic overlaps between the ceramics of the "Stone Axe Culture" (Neolithic) and the "Megalithic" (Iron Age) at the important site of Brahmagiri, some 30 kilometers south of Bellary (Wheeler 1947, and see Wheeler 1954, Morrison 2005). Further, "Megalithic" ceramics overlapped depositionally with ceramics of the "Andhra Culture" (Early Historic), so much so that in habitation contexts "Megalithic" ceramics *never* occurred by themselves without an admixture of "earlier" or "later" types.[13] Thus, if we consider only levels containing Neolithic and Early Historic materials, there was at both Brahmagiri and VMS-110 (an excavated site from the western Daroji Valley discussed in Chapter 5) no *physical gap* between the deposits of these two time periods. At the site of Watgal, similar depositional patterns were noted (Devaraj et al. 1995). All this seems to indicate a kind of "missing" Iron Age, a period of 500 more years, depending on one's favored chronological scheme. There are, however, locations with clear evidence, including radiometric dates, for permanent habitation during the Iron Age (Maski and Kadebakele, for example), indicating some regional restructuring of large habitation locations in the Iron Age. These patterns suggest important changes in regional land use in the period after about 1500 BC and before the first or second century AD, but at present it is difficult to say much more than this.

We are left, finally, with the problem of distinguishing the Iron Age in the absence of radiometric dates, in that is has no fully diagnostic ceramic types. Thus, we have no basis for suggesting an Iron Age (again, here conceived narrowly as a time period) occupation of VMS-110, nor indeed, of the Daroji Valley. Looking further afield to the intensively surveyed area, there are also only a few locations containing what may be Iron Age materials (that is, having Black-and-Red Ware without also containing Russet-Coated Painted Ware). Obviously, however, our bases for distinguishing this long period of time are weak. It is clear from our recent excavations at Kadebakele that this region was occupied during this time and may have seen some contraction of settlement into fewer, larger towns. These fewer, larger settlements were apparently occupied continuously, though many megaliths contain horse gear and other suggestions of some continued mobility.[14] It also seems probable that it was during the Iron Age that rice agriculture first became important in the region. Our inability to date places independently of this problematic ceramic chronology is still a serious problem. However, we may certainly assume that economic strategies, settlement forms and locations, memorial practices, and the form and tempo of landscape use changed significantly through the Neolithic into and through the Iron Age.

The Early Historic

Following the Iron Age is the Early Historic (*c.* 500 BC-AD 500), so-called because it is the time when written documents first appear in the subcontinent. The Early Historic was also a period of dramatic change in the south. This is the period in which institutionalized religions – Buddhism, Jainism, and Hinduism – gained a hold in the south, and when we see for the first time really large permanent settlements, more intensive forms of agriculture, and increasing long-distance relationships involving exchange and perhaps political domination and plunder from outside the region.[15]

The oldest known written material in South Asia are potsherds from sites in Tamil Nadu (see Mahadevan 2003 for a review) inscribed with characters of the Brahmi script, apparently in Tamil. Aside from these, however, the earliest texts are the public inscriptions or edicts of the emperor Ashoka, ruler of one of the first expansive polities in South Asia, the Mauryan empire. Curiously enough, this polity, with its base far to the north on the Gangetic plain, seems to have had some interests in our region though it seem unlikely that this area was really controlled by the distant empire. Ashokan edicts cluster in several areas, most of them clearly part of the Mauryan polity in some way (for a fuller discussion, see Thapar 1997, Morrison 1997a; Sinopoli 2001). However, there is a single cluster of edicts located in northern Karnataka, including two (Nittur and Udegolam) just to the east and north of the Daroji Valley in a level area south of the Tungabhadra River. Additional edicts are located at Maski, Koppal, and Brahmagiri (Figure 9). Ashokan edicts convey highly repetitive proclamations, so much so that they are numbered by content; only the Maski edict is in any way distinctive, being one of the few to specifically mention Ashoka by name (Hulzsch 1991; see Sugandhi 2003 for a detailed discussion of the differences between the various southern edicts).[16] Whatever their political implications, these texts, which carry a message of Buddhism as well as subordination to Ashoka, illuminate the presence of connections between this region and the larger world. The recent find of a Mauryan imperial issue silver punch-marked coin near the Nittur and Udegolam edicts (Sugandhi personal communication) also seems to mark this connection.

In some sense, it seems that during the Early Historic some of the basic and enduring contours of south Indian life were established. There was a general pattern of nucleated villages and towns. We have located several settlements of this period ranging in size from a few hectares to more than 40 hectares; several of these settlements had evidence for long-distance exchange, including lapis lazuli beads from distant Afghanistan and Rouletted Ware (RW) ceramics made in coastal Bengal (Gogte 1997). These habitation sites tend to be clustered along the Tungabhadra River (Figure 9), some on high outcrops. While excavation of these sites is just beginning, there is a clear pattern in the region of superposition of Early Historic (and probably Iron Age as well) deposits over Neolithic ones.[17] This is clear at the excavated sites of Brahmagiri, Watgal, and Sanganakallu, among others, and from the presence of extensive Early Historic surface remains near the excavated Neolithic site of Tekkalakota, just to note a few examples. During the Early Historic, and in contrast to its visibility in the Neolithic, the Daroji Valley appears to have been a secondary focus of occupation, an area where specialized activities such as iron smelting were carried out away from the main corridor of settlement along the Tungabhadra River to the north. The valley, further, seems to show a contrasting pattern to the occupational continuity (or re-use) noted above for Brahmagiri, Watgal, Sanganakallu, and Tekkalakota, with Neolithic places *not* re-used or re-occupied later. Why this may be is an interesting question and may have much to do with the contrast between the larger, more continuously settled places of the Neolithic that have usually been the focus of excavation and the smaller locations of the Daroji Valley and elsewhere.

Although much more could be said about the form and significance of Early Historic use of this region, I close my review of this era with one additional point. This is that, in terms of

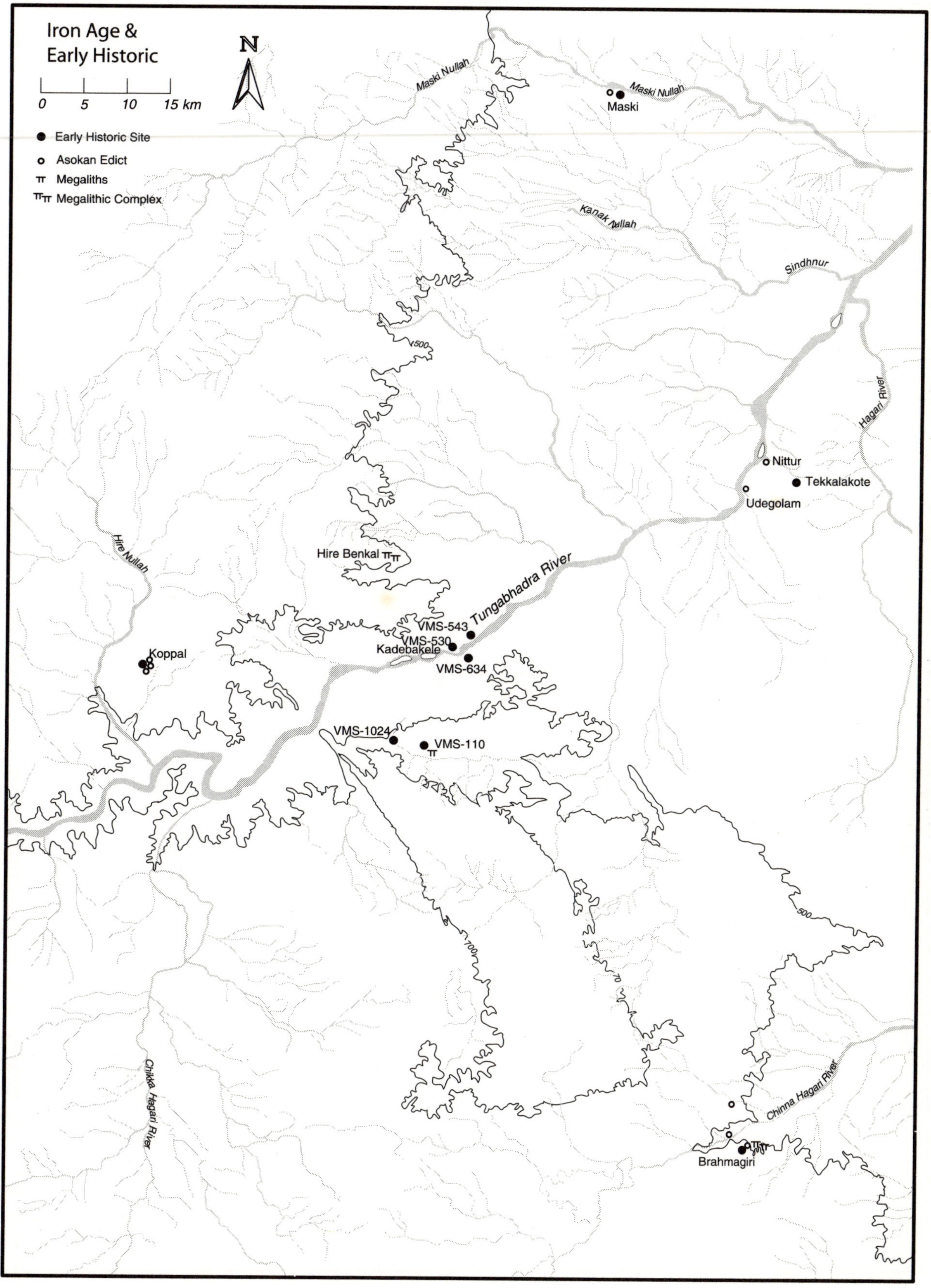

Figure 9. Distribution of Early Historic sites and features in the study area.

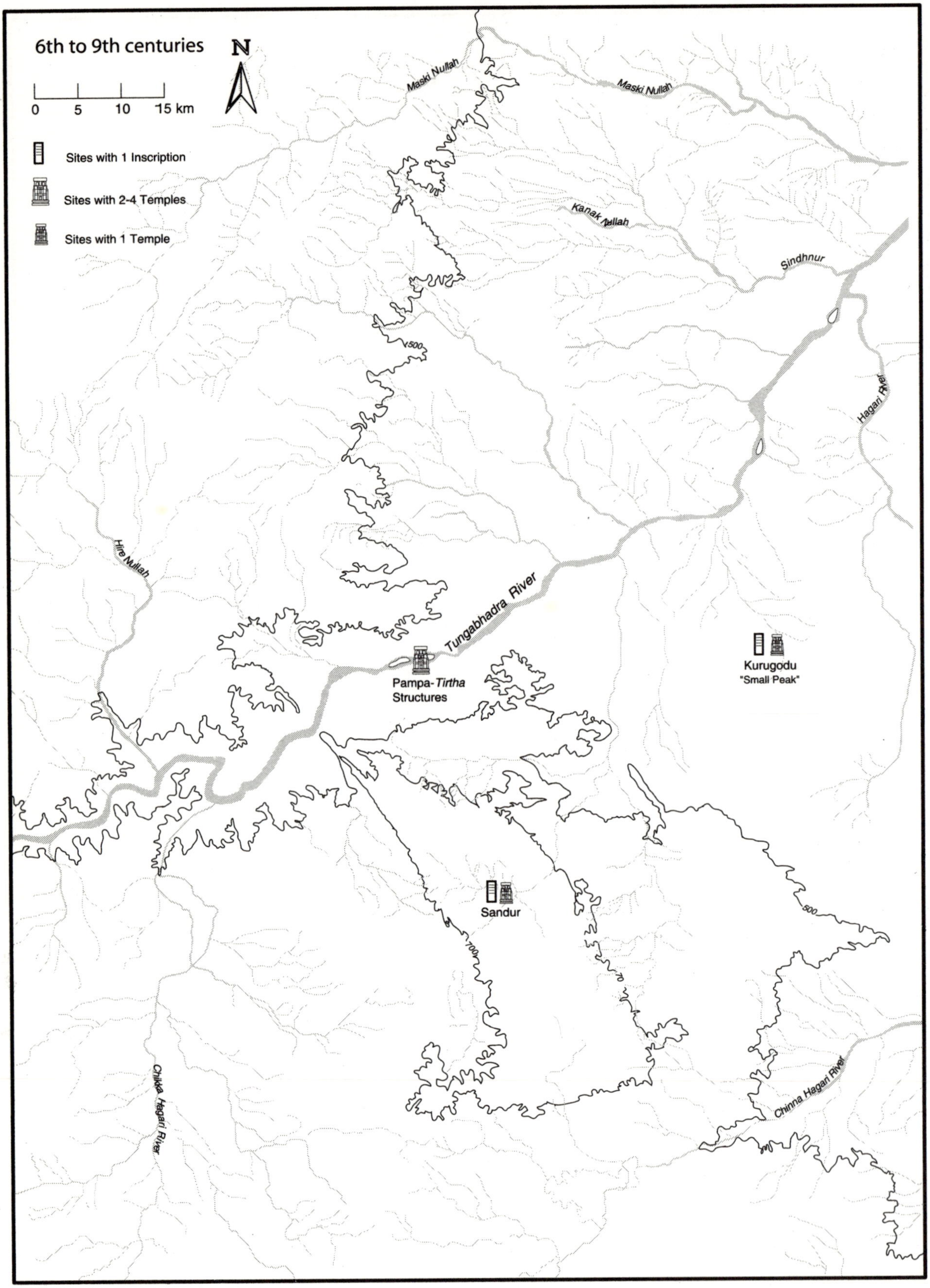

Figure 10. Distribution of sites and features, 6th-9th centuries.

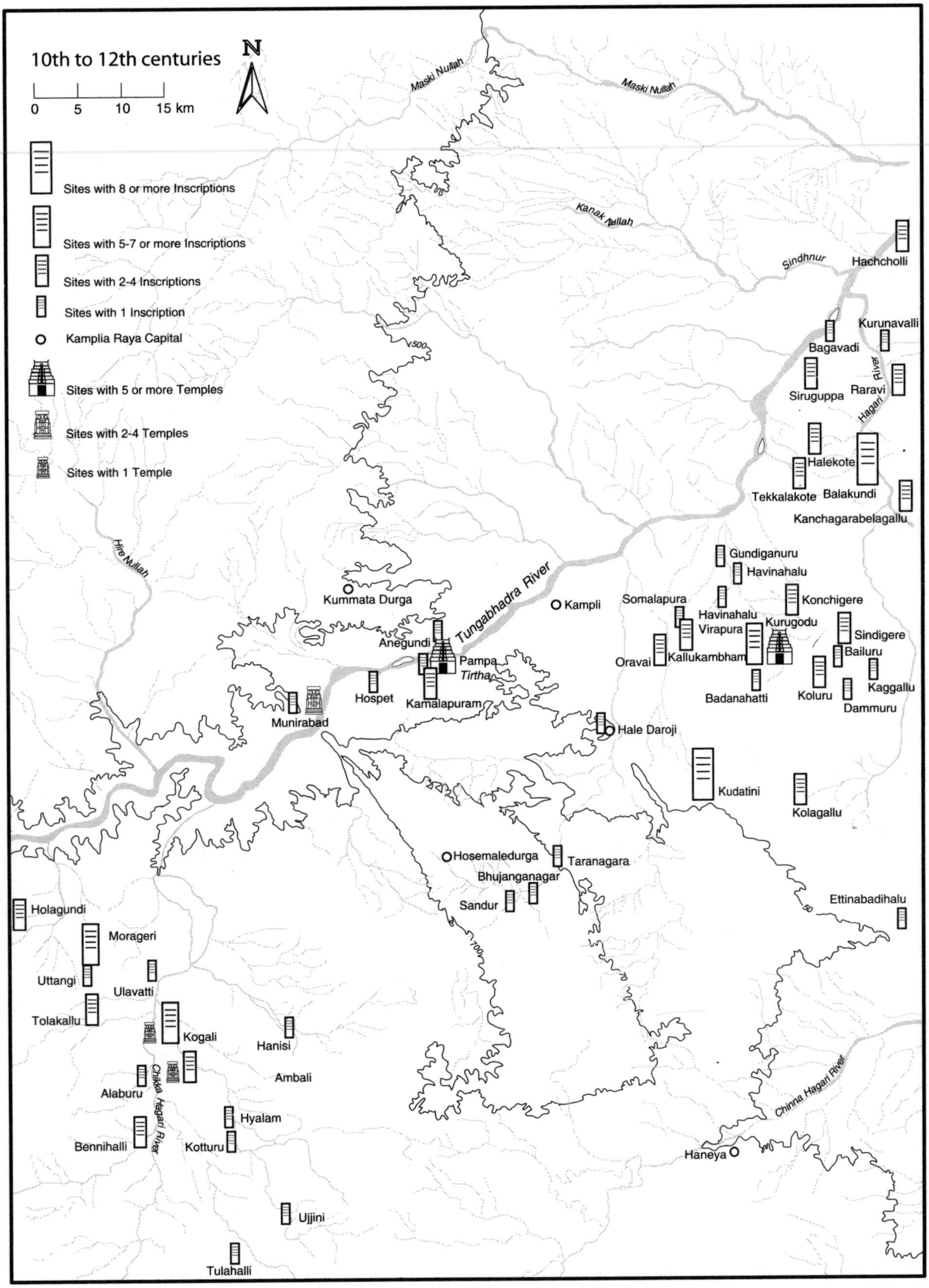

Figure 11. Distribution of sites and features, 10th-12th centuries.

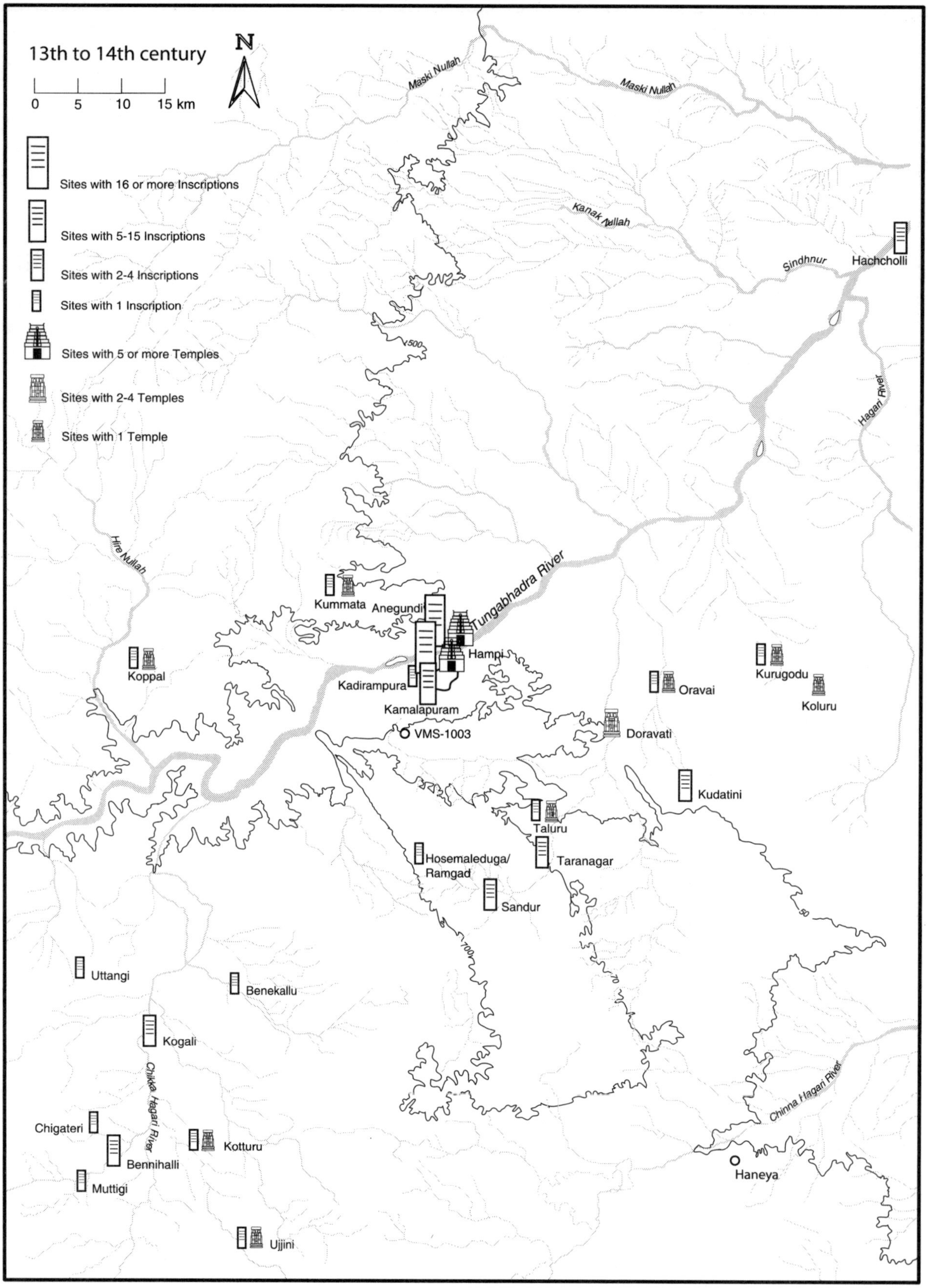

Figure 12. Distribution of sites and features, 13th-14th centuries.

agricultural practice, the location of Early Historic (and Iron Age) settlements seems to indicate some use of river water in farming, perhaps employing areas seasonally inundated for water-loving crops. Before the construction of the Tungabhadra Dam, floods were a regular feature of the river's annual regime; there is no evidence for Early Historic canals or other water control features but these could certainly have been destroyed by later cultivation. This shift seems to reflect the increasingly aggregated nature of settlement and more intensive localized production, perhaps of a new crop mix involving rice. Thus, although there are important indications of continuity, certainly the agro-pastoral landscape created by activity in Neolithic differed in important ways from the structure of agricultural production of the later Iron and Early Historic periods.

The Early Middle Period and the Doravati Nadu

By the tenth century AD, the broad level plain to the northeast of the Daroji Valley had become a major focus of settlement and the core territory of a series of small polities.[18] By AD 1149 this region was known as the Doravati Nadu[19] or Doravati-70 and was ruled over at that moment by Kacharasa, an officer (*mahamandalesvara*) subordinate to the Chalukyan kingdom with its capital at Kalyan, to the north (Patil 1996a: 243).[20] Doravati fort was the name of what is now known as the Daroji fort, the latter having a more or less continuous history of use and construction from before AD 1104-5 to the eighteenth century (Patil 1996a). The name Doravati was used to refer to this entire region; we can begin to see at least part of the Doravati Nadu quite clearly in Figures 10, 11, and 12, which show the distribution of inscriptions from the sixth through fourteenth centuries. During the Vijayanagara period, although the Doravati Nadu designation was retained, as is clear from a sixteenth-century inscription from Kurekuppa (discussed in Chapter 7), the region lost its centrality, and its name changed from being the name of an entire area as well as of a particular fort and settlement, to become the name of only a specific place, indeed one somewhat peripheral to the main locus of settlement, production, and power to the north. At some point soon after the fall of the city of Vijayanagara, the name Doravati became transformed into Daroji, as discussed in Chapter 7. Although the administrative center of this region again shifted following colonial incorporation, to the town of Bellary, the Daroji Valley continued to be something of an interstitial space in the region. I use the name "Daroji Valley" in order to emphasize the key role of the Daroji reservoir as its culmination. Perhaps it is a more appropriate name than I first realized, linking the Vijayanagara-period history of the valley with its temporal antecedents and emphasizing the way in which this area has passed from center to periphery, playing different roles in regional dynamics at different times and, all the while, being itself transformed.

The Early Middle period history of this region has been largely worked out by C.S. Patil (1991b, 1991c, 1992, 1996a, 1996b) and the following account is greatly indebted to this work. Unlike earlier periods, where archaeological data form the basis of our historical knowledge, the Middle periods are primarily known on the basis of textual and architectural data. Because there are few texts, aside from the Ashokan edicts, and no formal architecture from the Early Historic, both this and the preceding periods have generally been the domain of archaeology.[21] However, with the advent of both texts and formal structures, history, epigraphy, architecture, and to a lesser extent numismatics become the dominant disciplinary bases of knowledge. Obviously, our archaeological work is an exception to this, but because of the distribution of Early Middle settlements all around, but not in, the Vijayanagara core region, we have actually documented few remains of this period and these primarily temples.

Between about AD 550 and 757, the Doravati region came under the control of the Chalukyas of Badami (Patil 1992: 5), a polity based at city of Badami, some 150 kilometers to the north. There are few architectural remains from this period and none from the intensive survey area (Figure 10). It is clear, however, that the sacred *tirtha*, or river-crossing, that would eventually form the kernel of the city of Vijayanagara had already attained its identity by this time. This place, named after the river goddess Pampa (later known as Hampi) lies under the occupied village of Hampi which is still a major pilgrimage center. The earliest known textual reference to the Pampa *tirtha* is from a copperplate inscription issued by the Chalukyan ruler Vinayaditya I in AD 689-90 and found at Togurshode, in Kurnool District, Andhra Pradesh (Wagoner 1991: 141). The inscription records a gift given by the king while he was residing at his "victorious camp" which was "located at Pampa's crossing" (Wagoner 1991: 141). A seventh-century inscription from Kurugodu (Patil and Patil 1997: 19-20) specifies the land measure (a span measured by the extended thumb and little finger) as well as the type of coin (the *Navila-pon*, a gold coin) to be used there, suggesting at least some regulation of local economic matters and presumably the existence of some resource flows from land revenue to Badami.

After 757 and up to AD 973, this region came within the orbit of the expansive Rashtrakuta empire, a polity again based to the north of Doravati. It is in this period that the first stone temples were built in this region, at least the first that we have any evidence for. The Kumaraswami temple in Sandur has a ninth-century inscription built into the north wall of one shrine; this brief notice is written in Sanskrit in Nagari characters. The Pampa *tirtha* itself has a small cluster of nine ninth-century temples (Michell 1985a; Patil 1991c; Wagoner 1996); to these an additional and complementary group of six temples was added in the eleventh century, during the reign of the Western Chalukyas (Wagoner 1996: 142-52). Wagoner convincingly argues (1996: 148-9) that these two sets of shrines and their deities, belonging to what he calls "phase I" of the transition of this *tirtha* to an imperial capital, and hence the *tirtha* itself, relate primarily to death rituals, noted to be a primary motive for all pilgrimages to river crossings, real or metaphorical.

Beyond the Pampa *tirtha* itself, during the tenth and eleventh centuries the Western Chalukyas waged almost incessant battle with the Chola armies of the south. Although the approximate boundary of the two polities is often said to have been the Tungabhadra River, Patil (1992) sees the Doravati region as having been primarily under the direction of the Chalukyas. Certainly this region was the scene of many military conflicts; by the early twelfth century those conflicts came to include battles by the Chalukyas against the increasing ambition of the Hoysala chieftains, based in the southern part of what is now Karnataka. The practical end of Western Chaluykan rule in this region came in AD 1162 when Bijjala II, a provincial ruler under the Western Chaluykas and son of another high officer and relative of the ruling dynasty, seized power in what is sometimes referred to as the Kalachuri interregnum (after AD 1182 there was a brief, year-long effort to revive rule by Somesvara IV, son of the previous Chalukyan king; Patil 1992: 9).

The political situation of the twelfth and early thirteenth century was complex and somewhat fragmented, with the Seunas (also known as the Yadavas), who formerly acknowledged the suzerainty of the Rashtrakutas and later the Western Chalukyas, controlling the area north of the Tungabhadra and the Hoysalas, also formerly subject to the Chalukyas, the area south of this river (Patil 1992: 11-12). Although the Hoysalas are now known as great builders, having supported the development of a distinctive style of highly ornamented temple architecture, there are very few temples in our entire region that were built in this style (Patil 1992).

Although this account of a territorial division along the banks of the river seems fairly straightforward, in practice the political situation of the immediate pre-Vijayanagara period was considerably more complex. As in earlier periods, local leaders wielded considerable power in their home localities and often operated quite independently from distant imperial powers.[22] In this regard it is worth mentioning some of these families whom Patil terms "minor dynasties". Locally significant were the Nolambas who served under various dynasties for nearly three hundred years between the eighth and eleventh centuries

(Patil 1992: 12-13) and occasionally wielded independent dominion over an area that included parts of Chitradurg and Bellary Districts, in the eastern and southeastern part of the region depicted in Figure 11. An inscription of AD 1018 notes that the Nolamabas (then under the Chalukyas) moved their capital from Hemavati (now Anantapur district, Andhra Pradesh) to Kampli, on the northwest edge of the broad Bellary plain (Patil 1992:13, see Figure 11). The Nolambas disappeared in the later eleventh century to be replaced by the Pandyas of Uchchangi, based in the area just to the west of the region depicted in Figure 11. The Sindas of Kurugodu, a branch of the same family which was ruling at Erambarage to the north of the Tungabhadra River (Patil 1992: 13), controlled the Ballare Nadu, the region around Kurugodu, an important regional center in the twelfth century.[23] The division of which Kurugodu was the capital was known as Sindavadi-1000 (Patil 1992: 13).

Finally, we can mention the small kingdom of Mummadi Singeya-nayaka (AD 1280-1300) and his son Kampiladeva, also known as Kampilaraya (*c.* 1300-27), a dynasty of particular significance to this study. Patil has traced the movements of these little kings between their three fortified strongholds and capitals – Kummata, Hosamaladurga, and Doravati (1991b, 1991c, 1996a, 1996b). Kummata Durga (fort) lies to the north of the river atop a high outcrop and not far from the huge megalithic complex at Hire-Benakal, while Hosamaladurga has been identified with Ramgad in the Sandur Hills. Doravati is, as noted, Daroji. Note that all of these families governed relatively small areas and that there seems to be a certain amount of territorial overlap between them notwithstanding their mostly delimited spheres of influence.

To this complex situation which we may call for simplicity the Hoysala period was added, in AD 1295, the beginning of a series of raids by armies of the Delhi Sultanate, a northern polity whose rulers were Muslims. Carried out by a series of generals, these raids were organized to collect riches and, as such, they often targeted wealthy Hindu temples. The Seunas were eventually brought under sultanate rule though they continued their patronage of temples and other religious institutions (Patil 1992: 11-12). The Yadava (Seuna) kingdom of Devagiri (renamed Daulatabad) was annexed to the Delhi Sultanate in AD 1313, prompting Kampiladeva to assert his independence. In AD 1311, general Malik Kafur made the first raid into the far south; in this strike, the Hoysala capital Dvarasamudra (Halebid) was besieged and the Hoysala king Balalla III had to sue for peace and agree to pay an annual tribute. At one point (1326 to 1327), the rebellious nephew of the Delhi Sultan Muhammed Bin Tughluq took refuge in the kingdom of Kampila, at the Kummata fort, which was besieged by an army of the sultanate. Patil (1991b: 180-1) notes:

> The Sultan sent a powerful force against Kampiladeva. The latter offered heroic resistance. He defeated the imperial troops twice. Again his fort was surrounded on all sides by the enemy. Lack of provisions within the fort made it impossible for Kampiladeva to hold out for more than a month. On his advice the ladies of the royal family died by the fearful *jauhar* ceremony and the wives of the ministers and noble men followed their example. Then Kampiladeva and his followers sallied forth and died fighting to the last. Kampila's kingdom was annexed and constituted into a separate province with Malik Muhammed as its governor.[24]

This brief account of political history brings us up the beginning of the Vijayanagara period, which is discussed in the following sections. Here, however, we need to step back and consider how residents of the Daroji Valley and its surrounding region were distributed on the landscape and how they shaped and used that landscape. I have noted the spatial association of larger Early Historic settlements with rivers – those in our intensive survey area are all located near the Tungabhadra while Maski lies on the Maski River and Brahmagiri on the Chinna Hagari. Only Koppal, for which we have evidence of two edicts but not of a town, lies some distance from a river. VMS-110 (also not on a major drainage) was a specialized iron-smelting location and not a substantial settlement.

Between the sixth and ninth centuries we

have even less evidence for patterns of regional settlement than we did for the Early Historic, partly because of the lack of archaeological observations for this later stretch of time. It should be noted that the three locales with inscriptions and/or temples – the Pampa *tirtha*, Sandur, and Kurugodu – were all places which continued to be important in the following four centuries and it may be the case that regional land use between the sixth and ninth centuries was similar to that of the tenth through thirteenth. This is, however, impossible to assess at present.

In the tenth and eleventh centuries, we can see even in the rather imperfect map of regional settlement presented in Figure 11 that locations with datable temples and/or inscriptions – which is to say, villages, towns, forts, and religious centers of any importance – cluster on the broad, level plain of black soil north and east of the Daroji Valley. Note that data points for Raichur district, north of the river, are fewer, which does follow the balance of research but which appears also to dimly reflect settlement history. The Bellary plain contains the important town of Kurugodu, seat of the Sindas, which is situated atop an isolated high granitic outcrop. Although the temples and inscriptions of Kurugodu have been studied by Patil (1992), there has been no surface survey; it would not be surprising if archaeological research showed the presence of earlier settlement here. The Doravati fort seems to be associated with a settlement at the base of the high outcrop which supports it (discussed in Chapter 7); this was also a place of some importance, as was Balakundi on the Hageri, where numerous inscriptions have been found.

The second major locus of Early Middle period settlement is largely off the maps presented here, to the west. This is the area around Hagaribommanahalli and areas to the west which have abundant architectural remains and inscriptions (Patil 1992). The towns of Kogali, Morageri, and Ambali, seen on Figure 11, are all associated with multiple temples; both Kogali and Ambali lie on the Chikka Hagari River.

Agricultural strategies of this period seem to have focused on the exploitation of seasonal streams and the small, permanent water channels sometimes rather optimistically called rivers. Except for forest forts such as Hosamaladurga, Sandur, Doravati, and Kummata and river-crossings such as the Pampa *tirtha*, almost all of the eleventh, twelfth, and thirteenth century settlements are located along smaller drainages, not, with a few exceptions, on the banks of the Tungabhadra with its marked flood cycle. This strong pattern contrasts markedly with the pattern of riverside settlement in the Early Historic, though it should be noted that the Early Historic towns and villages we recorded did tend to perch atop high outcrops near the river banks. The Early Middle period settlements that do not sit astride large drainages are generally situated (on smaller drainages) at the base of large, isolated granitic outcrops of the black soil plains where they could harvest the runoff from those features.

In the Daroji and Avinamodugu valleys there is little evidence for the use of reservoirs prior to the thirteenth century. Reservoirs were certainly known and written about in these centuries; they were common in the far south and inscriptional data suggest that there were Early Middle period reservoirs in this region. Inscriptions from Morigere, Tallakallu, Kogali, Bagali, Ambali, and Sogi all mention eleventh and twelfth-century reservoirs (Patil 1992: 14). It should be noted that all of these are located west of the Daroji Valley either in the cluster of settlements on or near the Chikka Hageri in Hagaribommanahalli Taluk or in Hadegalli Taluk, further west – none are on the Bellary plain. It is also probable that these earlier reservoirs tended to be smaller than later ones and are thus less visible on maps; additional research on areas of dense Early Middle settlement is urgently needed. Perhaps some reservoirs of this period were refurbished in the Vijayanagara period and are thus invisible today. It is possible that the massive Daroji reservoir overlies the location of an eleventh, twelfth, or thirteenth-century reservoir, but even admitting some of these possibilities it is clear that there were major differences between agricultural strategies, organization, and the technologies of production in the Early Middle and Later Middle (Vijayanagara) periods.

There is clear evidence for the use of river-fed canals in the pre-Vijayanagara period, but again these features are few in number and their size appears to have been limited. An inscription of AD 1088 on a temple at Munirabad, north of the Tungabhadra near Hospet, records the construction of a canal near Pulige (Hulige). This is apparently the more than 6 kilometer-long Premogal channel, which is still in use. The inscription describes how the donor, Chauvedi-Bhattar, being convinced of the potential for harnessing the perennial river flow, surveyed the river bank and arranged for the excavation of a canal and subcanals. These channels are described as looking "like the threads drawn out after cutting asunder the stalk of the lotus" (Kotraiah 1995a: 19).[25] It is worth noting that the potential for perennial river irrigation in this area was apparently not well-established at this time; later inscriptions proceed on the assumption that such irrigation is indeed possible. Patil (1992: 14) also notes an inscription of AD 1199 from Hampi recording the gift of wet land under a weir called *Hampeye-katte,* indicating some irrigated land near the Pampa *tirtha.*[26]

Despite the evidence for some reservoirs along the Chikka Hageri, possibly at Hampi, and some further west, and for a limited zone of canal irrigation near the Tungabhadra, it appears that streamside fields and dry agriculture were probably the primary forms of agricultural production between the sixth and thirteenth centuries. Although these limited zones of formal irrigation were certainly of great importance, especially for what we can call the "western cluster" of Early Middle period settlement, it is also clear that the "eastern cluster" – the Doravati Nadu – was an area of dry farming and grazing, the former probably involving some control of runoff from the granitic hills and a focus on the heavy but water-retaining and level soils of the Bellary plain. The small polities of these settlement clusters did not have resource base of the later Vijayanagara Empire, resources to construct great irrigation facilities and the resources that resulted from those facilities. Such facilities are built at great cost, a cost both institutional and social (cf. Morrison 2007). Cattle and other livestock were probably very important parts of regional economies; hero stones and texts record valor not only in war but also in cattle raids and their consequences (e.g. Settar and Sontheimer 1982). Thus, grazing land would have been important and we can expect some mobility of herds and herders (among others) across the region.

We can conclude this historical account by noting that although the Pampa *tirtha* was certainly a culturally important place in the five or six hundred years before the founding of Vijayanagara, it was not a major locus of settlement. As noted, it is possible to isolate two main settlement clusters in this region, the Doravati-Kurugodu area and the area near Hagaribommanahalli to the west. Later Vijayanagara settlement would center around the Pampa *tirtha,* an appropriation of an existing sacred place which was certainly an important strategy of legitimation and positioning *vis-à-vis* the past and the local sacred power. However, it is also interesting that the city was situated in a kind of interstitial place between two earlier settlement clusters, a choice which seems to represent a deliberate break. In fact, both Vijayanagara historiography and traditional founding stories often mention the *de novo* character of the city and the empire – it seemed to burst out from nowhere (this region was never a political center before) and was built on nothing except a sacred river crossing. This is not exactly true. As we have seen, the site which would become the Vijayanagara urban landscape contained a long history of settlement and agriculture, built in a landscape already known, named, and memorialized, with cleared fields, temples, and occupied places. But this historiographic focus is correct in the sense that there was, in part and in conjunction with a deliberate appropriation of the past, a deliberate divorce with the past, a statement of founding and establishment of something new. In the following sections we will see that Vijayanagara period saw a massive transformation of the agricultural landscape, a significant shift in the kinds of facilities used, their distribution, in the scale of forest clearing, and indeed in the very structure of the landscape itself.

THE VIJAYANAGARA PERIOD: LOCALITY, CITY, EMPIRE

Politics and Origins

The many origin stories (Morrison 1995a: 37) for the city, despite their differences, all work to link city and polity with pre-existing landscapes and politics. Most accounts relate the story of two brothers, Hakka (or Harihara) and Bukka, local leaders who are said to have established the city and, shortly afterwards, the empire in the early fourteenth century. Of interest here is the oft-cited connection between the Hoysalas and the Kampila rulers of Doravati, Kummata, Hosemaledurga, and Haneya, rulers who, in some accounts, would go on to become the founders of the kingdom, a polity whose scope and fame eventually eclipsed those of the earlier Hoysalas. Other accounts link the brothers to other polities, including an account that has them convert to Islam (and back). It seems likely that these early rulers were local leaders formerly in the service of Kampiladeva and later subjects of the Hoysala kingdom with its capital at Dvarasamudra in what is now southern Karnataka. Members of this new Sangama dynasty began claiming royal titles only after several rulers and only as the Hoysala power waned (Stein 1980). Just as all the founding accounts suggest links to established powers, most also stress the novelty of the urban foundation as well as its supernatural sanction. Various well-established literary tropes (a rabbit that chases dogs, for example, signifying the special martial qualities of a particular. place) serve to highlight the distinction of the *locale itself*, a factor stressed more strongly in founding stories than specific political contexts, even though the latter have been of most interest to historians (Kulke and Rothermund 1986; Stein 1980; Venkata Ramanayya 1929, 1990 [1933]).

Expansion and Consolidation

Whatever the precise details of the establishment of the city of Vijayanagara (Figure 12), it is clear that this small polity, initially subordinate to existing larger states, rapidly expanded militarily. Military success was accompanied by demographic shifts with the formerly sparsely settled area around the Pampa *tirtha* quickly becoming the locus of a large city. As discussed below (and see Fritz, Michell and Nagarajo Rao 1985; Morrison 1995a, 2001), this rapid urban growth had a substantial impact on the landscape. If it is possible to trace a direct political legacy to the Hoysalas and a local connection to the Kampila rulers of Doravati, Kummata, Hosemaledurga, and Haneya – the study area – other kinds of links were also invoked by Vijayanagara kings and elites. One striking claim to an imperial legacy was established by evocation of the imperial Cholas, who ruled regions far to the south between the ninth and early fourteenth century. This evocation is seen in the "revivalist mode" of religious architecture (Michell 1994) whereby a distinctive Vijayanagara temple style was established through direct emulation of the monumental Chola style. This hearkening back to the expansionist Cholas was matched by a more general move toward "archaism" (Michell 1985b) in temple architecture that drew relatively clear connections between the ambitious new polity and older, established powers. The close connection between temple architecture and political ambition is no coincidence, as claims of authority were intimately connected to the *dharmic* role of kings and other leaders (see Appadurai 1978 for an analysis of how relationships between temples and political leadership were expressed in regional contexts). Other kinds of claims and connections to supralocal contemporaneous powers of South Asia, including Muslim polities of the north, were also established, using the idioms of elite, non-religious architecture (what Michell 1992 calls the Vijayanagara courtly style) and modes of royal dress and comportment (Wagoner 1996).

Both the long-term connections and the innovations of the Vijayanagara period can be discerned in landscape itself. As noted, the capital city was built on and around an important pilgrimage spot on the Tungabhadra River, a place with long-standing sacred associations. Although Early Historic settlement along the banks of the Tungabhadra was dense, there is no evidence for a major settlement or mortuary site in this exact location. The earliest architectural remains here are from the area on and near Hemakuta Hill, which contains several small pre-Vijayanagara and early Vijayanagara temples. The oldest of these may have been built in the ninth century (Michell 1985b: 274). The core of the great Virupaksha temple of Hampi, adjacent to Hemakuta, also dates back this far although most of the structure was built during the Vijayanagara period itself. As Michell (1985b: 274-5) notes, these early temples followed local, Deccani temple styles. It was not until the sixteenth century – a period of major expansion of the Vijayanagara empire – that the emulation and adaptation of Chola temple styles into a recognizable Vijayanagara idiom was really developed (Michell 1995: 191).

Most of the increase in urban and peri-urban population came from in-migration, some perhaps from the two settlement loci to the east and west of the Pampa *tirtha*, but the rest from other parts of southern India and beyond.[27] Initial military successes were concentrated to the south of the city where established political orders were in disarray; to the north the cohesive Bahmani empire effectively limited Vijayanagara expansion to a back-and-forth exchange of territory in the Raichur Doab, the fertile land between the Tungabhadra and Krishna rivers. Military success as well as a successful deployment of cultural markers of kingship (cf. Stein 1989a, 1989b) helped establish the rulers of Vijayanagara as (Wagoner 1996) "sultans among Hindu kings", or paramount rulers. Eventually, Vijayanagara would claim a significant part of the peninsula south of the city, with the exception of the western coast beyond the Ghats; ongoing conflicts with the Bahmanis and their successors (the Deccani Sultanates) as well as with the Hindu-ruled polities in the northeast meant that territories north of the city were often at issue. This pattern of conquest and consolidation meant that the capital city was always somewhat precariously located near the edge of the empire, a situation which eventually led to the abandonment of the city and several shifts of the capital further south.

Considerable disagreement exists about the degree of control exercised by the Vijayanagara kings over the territories claimed by them. Certainly, like all previous polities, subordinate rulers often maintained considerable autonomy and occasionally broke free of even nominal rule (Stein 1989a). At the same time, it is also clear that the Vijayanagara state maintained a much tighter grip over the administration and revenue extraction of at least part of the empire than had most previous rulers (Champakalakshmi 1981; Inden 1990; Karashima 1992, 1999; Palat 1987). Nilakanta Sastri (1966) famously referred to Vijayanagara as being the closest thing to a "war state" of any Hindu-led polity, a characterization aggressively contested by Stein (1980, 1989) whose adaptation of Southall's "segmentary state" model stressed the ritual character of the polity and the lack of any revenue flow from the provinces to the center. Most recent perspectives take more of a middle course, focusing on temporal, spatial, and resource-specific variability in efforts toward centralized control and revenue extraction (Sinopoli and Morrison 1995).[28] Certainly both war and ritual constituted important mechanisms of control, a fact embodied in royal patronage of both temples and fortifications, as well as other features equally, if less obviously, martial and religious – reservoirs, roads, and canals.

The Sangama dynasty would eventually be followed by three others, though the period of Vijayanagara rule over this region lasted only until the late 1500s, when the borders of the shrinking state moved further south. In these centuries, the demands of a huge and, at times, rapidly growing population greatly taxed the productive capacity of this semi-arid landscape.

Agricultural Production in the Heartland

The problems of supplying the populous city of Vijayanagara with foodstuffs must have been considerable. Archaeological research has shown just how extensively the landscape was modified in order to make this possible. With its large population of elites and specialists, the capital city needed a constant influx of grains, animals, vegetables, fruits, and condiments.[29] Outside the few areas such as the coast where water transport was possible, the transportation costs of moving bulk grain supplies were considerable. Goods were usually carried by bullock trains except where roads could support wheeled traffic. Our research has revealed the existence of many well-built roads around the city of Vijayanagara, but it seems unlikely that there were many similarly-built long-distance roads (Morrison in press a). As we shall see, much of the settlement and agricultural history of the region outside the city can be understood as a response to the demographic and political demands of urban markets and elites; the Daroji Valley is no exception to this pattern.

By the Early Middle period, some of the basic productive strategies on which Vijayanagara farmers relied had already been established. These strategies include specialized techniques such as the production of rice in paddies, probably with transplantation. It is worth reiterating, however, that reservoirs were *not* widespread in our survey area before the fourteenth century, and there was, as far as can be determined, only one large canal at this time. Throughout the Vijayanagara centuries, farmers continued to innovate and to respond to urban demands for specialized produce (wheat and barley for elite palates and foreigners, special types of rice, flowers for offerings and decorations, medicinal and flavoring plants, new crops such as maize and perhaps chiles). In the process of such change, we see the introduction of crops and facilities (such as aqueducts) new to this region, as well as reorganization of existing foci and forms of production. Among the latter we may count the quasi-commercial (large-scale) production of rice and other food grains, sugar cane, cotton, and vegetables, the extension of canal irrigation, the growth of dry land farming, and the phenomenal expansion in reservoir irrigation.

The greater metropolitan region supported a complex and internally differentiated agricultural economy involving multiple modes of cultivation (Morrison 1995a); at the same time, particular areas faced serious constraints on production which greatly limited their productive options. A major form of food production around the city was wet cultivation (*beddalu*, in Kannada), supported by a permanent, artificial water supply. All of the wet rice, sugar cane, vegetables, and high-value tree crops such as coconuts, areca nuts, and mangos depended on water from the Tungabhadra River (delivered via canals, canal-fed reservoirs, and aqueducts) or from wells. Wet agriculture was marked by a high degree of investment by institutions such as temples and by elite groups of various types (Morrison 2001, 2006a; Morrison and Lycett 1997).

Garden crops are primarily non-grain irrigated cultigens such as vegetables, spices, fruits, flowers, and medicinal plants; some gardens were watered by wells, a labor-intensive process. There is evidence for well watering in the Daroji Valley, as discussed below, where a few wells were fitted with special ramps for cattle to lift water (Morrison 1995a). Garden crops could potentially have been grown under the more reliable reservoirs. Prior to the twentieth century, the Daroji Valley supported virtually no wet crops and only limited areas of garden crops, a fact which is certainly key to understanding its history.

Most of the Daroji Valley relies on some form of dry cultivation (*gadde*, in Kannada), a practice ultimately limited by seasonal rainfall but marked, as we will see, by a wide array of ingenious devices for harvesting, storing, and conserving water. Although excavation data are lacking, historical evidence and basic crop requirements suggest that the dry crops grown in the valley included cotton, sorghum, various millets, pulses, and oilseeds. The degree of market participation by dry farmers appears to have increased significantly in the sixteenth century with the imposition of cash taxes on non-rice agricultural products (Morrison 2001), but it is probable, as discussed below, that expansion into the Daroji Valley was always meant to extend commercial food production. Sorghum and millets, the basic dry grains, have been the staple food of the majority of the population in the Vijayanagara region for at least the last several hundred years.

In another work (Morrison in press b), I discuss how practitioners of what I call a 'dry farming complex' worked, through their various productive activities, to provide basic economic and social support to the Vijayanagara state. Part of this role emerged from their participation in a complex web of patronage relationships, including the role of tax payer. As noted, there is some reason to think that even the so-called "inferior crops" such as millets had a considerable market and thus we must see even small-scale dry farmers, herders, and others as being caught up in larger supra-valley forces.

Elsewhere I discuss the financing of agriculture and its political and social implications more fully; but we may note here that larger projects were often financed by elites of various kinds and almost always for overt political and religious reasons.[30] While the construction of large canals was undertaken almost exclusively by kings, the financing of reservoir construction and maintenance was a matter of more general elite participation (Morrison and Lycett 1997) with *nayakas* constituting the largest group of reservoir donors. Having a reservoir built was an act of particular religious merit, perhaps all out of proportion to their utility in this landscape. Temples, too, undertook agricultural projects, in part as a consequence of their roles as landholders but also as a more general investment strategy. Temples were typically controlled by a board or committee, and political leaders were often involved in temple affairs so that it is not possible to say that "temples" and "the state" constituted entirely distinct arenas of political action. However, there was substantial independence and even tension between these two broad institutions (Saletore 1934; Stein 1980). Importantly, neither temples, with their diverse religious affiliations, nor political leaders, with their divergent interest and family groups, can be thought of as monolithic and we can thus identify multiple interest groups competing for access to and control of land, water, capital improvements, labor, and produce.[31]

For cultivators, outside capital improvements made agriculture more productive and could even change the form of cultivation that could be practiced. Although irrigation development increased both the number of demands on farmers' harvests and potentially the proportion of crop due, there is reason to believe that cultivators' shares also increased. The construction of a new reservoir would have been significant for agriculturalists not only because it might allow more secure production or the production of more desirable crops, but also because villages were generally situated near reservoirs. Proximity to farmland was one issue, but villages also required secure water sources for people and livestock, and the raised water table created by a reservoir made wells more viable. Thus, expanding reservoirs created both new opportunities and constraints for village placement.[32]

This outline of investment in reservoir construction and maintenance is primarily derived from the stone and copper-plate inscriptions of the period, most of which are associated with temples, although many are also built into agricultural features, such as the Dharmasagara reservoir in the Daroji Valley. Historical scholarship has focused disproportionately on temple inscriptions, a situation which has somewhat skewed our understanding of the range of textual concerns (Morrison and Lycett 1997). Even so, inscriptional information is available only for the larger reservoirs; many of the thousands of smaller reservoirs cannot be specifically tracked in the historical record. Similarly, the wells, terraces, check-dams and other features associated with dry farming and with reservoir watershed protection, find no mention in texts. It is thus difficult to extend this discussion of investment to these smaller features or to say whether or not construction of a terrace, for example, carried any of the *dharmic* implications that reservoir-building did. It seems possible, even likely, that many small reservoirs were financed by local people or families of substance, but people not as connected as the officially-appointed stratum of *nayakas* and less able or likely to leave written boasts of their actions. Smaller features may have been built by households, kin groups, or other local cooperative organizations. Perhaps village assemblies had a role in sanctioning the placement or form of such facilities – such bodies clearly played close attention to local issues of land use and water management (cf. Saletore 1934) – but it is difficult to be certain of this. In any case, it is clear that there were

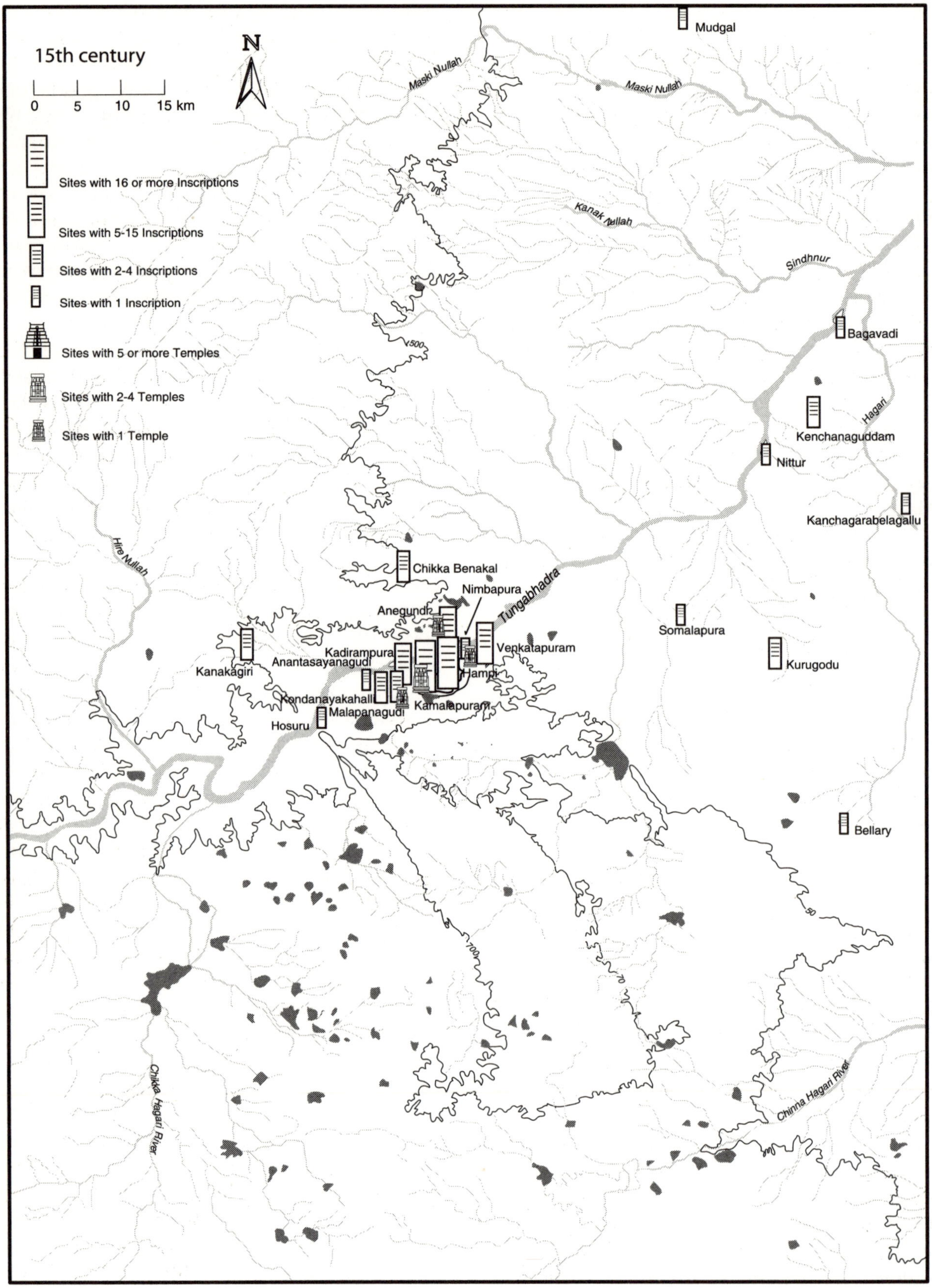

Figure 13. Distribution of sites and features, 15th century.

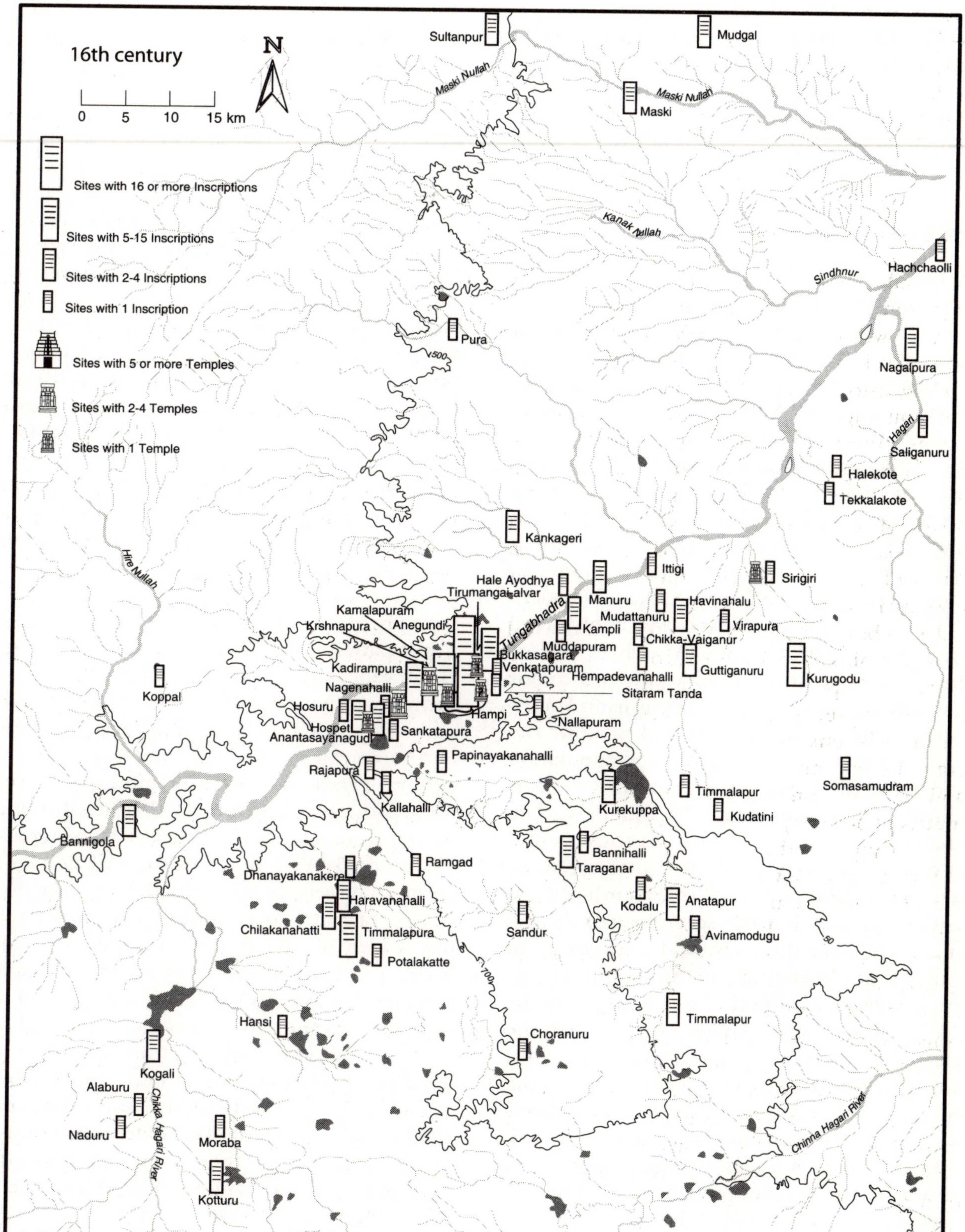

Figure 14. Distribution of sites and features, 16th century.

a large number of cross-cutting levels of investment, control, and involvement in local agricultural activities, and that even the small-scale dry farmers of the Daroji Valley were caught up to some extent in political and economic forces that reached in from beyond the valley and indeed, out from it as well.

Settlement and Change

As noted, Early Middle period settlement in our region was primarily concentrated in two areas east and west of the Pampa *tirtha*, both relatively more level than the site of the city which was tucked into a wide bend in the river. This location suggests both a desire to invest in canals – this is one of the few areas along the Tungabhadra where such an extensive canal network could have been constructed – and also no doubt an eye toward defense. Within a short time, Vijayanagara came to be one of the largest cities of its day with population estimates ranging from 100,000 to more than 300,000.

Using both survey results as well as historical and paleobotanical data (Morrison 1995a, 1996), it is possible to establish two major periods of settlement expansion and agricultural intensification in and around the city. The first major expansion of population and burst of construction came in the early fourteenth century (Figure 12), with the formal establishment of the city and the construction of the urban core walls. In the survey area, we see a distinctive pattern of fourteenth-century settlement that includes several small villages and towns near the river, and a scattering of walled towns further inland. Agriculturally, the Early Vijayanagara period was marked by the construction of several major canals and by the Kamalapuram *kere,* a large canal-fed reservoir, one of only two such perennial facilities in the entire region. Settlements cluster most closely near these zones of intensive irrigated agriculture. However, we also see the construction of a number of runoff-fed reservoirs in this period (especially north of the river) and have reason to believe that there was also dry farming of millets in upland zones further away from the river. In a sense, the Early Vijayanagara period established a spatial framework of roads and settlements, of temples and agricultural zones, that was only slightly filled out during the fifteenth century, or Middle Vijayanagara period.

The fifteenth century (Figure 13) is a period of relative stasis (Morrison 1997b) in the material record, and only one settlement, Mallapannagudi, associated with a large reservoir (VMS-4), clearly dates to this period. During the beginning of the sixteenth century, however, urban and rural population grew dramatically. The impact of this dense population aggregation on the surrounding landscape was considerable and it may be fair to say that the people of the sixteenth century transformed the land in ways that have significantly restructured all subsequent experiences of it.

The early sixteenth-century expansion of the city of Vijayanagara (Figure 14) is reflected both by construction of monumental architecture, including several large temple complexes, and by a pattern of filling in and spilling out of the walled space of the city. In the survey area, we see a phenomenal growth of settlement – again a dual pattern of infilling and expansion – with entire valleys becoming saturated with villages, complex systems of interconnected reservoirs and other agricultural facilities, temples, roads, and fortifications. Clearly, much of the agricultural production in the region was geared toward the provisioning of this massive city. As the botanical and historical data suggest (Morrison 1995a), much of the irrigated land seems to have been focused on the production of rice, orchard crops, and vegetables. Cotton was grown on dry fields for industrial-scale textile production, and large flocks of animals destined for the city's markets were grazed in area outside the city. Vijayanagara served as a major locus of consumption, not only of local produce, but also of craft goods from across South Asia and even beyond (Morrison 1997a; Sinopoli 2003). The sixteenth century, in particular, was a time of increasing monetization of the economy (Karashima 1984; Palat 1987), and agricultural production and exchange were partly, though not entirely, enmeshed in cash-based market relationships. These relationships varied significantly across classes of produce, especially rice versus other

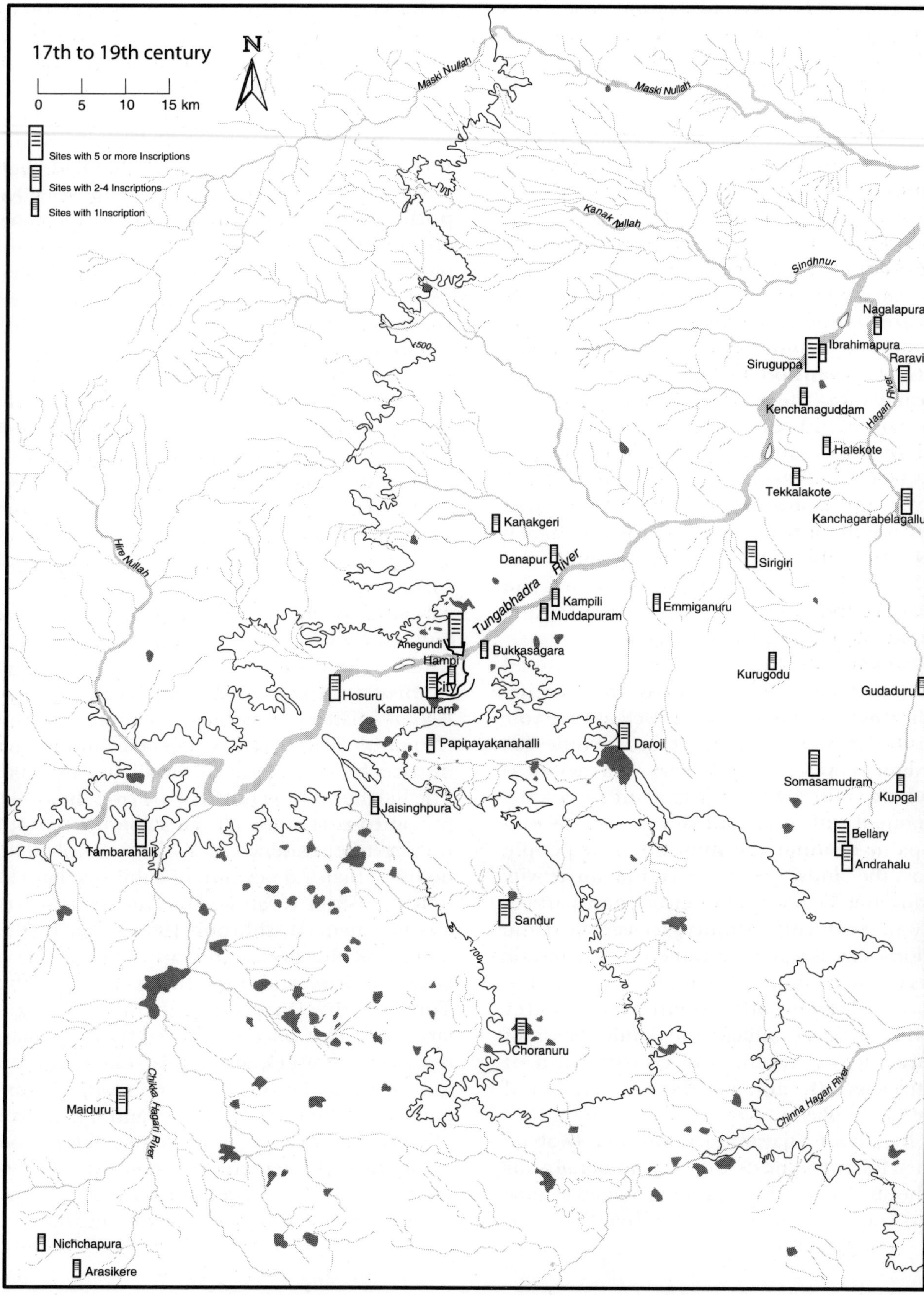

Figure 15. Distribution of sites and features, 17th-19th centuries.

food grains (Morrison 2001), and also across regions, so that areas further from large towns and cities were less involved in large-scale exchanges of foodstuffs (though not necessarily other goods).

Late Vijayanagara agricultural change played out differently across the study area. For example, north of the river agricultural intensification took the form of an expansion of canal irrigation, with the construction of the Anegondi channel as well as a large aqueduct. The Anegondi canal made many reservoirs in this area redundant, and they fell out of use. To the south, however, a major form of agricultural expansion into areas out of reach of canals was the construction of chains of reservoirs; both the Daroji Valley reservoir systems and the Dhanayakanakere system date largely to the sixteenth century. The construction of agricultural facilities, both these large ones as well as the many smaller features such as terraces, check dams, bordered and gravel mulched fields, dramatically reshaped the surface of the land, altering patterns of drainage, soil development, and vegetation.

Roads and fortification walls also constituted prominent features of this landscape. The impediments created by walls, as well as reservoir beds and muddy fields, and the possibilities for movement presented by formal roads as well as the long, raised embankments of reservoirs, combined with organic features such as outcrops to channel the movement of people across the landscape. In short, human activity during the Vijayanagara period, and particularly the sixteenth century, transformed the regional landscape in a number of dramatic ways – for example, through slope modification, changes in the patterns of water movement and drainage, the manipulation of routes of movement, the construction of temples and shrines, and the consecration of new sacred places.

The city of Vijayanagara was largely abandoned following the defeat of the imperial army in the AD 1565 battle of Talikota, waged against a military coalition of the five Deccani Sultanates, small polities on the northern border. The city was burned and looted and sporadic attempts at reoccupation proved short-lived. Most of the small agricultural settlements in the region continued to be occupied, however, including Hampi and Kamalapuram, small, early aggregated villages that had been absorbed into the metropolis. Only selective portions of the agricultural landscape were abandoned – for example, the reservoirs of more distant valleys such as Daroji and Dhanayakanakere. On the other hand, the canal system continued in use, and was expanded somewhat under British rule. Although there was some continuity in facility use, it is also clear that the contexts of agricultural production changed significantly with the abandonment of the city and the loss of urban food markets.

After the abandonment of the city and as the zone of Vijayanagara control moved toward the south, the capital of the empire was also shifted southward in a series of moves as the power and spatial scale of the empire slowly contracted. The study area came under the control of the Sultanate of Bijapur and later, various local leaders (Figure 15). Although the territory south of the Tungabhadra (part of present-day Bellary district) was briefly claimed by the Nizam of Hyderabad, it became one of the districts ceded by him to the British in 1800. The Raichur district north of the river, however, remained part of the Nizam's dominions until Indian Independence in 1947. Up until 1930, no more than 2.5 per cent of cultivated land in Bellary district (even less in Raichur District) was irrigated (Washbrook 1994: 132). In the middle of the twentieth century, spanning a period before and after Independence, the Tungabhadra Dam was built, submerging a large area that once contained towns, canals, reservoirs, temples, and roads. The irrigation supported by this dam, together with the expansion of the town of Hospet and the growth of mining in the area, have led to a new period of intensive settlement and landscape transformation that both builds from existing landscape forms and is rapidly transforming them.

NOTES

1. By places as such, I mean to say that which makes somewhere part of one place and not another, that which makes a location identifiable, named, recognized. This boundary construction, or what might be seen as a kind of precipitation of place out of the vast field of spatial possibility, need not of course be mutually exclusive so that multiple constructions of place may overlap and differentially incorporate a physical feature or features.
2. All of these temporal divisions are explained and discussed in the following sections.
3. Note, also that Caratini et al. (1991) found the onset of dessication to be some 500 years earlier in the south (at 16° north latitude, the same as the Daroji Valley). This may reflect sample resolution, dating error, real regional differences, or some combination of these factors. Sukumar et al.'s (1993) analysis of carbon isotopes from Nilgiri peat deposits (11° north latitude) suggested that monsoon weakening began even earlier, around 4000 BC, although this date is not yet matched by other studies.
4. The timing of this broad trend as well as the possibility of significant spatial variation in rainfall shifts clearly still needs additional work; here I work with the estimate of Caratini et al. 1991, as it is the closest study to our region that reflects a large-scale pattern of vegetation (Sukumar et al.'s study, while interesting, is apt to reflect primarily local conditions).
5. The "Little Ice Age" was a period of cooler temperatures and modified rainfall regimes that had profound effects on Europe and the Americas between the fourteenth and late seventeenth centuries. Although its effects varied by region, Lamb (1977) argues that they were globally synchronous. It is not, however clear that this is the case.
6. The terms C3, C4, and CAM refer to three different photosynthetic pathways, each of which is characteristic of a particular group of plant taxa. Worldwide, C3 plants constitute the largest group, which includes both rice and wheat. This class of plants follows a specific photosynthetic pathway named after a three-carbon compound formed early in photosynthesis. C3 plants tend to lose a large amount of carbon through photorespiration and are best adapted to cooler, moister, less bright conditions such as the temperate zones. CAM plants open their stomata for carbon uptake only at night, and as a consequence are well-adapted to dry climates. C4 plants comprise only about 1 per cent of the world's plant species. The C4 photosynthetic pathway leads to efficient net photosynthesis during strong light intensities; thus C4 plants are most often associated with the tropics. Many C4 plants are, in fact, tropical grasses such as maize, sugar cane, sorghum, and many of the millets. Climate-isotope signature relationships are far from simple, however, and anthropogenic actions can also alter plant compositions, which translates into changed carbon isotope ratios.
7. To say nothing of the fact that many paleo-climate studies employ vegetation indices as proxies for climate change. The record does show, however, that a variety of paleoclimate techniques have tended to produce broadly similar results, which should increase confidence in the patterns of change they isolate.
8. The precise construction dates of these temples are not known, but they were built some time between the early fifteenth and early sixteenth centuries.
9. Black cotton soils form deep cracks in the dry season; loose bits of soil fall into these cracks and thus the soil, in a sense, turns itself over every year or in some local expressions, it "plows itself".
10. Fuller (2003) lists the following staple crops for the early part (2800-2200 BC) of the Southern Neolithic; *Vigna radiata* (Mung bean), *Macrotyloma uniflorum* (Horse gram), *Bracharia ramosa* (Browntop millet), *Setaria verticillata* (Bristly foxtail millet), and *Dioscorea* sp. (Yams). In the middle part (2200-1800 BC) of the Southern Neolithic, he argues, *Lablab purpureus* (Hyacinth bean), *Pennisetum glaucum* (Pearl millet), *Triticum* sp. (Wheat), *Hordeum vulgare* (Barley), and perhaps *Lathryus sativus* (Grass pea) were added to crop repertoires. By the late (1800-1000 BC) period, *Cajanus cajan* (Pigeon pea), *Gossypium* (cotton), *Linum usitatissimum* (flax/linseed), and perhaps *Eleusine coracana* (Finger millet, an African import) were added to the mix.
11. Parts of what was formerly the Raichur District have just been incorporated into a newly-designated Koppal District. However, as this name has not yet made it into the literature, I will continue to refer to the area north of the Tungabhadra discussed here as part of Raichur district.

12. This boundary is based on a radiocarbon date from Maski, one of the earliest known dates for iron in India (see Chakrabarti 1992). Even if this rather controversial date does not, in fact, accurately date the presence of iron, it is useful as a general temporal boundary.
13. Importantly, Black-and-Red Ware is found without Russet-Coated Painted Ware or Micaceous wares (with a few key exceptions, see Wheeler 1947: 300) in one context – megaliths. There is some reason then to view at least some BRW vessel forms as specialized mortuary forms.
14. Of course, such megaliths might be chronologically restricted and, more importantly, the association of certain megaliths with horse gear is more likely to reflect some aspects of elite culture and ideology than any general mobility pattern (cf. Leshnik 1974).
15. Which is not to say either that Early Historic Hinduism was exactly like contemporary forms or that none of these religions have changed since the Early Historic. Certainly the history of what is broadly glossed as "Hinduism" is extraordinarily complex; I intend only to point to the increasing institutionalization of religious forms and practice on the one hand, and their dispersal throughout the subcontinent on the other (see Nilakanta Sastri 1966, 1992[1963] and Champakalakshmi 1996 for further discussion).
16. The edicts in this region are as follows: Maski contains Minor Rock Edict I, Gavimath (Koppal) Minor Rock Edict I, Palkigunda (Koppal) Minor Rock Edict I, Udegolam Minor Rock edicts I and II, Nittur Minor Rock Edicts I and II, Brahmagiri Minor Rock Edicts I and II, Siddapura (Brahmagiri) Minor Rock Edicts I and II, Jatinga-Ramesvara (near Brahmagiri) Minor Rock Edicts I and II (Sugandhi 2003). Clearly, the texts are highly repetitive. Only at Sannati (Separate Rock edicts I and II and Major Rock Edicts XII and XIV) and Erragudi/Rajula-Mandagiri (to the east, in Andhra Pradesh, Major Rock Edicts I-XIV, Minor Rock Edicts I and II) are there different edicts.
17. Many of the megalithic complexes we located and described were found in close proximity to these settlements; in one case, both sharing the same granitic outcrop. Ongoing excavations at Kadebakele point toward the existence of Neolithic deposits underlying the Iron Age levels; this is, however, not confirmed as yet.
18. The first millennium AD is a rather difficult time period in that textual sources are still quite rare and stone construction sparse (Figure 10). Much of our difficulty, too, probably stems from the utter lack of research on quotidian ceramics from this period. Still, it is clear that settlement in the intensive survey area was very light in these centuries, as was the entire surrounding region.
19. *Nadu* is a term referring to a territorial unit. Up until the Vijayanagara period numbers were also sometimes affixed to the names of territorial units, especially in (what is now) Karnataka, although this practice is also seen in Andhra. These are variously argued to represent the number of villages in that unit or, somewhat less convincingly, the number of conquering or founding households (Dikshit 1964: 20-1; and see discussion by Stein 1980: 127-30). Some of the numbers are very large – Gangavadi 96,000 for example – and cannot refer to either of these. Certainly there is a conventional element to these (round) numbers; it seems probable, however, that they are not simply arbitrary.
20. The Chalukyas of Kalyan (AD 973-1162) are also known as the Late Chalukyas to distinguish them from the earlier Chalukyas of Badami (AD 543-755).
21. There is certainly formal architecture dating to the Early Historic, but none of it is found in this region. Most famous are the rock-cut "cave temples", monastic complexes, and *stupas* primarily associated with Buddhism (Morrison 1995b). The closest known stupa is at Sannathi. Clearly, and despite the many Ashokan edicts in the area, this region was no Buddhist center. There are also texts other than edicts that date to the Early Historic but again none of these come from this region.
22. To call the Chalukyas, Rashtrakutas, and Hoysalas "imperial" is not to claim that they exercised close control over areas claimed by them and whose leaders acknowledged their overlordship. Rather, it is to point out the expansive and incorporative character of these polities. Certainly the Rashtrakutas were the most aggressive and successful of these three empires (Inden 1990).
23. Note the connection with the name Bellary.
24. Patil's sources include inscriptions, foreign accounts, and contemporary texts as well as architecture and art history. This account points to the value placed on heroic action in battle, a value materialized in hundreds of hero stones dating to the Early Middle period. Female heroism largely, but not entirely (see Zagarell

2002), involved self-sacrifice, especially *sati* or self-immolation, and was also memorialized on stone markers (see Settar and Sontheimer 1982).

25. The association between the lotus, an aquatic flower, and reservoirs is an important one, as discussed in Chapter 4.
26. This could also be a reservoir. Kotraiah (1995a: 20) suggests that it is a reservoir, which might be identified with the large and heavily disturbed reservoir in the "irrigated valley" (Fritz, Michell, and Nagaraja Rao 1985) south of Hampi.
27. The city of Vijayanagara was a cosmopolitan place where people of diverse backgrounds, occupations, and creeds lived and worked (e.g. Michell 1990; Sinopoli 2003; Stein 1980); clearly not all of the residents of the city came from southern India.
28. One relevant factor in these debates is the fact that much historical scholarship has been focused on the Tamil provinces rather than the imperial heartland itself. For example, Appadurai and Breckenridge's (1976, Breckenridge 1985) early work was critical for establishing the importance of Hindu temples in agricultural investment. Subsequent research in the northern part of the empire, however, has shown that, in contrast to the large southern pilgrimage centers studied by Appadurai and Breckenridge, around the city agricultural facilities were more often patronized by *nayakas*, or local political leaders (Morrison and Lycett 1997).
29. Here we should also note related demands for firewood, dung, fodder, and construction materials that would have been met primarily by production in the urban hinterland.
30. These themes are introduced in Morrison 1995a, 2001, and Morrison and Lycett 1997; they are elaborated more fully in Morrison in press b.
31. In addition to various Vaishnavite, Shaivite, and Devi (Goddess) temples, there were several Jain temples in and around the city. I do not mean here to exclude Muslim religious foundations; unfortunately we know very little about their landholding or involvement in agriculture in this region. It seems possible that these were primarily urban and peri-urban institutions; exceptions to this pattern will be noted in the following Chapters.
32. Like large dam projects today, the submergence of fields and structures was also a concern in the extension of reservoirs.

Chapter Three

ROLES AND MEANINGS OF SOME SOUTH INDIAN PLACES

> There exists a widespread though tacit assumption that the past is a limitless and plastic symbolic resource, infinitely susceptible to the whims of contemporary ideology. . . . This assumption is false. My own argument . . . takes for granted that discourse concerning the past is an aspect of politics, involving competition, opposition, and debate. But the central question with which I am concerned is: *how is such debate culturally organized*? (Appadurai 1981: 201-2, emphasis in original)

Inasmuch as this book is about the making of places and of their long-term histories, it is worth examining in some more detail what, precisely, constitutes a place and how this rather ambiguous concept may actually be deployed in specific cultural and historical contexts. The city of Vijayanagara, clearly, became a (named) place both through the lived experience of its residents and visitors, the representations of residents and others, and the imaginations of those who read or heard about it. But even after the abandonment of the city in the late sixteenth century and the restructuring of space and place in the surrounding region, the city has continued, in some sense, to be a salient place though the precise contours of that place, its significance, and import have changed radically through time and vary radically from person to person. It may be clear that, on the one hand, the contemporary pilgrims who arrive by the busload every year visit certain sacred locations see the region in a particular way while the international tourist, lured by the site's (threatened) designation as a UNESCO World Heritage Monument conceives of the city as another kind of place altogether. Indeed, by insisting that Vijayanagara be thought of as an abandoned *city*, I am arguing against a common contemporary view of the region as a vast stage-set for scattered piles of ruins and isolated structures; indeed, even my own archaeologically-informed sense of place differs from those of other scholars who have not, for example, had the experience of systematically documenting the landscape all around the city and who thus conceive of the city's place in the region very differently.

This distinction involves both time and standpoint and, taken, to an extreme, seems to mitigate against the possibility of shared definition, of any useful fixity to the concept of place at all. This is not my intent. I suggest instead that variation in perception and experience, contestation and disagreement about the meanings, nature, and very contours of places are analytically significant primarily because there usually *is* some set of larger definitions of place, definitions which are or aspire to be normative or hegemonic. Thus, I will argue that, on the one hand, the Daroji Valley became an identified place only in the Vijayanagara period while the Doravati Nadu, to which the valley as a place was closely allied, had already achieved an independent identity by the Early Middle period. In this I am identifying temporal flux in the specific contours of place in one small region. On the other hand, I also suggest that we can identify specific south Indian *kinds of places*, among them ashmounds, megaliths, villages, temples, inscriptions, reservoirs, tombs, and many others. While only some of these categories are unique to south India, the specific forms, functions, and meanings of such places in a south Indian context will differ to a greater or lesser extent from their manifestations elsewhere. Lest this assertion raise alarms among those who fear essentialism and reification, let me hasten to add that all places are contextually defined, in both time and space, and that there are thus as many kinds of places as there are people (in time) to make, experience, and redefine them. South Indian places, as I characterize them here, are no more a unitary category than any other. This said, however, there are always, certainly, shared cultural experiences of relevance in the making of places; to deny this is to deny the relevance of cultural understanding entirely, and it is for this reason I feel the need to consider some of the kinds of landscape elements we will encounter in and around the Daroji Valley and to make some general comments about their characteristics. The materialized landscape and the kinds of places it contains – built and otherwise – constitutes a kind of initial repertoire for further action and construction, a certain concretized form of "the past", that, following Appadurai (above), consists of certain *a priori* culturally-significant structures that are part of the raw material for the present. To understand any present, then, we might begin with its location and so now to the valley itself.

THE DAROJI VALLEY: A LANDSCAPE IN HISTORY

For most periods of its history, the Daroji Valley lay at the edge of a center – spatially, strategically, and socially, a pattern that was certainly true for the Vijayanagara period. This small valley is situated along the southern edge of the productive and densely settled irrigated landscape surrounding the city of Vijayanagara. The dry farming, grazing, and other economic strategies practiced by Daroji residents were not among the most financially rewarding nor were the social positions of valley residents among the highest in the region (Figures 16 and 17). Nevertheless, the Daroji Valley was no isolated backwater, serving as a route of passage, a defended field of action and a landscape of some complexity and productivity that was closely linked to the economy of the nearby metropole.

The Daroji Valley as an historical place, an anthropogenic landscape whose history can be traced for at least four thousand years, can in some sense only be understood in relation to the larger world of which it was a part. I have already briefly discussed this larger context here; it is necessary now to focus more closely on the structure and content of the valley landscape itself. The agricultural history of the Daroji Valley is of a sort that often goes unrecorded and indeed virtually unnoticed in South Asian archaeology; a kind also largely overlooked by historians. The valley is a place of widely scattered surface remains, without much monumental architecture, noted in texts only briefly and in passing. Nevertheless, this valley formed an important part of the regional picture of the Vijayanagara empire and indeed has functioned as a productive landscape ever since the Neolithic.

As I have mentioned, my objective in this study is not to construct a fully realized history of the Daroji Valley, but instead to use this small region as an example of the way one predominantly agrarian landscape was structured and used over a long span of time. However, within this broad temporal frame, I focus most specifically on the Middle Periods, especially the Vijayanagara period, as this is the era when the Daroji Valley was most significantly transformed. Although I give weight in this analysis to a large number of types of features, my discussion focuses somewhat disproportionally on a single important and distinctive form of agricultural feature, a feature perhaps most highly developed in southern India and Sri Lanka – the reservoir. Within a discussion that covers several millennia, the vast majority of our information comes from the Vijayanagara period of the fourteenth through sixteenth centuries AD, when reservoir construction reached its maximum extent and when the valley attained the basic productive contours that would persist until the middle of the twentieth century.

This study includes a great deal of descriptive detail; it is my intention to present here primary information that must lie behind any interpretive study of precolonial rural landscapes and to show, at least in outline, how such information might be used as both a foil and a support to the perspectives we derive from text-

Figure 16. View from fort VMS-1009 across the village of Papinayakanahalli and the Daroji Valley; Sandur Hills in the background.

Figure 17. Recent threshing surface, fallow dry-farmed field in the Daroji Valley; Sandur Hills in the distance.

based history. Agrarian history has a long and distinguished record in India (e.g. Baker 1984; Charlesworth 1985; Guha 1985; Habib 1963, 1995; Ludden 1985; Robert 1983; Stein 1980; Stokes 1978; Washbrook 1994). I am fortunate to be able to build on this research tradition and on existing works on environmental history both in India and beyond. However, my project departs from all of these in emphasizing the actual physical remains of landscape transformation and in documenting an anthropogenic landscape on the ground, rather than solely through texts, memories, or ecological models.

The Daroji Valley as Place: Doravati, Vijayanagara, and the World Outside

What makes the Daroji Valley a place of any integrity? In some sense it is not, having been defined and even named for this project; for many of the periods of time that people used the valley it probably had little to no identity as a place at the scale discussed here. Like all other archaeological studies, this is a study of a particular area – of a physical space rather than of any particular anthropic landscape. My assertions about time, change, and meaning are, of necessity, inferential and it is always the case that the borders of any spatial analysis are to some extent arbitrary. However, it does seem fair to say that the Daroji Valley "became" a place during the Vijayanagara period and that it had a particular unity at that time. Furthermore, because of that unity resulted in the construction of several chains of interconnected reservoirs, enduring landscape features, it still has something of that salience as a spatial unit.

A place as opposed to where? It is a common place that spatial identities vary considerably with scale are always framed with reference to some other place. Thus, in one sense, the entire region considered in this book may legitimately be called south India, a term which, while it uses contemporary socio-political nomenclature, can be matched in other time periods by similar large-scale geographic conceptions. This analytical scale is not, however, very useful here. I operate, instead, on a smaller, more intimate scale in considering the structure of the Valley landscape and its change through time, the primary focus of this book. However, we also need to match this focus, what in archaeological work is usually referred to loosely as the region – the Daroji Valley is after all more than 80 square kilometers, or 180 square kilometers including the Avinamodugu Valley, an area posing serious logistical challenges to fieldwork – with a more meso-scale unit, called here the macroregion. The macroregion appears in various maps in this volume and as an implicit or explicit basis for comparison. An argument that the Daroji Valley only emerged as a place of any integrity during the Vijayanagara period must also, then, consider the city of Vijayanagara. When and how did the "city of victory" itself become a place and how has that changed? Although this subject is outside the primary focus of this work – after all, the logic of this argument would eventually expand to encompass the entire world – I do consider the city as a place briefly below; this subject also arose in the historical discussion of Chapter 2 but in this Chapter I deal more explicitly with the physical structure of the city and its remnants.

The unity of both the Daroji Valley and its sister Avinamodugu Valley is, first of all, topographic and hydrological. As watersheds, the Daroji and Avinamodugu Valleys form a more or less self-contained hydrological unit. The east-west oriented Daroji Valley (Figure 18) draws runoff from two ranges of hills; the western end of the valley is marked by a gradual upward slope, while the eastern end, once open, has been dammed by the Daroji reservoir. The north-south Avinamodugu Valley, which drains into the main valley just before the latter's eastern edge, may be seen as a kind of appendage to the Daroji Valley, feeding it with excess water flow and not itself having any significant access to outside areas (at least topographically and hydrologically; clearly human beings moved freely in and out of this side valley). The hydrological features of the Daroji Valley follow from its distinctive topography as do possibilities for human

Figure 18. Topographic overview of the Daroji Valley.

mobility; there are only a limited number of gaps in the rocky hills defining the northern side of the valley that would easily carry roads, even fewer on the south.

The boundedness of the Daroji Valley marked by natural flow of drainage and runoff was, by the end of the Vijayanagara period, also limited by human constructions. The eastern edges of the valley are clearly marked and defended by fortification walls and forts, making the valley both a naturally and culturally defined space. The Avinamodugu Valley, for the most part, lies outside this fortified area and was evidently separate from the Daroji Valley. Though at one level we may see the Daroji Valley as a place in itself, as an area situated less than 10 kilometers from an imperial capital, the Daroji Valley at this time was also oriented toward production for the urban markets and its inhabitants were responsive to changes in the conditions of production, consumption, and distribution caused by, for example, the dramatic expansion of the city of Vijayanagara and the Vijayanagara polity. Thus, the boundedness of the valley can easily be overemphasized. Some of the connections between the Valley and the city can be traced textually, others have left more material traces. Thus, although the Valley has a coherence as an analytical unit, both geographic and archaeological, we will constantly have to move back and forth between extremely local considerations of land use and their larger contexts.

Close study of the Daroji Valley has shown that people lived and worked here prior to the Vijayanagara period, and we can begin to consider the structure and timing of that land use history; clearly, the Daroji Valley and its environs were differently integrated into regional spatial conceptions at different times. Most immediately, the area in and around Daroji can be seen to have been the focus of the Doravati Nadu, a territorial division that while perhaps taking in part of the main valley, was oriented toward the east and the Bellary plains where population was concentrated in the Early Middle period. This political unit was absorbed into the expanding Vijayanagara polity, retaining its identity as a place while being transformed politically, socially, and economically. Even earlier, we can see Neolithic farmers and herders living and moving through the valley, Early Historic iron workers using local ores to make metal objects for use elsewhere, and megalith-makers marking locations and burying their dead, activities carried out on the margins of places along the river where most human activity was centered at that time.

SOME SOUTH INDIAN PLACES

My discussion of various kinds of places in this chapter is necessarily selective and incomplete. In most cases, there exists a vast (but often scattered) literature discussing the features of such places. This, chapter, then, should be considered an overview only, but one where material features not usually considered together – ashmounds and temples, for example – take their places side by side, as they do on the ground. In each of the following cases discussed below I will attempt to summarize not only the salient physical characteristics of each feature but also to contextualize aspects of its potential economic function, political and social contexts, and cultural meanings. In all cases, we must ask, "Whose use? Whose meaning?" because such concerns are necessarily contextual and the significance of a marked object/place such as an inscription will be variable and contested even at a single point in time (Lycett and Morrison 1998). History, too, matters as places are remembered and revisited, forgotten and abandoned (Alcock 2001; Nelson 2000). Even where places continue to be used and lived in, they inevitably become transformed. Structures are remodeled or used in new ways. Thus, I pay particular attention in this book to the continuities and discontinuities in the historical trajectory of this region. Which places continue, century after century, to be marked, built, and rebuilt; which now lie abandoned or radically transformed? Another way to phrase this question brings us into contemporary classifications of places and this is – which places are now "archaeological sites" and which are "living"? When do such breaks occur and what might such patterns tell us?

The context of a place also changes it even in the absence of major remodeling so that what were once forest temples on the Sandur Hills now sit amid open grasslands, houses, and the scars of mining. Forests, again, carry cultural baggage, not just in south India, but for almost all people, and one of the hidden features of landscape transformation is often this kind of environmental context. A landscape history of this area thus requires consideration of, for example, the degree to which the granitic Hampi-Daroji Hills may once have held developed soils and of the nature and extent of past vegetation cover. Changing physical contexts may be "natural" (the climate of the Southern Neolithic seems to have been significantly drier than that of later periods, for example, and this had an effect on the lived experiences of area residents), "cultural" (the construction of the Tungabhadra Dam in the twentieth century had a significant impact on the region, both extending canal irrigation and flooding many villages), or some combination of both. One hillside temple near Hospet, for example, has even changed color as a result of strip mining in the Sandur Hills and subsequent erosion of iron- and manganese-rich sediments, the newly-exposed red sediment indelibly staining the structure and even the resident troops of rhesus macaques a dark red color. As we will see, color is a dimension of great symbolic significance in temple architecture and Hindu ritual more generally; a temple that changes color must surely also change in other ways.

In many cases, we can know or guess something of the expressive nature of a landscape feature. Temples and reservoirs may have been endowed by a single person or a group of people. They were planned and built. Inscriptions and sculptures, as well as rock art, were meant to be seen and "read". However, much literature on landscapes, at least the strand that does not reify construction as abstract labor value, often ignores the material nature of landscape elements and of places, even in many cases, the materiality of the built environment. Clearly, the construction of places is a key concern. How are resources, including knowledge, labor and material, generated, allocated, mobilized? Who has the ability to place landscape elements such as, for example, a temple in a particular location? What is the nature of the social and political organization of builders, donors, scribes, worshipers, and others who make, use, and see a place? Indeed, what is the tempo of the productive process? Are objects and places made quickly, slowly, singly, collectively, officially, unofficially? Answers to all these questions, even ignoring for the moment the great variability in individual situations, will be long and shot through with qualifications. I thus reiterate my caveat that this discussion should be considered a springboard only; in the following chapters I move directly to some concrete examples.

Ashmounds

The term ashmound is a misnomer. Although these Neolithic features, unique to this part of southern India, are indeed mounds, they are not made of ash (Figures 19 and 20). Their only ash-like characteristics are their color – a kind of variegated light gray – and association with fire. As noted, ashmounds are durable accumulations of fired dung, monumental features in their own right. There is no accepted alternate term for ashmound and so I use it here – indeed, as I discuss below, this very name provides an interesting link with later senses of these places and of the residues of significant fires. However, I will refer to the physical substance of the mound as vitrified dung or slaggy[1] material in order to emphasize its actual physical properties; lightweight, hard, scorious, and coherent. Although, as noted in Chapter 2, a coherent account of ashmounds in their original socio-economic contexts cannot be separated from associated evidence for settlement (artifacts, postholes, surfaces, etc.), in more contemporary notice it is the ashmound alone which seems to command attention; the original functions, significances, and meanings of the features in Neolithic worlds having been completed erased.

Objects of antiquarian curiosity since the late nineteenth century, various origins have been suggested for south Indian ashmounds. The

Figure 19. VMS-1035, Kudatini ashmound, showing road cut.

Figure 20. Kupgal ashmound, with tree shrine.

British historian and antiquarian Robert Sewell, for example, noted local accounts that they were the funeral pyres of giants, demons, or other supernatural figures, adding that they might represent the remnants of "enormous human or animal sacrifices performed by holy *Rishis* [sages]" (cited in Foote 1916: 92). Other hypotheses included metal working, or the remains of old funeral pyres. The actual origin of these mounds as dung accumulation was worked out by Robert Bruce Foote, a British colonial officer working for the Geological Survey. Foote, a pioneer in the archaeology of southern India who documented evidence for the earliest human occupation of the peninsula and whose catalogues of prehistoric antiquities (1914, 1916) still remain valuable resources, argued that the ashmounds consisted of burned cattle dung and correctly assigned them to the Neolithic.[2] This compositional supposition was later confirmed through chemical testing (Zeuner 1959).

Although many ashmounds had been probed by amateur enthusiasts, the first systematic excavations in and around these features was in the 1950s. Excavations by Raymond Allchin at Piklihal and Utnur (1960, 1961 and see Allchin 1963), then in the dominions of the Nizam of Hyderabad (later to become Raichur district, Karnataka) revealed not only more secure evidence for the chronology of ashmound sites, but also yielded cattle footprints captured in the hardened slag, a kind of frozen moment in the transformation of wealth in cattle to monumental form.[3] Since then, several more ashmound sites have been excavated, the closest of these to our region being the settlement and twin ashmounds at Kupgal (Majumdar and Rajaguru 1966), near Bellary. Most recently, excavations at Budihal and Watgal (Paddayya 1993a, 1993b, 1998; Devaraj et al. 1995), both in Raichur District, have contributed greatly to our understanding of ashmounds (and see Paddayya 1973 for a regionally-oriented analysis; Korisettar et al. 2001 for a recent review of the literature) and Neolithic life more generally; neither of these projects is yet fully published.

Ashmounds both blend into and stand out from the organic landscape of this region. They often occur, singly or in groups of two or three, at the bases of the granitic hills which shape local topography, but many also sit perched on the sides of these hills, especially on the saddles between peaks. It may not be too fanciful to suggest that ashmounds were meant to invoke or represent the ubiquitous hills of the region, especially since the distribution of these features across southern India is quite limited and does not extend much beyond northern Karnataka. Unlike the granitic hills, however, ashmounds are light in color, perhaps almost white when fresh, as broken chunks are significantly lighter than their weathered surfaces. They would, then, have stood out visually, especially those located on hills. In general, plants do not prosper on ashmounds. They are hard and not absorbent; even now, some four thousand years after most of them were made, only a few are hidden by vegetation cover. Some ashmounds in our region, however, have one or more trees growing atop them, often trees with sacred associations such as Neem (*Adazirachta indica*). Taken in association with the small shrines that generally accompany such trees, it is clear that these ashmounds (still?) have sacred associations (Figure 20). As will become clear, however, other ashmounds in the region are either not being used at all or are being mined as raw material for the production of lime.

Several observers of ashmounds have described the occasional occurrence of a "vallum" of vitrified dung surrounding ashmounds and their associated settlements. This is an interesting feature, seemingly something of a low wall defining a space containing the mound (or mounds) as well as the houses, work areas and open spaces around it. In his 1963 review, Allchin described some of the ashmounds of the Daroji Valley (and see Foote 1914), noticing vallums of slaggy material at some of them. Unfortunately, these features are no longer evident at any of the ashmounds I have visited. It is possible that these features are limited to low-lying ashmounds and that their disappearance is thus due to burial by colluvium over the last 50 years; another explanation for the absence of such features is destruction by the expansion of plowed areas, but this seems less compelling because if the "ash" vallums were actually as highly fired as the mounds, then they would be unlikely to be destroyed by the light plows of this region.

How were ashmounds made? It may not be incorrect to say that they were built, in the sense that they must have begun with large piles of dung, piles heaped up deliberately. At Budihal, the only site with extensive horizontal excavations, Paddayya (1993a) has described the topography and stratigraphy of this site's two ash mounds, each of which was surrounded by, and occasionally interlayered with, habitation deposits. Ashmound I consisted of both softer and more vitrified dung deposits: Paddayya (1993a: 78) notes that there are at least five major phases of dung accumulation, and three major episodes of firing. However, he also notes (Paddayya 1993a: 78) the presence of "discontinuous lenses or pockets of soft/ granular ash, the implication being that each one of these layers involved several minor episodes of cow-dung accumulation and burning". Thus, we can posit both major accumulation and burning – activities involving sustained collection of material and a rather spectacular incineration – as well as much smaller dung piling and burning events. The form of the Budihal mounds, then, is far from the "layer cake" model described by Allchin (1963; cf. Paddayya 1993a: 79), a fact also reflected in the overall form of the mounds which consist of both a larger, lower area topped by a higher, smaller area. Other ashmounds, such as those at Kupgal, seem to consist solely of two discrete piles of slaggy material without a lower apron of fired dung. In any case, notwithstanding Allchin's (1963) characterizations of ashmounds as cattle pens, it seems wildly improbable in the context of a mobile, extensive land use system that cattle would be so closely corralled that they would have to stand on piles of dung much higher than any contemporary stockyard in the western United States, places of incredibly dense concentrations of animals. Cattle must certainly have been penned or confined somehow, or such a quantity of dung could not have been gathered, but the deliberate, built nature of the mounds seems beyond dispute.

Evidently, the piled-up dung was burned, sometimes while still relatively fresh, as evidenced by the footprints. In many cases, ashmounds reveal internal stratigraphy, indicating the accretional nature of their construction. Layers of vitrified dung may be interspersed with rocks, dirt, even a few artifacts, evidence for gaps between episodes of burning. Kudatini ashmound, for example, discussed in Chapter 7 (and see Figure 19), has at least four major layers of vitrified dung (Allchin 1963: 55) separated by several thin interstitial layers. Allchin also argues that this entire mound was built over a prepared surface. If construction of ashmounds was often accretional, it is also the case that most dung layers are quite substantial, suggesting that heaping and burning episodes were large-scale and dramatic. The firing of a dung heap must have provided a very powerful sensory experience. Not only would a large, hot fire have been produced, but dung fires create very substantial quantities of smoke with a pungent, characteristic smell. Even today, when dung is far too valuable to be fired in quantity and is used both as manure and as a source of fuel for those who cannot afford other sources or for temporary fires such as those built by night watchmen to keep warm on the job, the smell of a dung fire is powerfully evocative of the South Indian landscape. The pillar of smoke, even more than the smouldering fire, must have been the primary visual impact of ashmounds in the Neolithic landscape. Later on, of course, the durable, rock-like mounds survived as markers of these places, places which as this study will emphasize, were often visited again and again and were in many cases reoccupied during the Iron Age and Early Historic.

The labor requirements of ashmound construction are very difficult to estimate, especially since our grasp of their lifespans is so tenuous. However, it is certain that these large mounds – the largest ones in the region approach 1,500 square meters in surface area and have volumes of up to 15,000 cubic meters (and see Johansen 2004 for a list of ashmound sizes and estimated volumes)—would have required some coordinated labor effort, perhaps possible only at times of population aggregation.[4] The clear need for large quantities of dung (and hence cattle), as well as the presumably limited nature of forage during a dry phase in the generally dry climate of northern Karnataka, suggests that large cattle aggregations must have been episodic rather than constant; the accretional nature of the mounds and the fact that some occur with only limited artifact scatters (even though there existed some large permanent settlements) also indicates that mounds must have been revisited by groups of people and animals moving across the landscape, visits that may have continued for as long as a thousand years.[5]

Recognition of the likelihood that Neolithic ashmounds emerged as by-products of periodic human and cattle aggregations has provided ground for the most common explanations of why ashmounds might have been made. As noted, Allchin sees them as cattle pens but suggests that their firing was ritual in nature, drawing a direct parallel with the later Hindu festival of Holi, when large bonfires (not involving dung, however) are often made. Paddayya has suggested a somewhat different explanation, postulating the existence of periodic cattle fairs and subsequent dung disposal. Why, then would the dung be burned? To get it out of the way in a context where abundant wood was available for fuel and manure was nor required for agriculture. This may be – it is obviously difficult to evaluate arguments about why something happened in such a distant time – but it also seems probable that the "reasons" for making ashmounds (and there must have been many), had to do with either the smoky fires they made, the distinctive features they created, or both, as well as other factors we have not yet considered. Slaggy material may also have been moved around, which suggests that the mounds themselves had a significance beyond the fires that made them. Excavations at the site of Brahmagiri (Wheeler 1947), which has a very large Neolithic settlement but no visible ashmound, yielded some loose fragments of vitrified dung in the settlement itself.

Arguments purporting to explain the import of monumental features and structures often revert to functionalism. In archaeology, the legacy of structural-functional anthropology is especially strong so that monuments such as tombs are sometimes "explained" in terms of some economic or, preferably, social function such as marking of communal or individual land tenure or maintaining social organization, either through enforcing an egalitarian ethos, concealing stratification and inequality, or glorifying an elite, even in research traditions which decry the functionalism of "processual" archaeology (e.g. Bradley 1987; cf. Lycett 1995). While such accounts are of some interest, it is not entirely satisfying to argue that landscape features can be accounted for by the presumed socio-political "functions" they served. Aside from the fact that such explanations tend to emphasize, in a conservative way, stability and the maintenance of a *status quo* which seems obviated in every case by evidence of change, invoking the "function" of features can in no way account for their specific forms and worse, tends to elide specific cultural contexts altogether. That said, it is at this point in our knowledge impossible to discuss possible social roles of ashmounds during the Southern Neolithic, an assertion I hope will soon be changed by new fieldwork and analysis.

Whatever they meant and however they operated in Neolithic society, ashmounds certainly mark the landscape in obvious ways. As noted, they are generally highly visible because of their color, elevation and sometimes location. In the eastern part of the Daroji Valley, where there are several ashmounds, it is possible to see from one the hills containing several others; this is also true for some of the closely spaced ashmounds and Neolithic settlements near Bellary. Such intervisuality would have been accentuated by plumes of smoke and fires though we cannot at present say if all these were in use at precisely the same time. This chronological uncertainty is highlighted by the occurrence of several locations that have undeniable Iron Age/Early Historic ceramics and occupational debris but also have large areas of slaggy material identical to that found in ashmounds.[6] Several places like this were documented in the intensive survey area north of the Daroji Valley. These might, of course, be reoccupied Neolithic locations, as is VMS-

110 in the western Daroji Valley described in Chapter 5, but preliminary surface work has failed to yield Neolithic ceramics, suggesting that dung-burning activities, perhaps not identical to those of the Neolithic, may have continued into later periods. In these cases, the slaggy material is not in the form of a large mound but a low stratum of solid vitrified dung. Unfortunately, because so many ashmounds are under attack as lime sources and our sample of Iron Age/Early Historic sites with slaggy concentrations is small, it is not possible to say if there ever were mounds in these places or not. In either case, the continuation in some contexts of dung-firing, or the re-use of ashmound locations, we have striking evidence for the continued salience of these features for later residents of the region.

Although the ashmounds of the Southern Neolithic have created a great deal of interest and have invited much discussion about their original construction and use, much less work has been directed toward their later integration into landscape features and practices, this discussion mostly being limited to showing the subtle humor of local people's misinterpretations.[7] Indeed, one may ask why these features are called ashmounds at all, a singularly inappropriate name but one which encodes much of their later signification. The term ashmound emerged in the nineteenth century as an alternative to, for example, Foote's (1916) much more apropos "cinder mounds" and "cinder camps".[8] In any case, the term "ashmound" directly links these features with other significant fires, especially cremation fires and with the ash from such fires.[9]

As is well known, many, but not all, Hindu communities practice cremation. On the one hand, cremation grounds are seen as polluted, impure, and dangerous – cremation grounds are usually placed outside settlements, outcaste people may be forced to live near them, and they are often situated in inauspicious or otherwise negatively-associated locations such as the north side of settlements (e.g. Kramrisch 1976). On the other hand, funerary fires can also be associated with bravery and auspiciousness, the highest form of this being as places where strong, virtuous women committed *sati*, or self-immolation. Sati events are often marked through the construction of memorial stones (see below) and sometimes temples. Local women, even ordinary, non-elite women, are thus remembered and deified. The ash from places thought to be locations of *sati* may be thought to have special properties; Chidanandamurti (1982) recounts the story of a young woman from southern Karnataka whose revenge on her husband's killer and subsequent *sati* was marked by both a memorial stone and a temple where her bravery is annually remembered in a festival. Her sacrifice is said to have taken place in the bed of a dry reservoir and the water of this reservoir is considered have magical properties because of its association with the ash of her pyre.

In a slightly different vein, the Nimbapur ashmound (VMS-34) located within our intensive survey area near the Tungabhadra River, is locally known as "Valighat", the funeral pyre of the monkey-king Vali of *Ramayana* fame, the same Vali killed by Rama. This region is locally believed to be mythical Kishkindha, the monkey kingdom ruled, after the death of Vali, by Sugriva, who was ably assisted by Hanuman.[10] Like many other places in India, certain episodes of the *Ramayana* story are supposed to have taken place in this area (Dallapiccola 1994). As I discuss below, one of the pervasive ways in which local places are linked to larger worlds, mythic and otherwise, is through retellings of pan-South Asian epics, tellings that link local places, physical remains of very precise provenience, to sagas with supralocal significance. In this way, the larger tradition is also domesticated, brought home and made concrete in a way that even performance and recitation do not accomplish. Significantly, local sites with sacred associations may also be more widely accessible to diverse members of a community and access to them more difficult to control in the same way that literacy and education clearly were. It may be, then, that the physicality and concreteness of, for example, *Ramayana*-associated places constitutes yet another basic form in the diversity of the *Ramayana* tradition (Richman 1991) and indeed in the tradition of questioning *Ramayanas* (Richman 2000) – constructing new versions which may challenge existing norms regarding hierarchy, right behavior, or other "lessons" embodied in the authoritative[11] versions of the text.

Several villages near ashmounds also have names that incorporate words for ash – Budihali, Budikanama, Budigunta, and so on, suggesting not only an awareness of their presence but also a sense of their cultural importance. As noted, some ashmounds have shrines built on them but most do not, and many have no evidence of contemporary or recent use whatsoever. One comes across scattered references to the contemporary ritual significance of "hills of ashes" used in present-day worship (e.g. Feldhaus 1995: 79), but such sources are generally not archaeologically aware and may not be referring to ashmounds at all. The most common use of ashmounds today, however, is as sources of material for lime kilns. Lime kilns produce material for plaster, usually from calcium carbonate nodules, *kankar*, but also from chopped-up ashmounds. Such practices are the greatest threat to the continued physical existence of Neolithic ashmounds; with this form of use the original meanings and significances of these features are irrevocably lost.

Megaliths

Although there are scattered nineteenth-century reports on the possible composition of ashmounds and speculations on their origin, fascination with the south Indian megaliths was much more widespread, at least among Europeans, and what can only be described as the looting of megaliths was a common past time of the colonial elite, a holiday excursion also in fashion in England at that time (Trigger 1989). South Indian megaliths – the word of course refers to large stones – actually consist of a wide range of features, only some of which employ massive lithic elements. Of these, a very small subset shares certain morphological features ("port-holes" for example) with European megaliths (Figure 21). If it was not precisely this presumed link to Europe that prompted the mania for megalith-opening, it was certainly this potential link (as well as others) that has continued to animate scholarship on megaliths ever since.[12]

In 1947, the year of Indian Independence, V. Gordon Childe, the eminent archaeologist of Europe and the Near East, published a paper in the journal *Ancient India* suggesting some possible connections between the enigmatic megaliths of southern India and those of Europe. In this article he noted some of the morphological similarities between megalithic features worldwide, suggesting that sea travel must have been an important mechanism of diffusion, a process necessary to disperse knowledge of megaliths from the one (or a few, Childe 1947-8:12) location of their origin, probably the eastern Mediterrannean. This paper illustrates quite clearly the dubious logic of diffusionism, which views material culture as nothing more than objectified ideas, ideas specific to both a "people" and an "age", a perspective which, among its other flaws, clearly erases the physicality of these features. Given the allied presumption that humans are only minimally inventive and creative, in order for similar structures or objects to have been made in widely separated times and places, these discrete ideas (or bundles of ideas often called "traits") must thus have moved about on the landscape, either in human form – migrations and invasions – or through the somewhat vaguer process of diffusion. Although it is now clear that there were in fact *no* direct connections between south Indian megalith builders and their Western European counterparts, the timing of Childe's paper, as well as that of another report published in that same issue of *Ancient India* (of which more below), is significant as it brings the European fascination with south Indian megaliths right up to the moment of independence and isolates a theme – that the makers of megaliths were a distinct "ethnic" or even biological group, a "people",— that endures even in some contemporary scholarship. As Lycett and Morrison (1998) have argued, however, megalith making and using may more usefully be seen as a sets of actions and practices rather than ethnic or racial markers and, as we shall see, the term megalith draws in a vast range of morphological and temporal variability which argues against any simple account of their uses and meanings.[13]

Megaliths, as such, are largely confined to southern India though there is also a cluster of similar features in Vidarbha, Maharashtra, as well as some constructions involving large stones in northeastern India that are sometimes seen as a "living continuation" of Iron Age traditions (e.g. Krishnaswami 1949). The region discussed in this book lies right within the heart of megalith country, its ubiquitous granite providing raw material for a bewildering array of structural forms and its granitic outcrops the settings for transformed landscapes that range from isolated cairns and cists to subtle modifications of the existing rocky hills, to vast complexes consisting of hundreds and even thousands of megaliths. Because the majority of megalith excavations were carried out early on, there has been to date little systematic study of megalith distributions *vis-à-vis* is one another, settlements, or environmental features. In our study area, megaliths are located, along with Iron Age and Early Historic settlements, in a dense band along both banks of the Tungabhadra River, but we also find them in other areas, for example along the northern hills bounding the Daroji Valley. While a few megaliths lie within settlements, the majority are placed on the slopes and tops of granitic outcrops; many of these clearly intervisible. Given the vast temporal extent of megalith construction (Chapter 2) and the large degree of variation in this analytical category, it is difficult to believe that these features had uniform functions and meanings. As we have noted in another context (Lycett and Morrison 1998: 2):

> . . . it is this staggering variation in morphology, scale, and context of megalithic features and landscapes that we wish to emphasize. Individual features range from small rows of cupules to long crack features and boulder alignments, from isolated but formally constructed passage-chamber megaliths to large groups of interlinked stone circles formed by slight rearrangements of existing fields of boulders. Clusters of features—sites—range from single megaliths to large complexes approaching 40 hectares. This variation in both the scale of individual features and in the scalar effects of overall landscapes mitigates against simple notions of megalithic mortuary features, features of commemoration, as simply piled-up power, power that can be measured as an accretion of human labor. Alternately, such features and the landscapes they help create cannot be seen as simple messages to be decoded, either messages about their builders or about the societies from which those builders came. Megalithic features and landscapes might better be understood as *meaning put in play*, as arguments or claims that were ambiguously and multiply interpreted, even contested, over the long time spans such features were constructed and used.

Using the terminology of Krishnaswami (1949), our region contains both his types D (dolmenoid cists) and C (stone circles) megaliths, often in combination.[14] Dolmenoid cists typically enclose single or multiple burials (sometimes cremations or inhumations, more often secondary burials); burials may be loose, in urns, or in clay sarcophagi. Although all the cist-burials excavated by Wheeler at Brahmagiri (1947) were below ground (only the tops of the upright slabs were visible prior to excavation); the complex at Hire Benkal consists almost entirely of above-ground cists, though these are, like many from Brahmagiri, made of chipped slabs arranged in a *swastika* pattern and have both port-holes and a large flat dolmen or roof also of chipped granite (Figure 22).[15]

Excavated burials typically contain Black and Red Ware ceramics as well as plain black and plain red wares,[16] iron objects, and sometimes ornaments of gold. It is clear, however, that many of the stone circles and passage-chamber megaliths we have documented were not used for actual burials – many of these are built right on sheetrock and there are generally no artifacts or human remains associated with these. Passage-chamber megaliths clearly represented some kind of special, limited feature within the overall assemblage of megalithic forms. Every large complex has a few, and these tend to be located on hilltops, often commanding spectacular views over the river. Some are isolated while the only megalith inside the more than 40 hectare Iron Age/Early Historic town of Kadebakele is a passage-chamber form. More common are stone circles of various sizes, some forming vast fields of

Figure 21. Port-hole cists, Hire Benkal.

Figure 22. Solid slab megalith, Hire Benkal.

overlapping rings; the occasional large stone spirals found in such complexes may also be related to circles in some way.

What we have called enclosures (Lycett and Morrison 1998) seem to be elaborated forms of what Krishnaswami (1949: 38) refers to as "transcepted cists" (cists with internal dividers) and "transcepted cists with antechamber". In the survey, we documented a great many features which resembled rooms and small room complexes, some defined by "walls" of upright chipped slabs, others by boulder alignments. One large complex we estimate at some 40 hectares contained not only many square, round, and rectangular enclosures, but also long bounding walls, a stone spiral more than 10 meters in diameter and at least three courses high, several passage-chamber tombs, and other associated features.[17] Parts of these complexes may look a great deal like settlements, an assessment belied by the utter lack of artifacts found in and around them. One other megalithic complex, VMS-543, lying adjacent to a settlement, included walled rock shelters and an 8 by 8 meters brick platform enclosed within a wall of boulders.

Most large complexes, and many settlements also include runoff-fed reservoirs, the earliest known examples in south India (Figure 23). These are, however, solely catchment basins without provision for water distribution. They differ in form, placement, and construction from Middle period reservoirs; their presence on hilltops and in large megalithic complexes suggests that both ritual and domestic water use rather than, for example, agricultural use. The sides of these features are often built of piled-up earth and small chips of granite.

While stone circles, cists, and to a lesser extent, reservoirs are well-known features of the south Indian megalithic repertoire, we also documented some more subtle modification of the landscape (Figure 24) which suggest that spatial and visual scales greater than that of the individual feature were at issue:

> In most of the large complexes recorded, there were also a number of more subtle forms of landscape modification that, although they involve stone, might not be called megalithic. In all cases, these features emulate natural aspects of the granitic landscape. In this region, the weathering of granitic ridges has led to a dramatic series of parallel rocky outcrops separating colluvial valleys; megalithic complexes work on and with the morphologies of these hills. What we provisionally refer to as crack features consist of rocks stuffed into natural cracks in the outcrop. Crack features range from a few meters to nearly a hundred meters long. Crack features tend to emphasize horizontal space. However, in rock shelters and rock overhangs we also find smaller cobbles and even boulders used to close up natural openings, some of them vertical rather than horizontal. We recorded crack features very conservatively, as we were reluctant at first to see them as cultural features, but even so they are very common wherever megalithic remains occur.
>
> Another feature we noted that has previously not been discussed in the archaeological literature are smaller rocks wedged under larger rocks. Again, these "rock wedges" at first appear similar to natural landscape features. They range widely in scale and degree of evident modification. In some cases, chipped flat slabs lie atop smaller cobbles in what are clearly human products, while in other cases, several smaller boulders might be wedged under a large one that could not have been moved by a single person. Rock wedges cluster in distinctive patterns within mortuary complexes and sometimes occur in and near settlements.
>
> Other small-scale features associated with mortuary complexes, settlements, and other sites include lines of small pecked cupules. These are sometimes arranged into intersecting patterns and always occur on flat boulders or sheetrock. Other pecked features include a range of images on boulders or slabs. Painted designs in red or white also occur, ranging from lines and geometrics to representational art. That at least some, if not most, of these painted shelters and overhangs date to the Iron Age and Early Historic seems likely on the basis of associated artifacts and proximity to settlements and mortuary complexes. (Lycett and Morrison 1998: 3)

All these transformations worked to make entire hillsides into artifacts; working with the natural features of the landscape, thousands of small changes subtly reworked the shape and appearance of these outcrops, marked and memorialized places in way which, until recently, have mostly gone unnoticed by contemporary residents (see below). Unlike the

Figure 23. Hire Benkal, field of chipped slabs, upright cist megalith, and reservoir.

Figure 24. VMS-543, overview with F12 and F13.

monumental ashmounds of the Neolithic, Buddhist *stupas* of the Early Historic, or the lofty temple towers of the Middle Period, megaliths created a very variable and often very subtle field of visual impact. A great many of the modifications described here take a practiced eye to detect; few are visible across great distances.

We are, of course, severely limited in our ability to discern meaning from megaliths, the more so because of the poor quality of early excavations. However, some clue to their ongoing significance can be derived from their later histories. As noted, it is difficult to say precisely when megalith building came to an end, but there are some significant superpositionings which fossilize, in some sense, moments of change. At some Buddhist religious sites in Andhra Pradesh, megaliths have been reported to underlie stupas (e.g. R. Subrahmanyam 1975: 165), a pattern which perhaps suggests appropriation of existing sacred places and features, a pattern by now very familiar. At Aihole, one of the settlements and religious centers that constituted the core domain of the sixth to ninth century Chalukyan polity (Chapter 2), a partially rock-cut, sixth-century Buddhist temple is built near the top of a large hill. At the peak of the hill is Meguti temple, whose foundation inscription of AD 634 makes it the earliest dated structure in south India (Michell 1997: 278); this Jain temple sits within an enclosing wall that defines a large level area on sheetrock, now almost completely featureless.[18] Just outside the wall, however, is a large megalithic complex, consisting of hundred of low dolmenoid cists. While the co-occurrence of this early shrine and the megalithic complex may be simple coincidence, this seems unlikely given their probable temporal proximity as well as the excellent visibility of the Aihole megaliths which are built on a large, level, vegetation-free terrace covered with sheetrock.

Curiously, we see none of these interesting superpositionings in our study area; all the megalithic complexes we documented seem to have been entirely abandoned and none show any significant degree of later construction. The only exception to this is VMS-643, a large complex which has a few Vijayanagara-period walls and structures built on its edge alongside a contemporary roadway. Here there is also a large fortification wall with steps which was built of reused boulders and slabs from the nearby megalithic complex, a process which led to the destruction of a large part of it. In general, however, there is little reason to believe that megaliths held much salience for people of the later Middle period and certainly they hardly feature at all in contemporary local imaginations. This is not to say, of course, that local people are unaware of megaliths. They are, and by far the most common account of such features is that they are somehow associated with the Pandavas of the great epic, the *Mahabharata*. Other stories, sometimes linked, mention races of giants or dwarves; Sundara (2001) notes that people he talked to in this general region associated megaliths with Mauryas, a pattern he takes to mean that they date to the Early Historic (though it is not clear from his text that people are really referring *the* Mauryas of the Gangetic plain). This I find rather unlikely, as there is every reason to think that although the transition away from the construction and use of megaliths was long, complex, and contested – perhaps taking place over a period from around the fifth century BC to perhaps the tenth century AD, although these dates are largely speculative – historical memory of megaliths is now completely absent. Indeed, this is why Wheeler felt the need to excavate Brahmagiri and provide a firm chronological baseline for the enigmatic south Indian megaliths.

Villages and Towns

There is a long history of nucleated settlement in southern India. By some time in the Southern Neolithic, there emerged large nucleated villages alongside the smaller seasonal camps and stopping places. Brahmagiri, for example (Wheeler 1947, Morrison 2005), was a very large place during the Neolithic, though it would be useful to know if this large, deeply-stratified place was continually or periodically re-occupied and how it may have articulated, in regional patterns of mobility, with ashmounds and other places.[19] Unlike, for example, the humid southwest coast of India, this region never saw a dispersed agricultural settlement pattern and whenever people in the semi-arid *maidan* east of the Western Ghats maintained a primary focus on agriculture, nuclear settlement patterns were the norm.[20] Clearly, the "village" as a special form and focus of life existed in some sense during the Neolithic, but the term probably only makes sense in light of later, Iron Age, differentiation between what may be seen as "towns", places with larger populations and greater social diversity, and smaller agrarian-focused nucleated settlements. By the Early Historic, most settlement seems to be in nucleated villages or towns and there is less evidence for extensive mobility, at least in our intensively surveyed area.[21] The distinction between locations of permanent settlement and other places is not only very marked in literature, it is also very clear on the ground. Settlements in this region tend to be highly coherent, suggesting a somewhat tethered mobility of their residents to fields, grazing areas, and other resource areas. Still the specialization and localization of *places* does not necessarily imply a lack of human (and animal) mobility. People in all time periods clearly moved significant distances, sometimes staying for long period of time, to distant places for pilgrimage, travel, and trade. Such movement, well-documented textually, is also marked in the material record in the form of, for example, objects of trade, inscriptions on Buddhist monuments, and widespread ceramic, sculptural, and architectural styles.[22]

One remarkable feature of settlement in southern India has to be its pattern of long-term continuity. In our survey, we found only a few Vijayanagara-period villages that had been completely abandoned (Figure 25); a larger number now lie underneath an occupied place, more often than not a place with the very same name. Reading through archaeological site reports from the area, one is struck by the consistency of reoccupation; deeply-stratified sites are common, some with sequences beginning in the Mesolithic and extending into the Middle period.[23] However, not all locations on the landscape that once saw year-round settlement were maintained as parts of regional settlement geographies. At certain times and in specific locations, places seem to have fallen out of the settled world, to have been, if not forgotten altogether, then at least abandoned as places of permanent habitation. In such cases, there is sometimes a later reoccupation, sometimes *much* later, a process which begs the question of the intervening centuries or even millennia. Was that place somehow marked and recalled, or are such re-occupations entirely fortuitous? Some clues inhere in practices of naming. In historically-documented cases, we may see, for example, the official founding and naming of a town in a place where, archaeological data make clear, people had long been living. In other cases, the same name is used for settlements which seem to wander about in space, shifting subtly or not-so-subtly across the landscape, moving physically but not conceptually.

When and why did this happen? Regional-scale and long-term landscape histories make it possible to hazard some guesses about these sharply defined patterns of continuity and disruption. The bulk of this volume is dedicated to laying out the details of one such landscape history. In this case, it seems that there are some correlations between specific types of locations and human habitation, correlations relying heavily on forms of production, distribution, and consumption. On the other hand, it is also clear that resource distributions do not *fully* account for material pattens; there seem to also be competing, and perhaps often coordinating, historical forces – powers of place and memory, marked by, for example, existing structures, names, and landforms.[24] Chapters 5 to 8 detail evidence for both rupture and continuity in landscapes of the Daroji Valley; broader patterns and processes are considered in Chapter 9.

In this study, there is a single nucleated settlement, the city of Vijayanagara, that looms over all other places of human habitation for a period of some three hundred years. This vast city constituted the seat of political power in the region, to be sure, but it was perhaps the demand for produce and the lure of economic opportunity exerted by this place that had the

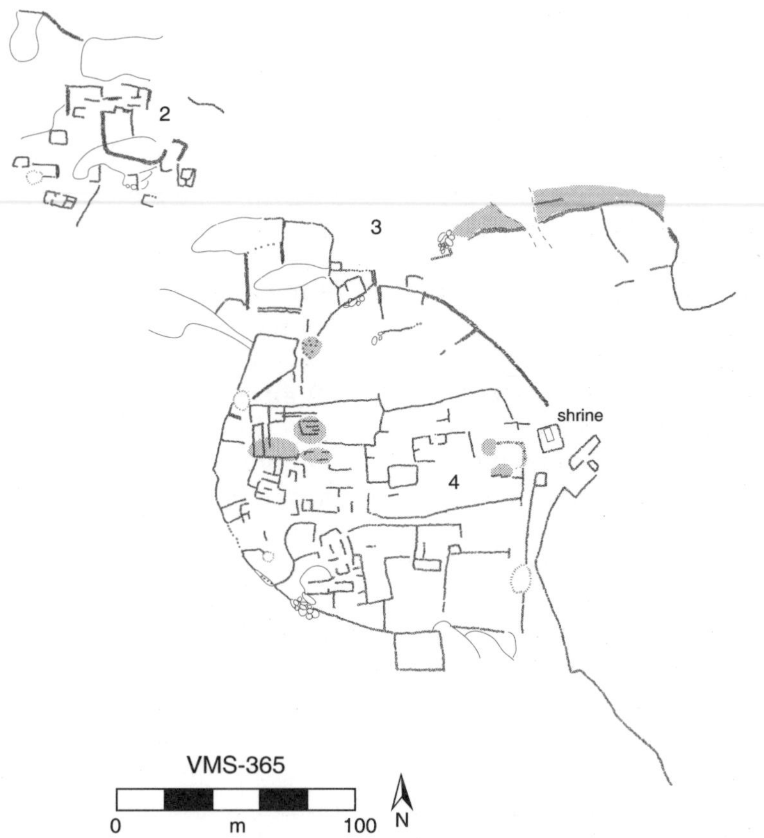

Figure 25. Now abandoned walled village, VMS-365, in dry farmed area southeast of city.

Figure 26. 16th-century Krishna temple complex, Vijayanagara city, now under jurisdiction of the Archaeological Survey of India.

greatest effect on the people and places of the Daroji Valley. The city, as discussed in Chapter 2, was simultaneously represented – both in words and in the more subtle messages of the built environment – as *both* new and old, as a place "founded" as a deliberate act but also a place drawing on the sanctity of the existing Pampa *tirtha* (and see below). A deliberate manipulation of history and place is also evident in architectural traditions, with, on the one hand, temples built in the archaic Chola imperial style rather than more modestly-scaled local traditions and, on the other, the developments of a new "syncretic" architectural style for secular, elite monuments, the style Michell (1992) terms the "Vijayanagara courtly style" and which older art historians called "Indo-Saracenic".[25] This latter style linked the city to contemporaneous rulers across the subcontinent, especially the neighboring sultanates and other powerful north Indian rulers.

This overt manipulation of the built environment of the city was not restricted to new construction; witness the use of captured objects and even entire buildings as "loot" in the capital city.[26] Examples include the monumental Krishna temple complex (Figure 26), built to house a Krishna image taken from Udayagiri by Krishna Deva Raya in 1513, and perhaps the chlorite step tank (Figures 27 and 28) in the middle of the Royal Center (Fritz, Michell, and Nagaraja Rao 1985), a structure built in what seems to be a non-local style and in which each block is marked with (re)assembly instructions. Such objects insert a new sense of history and place into a locality quite forcefully and, as Alcock (2001) has pointed out, also leave "holes" behind in the places of their origin. In some sense it is possible to view these appropriations in the same light as my assertion that the "myth" of the city partook simultaneously of a sense of the creation of something new while at the same time, borrowing, appropriating, modifying, and building (literally and metaphorically) from assorted elements and forms of existing signs of authority, of locality, urbanity, and so on.

Although it is not possible to do justice to the complexity of spatial practices in South Asian towns and villages (and to the historical and situational variability of such practices), it is worth noting that status relationships have often been explicitly mapped in terms of house location, routes of movement, and especially access to shared water sources such as wells. Water, in particular, is a potent medium for pollution and thus the control of water sources, including reservoirs, seems to have been important throughout the Middle period and into the present.[27] As I have already noted, temples, too, were commonly access-restricted, either in milder (with the outer courtyards being relatively open and only inner spaces highly controlled) or profound ways (when, for example, entire classes of people, or genders, are excluded).

The residences of people considered by others to be low, and ethnographically and historically this means especially those of lower castes or "outcastes", are often relegated to the outskirts of settlements, sometimes to locations outside fortification walls or conceptually beyond the boundary of the settlement. For example, the *Mayamata*, dated to between the ninth and twelfth centuries AD (Dagens 1985: 46), provides detailed instructions for town layout, specifying that "The candala and kolika huts must be two hundred poles beyond the town to the east and southwest." Similarly, occupational, religious, kin, or other groups are sometimes concentrated in particular neighborhoods or on particular streets.[28] This does seem to have been the case for the city of Vijayanagara – at least the pattern of concentration of occupational specialists – and it also seems probable, based both on textual and archaeological patterning, that residence was strongly patterned along status lines. Nevertheless, this pattern could be complicated; for example, serving personnel clearly lived in elite neighborhoods alongside those they worked for (e.g. Sinopoli 1993). Residential space, then, can be seen as both socially and ritually charged; spatial practice is rarely, in this context, neutral.

Figure 27. Chlorite step-tank, overview, Vijayanagara Royal Center.

Figure 28. Chlorite step-tank, detail with inscription.

Hindu and Jain Temples and Shrines

The term Hinduism is a rather imprecise, post hoc category that encompasses extensive historical, spatial, and group-specific variability in practice and belief. Although foundational texts such as the Vedas are often seen as having a very great antiquity, as much as three thousand years, there is not only little empirical basis for this specific date, it is also the case that what has been called "Vedic Hinduism" was quite different than the Hinduism of today. When, precisely, more contemporary forms developed is a matter I am not prepared to discuss in detail but it can be said that the Middle periods saw a major part of the transition from Vedic (and perhaps "late Vedic") forms centered around sacrifice involving both priestly officiants and kings to more personal, devotional forms of worship and belief (the *bhakti* traditions, discussed below) centered primarily around manifestations of the deities of Vishnu, Shiva, or the goddess (Devi).[29] Indeed, the distinction between Vaishnavite, Shaivite, and goddess sects could be quite salient, sometimes even involving significant conflict, so that for periods after about the thirteenth century I shall primarily make reference to individual sectarian divisions rather than to "Hinduism" as such.

In the material record, we can see changes in sectarian affiliations of shrines and temples, sometimes related to changes in regional power relations. For example, just after the Vijayanagara period in the region in and around the capital city, many of the officially-sponsored temples dedicated to Vishnu were either abandoned or converted to Shaivite shrines, a change which highlights some disjunctures between the practices of elites who fled the city and the farmers and others who stayed. Such regional patterns of dedication and their changes through time say a great deal about the ways in which political power, community affiliation, and personal devotion were expressed and concretized on the landscape. In the longer term, such change also involved the initial establishment of Hindu sectarian traditions as well as Buddhist, Jain, (and later) Muslim, Christian and other practices from a presumably already diverse landscape of belief and practice materialized in as-yet poorly understood ways through the construction and use of megalithic complexes, rock art and no doubt many other features we are unable to decipher.

Jainism, like Buddhism, is sometimes described as a "heterodox" religious tradition, arising in protest against some of the practices of Brahminical Hinduism in the Early Historic period. Unlike this latter tradition, both Buddhism and Jainism have historically-known founders, Gautama and Mahavira, respectively, both born around the sixth century BC. While Buddhism spread rapidly throughout south India and became particularly important in the coastal regions of Andhra Pradesh and Tamil Nadu (e.g. Ray 1986, 1994; Soundara Rajan 1994), it apparently never established much of a foothold in our region. The only material signs of Buddhism in this area are several sculpted limestone panels, not in primary context, excavated from the center of the city of Vijayanagara.[30] The nearest site with Buddhist religious architecture (*stupas, viharas*) is Sannathi, several hundred kilometers to the north (Howell 1995; Devaraj and Talwar 1996). South of the study area and throughout much of what is now the state of Karnataka, Jainism was always more important than Buddhism; Jain traditions relate that Chandragupta Maurya converted to Jainism and spent his last days at Sravanabelgola, a major Jain religious center in southern Karnataka.[31] There are a number of Jain temples in and around the city of Vijayanagara, many of them dating to the fourteenth and fifteenth centuries. However, we have not recorded any Jain temples in the area around the city, suggesting that perhaps Jain practice was confined to urban traders and others in non-farming professions, a pattern evident even today.

The earliest stone temples in south India date only to the sixth century AD (Michell 1997),[32] although it is clear, for example, from the ways in which lithic roof beams follow the forms of wooden ones, that these build on a longer tradition of wooden structures, none of which have survived in this region. The development of southern architectural styles, too, entangles histories of Buddhist monasteries and sites of worship, Jain and Hindu temples, and even to a certain extent Islamic tombs, mosques, and towers in ways which indicate a large degree of architectural (and other) interconnection.[33]

If, however, we go back to the Iron Age and beginnings of the Early Historic, when there clearly existed (autonomous?) indigenous religious traditions here loosely glossed in terms of the construction and use of megaliths (although this must certainly underestimate the reach of such practices), the nature of the relationships between these local practices, their built forms and the newly-introduced traditions of Brahminical Hinduism, Buddhism, and Jainism, is much less clear. Several scholars have postulated a formal relationship between megaliths and early temples, a pattern presumably paralleled by forms of conversion and religious change. Kramrisch (1976: 150-5, 166), for example, draws a parallel between the sanctuary (*garbhagriha*) of Hindu temples and the dolmen or cist that forms the burial chamber of some megalithic forms (above), pointing also to the associations between temple form and certain natural places, which, although she does not mention this, are also common locations for megalithic features (1976: 167):

> The piled-up alter, the base, the dolmen-cell, the *Garbhgrha*, and the superstructure are the architectural constituents of the whole image of the temple; it rises like a mountain. Its mass diminishes while it is drawn along the vertical to a high point, straight above the center in the dark space of the interior. The image of the mountain and cave is known in nature, and is given form by the architect.

More recently, Wagoner (1996) has pointed out the association between sacred river-crossings (*tirtha*) and death rituals, associating such practices with some of the early development of the Pampa *tirtha* (Chapter 2). In an analysis of Kakatiya-period temples (AD 1163-1323) in neighboring Andhra Pradesh, he draws somewhat more explicit parallels between local megalithic forms and early stone temples (Wagoner 1995), a connection which seems more than probable, especially given the fact that megalith construction may have continued as late as the time of the first free-standing stone temples and perhaps even longer.

Tirtha: Temple and Place

Normatively, the placement of temples (Figure 29) always involves a great deal of thought and planning, and the connection between site and shrine is an intimate one. Places of pilgrimage, *tirtha* or *kshetra* (see Chapter 2), need not have any human modification at all, but the development of such places through the construction of temples, the carving of sculptures, engraving of inscriptions, and deposition of the materials of worship (ghee, milk, flowers, branches, food, and artifacts such as bangles and ceramic oil lamps) is common.[34] Kramrisch (1976: 143) notes, "To the pilgrim who goes to the temple, it is a *tirtha* made by art, as others are by nature, and often it is both in one", going on to add that the temple does not fulfill its function by being built, but by being seen,[35] though it would also be possible to dissect this notion of function a bit more and to suggest that, for donors, the construction (or restoration) itself as well as its public recognition are indeed one of the "functions" of the temple. Indeed, temples were often seen (Wagoner 1993), as one of the "sevenfold progeny", and the construction of temples as an especially meritorious act.[36]

The rhetoric of restoration is as critical for temples as it is for irrigation systems and indeed partakes of many of the same literary and political tropes. This point becomes quite clear in Michell's (1995: 25) discussion about the paucity of foundation inscriptions in the Vijayanagara period:

> . . . many religious buildings were, in fact, newly established during the centuries under consideration here. The patrons of such projects frequently advertised their pious bequests, but sometimes appear to have been more interested in presenting themselves as protectors and repairers of already existing monuments than as sponsors of entirely new foundations, even when this was actually the case.

Elaborate textual prescriptions for the installation of gods and the construction of temples were well-developed by the fifteenth century. Kramrisch (1976: 5 and see Dagens 1985), for example, discusses the *Visnu-dharmottara*, an early compendium which recommends:

> Installations [of gods] should be made in forts; in auspicious cities; at the head of shop-lined streets . . . ; in villages or hamlets of cowherds where there are no shops, the installations should be made outside in gardens . . . ; Installations should be made at riversides, in forests, gardens, at the sides of ponds, on hill-tops, in beautiful valleys and particularly in caves. At these places, the denizens of heaven are present. In places without tanks, gods are not present. A temple therefore should be built where there is a pond on the left, or in front, not otherwise. If a temple is built on an island, the water on all sides is auspicious.[37]

Water could, however, also be present symbolically, with jars of water used at the time of consecration (Dagens 1985; Davis 1997; Kramrisch 1976: 5), when the god enters into the image/artifact that thus becomes the living deity. Such consecrations also often take place at the edge of a body of water such as river, lake, or reservoir.

Although we can be certain that actual practices of siting and construction varied significantly, we might follow Kramrisch's discussion as a general guide to one philosophy of place and built form. There is, she notes (1976: 6-7), in principle a complex ritual plan, *Vastupurushamandala*, behind all temples, "Although this ritual diagram is neither the ground plan of the temple nor necessarily the plan of the site, it regulates them." Explaining, "*Vastu* is the site; in it *vastu*, bodily existence abides. Purusa is the universal Essence, the Principle of all things. . . . In bodily existence, Purusa, the Essence, becomes the Form. The temple building is the substantial, and the 'plan' (*mandala*) is the ritual, diagrammatic form of the Purusa." Before a temple is built or re-built, it is "ritually leveled" (Kramrisch 1976: 7) and the soil of the construction site is examined and prepared by grazing cows on it, plowing it, and planting seeds in it.[38] In this, the temple is located very specifically in soil of a certain color, smell, taste, and consistency; both soil color and the type of building material and its color are seen (in this text, although this seems improbable in terms of both locations and materials of actual temples) as being appropriate to different genders and especially different statuses.[39] The link between the local and the universal is explicitly theorized (Kramrisch 1976: 7):

> The form of the temple, all that it is and signifies, stands on the diagram of the *Vastupurusa*. It is a 'forecast' of the temple and is drawn on the leveled ground:[40] it is the fundament from which the building arises. Whatever its actual surroundings, forest glade, seashore, hill, or town, the place where the temple is built is occupied by . . . the *Vastupurusa-mandala*. That it is surrounded by the streets of a town, walls of a fort, ravines, or fields, becomes of secondary importance, for its particular topography is but the hinge by which a changeable panorama is linked with the structure of the universe.

In this linkage, between stability and change, the local and the universal, place and history, sanctified by textual tradition, we can see a parallel to the ways in which epics such as the *Ramayana* are harnessed to specific localities and features, as noted above.

The situation of the temple in its surrounding landscape and the possible ways in which this was conceived, not only by the original donors and builders, but also by later visitors and viewers, is also clearly of interest for this analysis. As a kind of cautionary tale suggesting that a more integral, holistic view, precisely the position advocated in many "landscape approaches" to archaeology, might not in fact be the most appropriate, we might look to Tillotson's (1998) analysis of eighteenth- and nineteenth-century Indian and British conceptions of structures in their landscapes. Using pictorial representation as a guide, Tillotson convincingly shows that the conventions of British landscape painting and the those of both Muslim and Hindu Indian artists differed significantly. The English picture (Tillotson 1998: 66) shows "a single view or act of seeing. The Indian picture corresponds to our visual experience only if we include the dimension of time: we cannot in life see all the parts at once but we can explore them in turn; and the painting draws together our sequence of perceptions and understandings." In this sense, the paintings of temples he examines are more like maps showing the route the worshiper takes through the complex than they are like naturalistic representations.[41] He goes on to note that representation of temples commonly concentrate on those features (the image of the gods, the tanks) which are seen as the most important, with multiple perspectives being adopted to fit all these elements into the image (Tillotson 1998: 66). Interestingly, some features are shown in elevation, as one actually sees them, and others in plan, suggesting that the role of both seeing and moving are complex and that Tillotson's (1998: 67) analysis that "such images suggest an approach to architecture which is less aesthetic than functionalist" might be incomplete. Indeed, temples are clearly meant to *both* be seen (and appreciated, an experience which is at least partly aesthetic) and to be experienced in certain ways. With this tempering in mind, Tillotson's conclusion (1998: 67) still gives pause to the scholar attempting to situate temples within a larger landscape:

> In images such as these, buildings are not seen as quasi-natural or as continuous with their environment, but as avowedly artificial, as isolated places apart. They are not shapely, formal objects, but spatial ordered areas. They are not pictorial, things to be looked at, but comprehensible, things to be understood.

The Lives of South Indian Temples

If Indian images can be said to have lives (Davis 1997), then so, it must added, do temples.[42] Perhaps more than any other kind of built form in the south Indian landscape, temples tend to be made and remade, reconfigured, rededicated, repaired, and otherwise reintegrated into contemporary worlds. This is not to say, however, that temples are never abandoned or forgotten, never neglected or destroyed. They are, and these kinds of material transformations, as well as more subtle but perhaps no less powerful changes such as re-alignments of processional ways speak to changes, not only in ritual practice, but also to patterns of regional settlement and production, to power relations and patronage in ways which textual accounts stressing continuity tend to elide.

Temples sit on and in landscapes not only singly, but often in terms of clusters or complexes, groupings which may be planned, accretional, or some mixture of each.[43] It would be possible to cite many examples in which individual shrines or larger complexes were remade (or unmade) through practice; here I just mention a few illustrative cases. Perhaps the most extreme example of a structure which literally appropriated older elements in a changeable life history may be the Uncappamatha in Anegondi, just north of the Tungabhadra River from Hampi (Chapter 2) and traditionally, a base of the Kampila kingdom.[44] This structure incorporates elements ranging from twelfth-century Chalukyan temple pillars to Vijayanagara-period temple elements, all of which were later made into some kind of an "Islamic" Deccani-style building, presumably (though not certainly) after 1565. Dhaky (1996: 189) remarks:

> The so-called Uncappa-matha is a mysterious building. Its west wall and side walls do not exist. A large number of plain Vijayanagara pillars, a few partly defaced and reused sculptural fragments in typically Vijayanagara narrative style, have been built into the west sector of the building. The building's roughly central portion has an upper storey with a superstructure crowned with a śikhara, all of course in Vijayanagara style. The east façade, however, is an extension of the sultanate occupation period when the structure had apparently been converted into an Islamic building. Its central portion shows the upper section with a row of Bijapur arches inserted to suggest the mihrabs.

This eastern facade, a columned arcade, was itself built of reused high-quality Chalukyan pillars clearly taken from some eleventh or twelfth-century structure (Dhaky 1996: 190). These short and somewhat stocky Chalukyan columns are stacked two high (without bases or capitals) in order to create the more lofty proportions of a Vijayanagara-era hall. These older columns all face the exterior of the structure and are much more visible than the Vijayanagara-period columns along the

Figure 29. Overview of 16th-century Tiruvengalanatha temple; built in imperial style (Vaishnavite), but no longer in worship.

Figure 30. Towers of the Virupaksha temple from the Tungabhadra River.

interior. Just as the makers of the Vijayanagara structure appropriated and displayed older elements in a reconceptualized architectural scheme, so did the later Bijapur builders, who changed both the function and form of this building while at the same time explicitly displaying its older elements.

Returning to the Pampa *tirtha,* site of the earliest constructed temples in this region, it is possible to trace a north-south axis of small shrines leading from the Tungabhadra River to the south and approaching Hemakuta Hill (Wagoner 1991). As noted in Chapter 2, these temples range in date from the ninth to eleventh centuries and now lie beside the massive Manmatha tank, a stepped temple tank just north of, and outside the walls of the Virupkasha temple in the village of Hampi.[45] The north-south axis of this line of east-facing small temples (especially if the proto-Virupaksha temple is included in it) is now dramatically interrupted by the *prakara* wall (sixteenth century?) of the Virupaksha complex. That there was also a road passing by these shrines has been demonstrated by Wagoner (1991), who has traced this route to the south of the Virupaksha and through a gateway in the walled hilltop cluster of pre- and Early Vijayanagara temples on Hemakuta Hill (and see Fritz, Michell, and Nagaraja Rao 1985). This shift, then, represented a major re-orientation of space and re-focus of ritual space toward the newly-elaborated Virupaksha, where the eponymous god had almost fully replaced the goddess Pampa, now reduced to a version of the rather docile Parvati, wife of Shiva (see discussion by Wagoner 1996, Verghese 2000: 94-114).[46] The east-facing Virupaksha complex includes a long paved road extending beyond the *prakara* (enclosure) walls; this road served both as the processional street for the annual "car" festival in which an image of the god is brought out for worship (an event that still draws tens of thousands of pilgrims every spring) as well as a commercial and residential street, the Hampi Bazaar, that forms the center of commerce, movement, and tourism in this tiny village. The earlier route is all but forgotten and many (but not all) of the older temples have fallen completely out of worship.

Other changes, too, mark these spatial and conceptual shifts, among them changes in temple style. In what Michell (1994) has called "revivalist mode" of religious architecture, patrons of Vijayanagara-era temples resurrected the lofty, aggrandizing temple forms – especially the monumental towered gateways or *gopura* that could be seen for great distances – of the imperial Cholas, a model of architectural authority rooted in times and places quite distant, but apparently one still well-understood by many (Figure 30). The break, then, in the earlier north-south alignment of small, human-scales shrines built in local, Deccan styles toward the west-east alignment made by the Virupaksha temple complex and its car street, could not be more dramatic. That this re-alignment was deliberate seems not to be in question; the expansion of the Virupaksha was planned, the refocus of worship toward Shiva and the domestication of a local goddess can hardly have been accidental (cf. Stein 1978).

Other re-orentations in space seem to have a less deliberate character, happening because of change in the landscape around the temple rather than because of major construction projects. The routes of many older roads, for example, are dotted with shrines and temples as well as other features such as wells, villages, hero stones, etc. With the abandonment of a settlement or a shift in the course of a road, these shrines are left facing empty space, space devoid of the kinds of human features that once oriented them. This becomes more clear if we consider some of the general guidelines for the orientation of temples and gods:

> In the orientation of the temples three principles combine: (1) the orientation proper, for the temple should face the East, the rising sun; (2) the temple should face the Centre – of the settlement, the village or town, etc.; (3) God in his peaceful (*santa*) image should be located in and turn towards, the habitations of men; God in his wrathful (*ugra*) image should be situated outside and face away from the habitations of men. (Kramrisch 1976: 235)[47]

In fact, the actual orientations of temples in the study area follows this scheme rather closely. The majority of shrines face east though many also face roads or towns. In the latter case, changing human land use can change the setting of the temple rather dramatically, whether this means abandonment of settlement (which sometimes, but not always results in the end of maintenance of the structure and/ or the cessation of worship) or expansion of settlement which, presumably, could create potentially dangerous situations when a fierce (*ugra*) god or goddess comes to face human habitation directly.

In the Daroji Valley itself, as the following chapters describe in more detail, the majority of shrines with identifiable deities are dedicated either to some form of Shiva or to goddesses – there is only one temple dedicated to Vishnu. The latter sits near a gateway in a massive fortification wall that divides the main part of the valley and is thus arguably an "official" installation. By the sixteenth century, royal temple patronage was increasingly oriented toward Vaishnavism (Verghese 1995), even to the extent that the usually mixed iconography of outer pillars became increasingly restricted in theme and the broadly tolerant attitude of earlier rulers (most of the rulers of the Sangama dynasty were Shaivite whereas most of the Tuluvas were Vaishnavite) was reversed.[48] While a great many of the other Vijayanagara-period shrines in the valley are still in worship, this lone Vaishnava shrine is completely abandoned, witness to the general preference among local farmers, herders, and craftspeople for other gods and goddesses.

Elsewhere in the study area, preferences for forms of Shiva, goddesses, and local heros such as Hanuman are also marked.[49] Although the majority of the large temple complexes in and around the city are Vaishnavite, only the Shaivite Virupaksha temple is still in worship. Equally striking are patterns of worship outside the city. A review of some 45 locations[50] from the intensive survey area recorded as being currently in worship shows 11 Hanuman[51] shrines (Figure 31), 17 Shaivite shrines, 6 Goddess shrines, 3 of unclear affiliation, 4 Vaishnavite[52] shrines, 6 water-related shrines,[53] 1 Muslim shrine, and 1 Harihara (a mixed form of Shiva and Vishnu) shrine. Of the older structures which have clearly been converted from one sectarian affiliation to another, one Vaishnavite temple was converted to a Goddess temple[54] and one to a Shaivite temple. A columned hall of unknown affiliation was converted to an Islamic saint's shrine, one Shaivite temple was converted to a goddess temple and two to Hanuman shrines (one with many Naga stones as well). Clearly, patterns of change are complex and in some cases represent adaptations of the existing distribution of shrines and sculptures – older images are often gathered up to make composite shrines, for example, and the Hanumans found in this area are typically very large and thus extremely bulky and difficult to move – but there is also evidence of creative re-use and rededication, even creating innovative and non-normative arrangements such as Nandi facing Rama and Sita, or a broken Nandi head being set up as a *lingam*.[55]

Irrigation Facilities

As discussed above, the landscapes of southern India have, for the last four millennia, been to a large extent agrarian landscapes, and for most of this time, the growing of food has powerfully shaped the ways in which humans have made and maintained places. South Indian places and facilities related to agriculture are many; these include fields and pastures, canals and *anicuts*, aqueducts, check dams and terraces, gravel-mulched fields, field houses and storage facilities, haystacks and manure piles, and both canal-fed and runoff-fed reservoirs.[56] Because the latter are a dominant feature of the Daroji landscape, in some sense, *the* feature that made the Vijayanagara period occupation of this region possible, Chapter 4 is devoted to a more detailed discussion of morphological and functional issues of reservoirs as well as aspects of patronage, meaning, maintenance and re-use (see Morrison 1993, 1995a).

Other irrigation facilities also carried complex sets of associations. Canals, for example, seem to have evoked some of the symbolic associations of rivers, discussed in more detail in the next Chapter. There exists a large number and huge variety of facilities designed to assist dry farming, most relating to the capture and retention of soil and water.

Such features merit no mention whatsoever in texts and, furthermore, are rarely, if ever, associated with shrines. As such, it is difficult to say precisely, if, for example, the ritual meanings of these facilities could be in any way compared to those of reservoirs and canals nor is it really possible to consider the organization of labor that went into their construction and maintenance. It seems possible that many of these smaller facilities were built with family labor; however the great degree of facility integration across the regional landscape (Chapter 4) does warn us against simple correlations between facility scale and the social/political standing of the builder (see Morrison and Lycett 1997).

Inscriptions, Hero Stones, and Memorial Stones

Although, as discussed in the previous Chapter, lithic and copper-plate inscriptions have been objects of scholarly study for more than a hundred years and the contents of these texts are staples of historical research, much less attention has been paid to the physical and contextual aspects of these durable landscape features. To begin, it is worth noting that stone inscriptions tend to be held in continuing regard, objects of veneration that are often moved to temple precincts and other sacred places and where they still lie in fields, in reservoir embankments, alongside roads, and elsewhere, only a portion of them are utterly forgotten. Many inscriptions are cut into structures – large temple complexes typically incorporate many inscriptions (and in the case of regional pilgrimage centers, thousands of inscriptions) and even staircases and watch-towers sometimes have label inscriptions associated with them. Most common, however, are inscriptions cut into large granite slabs, boundary stones, boulders, or hero stones, large freestanding constructions which may or may not be associated with temples or shrines. A great many inscriptions lie in fields, for example, with these texts more commonly relating to grants of land than do inscriptions in other locations. In general, as we (Morrison and Lycett 1997) have already demonstrated, inscription *content* is powerfully shaped by inscription *context.*

Inscriptions clearly have a performative, demonstrative quality differing from copper-plates which were usually privately held and which are a great deal smaller and more portable. The *Bharatesha Vaibha Sangha*, a mid-fifteenth-century work in Kannada by Ratnakaravarni (Kotraiah 1994), which describes the life and rule of the king Bharatesa, one of the twenty-four Jain *Tirthankaras*, illustrates this point (Kotraiah 1994: 11-12):

> Proceeding further, the king [on a military tour] reached the spot of a mountain called 'Vrishabhadri'. On the rock-surface of that big mountain, the previous rulers had got engraved their names and their victorious achievements and there was no more (blank) space left for the present king to do similarly. On the king's command, one of the engravings was wiped off with the help of a *danda* [staff] and then the king's extolled account of victories was carved with *kakini*-gem by a writer who was duly rewarded by the pleased king.

In this aspect of public or semi-public display, inscriptions share a great deal with hero stones.[57] The cult of the hero seems to be of great antiquity in southern India, dating back to the first centuries AD or perhaps even longer. It was, however, in the Early Middle period that hero stones, commemorative sculptures depicting the heroic death of some local man or woman, came to be a common landscape feature in our region. Between the eleventh and thirteenth centuries, for example, hero stones (Figures 32 and 33) were often found scattered throughout towns and villages, along roadsides, and inside temple precincts. Hero stone construction and, especially, worship did continue much later than this, but the majority of hero stones in the study area appear to have been made in the Early Middle period.

These features, typically carvings made on flat, quarried granite slabs with rounded tops, tend to be highly stylized. Carving is almost always divided into separate panels and occasionally hero stones also include inscriptions giving the names and circumstances of the hero's death.[58] Deaths in cattle raids and in cattle protection are quite common, pointing

Figure 31. Vijayanagara period Hanuman sculpture in heroic style, in worship.

Figure 32. Hero stone near Dharmasagara, Daroji Valley (no longer present).

Figure 33. Hero stone, Early Middle period village under VMS-1003.

to the critical role of cattle husbandry in this dry region.[59] As noted, Early Middle period agriculture away from the larger rivers was primarily organized around stream side inundation with some small use of runoff-fed reservoirs. Grazing of animals would have taken place in the extensive dry uplands away from settlement, areas also subject to raids and plundering expeditions.

Minimally, there is a single panel depicting either a man, often on horseback holding a sword or some other weapon, or a woman, the latter generally with an upraised right hand indicating death on her husband's funeral pyre.[60] More elaborate hero stones have two or three panels, typically with the hero(ine), assisted by heavenly beings, ascending into heaven in the central panel and, in the upper panel, worshiping a Shiva *lingam* in the company of Nandi and perhaps others. One salient feature of hero stones is their local reference. These carved panel sculptures were generally made by professional sculptors and yet they depict local men and women of exemplary bravery and virtue.[61] It is not surprising, perhaps, that most hero stones have been maintained as objects of veneration to the present, some showing signs of active worship. In more than a few cases, the names and exploits of these heros continued to be remembered, though without contemporaneous inscriptions it is difficult to cross-check present-day accounts with older ones. Of course, some heroes are more famous than others, and one has only to mention the local Early Middle period folk-hero Kumara Rama (Sankar 1982; discussed below) to illustrate the continued salience of local men and women who have achieved, if not always deification, then something very close. The existence of a certain ambivalence about such heros is also evident in some of the historical accounts, for example, women who committed *sati*, although clearly deified were sometimes seen as *ugara*, angry, dangerous goddesses whose worship was as much a duty as a pleasure.

Although hero stones clearly continued to be made in smaller numbers into the Vijayanagara period, most of the ones scattered around the region today do seem to date to around three hundred years (AD 1000 to 1400) of the Early Middle period. This is not to say, however, that heroes were no longer important after the fifteenth century. Quite the contrary, is it evident that military service was a major avenue for advancement during the Vijayanagara centuries and that both military service and heroic death in battle were highly valorized. Again, following the abandonment of the city of Vijayanagara and the periodic dissolution of political power into smaller, warring polities, miliary prowess continued to be a major way of defining status and position (e.g. Narayana Rao, Shulman, and Subrahmanyam 1992). Still, it is interesting that hero stones, as such, never regained their former popularity and local behavioral exemplars came to be remembered and commemorated without them.

DISCUSSION

Although lengthy, this discussion of south Indian places has been far from exhaustive and served only as a general pointer. A fuller discussion might also include, for example, forts, walls, roads, bastions, and naturally defensive locations, places both built into and marked on the landscape. Another set of locations are the tombs, mosques, and *idgahs* associated with Islam, a religious tradition of great significance in southern India. Although the city of Vijayanagara itself contained many mosques, tombs and rest-houses clustered into Islamic neighborhoods (Michell 1990; Nagaraja Rao 1983; these areas also contained distinctive ceramic assemblages, Sinopoli 1986), it is clear that there were also Muslim-dominant settlements in the countryside all around the city. I do not dwell much on the meanings of such structures here not because they were not, or are not, important, but because they are much better known than the ashmounds, megaliths, hero stones, and other distinctive features of the south Indian landscape.

Finally, it should be pointed out that south Indian places of special significance are not limited to anthropogenic features and structures; the land itself is typically imbued with meaning and almost each hill has its own name and history. Natural features of the landscape such as rivers, hill tops, forests, and caves held special significance and often referenced oral or textual accounts from the great epics as well as histories and personages of more local renown.[62] Indeed, the distinction between the 'natural' and the 'built' environment is not always clear inasmuch as human and divine personages have all had a hand in shaping the present-day contours of the earth. The Ganges river, for example, as is well known, is said to have been brought down to earth by Shiva and as such might be construed as a constructed feature analogous to a canal. A small depression in the granite where water often pools is locally known as a place where Sita's jewels fell to earth (Dallapiccola 1994), a place of great religious significance and a goal of local pilgrims notwithstanding the fact that it is simply one of many small natural pools, not physically modified in any way. Clearly, there will always be vast fields of signification lost to the analysis of material remains alone, but the contrary example of features such as dryland agricultural facilities that apparently merited no textual notice whatsoever, should also warn us that both archaeological and historical work must be combined for the fullest possible understanding of the complex accretional landscapes of southern India and indeed, all places.

NOTES

1. However, this should not be confused with the slags that are by-products of metal working, vitrified objects of very different origin.
2. Though, of course, he had no way to actually assign calendar dates to this period.
3. As discussed in Chapter 2, cattle pastoralism was a mainstay of the Southern Neolithic economy and it seems improbable that the meanings of ashmounds were not in some way linked to the ultimate source of the dung that fueled them. We know nothing of the nature of control over cattle and little about the distribution of wealth and status in Neolithic societies except that there did not seem to have been massive disparities between individuals in burial treatment, for example. It is very important to note here that the cultural significance of cattle in the Neolithic was obviously much different from what it would later become. Cattle provided traction, as is evident from analysis of the bones of their legs and feet, but they were also butchered.
4. Although many ashmounds have been heavily disurbed, both by erosion processes and by human action, the tallest stand as much as 12 meters above the surrounding ground surface. Most, however, are between 4 and 6 meters high.
5. There is some indication that ashmounds are limited to only a part of the Southern Neolithic. It will be very important to clarify the internal chronology of such features, but we are a long way from being able to do this.
6. Critically, these sites have Early Historic material but cannot be independently diagnosed as being occupied during the Iron Age without excavation.
7. And here I should note that I strongly assert that ashmounds became meaningful in different ways to later residents and that these meanings are just as valid in their own way as those of the original builders. However, ashmounds were all built around the same time, during the Southern Neolithic, and thus local people are indeed wrong when they assert otherwise. Meanings and significances of places change, but this does not mean that "the past" is totally unknowable, simply that the tidy time-parceled view of the past that archaeologists like to create is just one way of seeing, one that does some violence to accreted landscapes, albeit a violence that is analytically necessary for some kinds of questions.
8. He thought that some places only had mounds while others had mounds and residential occupations. All the mounds I have visited have some artifact scatter associated with them, though this may be quite light; thus Foote's distinction does seem to have some value in highlighting locations with intensive *vs.* extensive habitation debris.
9. Ash is also important in Hindu rituals and is often offered as *prasad,* sanctified substances offered to a deity and returned to worshipers (Flood 1996; Fuller 1992; see also Morrison 2001).
10. Kishkindha is located near the river, with Hanuman's birthplace lying atop a high outcrop just north of the Tungabhadra. It is not clear where the precise boundaries of this polity are believed to have been so I cannot really say if the Daroji Valley was seen as part of Kishkindha. Certainly, as I will suggest, we can at least think of Hanuman as a local god of sorts, notwithstanding his larger reputation. When this

association began to be asserted is an interesting and important question. Certainly it is well-established today and the presence of, for example, significant *Ramayana* narrative panels (Dallapiccola et al. 1992; Dallapiccola 1994) in the fifteenth-century Ramachandra temple in the capital city suggests that it was also a way of seeing the region by the time of the Vijayanagara period.

11. Richman (2000: 8-10) contrasts "authoritative" versions of the *Ramayana* with "oppositional" tellings, while at the same time arguing for a "many *Ramayanas*" perspective which refuses to view some tellings as derivative of, in particular, the Valmiki *Ramayana*, the earliest written version of the epic.
12. One cannot fail to see the parallel between the drive to find a connection between the south Indian megalith-builders and ancient Europeans, and the success of the "genetic" analysis of Sanskrit by Sir William Jones in 1786, which proved the unity of what would come to be called the Indo-European languages. With the exception of the Vidharbha megaliths from northern Maharashtra (and some other scattered features which, however, differ quite substantially in form), megaliths are clearly unique to southern India, where Dravidian (non-Indo-European) languages prevail. This pattern has continued to confound attempts to see south Indian megaliths as derivative and megalith-builders as foreign invaders. The dating of the earliest iron in India, too, seems to suggest a movement of smelting practice from south to north, an anomaly in the generally presumed pattern of north-to-south "influence" and "advance". Although diffusionist speculation continues, the south Indian megaliths continue to resist such analysis—a fact which points again to their home-grown qualities.
13. The following discussion draws heavily on Lycett and Morrison (1998).
14. Krishnaswami (1949: 43) defines a dolmen as "A single slab of stone supported by several orthstatic boulders or slabs built on the surface of the ground in such a way as to enclose a space or chamber beneath the capstone. It may or may not be wholly or partially covered by a barrow or cairn. A dolmen may be with out without a port-hole." In what we are calling passage-chamber megaliths, the "orthostatic boulders" are commonly two long rows of small square blocks laid side-by-side and the "dolmen" consists of a series of parallel rectangular slabs laid crosswise across the narrow opening so formed. A heap of smaller, irregularly shaped but often chipped cobbles is piled over the entire thing, covering the rectangular passage. Such features are often built over sheetrock.
15. Chipping or percussion of the granite is a characteristic feature of Iron Age and Early Historic construction in this region. While later structures used quarried blocks and slabs, earlier builders employed either unmodified boulders or carefully reduced slabs and small tabular blocks. As might be expected, this kind of lithic reduction created large quantities of debris. Such debitage seems to itself had some special value–stone circles made of boulders might ring a field of granite chips, and, at Hire Benekal, the ground itself is completely covered with undulating mounds of chips (some no doubt covering megaliths) making it impossible to walk quietly across the site.
16. Other ceramic types have, however, also been reported. Krishnaswami (1949: 39), for example, mentions a port-hole cist from Cochin "which has yielded the red-ware, decorated with yellow wavy lines, dating probably from just before the Christian era to the first or second century AD". Wheeler, too, (1947: 300) notes this anomalous ceramic association.
17. VMS-643, 646, and 647. This complex covers the tops and slopes of two adjoining granite ridges; the area in between is now devoted to dry farming but was clearly once part of this massive complex, one of the few areas where we can trace megaliths across lower ground. It is probable, of course, that later land use has obscured much of this pattern; most of the megaliths at Brahmagiri, for example, lie to the east of the settlement in what are now level fields.
18. No megaliths lie inside the wall, undoubtedly a product of later archaeological clearing.
19. No ashmound has been reported from Brahmagiri and indeed, there is no ashmound evident on the surface today even though sites with ashmounds are common in the region. However, in a recent re-analysis of the Wheeler's (1947) Brahmagiri collections, I found large chunks of vitrified dung that clearly derived from ashmounds: This material may have been collected elsewhere and brought to the settlement; activities producing dung slag may have taken place locally but not on a large enough scale or for a sufficient length of time to make an ashmound; or, as is also common,

the ashmound itself may have been attacked for lime production or some other purpose.

20. The mountainous and hilly regions in and along the eastern foothills of the Ghats are known as the *malnad*, the lower, drier regions of the interior Deccan and Karnatak plateaus, the *maidan*, a term that was also used by the British to refer to open, level areas such a playing fields and exercise areas.
21. This should be considered provisional, however, as some of the areas closest to pre-Middle period settlements lie along the Tungabhadra river and have been subjected to intensive land surface modification for irrigated agriculture.
22. Hundreds of short inscriptions on many Buddhist structures indicate that they were supported by many small donations from farmers, craftspeople, and other less wealthy members of society, many of them women, a pattern which contrasts markedly with that of the Middle period (Dehejia 1992; Morrison and Lycett 1994, 1997; Willis 1992).
23. Most of the Mesolithic components consist, however, only of scattered stone tools and these tend not to be well-studied. Furthermore, such Mesolithic places presumably played a very different role in regional mobility patterns than did the larger, more permanent settlements which overlay them. Note also that many places now seen primarily as archaeological sites are places which did experience some disruption in occupation, commonly around the Colonial period; they thus could be reclassified as historical places.
24. By some time in the Middle period, and increasingly regularized under the British, each village was (and is) associated with specific lands, lands which are said to "belong" to the village even though individual ownership often crosses such lines. This seems to be why abandoned villages were kept on colonial settlement rolls for long periods of time; as long as some of the lands associated with the village were under cultivation, and taxes were being remitted, there was a need to maintain information on names, populations, and revenues. It is clear that such places did eventually get dropped from these lists though topographic maps tend to retain place names and village locations for a very long period of time after abandonment.
25. Recall that the homeland of the Cholas, in what is now Tamil Nadu, was located thousands of kilometers away from the city, so that distance was both temporal and spatial.
26. The English "loot" is, in fact, an Anglo-Indian contribution, from the Hindi (Yule 1903: 519-20); my use of the term here is indebted to Richard Davis (1993, 1997).
27. In his analysis of the seventeenth-century Tamil text, the *Tiruilaiyatarpuranam*, Shulman (1985: 230), describes an episode in which Indra, suffering from the sin of Brahminicide, "distributes the evil among the usual carriers (trees, earth, women, and water)". Although each of these is then given a possibility for expelling the unwelcome gift (cf. Raheja 1988) (evil flows out of the water as foam, out of women as menses, etc., Shulman 1985: 230), that these are considered common carriers of inauspiciousness/ pollution appears to be fairly typical.
28. The *Mayamata* (Dagens 1985: 33-4) notes of village layout, "The cowshed should be to the south, the flower garden to the north and the dwelling of ascetics either near the eastern gate or to the west. A tank or reservoir should be placed wherever water is required. The quarter for the vaiśya is to the south and that for the sudra on the periphery. The potters' houses are either to the east or to the north, where are found barbers and other artisans; the fishermens' quarter is to the north-west and that of the butchers to the west and, lastly, the oil-makers quarter is to the north."
29. The names and attributes of goddesses are legion. Gopinatha Rao (1969[1914]), for example, lists 78 forms of the goddess in his *Elements of Hindu Iconography.* This list certainly omits the more local, village-specific forms.
30. Limestone is not locally available.
31. Verghese (1995: 7) explains, "For about fifteen centuries Jainism had been the dominant religion in this region. Its advent into Karnataka is traditionally attributed to the migration of Bhadrabahu and Chandragupta Maurya in the third century BC. . . . But the Hindu renaissance in Tamil Nadu . . . and the Saiva revival in Andhra struck a death blow to Jainism and it had virtually disappeared from these regions before the fourteenth century AD. Its last stronghold in the south was in Karnataka. . . ."
32. As noted in Chapter 2, however, the earliest temples in the study area date to the eighth century.
33. This is most clearly seen in the early Buddhist focus on rock-cut "cave" structures; by the first few centuries AD these excavated structures are as likely to be Shaivite or Vaishnavite as Buddhist.

34. The preparation of food, too, tends to leave traces such as hearths and grinding slicks.
35. Seeing, *darsana*, or looking at the temple and the god as well as worship, *puja*, are the primary acts associated with visits to temples. The value of seeing is discussed in detail by Eck (1981). Hardy (1998: 107), too, notes the admonition of the *Brhadaranyaka Upanishad* that "truth is sight".
36. The value of antiquity is also discussed by Appadurai (1981). Note that the Kurekuppa temple (Chapter 8) is exception to this pattern.
37. Inden (2000) sees this text as rooted in seventh and eighth-century Kashmir (see also Mukherji 2001).
38. "At the beginning of the various phases of construction and consecration of the temple the 'rite of the seeds and their germination' (*ankurarpana*) is the most important. It precedes the building of the temple . . . and again the rite is observed before the last brick or stone is put into the superstructure . . . and once more prior to the installation of the main image and before the rite of opening its eyes . . . and also prior to the consecration of the sacrificial vessels." (Kramrisch 1976: 15). These seeds are said to include "different varieties of rice, kidney-bean, pulse, sesamum, mustard, etc. also barley, wheat, and other alternatives" (Kramrisch 1976: 15).
39. This refers primarily to the gender and status of the donor, although it is also an important question to what extent members of a certain community or other ascriptive category were allowed or denied access to temples at different times. By the nineteenth century, there seems to have been a significant degree of exclusion in access to places of worship as well as to water from wells and reservoirs; the extent to which this kind of discrimination may have been practiced in prior centuries is not yet well understood.
40. Although some north Indian temples were obviously sketched out this way—at Bhojpur, for example, one can still see the outlines of planned temples incised into sheetrock—I am not aware of any temples in the study area that show evidence of this kind of laying-out.
41. The route of worship through a complex is generally well-scripted, with controlled movement in toward the increasing restricted space of the central image and a prescribed clockwise perambulation (*pradakshina*) around that image.
42. In this, Davis (1997, and see Davis 1993) refers both to role of images as living beings—following certain rituals, gods may come down to animate and occupy images, serving not only as loci of worship but also the "rulers" of temples (and even kingdoms) and owner of its lands and goods—and to the changing contexts of use, ownership and meaning when, for example, an image is taken from a temple for safekeeping, hidden, and later perhaps transformed into a museum piece. Temples, too, have such dual "lives", the one animate and directed, the other as objects of human construction and appropriation.
43. ". . . The Hindu temple is more a solid monument than a work of architecture. . . . A monument stands in space, it does not face it. The Hindu temple too, has strictly speaking no facade; the four orients and the immediate directions of space step forth in buttresses and images from the body of the temple in a continuous integrity of the mass analogous to the variable pattern in which the divinities are laid out on the *Vastupurusa-mandala.*" (Kramrisch 1976: 103)
44. A *matha*, sometimes loosely translated as monastery, is a place of religious instruction and scholarship as well as worship and contemplation.
45. The Virupaksha, too, is a complex accretional product, with a core dating to perhaps as early as the ninth century, major fourteenth, fifteenth, and sixteenth-century additions, and what may be a nineteenth-century *gopuram,* all in active use today.
46. Virupaksha is a form of Shiva; the central image in this temple is a Shiva *lingam.*
47. Both Shiva and Vishnu, and especially Devi, have both beneficient and more dangerous, fierce forms. Many locally-important goddesses, for example, are associated with smallpox or other diseases and thus may be feared and propitiated as much as adored. Some of these various forms (e.g. Narasimha, the man-lion) were created out of specific historical necessity in order to rid the world of dangerous demons.
48. All of the pre- and Early Vijayanagara temples on Hemakuta Hill, for example, are dedicated to Shiva, as is the Virupaksha temple itself.
49. Hanuman is of course associated with Vishnu. Nevertheless, he is still very popular as are, to a much lesser extent, Rama, Sita, and Lakshman.
50. These 45 places were drawn from a sample of 470 recorded sites; more than one shrine was present in some places.

51. Quite a few of these also have associated images, especially Ganesha and Naga stones. Several shrines also contain hero stones or hero stone fragments (see below).
52. Two of these are located in the village of Bukkasagara; VMS-116 is a Vijayanagara-period temple with Vaishnavite door guardians. Inside the sanctuary are two Hanumans, a Naga, and a Ganesha. The complex also includes a shrine to Ganesha (son of Shiva) and one with a *lingam* and Nandi (Shiva and his vehicle). VMS-118 also lies within Bukkasagara; its sanctuary houses Vishnu, Narasimha (a form of Vishnu), Hanuman, and many small contemporary whitewashed cow figures made of unbaked clay. A subsidiary shrine is dedicated to a goddess. VMS-270 lies in the village of Kamalapuram; its Vijayanagara-period Vaishnavite door guardians now flank recent images of Rama, Sita, and Lakshman. VMS-367 is a Vijayanagara-period structure whose central image, a slab sculpted with Rama and Sita, may have once been built into an exterior wall. Curiously, a Nandi is set up to face the couple, as if these (Vaishnavite) images were forms of Shiva.
53. Five reservoir sluice gates in worship as well as one step well. Note that this sample does not include all the recorded sites even within the intensive survey area.
54. This does not seem to be an "orthodox" Vaishnavite goddess; there is no sculpted image at all, just paint along a crack in a large boulder. It is clear, however, that this is women's shrine in active use and local residents seem unaware or uninterested in the Vaishnavite door guardians.
55. Normatively, broken images should never be in worship. However, it is very clear that in the countryside, such prohibitions are not necessarily in place.
56. *Anicuts* are dams which divert water into canals. In this region, *anicuts* are usually placed across one of the braided channels of the Tungabhadra, sending a portion of the river water into the canal. These low dams were built of stone, sometimes clamped together with iron hooks. At times, water flows right over the *anicut*, preventing serious breaches during times of high water. Many *anicuts* are also fitted with postholes, in which upright poles could be placed, a framework for an easily replaceable screen of brush which would raise the volume of water diverted.
57. Given that many inscriptions are in temples, the degree to which temple access was restricted to certain groups before about the sixteenth century remains an important and largely unresolved issue. It is worth pointing out that some inscriptions have multiple copies such that one copy of a land grant, for example, may be placed in a field in the grant area and another copy in a temple. Whether these were intended for different audiences or simply meant to reinforce the terms of the grant is an open question. Similarly, some inscriptions refer to quite distant places, pointing to the social and other links that were also being made between the place of donation and the actual location of the inscription commemorating that donation.
58. The majority of hero stones have no inscriptions. Still, the link between inscription formats and hero-stone formats is very clear. The narrow, rectangular slab with a rounded top comes to be the basic slate for free-standing lithic inscriptions and Shaivite inscriptions especially, replicating the upper worship panel of hero stones. The link is obvious; what is not clear is if hero stones deliberately used the conventions of stone inscriptions, vice-versa, or if the two simply emerged together.
59. Shulman (1985: 351) notes of the Tamil country that the hero "shades off into the cattle thief", notwithstanding that fact that hero stones, "abode[s] of a sacred presence", often memorialize the hero's defense of the village cattle. Clearly, heroism is strongly situational and rooted in place.
60. Sati stones often also show the woman holding a lemon or a mirror; at times the woman herself is stylized into a kind of pillar with an extended and raised right arm. Many scholars have presumed that these women killed themselves following the heroic death of their spouse, a supposition supported by some textual accounts as well as by the relatively common occurrence of both a man and a woman on some hero stones. Zagarell (2002) notes the existence in the Nilgiri Hills of the Western Ghats of hero stones with armed women, suggesting that different norms of male and female heroism may have existed in these upland areas. No such depiction has yet been recorded in our study area, suggesting perhaps more "conventional" gender role expectations in the region.
61. The existence of professional sculptors and their involvement in hero stone manufacture has been established by Settar and Sunkad (1982);

it seems that commissioning of such sculptures was probably the norm, given the generally consistent level of workmanship. Zagarell (2002), again notes the poorer artistic quality of Nilgiri hero stones and postulates that these were not made by professionals.

62. Some of these significations are discussed in the following chapters.

Chapter Four

VIJAYANAGARA RESERVOIRS: FORM, FUNCTION, AND MEANING

> [The seven most exemplary acts one can perform are] begetting a son, writing a literary work, planting a forest, establishing an *agrahara* [village for Brahmins], acquiring hidden treasure, building a Shiva temple, and building a reservoir. (Randhawa 1980: 99, citing an inscription from the sixteenth-century Porumamilla reservoir)

In this chapter I discuss the morphology, function, and aspects of the contemporary meanings of Vijayanagara reservoirs, as well as some practical issues of dating these features. Beyond their historical visibility as objects built through elite generosity, loci of elite sport and play, and areas of concern for kings, reservoirs, and irrigation facilities more generally, were also physical features that had (and have) a considerable impact on the landscape. The consideration of form, function, and meaning in this chapter is intended to complement the more institutional and organizational approach of Chapter 2 and to lay the groundwork for the descriptions, in following chapters, of the material landscapes of the Daroji Valley. In laying out my discussion this way, I want to emphasis not only that reservoirs operate in situated social, political and ritual contexts, but also that they are material features, built of physical substances with human labor, features that have a certain permanence and that transform landscapes in significant ways. These transformations include changes in productive potentials, in webs of rights and obligations, in the meanings, visibility, and even definition of places. They also include changes in runoff, edaphic conditions, plant and animal communities, and transportation patterns. As such, the landscape transformations effected by reservoirs are both intended and unintended and while some have disappeared from the contemporary landscape, others endure.

RESERVOIRS IN SOUTH ASIA

Devices to capture or harvest water, especially runoff from rainfall, have probably been around nearly as long as human beings have, but I mean to restrict my discussion of reservoirs here to a particular range of constructed forms that consist of artificial embankments built across paths of gravity water flow, whether streams, rivers, or simply slopes that might carry runoff after a rainfall. These features may or may not involve excavation of a basin to contain this water, but they are all storage or storage/distribution devices built on a relatively large scale and meant to contain water *behind* (an embankment or dam) rather than *within* its major construction and for this water to come from gravity flow rather than water tables. In this, I differentiate between cisterns (which collect and store water within a rock-cut or other constructed facility), wells (which tap the water table), reservoirs (defined above), and tanks. The term tank is widely used in the South Asian literature and it may be worth explaining why I avoid it here. Simply put, the word "tank", can be (and is) used to describe almost any water-holding feature, although the term most frequently refers either to reservoirs or to temple tanks, large masonry structures, often stepped, that hold water for ritual ablutions and other functions associated with temple worship. Temple tanks often derive their water from the water table (wells), although they may have other sources of supply. As such, temple tanks and reservoirs are wholly different in construction, morphology, and operation, similar only in their capacity as water holding devices and in certain parallels of meaning and symbol.[1] I thus reserve the term tank to mean something more like temple tank, and employ the term reservoir only for water-retaining embankments, a usage consistent with the meaning of the term elsewhere in the world. In this work I use the English term *reservoir* and the Kannada term *kere* interchangeably.[2]

The use of reservoirs as facilities for water collection and storage is common in areas in which there are rainfall shortages relative to crop requirements, and particularly where marked temporal inequities in rainfall exist. Reservoirs have been (and are) employed throughout the world wherever water harvesting and storage are important for agricultural production and/or domestic consumption. A great deal of morphological and functional variability is subsumed within the single term of reservoir, although the overall goal of water collection and storage remains consistent.

As noted, a large number of water storage facilities, from the plastered baths of the elite to vast artificial lakes held back behind dams, are termed "tanks" in South Asia. Here, however, I reserve the use of the term reservoir for just one category of "tank", an artificial lake or pond created by the construction of a dam and fed by either runoff or some other source of water.[3] Reservoirs were clearly present by the time of the earliest historic sources in India, and played important roles in the structure of agricultural production in the early states and empires of India and Sri Lanka (e.g. Brohier 1934; Gunawardana 1979; Ludden 1985; Mahalingam 1951; Nilakanta Sastri 1966; Seneviratna 1989; see also Leach 1971). In part, that role varied with the ecological context of the settlement. In the dry zone of Sri Lanka, for example, reservoirs fed both by canals and by runoff were vital to the support of intensive agriculture and thus to the existence of such early cities as Anuradhapura and Polonnaruva (Seneviratna 1989; Brohier 1934; Myrdal-Runebjer 1994). In more well-watered portions of south India, including the deltaic regions of the east coast that came under Vijayanagara imperial control early on, reservoirs were often found at the terminus of a canal (Ludden 1985). The storage capabilities of these reservoirs enabled temporal fluctuations in river flow to be minimized, reducing production risk. In dry regions without permanent water sources, reservoirs facilitated the collection and distribution of surface runoff, a strategy that also helped mediate the risk of crop failure in these zones of low and variable rainfall.

While the collection and containment of water did serve to minimize some kinds of production risks – a critical aspect of their operation – viewing soil and water control features *solely* in these terms leaves us with a partial and unsatisfactory account. Risks of crop failure had to be offset against, for example, the investment in construction and maintenance of these costly facilities and the kinds of social and ecological reorganizations that the presence of reservoirs in a region created. Logistic considerations of reservoir construction, maintenance, and water allotment varied with both the type and size of the reservoir and created a dynamic of their own so that the socio-political context of construction, operation, and maintenance must be considered in any attempt to trace out the role of reservoirs in the development of South Asian agriculture. Variability in this class of agricultural facility, then, must be considered along a number of different axes, including environment, the history of land use in a specific area, and the socio-political context of the construction, operation, and maintenance of reservoirs.

RESERVOIRS AS PHYSICAL FEATURES: FORM AND OPERATION

Types of Reservoirs: Inflow and Connectivity

Sharma and Sharma (1990: 20) categorize South Asian reservoirs into three types: (1) *system reservoirs*, which receive water from a river or canal and thus are not primarily dependent upon runoff and may not even have a significant catchment area; (2) *non-system reservoirs*, or "isolated" reservoirs dependent solely on runoff from their own catchment; and (3) *grouped reservoirs*, which consist of series of interconnected reservoirs receiving water from those upstream (although these may also obtain a significant supply of runoff from individual catchments). Most of the reservoirs in the Daroji valley are grouped reservoirs, although there are also some non-system reservoirs.

I propose here to extend Sharma and Sharma's (1990) classification of non-system (isolated runoff-fed) reservoirs to include both *distribution* reservoirs and *containment* reservoirs. These categories are distinguished by the presence or absence of sluice arrangements so that containment reservoirs simply hold water behind an embankment, while distribution reservoirs both hold and redistribute water to areas below the bund. Containment reservoirs almost always have much smaller embankments than do distribution reservoirs.[4] Previously (Morrison 1991), I referred to these two kinds of facilities as "reservoirs" (here, distribution reservoirs) and "embankments" (containment reservoirs), but these terms now seem imprecise and potentially confusing and I would suggest abandoning them.

In part, the geographic distribution of these different types is linked to ecological conditions, since system reservoirs require an appropriate perennial water source, and non-system and grouped reservoirs are more common in drier regions. However, reservoir type is also a reflection of the intensity of land use, so that system reservoirs are found, for example, throughout parts of the state of Tamil Nadu where there exists a long history of intensive cultivation and construction of large-scale agricultural facilities such as canals (cf. Ludden 1985). There reservoirs represent something of a refinement of canal irrigation, more efficiently capturing and using river water. Intensification of areas previously more extensively farmed – especially areas under dry farming or in zones of grazing – may have also led to a process of infilling in valleys suitable for the support of long chains of reservoirs (grouped reservoirs). This seems to have been the pattern in the Daroji Valley. Of course, as large physical features, reservoirs may persist long after the initial conditions that led to their construction have passed. Thus, Vijayanagara-period reservoirs play quite variable roles in contemporary agricultural practice in the Daroji Valley. A few are still functional, while others support wells, trees, dry fields, cemeteries, roads, and/or shrines. Thus, simple correlations between facility size, type, and agricultural intensity are complicated by the accretional and historically situated nature of the agricultural landscape.

As discussed in Chapter 2, Vijayanagara agricultural facilities and strategies were diverse in both form and in scale, with areas of production ranging from vast networks of canal irrigation to small rain-fed plots. In terms of the classification of south Indian agriculture into wet, garden, wet-cum-dry, and dry production, reservoirs clearly cross-cut several of these categories. They can serve either wet, garden, or wet-cum-dry fields; they are often physically integrated with dry facilities. Further, they range widely in scale, from tiny ponds to vast oceans on a truly monumental scale. Thus, a focus on reservoirs themselves, their construction, use, maintenance, and abandonment, tends to work across analyses oriented around traditional land use categories and, to a certain extent, helps us to see that the land use histories of specific areas may change in rather significant ways so that understandings of underlying climatic, edaphic, and topographic conditions can only ever serve as the barest of skeletons that helped to shape the changing human landscape.

Catchment Areas and Basins

Reservoirs consist of a water-holding basin and a dam (*setu*) or embankment, discussed below. The basin is generally situated in a natural hollow or erosion channel; basins seem only to have been excavated to the extent that fill was required for the embankment.[5] Reservoirs in the Vijayanagara region are primarily of the non-system and grouped type, both fed by runoff from the monsoon rains. In this region there are only two system reservoirs, the Kamalapuram *kere*, near the city of Vijayanagara, and the Sangapuram *kere*, north of the river. Runoff-fed reservoirs are typically placed in valleys although they do occur on more level plains where they capture flows from ephemeral stream channels and drainages. The dominance of valley locations is particularly marked in the low, rocky, and dissected granite hills of the Hampi-Daroji ranges. Reservoirs in these dissected hills use to good advantage the rugged, rocky topography of the region, damming up valleys between ridges and capturing runoff from high granitic outcrops.

That valley locations are not universal is illustrated by the large group of reservoirs south and west of present-day Hospet (itself built around a sixteenth-century settlement). This group, dominated by the sixteenth-century Dhanayakana *kere*, tracks the many small streams or *nullahs* that run down from the Sandur Hills. As we shall see, the Daroji Valley reservoirs tend to avoid the steep slopes of the Sandur range – the distinction here seems to relate to topographic differences between the northern and western Sandur slopes and the degree of channelization, both influencing the velocity and tempo of runoff. Where reservoirs are placed perpendicular to valleys, the embankment may or may not span the entire width of the valley. As discussed in more detail later, only very large and long reservoir embankments managed to span the broad Daroji Valley; these trans-valley reservoirs had to be able to withstand occasional but torrential runoff and most have been breached and abandoned.

Wherever reservoirs were placed, particular attention was always paid to their catchment area. As noted, seasonal or more permanent streams were considered ideal candidates for collection behind reservoirs; however, many facilities in the study area actually gathered runoff from unchannelized areas of rocky or otherwise barren ground, relying on the scant annual surface runoff and the consequent enhancement of the water table in order to make a plot of land more congenial to plant growth. In either case, the catchment area of a reservoir was considered to be part of the land "belonging" to that facility.[6] Cultivation was rarely carried out in immediate reservoir catchments, but such areas were important for grazing and firewood collection.

Water depths are generally shallow, rarely reaching more than about 10 meters. Because of their extensive and relatively shallow waterspread, reservoirs in this region are marked by high evaporation rates (Sharma and Sharma 1990:20) and a high degree of overall water loss. The relatively shallow and seasonally shifting pools of water support many aquatic and semi-aquatic plants, both floating weeds and plants requiring solid ground to root in (N.P. Singh 1988). Besides the lotus, with its edible rhizomes, beautiful flowers, and useful leaves, many other aquatic plants also had value as food, forage, and thatching material and as enhancements to fish habitats.[7] However, other aquatic plants, most notably that New World introduction, the water hyacinth, could virtually overrun a reservoir, even to the point of clogging the area near the sluices and thus impeding reservoir function. Such plants are considered pests and periodic maintenance is required to rid the facility of these weeds.

The seasonal nature of runoff and the fact the rain often falls in brief, heavy showers means that water coming into a reservoir bed tends to carry a heavy sediment load. This sediment load will diminish the capacity of the reservoir over time, and maintenance of these facilities was largely oriented around cleaning out accumulated sediment. Because water and sediment enter the reservoir bed together, it is possible to track the locations and velocities of inflow from sediment particle size distributions on the reservoir bed. Where we have mapped particle size distributions, there is a clear pattern of diminished inflow velocity with distance from the edge of the reservoir, the slowest flows being located near the sluice gate(s). This creates a distinctive set of sediment bands, where gravel is localized around the edges of reservoir beds, sand a little further in, followed by a band of silt, and finally an area of clay up against the embankment.[8] From these patterns one may map the approximate extent of the water-containing reservoir bed and its change through time. From surface sediment particle size distributions, it is possible to determine either the maximal extent of the bed, or its most recent extent where there has been substantial accumulation of sediment covering earlier particle distributions. Reser-

Figure 34. Avinamodugu reservoir, overview, showing two easternmost sluices buried in accumulated sediment.

Figure 35. Avinamodugu reservoir, sluice 1, detail, buried in accumulated sediment.

voirs for which detailed subsurface particle size studies are available include VMS-231 (Kamalapuram *kere*) and VMS-1004 (the reservoir near VMS-110 in the western valley, see Chapter 5). In addition to clay, one of the non-agricultural products associated with reservoirs is silt (Mosse 1999: 318, others include trees and fish).

In several cases we have observed that the catchment areas of large reservoirs contained extensive agricultural terraces. Terraces walls tend to be low, no more than one or two masonry courses, but some terrace complexes cover very large areas. We do not know if dry crops were planted in these enclosed fields, although it seems likely. All the cases of terraced watersheds we recorded were associated with large reservoirs and with watersheds situated not on the virtually soil-free rocky hills but on more shallowly sloping, open ground. Terraces protected the reservoir bed from excessive siltation and served to slow and perhaps even direct runoff. Certainly, the terracing of reservoir watersheds is more important where vegetation cover on erosion-prone sediments has been denuded, as seems to be the case in all the examples we observed.

That sediment infill was a serious maintenance problem is clear, both from the large number of silted-in and abandoned reservoirs and from contemporary texts. Inscriptional sources often discuss arrangements for dredging sediment out of reservoirs and hauling it away; often this sediment was placed on the embankment to strengthen it. For example, two inscriptions, one from AD 1429 and the other 1432 from Timmanhalli, Hassan District, Karnataka (EC XV, Ak. 238), both found in fields near the village, record grants of (the income from) land which was used to maintain a reservoir called *Hiriya kate* ("big reservoir") by carrying away the silt and strengthening the bund. Typical of this genre of records is an inscription of AD 1371, also from Hassan District, that refers to arrangements for both labor and tools in maintaining the reservoir. Gopal (1985b: 138-40) summarizes the record:

> This is described as an arrangement (*samsthe*) made by the *mahajanas*[9] of Namjenathapura alias Hebbale about the maintenance of four carts for the tank, Hiriyakere, of the village by Bommagauda and three others (named) of Boluketanahalli, the hamlet. They were allowed collection of certain specified taxes like *aruvana* and *binugudere*, and were remitted from some others. . . . It was stipulated that the beneficiaries themselves were to meet the expenses of the buffalo (*kona*) [for pulling the cart], wooden implements (*kirumuttu*), iron (*kabbuna*), and oil for the carts. . . .

Responsibility for silt removal was also sometimes expressed in terms of the volume of silt individuals or groups were required to remove. These quantities are expressed in terms of pits (*kuli*) of specific sizes to be dug into the bed (and see Kotraiah 1995a).

Even more dramatic than textual discussion of maintenance is the physical evidence for bed siltation. Some abandoned facilities appear to have been given up precisely because of excessive sediment infill. The Avinamodugu *kere*, for example, has filled in with clay-rich sediment to a depth of at least 2 meters as is clear from the partly buried sluices (Figures 34 and 35, and see Chapter 8) and from our sediment coring. The abandonment of some of the Main Valley reservoirs also appears to be due to excessive siltation. Of course, sediment infill is an ongoing problem and even the twentieth-century Tungabhadra reservoir is not immune to loss of capacity caused by sediment accumulation. Local residents claim that this reservoir has already lost over half of its capacity in its brief, 50-year existence. In general, larger facilities with deeper water and more reliable sources of water (that is, without marked dry seasons, systems reservoirs being the prime example) are more difficult to maintain, their very strength – abundant flowing water – also being one of their greatest weaknesses.

Embankments: Construction, Size and Shape

Figure 36 illustrates a hypothetical reservoir in cross-section, showing all of the named elements. Water is retained by a massive earthen embankment, also known as a *bund*, usually containing a fine-grained internal stratigraphy caused by the accumulation of a great many small loads of soil and gravel. Most embank-

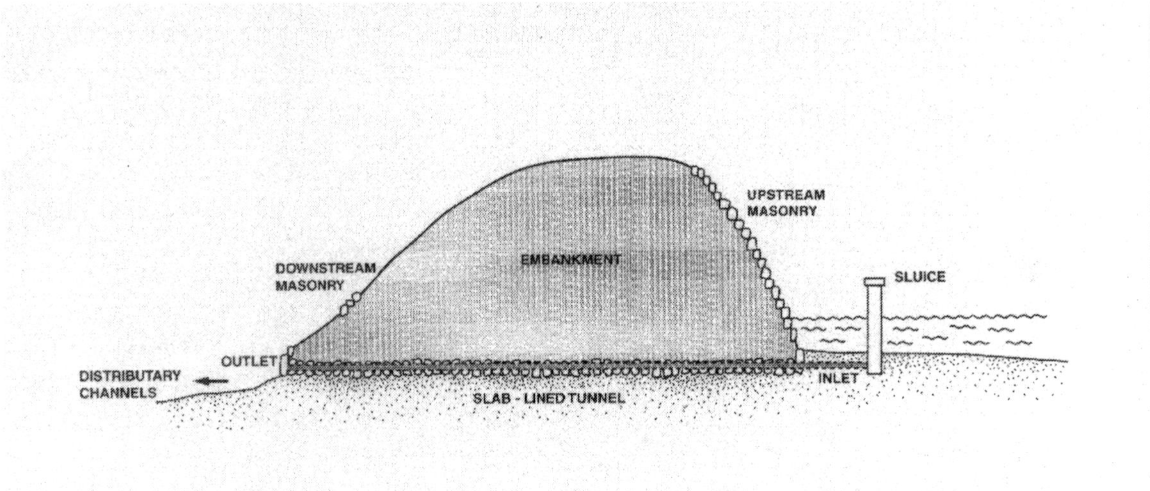

Figure 36. Hypothetical reservoir in cross-section.

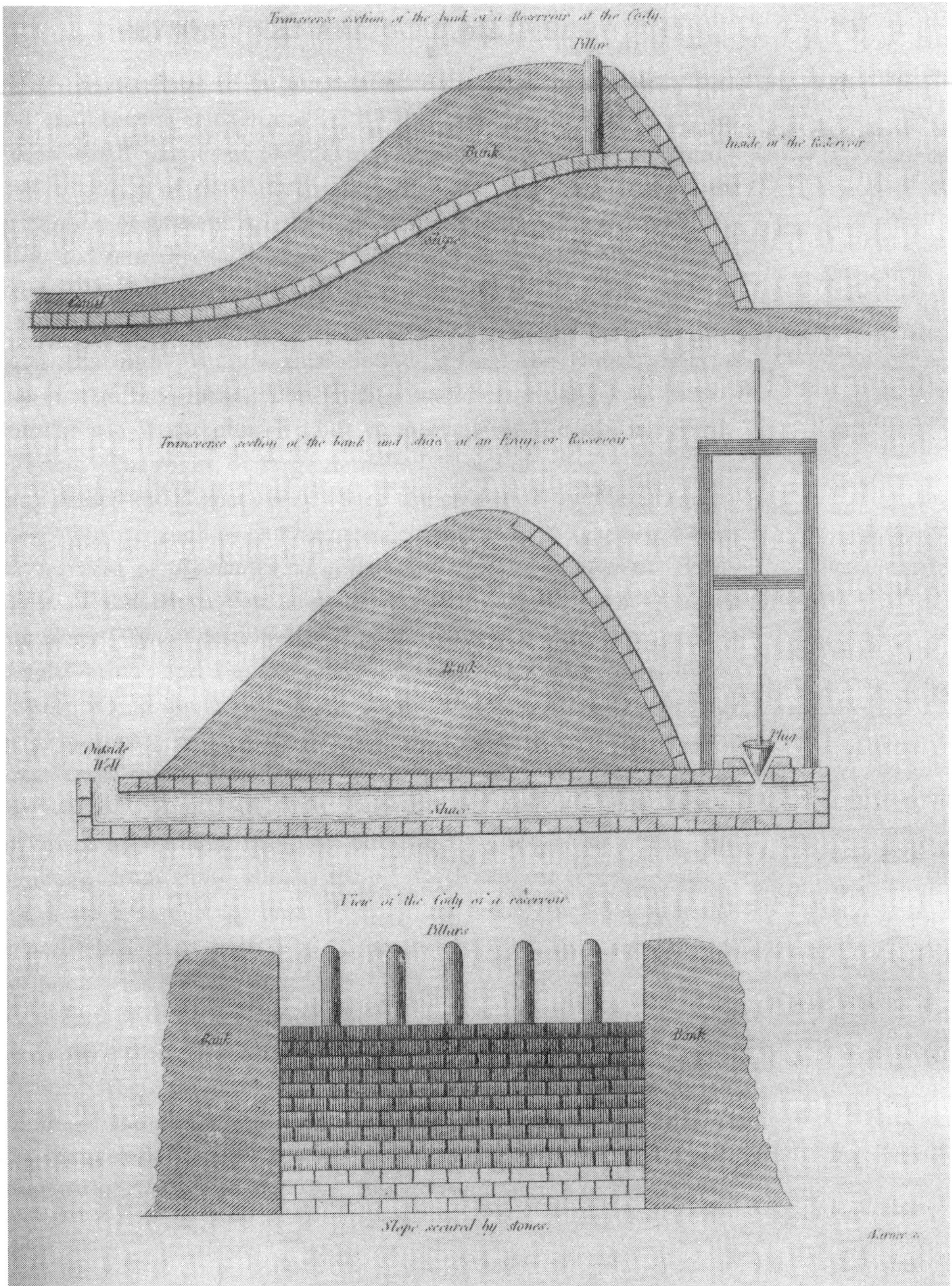

Figure 37. Buchanan's depictions of reservoirs in south India.

ments are constructed from soil and gravel found very near the facility itself; what bed excavation there is usually consists of borrow pits for embankment fill, although some inscriptions mention leveling of the bed and the undesirability of high spots in the bed.[10] Most embankments are built from sterile (artifact-free) soil, although there are a few that cut through and incorporate fill from earlier cultural deposits (e.g. VMS-1003, Chapter 5). Examination of breached reservoir cross-sections shows little spatial differentiation of fill by size or material within the body of the dam. In his trip across what is now southern Karnataka and northern Tamil Nadu in 1800, Francis Buchanan (1988[1807]: plate I) also examined reservoir construction. His diagrams are quite similar to mine (Figure 37); however, the kind of construction he illustrates for the waste weir or overflow sluice (he calls these *Codies*, from the Kannada word *kodi* for waste weir, 1988: 4) is not evident in any Vijayanagara period reservoir and appears to be a later feature. Waste weirs are discussed in more detail below.

Embankments located and described in the survey area vary in length from 2 meters to more than 3 kilometers long (Figure 38); the highest was 28 meters high. Thus, there exists a great range in reservoir size from the truly monumental to the very modest. Reservoir size appears to be determined primarily by hydrological and geological considerations rather than their positions *vis-à-vis* settlements; if anything, it is the reservoir that determines the location of the settlement rather than the reverse. It does seem to be the case, however, that very small reservoirs cluster in areas of dry farming and lower population density and as such, they appear to be part of small-scale agricultural strategies that operate around the edges of larger, more urban-oriented facilities. The Vijayanagara-period reservoirs that now exist close to the capital city are inevitably large; these were all highly productive facilities with reasonably secure water flows.[11]

Embankment shapes vary somewhat, depending on the situation of the reservoir and the velocity and concentration of runoff into the bed. A short *bund* blocking the mouth of a small box canyon (steep-sided valley enclosed on three sides) where runoff is fast and focused will be higher and the cross-sectional shape of the embankment at a more acute angle than a longer embankment crossing a broad valley. There the runoff, while greater in overall volume, will be slower and more spatially dispersed and the potential stress on the embankment will be different. Such large embankments tend to be wider and the cross-sectional shape of the embankment is more rounded and less acute. The upstream side of the *bund* usually slopes a little more steeply than the downstream side.

In plan, reservoirs are generally curved, with the open side of the arc on the upstream side of the feature. Again, this kind of construction helps prevent dam breaches. Sometimes embankments are built from a series of curved segments (see, especially VMS-1003, Chapter 5), or they may have a more complex form that responds to very specific local runoff and slope configurations. Embankments are always very carefully sited – each one is different. A few of the largest embankments have breakwaters, small extending arms that reach into the bed of the reservoir and serve to break up the currents and waves in locations particularly susceptible to damage (e.g. VMS-1015, Chapter 6).

Embankments: Masonry Facings and Features

Most earthen embankments are faced with stepped masonry on the upstream side, and occasionally on both sides. The masonry serves to protect the earthen bund from the rush of water flowing into the feature and from the constant lapping of waves against it. Small reservoirs may have only a few rows of roughly-coursed boulders, while large reservoirs may have more than twenty courses of stone. In general, masonry on Vijayanagara-period reservoirs is regularly coursed and stepped, so that the boulders, blocks, or slabs constituting the masonry lie flat (horizontally) while still following the slope of the embankment. This pattern is strikingly different from later reservoir facings, in which the stones that line the inside of the embankment conform to its slope;

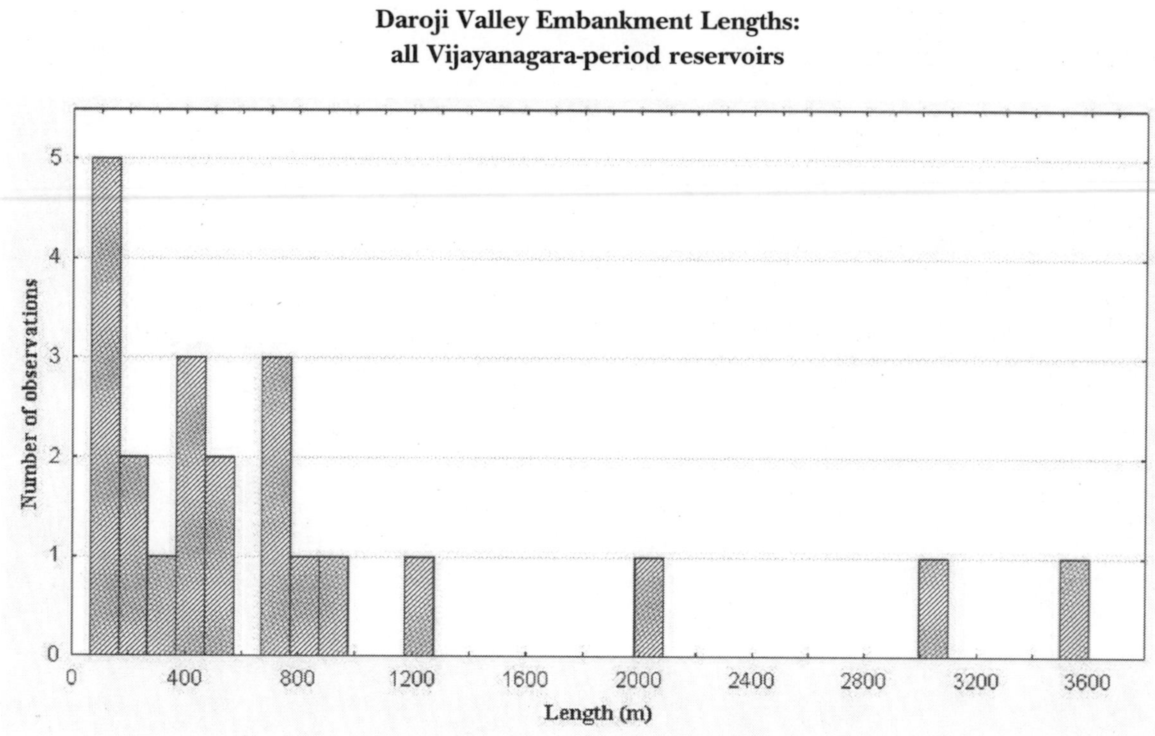

Figure 38. Distribution of reservoir lengths.

Figure 39. VMS-190, Halla *kere* embankment.

Figure 40. VMS-190, Halla *kere* sluice 2, with Gajalakshmi.

Figure 41. VMS-190, masonry detail, looking down, steps with carved lingam.

Figure 42. Raya *kere*, staircase and sluice.

this pattern is schematically illustrated by Buchanan (1988[1807]) in Figure 37. Masonry is either laid right on the earthen *bund* with no foundation deposit or else is seated on a gravelly base.

The stone that makes up the masonry is generally locally obtained, so that granite is the most common building material throughout the study area. Some reservoirs incorporate the dark outcropping basalts that are found in granitic formations, and some Daroji Valley reservoirs use the metamorphic rocks of the Sandur Hills. The choice of building material appears to be expedient in most cases; however, there is at least one very striking example of deliberate selection of lithic materials. This is the Halla *kere* (VMS-190), located in Block S to the north of Papinayakanahalli (Chapter 6; and see Morrison 1995a). Halla *kere* is a large reservoir, some 684 meters in length, that is now fed by the Right Bank Main Canal of the Tungabhadra Dam scheme. This reservoir is faced with up to 24 courses of masonry on its northern, upstream side. Alternate courses of split boulders are of grey, pink, and some black granite, creating a striped effect (Figure 39). Most striking about this striped masonry is the fact that stripes of "red" (or pink) alternate with stripes of "white" (or grey) – vertical (but not horizontal as in this example) red and white stripes were (and still are) often painted on temples and even the outer walls of fortified villages. The association of these stripes with both temples and reservoirs is no coincidence, as I discuss below; the Halla *kere* also has a sluice (Figure 40) with a sculpted Lakshmi and elephants (Gajalakshmi, see below).

The stepped masonry itself often consists of unmodified boulders of various sizes. Sometimes the boulders are split; less often, the masonry is composed of quarried or even quarried and dressed slabs. Features built into the masonry include projecting steps and staircases. Steps (Figure 41) usually consist of diagonal rows of rectangular slabs that stick out from the masonry face. When lithic inscriptions are built into the masonry, they may appear to be like protruding steps as inscriptions are usually sculpted on long stone slabs. Stairways (Figure 42) are more formal, usually built of long slabs, sometimes placed so that the height of each step is much shallower than the surrounding stepped masonry (which can be difficult to climb up and down). Stairways are always built opposite sluice gates, several even have balustrades. This placement certainly serves a practical value in that access to the sluice is necessary to control water distribution and further because sluices are always the primary foci of maintenance work. However, there is also a kind of spatial focusing created by staircase placement which makes sluices even more prominent.

Downstream masonry is usually much less elaborate than upstream revetment. Where such construction is present, it is rarely more than a few courses high and is usually located near the base of the embankment. The function of downstream masonry seems mainly to be to retard erosion of the embankment itself, especially since reservoir embankments are often used as roads and are thus subject to heavy disturbance.

Water Distribution: Tunnels and Sluices

Tunnels

For reservoirs equipped to distribute water, the primary means of conveying water downstream is through tunnels built into the embankment (Figure 43). Tunnels tend to be square or rectangular in section and are lined with stone slabs on all sides. The liner slabs are often encased in a brick-and-plaster sheath that protects the integrity of the tunnel from the tons of dirt that cover it. In a few cases I have observed round brick- or rock-lined vents on the tops of reservoir embankments above tunnel locations. These vents presumably facilitated water flow and perhaps tunnel maintenance. However, such vents are by no means common and in any case, they tend to be a meter or less in diameter, opening many meters above the tunnel, making it difficult to see exactly how one would reach the distant tunnel for repairs. In fact, it is not at all clear how blocked tunnels were cleared, since they tend to be both very constricted (.5 by .5 meter on average) and long (as much as 30 meters

Figure 43. Tunnel inlet, showing some brick in upper left.

Figure 44. VMS-231, Kamalapuram *kere*, showing sluice in use.

long). The tunnel outlet is often visible below the reservoir, while on the upstream side of the embankment, the tunnel inlet is under water – at least, when there is water. Obviously, the placement and number of tunnels had to be part of the initial plan for a reservoir. Adding new tunnels (and sluices) after the fact involved a significant reconstruction of the facility. A few inscriptions refer to investments in new sluices, undertakings no less costly and significant than the rehabilitation of a breached reservoir. In some approximate sense, the length of the reservoir can be used as a rough predictor for the number of tunnels, one to four being the typical range. The flow of water through tunnels is always regulated by sluices.

Sluices

Vijayanagara sluices (*madai, tumu*) are distinctive, and serve as one of the best indicators of chronology and degree of elaboration of a reservoir (Figures 1 and 2). A typical sluice consists of two stone uprights joined by two or three horizontal cross-bars. The tunnel opening is located between the uprights (under water), and all the cross-pieces are perforated by round openings above the tunnel opening. The tunnel can be blocked by lowering a wooden plug attached to a bar or rope into the opening. The end of the bar or rope may be secured to one of the cross-pieces, depending on the level of the water.

The upper cross-piece or lintel commonly consists of a three-part moulding sequence, similar to those seen in formal architecture of the period (cf. Fritz, Michell, and Nagaraja Rao 1985; Michell 1990). A three-part moulding consists of three superimposed stone elements: a lower moulding which angles in toward the center slab; a central inset slab; and an upper moulding which is a mirror image of the lower. Not all sluice gates have formal moulding sequences nor indeed any mouldings at all. These simple sluices appear to have been built throughout the Vijayanagara period and are thus not temporally diagnostic of any particular division of the period. It is, however, relatively straightforward to distinguish Vijayanagara-era sluice gates from earlier and later sluices, so at least this broad temporal assignment can usually be made.

Sluices with moulding sequences vary a great deal in both scale and form. One common sequence on both architecture and sluice gates employs the moulding type known as two-stepped with angled bevel, illustrated here on a sluice from the Kamalapuram *kere* (Figure 44). These mouldings often have center half-medallions and/or corner quarter medallions, but rarely any other kind of decoration. Two-stepped angled bevel moulding sequences are often found on sluice gates built on a rather modest scale, as is the case with the Kamalapuram *kere* sluice depicted here.[12] In all cases where this moulding sequence is associated with a dated reservoir (the dates coming from associated inscriptions), construction dates fall in the fourteenth or fifteenth century. This association between Early and Middle Vijayanagara period architecture and two-stepped with angled bevel mouldings is strengthened by analogy with the architecture of temples, palaces, and other elite structures from the city of Vijayanagara (Fritz, Michell, and Nagaraja Rao 1985; Michell 1990). As we shall see, this early moulding sequence is not common in the Daroji Valley, although it is outside the valley. This is one of the lines of evidence that leads me to suggest that the Daroji Valley expansion of reservoir irrigation was primarily a sixteenth-century phenomenon.

Other moulding sequences appear to have replaced the modestly-scaled and relatively simple forms of the two-stepped with angled bevel types. These sequences generally have rounded, or convex bevels set off by carved steps above and below; thus, these forms include named types such as three-stepped with convex bevel, four-stepped with convex bevel, and so on. Convex bevel forms may also have extra bands of decoration or the bevel may itself be elaborated (for example "jeweled" bands which look like strings of pearls, wave-like undulations, and ribbed or lobed designs representing lotus petals). Carved panels also tend to be more elaborate than half- or quarter-medallions; these include *makara-torana*, arched projections which at their most elaborate are stylized heads of *makara* (mythical crocodile-like animals, discussed below), but more often are simply medallions with rounded or pointed tops.[13] More details of sluice elaboration will arise with individual sluice descriptions; I simply wish to note that here that there is a broad range of decorative elaboration possible and that this is mostly associated with convex-bevel moulding types. The latter, again, are always associated with sixteenth-century reservoirs when the reservoirs can be independently dated. Further, these forms, while not unknown prior to the sixteenth century, do seem to follow the general pattern of decorative elaboration in sixteenth-century architecture (e.g. Michell 1995).

Beyond the mouldings themselves, there are also some distinctive sluice morphologies that seem to be restricted to the sixteenth century. These are the huge double sluices seen on at least four reservoirs in the Vijayanagara region; Dharmasagara (VMS-1015), Daroji *kere* (VMS-1019), Avinamodugu *kere* (VMS-1031), and a reservoir just northeast of Timmalapuram *kere*, in the Dhanayakana *kere* region southwest of Hospet (Figure 45). The double sluices at Daroji are distinctively roofed; this may be a later form, as discussed in Chapter 7. In general, there seems to be a set of distinctive sixteenth-century sluice proportions, with the taller and more monumental sluices all dating to this century. I am thus suggesting here that certain elaborate sluice mouldings, sluice proportion, and forms such as the roofed or double sluice indicate sixteenth-century construction.[14]

Other kinds of decorative elaboration on Vijayanagara sluice gates include sculptures of deities. Gods and goddess are almost always carved in the center of the uppermost cross-bar, facing the embankment. These sculpted sluices create striking echoes of temples, especially temple doorways; their door-like morphology, use of moulding sequences, and iconographic programs all evoke temple architecture. Temple door frames (also built of stone slabs) leading into both the antechamber (*antarala*) and the sanctuary (*garbhagriha*) are often decorated in the center of the lintel, facing out toward the worshipper, with either simple square panels, lotus flowers, or deities. The most common door deities are Lakshmi (goddess of wealth and prosperity), often flanked by elephants (this form is known as Gajalakshmi) and Ganesha (Ganapati, the elephant god who oversees beginnings, among other things). Interestingly, Lakshmi is associated with Vishnu while Ganesha is associated with Shiva – still, door deities often cross-cut the sectarian affiliation of temples.

Above-door deities are quite different from door guardians (*dvarapala*), fierce Shaivite or Vaishnavite beings who literally guard temple doorways. Door guardians often carry clubs or other weapons and are usually carved on either side of the door, on the stone door jambs. Door guardians generally stand on or near the floor so that if there are donor portraits (see below), they will be higher up. Sometimes door guardians are free-standing sculptures, but even then they are placed on either side of the door into the sanctuary or antechamber. Besides door guardians, one also finds sculpted vessels (*kalasha*, discussed below) flanking some temple doorways, usually placed on either side of the door near the base of the jamb.

Other kinds of sculptures carved into temple doorways include donor portraits, some of them also royal portraits. Donors or devotees (the latter may also be carved into the floor in an attitude of prayer, facing the sanctuary) are clearly distinguishable from gods and goddesses, having none of their iconographic attributes. Male donors in the Vijayanagara periods commonly wear tall pointed hats (cf. Wagoner 1996) and *dhotis*, a kind of draped lower garment. Female donors generally wear their hair in a large bun to one side of the head; both males and females hold their hands together in a prayerful, respectful mode (*anjali mudra*). The large, early fifteenth-century Malapannagudi reservoir (VMS-4) has a moulding sequence with two-stepped with angled bevel mouldings built on a rather modest scale. This reservoir contains donor portraits on either side of the uprights of the second sluice, corresponding to the typical placement of donors on temple doors. Interestingly, the donors – a male and a female (Figure 2) – are not facing the embankment, as dieties always do, but are instead looking out across the reservoir. On the other side of this same sluice, in her usual position facing the

Figure 45. Large double sluice from reservoir northeast of Timmalapur.

Figure 46. Exterior of Pattabhirama temple, showing door-like aedicules and *purna kalasha.*

bund is a carved figure; in this case it is the rather unusual choice of Sita flanked by Hanuman and Sugriva.[15] Unfortunately, we have no other examples of sluices with donor portraits, so it is difficult to say if the placement of these images is unusual.

In temples more generally, representations of door-like (or sluice-like) shapes are also important in larger decorative and iconographic schemes. Figures representing openings or entire buildings (Figure 46), and often forming niches filled with sculptures, are placed all around the exterior walls of temples and on the pyramidal superstructures over the sanctuary (the *vimana*) or temple gateway (*gopuram*). Hardy (1998: 110, 124) refers to the construction of temples, and south Indian temples in particular, as being characterized by *aedicularity*, "The principle of articulating the temple exterior as a matrix of interconnected shrine-images . . . progressively extended down a hierarchy from primary components to minor niches", with his shrine-images or *aedicules* corresponding to what I refer to as doorway or gateway figures (in two dimensions) or miniature temples (in three).[16] Hardy further identifies a basic historical trend toward greater aedicular density, proliferation, and fragmentation (1998: 124-5), a movement clearly seen in the increasing elaboration of Vijayanagara temples between the fourteenth and sixteenth centuries. Although temple aedicules tend to be more ornate than sluice gates, both kinds of aedicules consist of upright columns capped by a three-part moulding sequence and sometimes by a roof (Figure 45). In fact, it may not be too bold to suggest not only that sluices invoked temples, but also that temples invoked sluices, symbols of agricultural productivity and prosperity, of elite largesse and *dharma*, culturally-valued loci and landmarks in a world where gods and gardens were associated in both "mythic" and real space and time.

Waste Weirs

In addition to the water conveyed through tunnels and controlled by sluice gates, excess water can also be released from the reservoir by spillways, waste weirs or *kodi* (Figure 47). These "overflow sluices" may consist of very closely fitted stone aprons and low walls or, more commonly, appear to be a jumble of boulders and cobbles. Rarely, the waste weir is a more formal structure like that illustrated in Figure 47. The rocky landscape, the sparse vegetation, and the seasonality of precipitation virtually ensure that the velocity of runoff in the rainy season can be sufficient to breach even the largest reservoir.[17] Spillways allow the excess water to flow out of the reservoir with the minimum impact on the embankment. Some very small reservoirs do not have tunnels, but only spillways, and could have been used for only a very limited period of time each year. Spillways are typically located toward one end of an embankment, so that they are engaged only when the water level is high.

The waste weir illustrated by Buchanan (Figure 37) is quite formal and differs from those of most reservoirs discussed here. Note that Buchanan's uppermost illustration is meant to indicate how high the top of waste weir is *vis-à-vis* the top of the embankment (about three-quarters of the height, in this case) and to show how the *kodi* articulates with the *bund*; it is not meant to indicate that there is an internal masonry course running all of the way through the embankment. In the lowest illustration, the shading on the elements of the waste weir is meant to depict a slope down toward the viewer.

Very few reservoirs in the study area have such a formal overflow sluice; the few that do are still in use and these features may have been added later. At least two reservoirs in the Daroji Valley contain formal waste weirs; the other reservoir with a formal overflow sluice is the Kamalapuram *kere* which is fitted with a *c.* 25 meters wide chute paved with flat boulders. The surface of the waste weir is a few meters lower than the top of the earthen *bund* and it is located near the western end of that *bund*. The slope of the stone apron is not nearly as steep as that depicted by Buchanan. Here and there in this pavement are upright stone "needles" that could be used to support a temporary structure to retain water, much as described by Buchanan.[18] The Kamalapuram *kodi* is virtually non-functional since the reservoir has lost much

Figure 47. Kurugodu reservoir waste weir.

Figure 48. Kamalapuram *kere*, stone distribution basin below embankment.

capacity to siltation and, in the two decades I have been observing it, the water level only once reached the overflow sluice. The Daroji *kere* also has a formal waste weir, as described in Chapter 7. This feature may, however, date to the seventeenth century or even later. A much more common kind of *kodi* construction in our region, even on large reservoirs with formal sluice architecture, is a pile of boulders near one end of the embankment, often the end that is at a slightly higher elevation. The piled-up boulders do allow some water to pass through, making a kind of sieve for excess water flow – the position of such a feature at the very end of the embankment means that water would flow through only when the facility is already quite full.

Distribution Features Below the Reservoir

On the downstream side of the embankment, water either flowed out of the tunnel directly into the fields, conveyed by temporary earthen channels, or it was diverted into a small basin before being re-directed into feeder channels. Basins are made either of stone or brick and plaster, and are invariably square. Such basins are rare and tend to be associated only with larger reservoirs. Most large reservoirs, however, have no such basins, so they are obviously not required for successful operation. The Mallapannagudi reservoir, VMS-4, has two brick and plaster basins while the Kamalapuram reservoir, VMS-231, has one beautiful stone basin made of dressed and rounded slabs (Figure 48). In both cases, these reservoirs are very close to substantial settlements; it may be that the basins were meant for domestic activities such as drawing water and washing clothes. However, they do prevent the water coming out of the reservoir tunnel from eroding the damp ground immediately below it and serve to effectively distribute water into the small earthen channels that take it to the fields. The latter would have had to be constantly maintained and were presumably reconfigured occasionally, perhaps even annually, to reach the areas under cultivation at that time.

INTEGRATION WITH OTHER FACILITIES: RESERVOIRS AS ELEMENTS IN AN AGRICULTURAL LANDSCAPE

Vijayanagara reservoirs did not operate in isolation. Many of them were physically linked with other agricultural facilities such as canals, terraces, wells, or other reservoirs. System reservoirs, for example, integrated river-fed canals and reservoirs. Multiple-reservoir systems (grouped systems), such as those of the Daroji Valley or the Dhanayakanakere area are certainly among the most dramatic examples of interlinked facilities, but even these chains of reservoirs were connected to other kinds of facilities. In the Daroji Valley, it is clear that at its maximal extent in the sixteenth century, nearly half of the land in the main valley was once devoted either to reservoir beds or to fields watered by reservoirs so that even small facilities were linked to a spatially expansive system of soil and water control. Reservoirs are also often associated with wells. Reservoirs raise the level of the water table in their immediate vicinity, and associated wells may contain water even when the reservoir itself is dry. Wells may also have been important for supplying water to reservoir-side villages and to livestock. Because the bed of a reservoir always slopes down toward the embankment and the sluice gates, water tends to collect at the *bund* and to remain there longer into the dry season than elsewhere in the bed. Thus, the level of the water table is always most elevated near the embankment and, consequently, wells are always placed just below the reservoir; that is, downstream from the bed near the *bund.*

Some of the wells associated with Daroji reservoirs are quite large; most are square or rectangular and masonry-lined.[19] Many have provisions for lifting water, such as overhanging platforms for supporting lifting apparatuses. It is interesting that many, perhaps most wells associated with Daroji reservoirs have construction styles that appear to be post-Vijayanagara, suggesting that they were built either as the reservoirs began to silt in and their capacity was reduced, or perhaps even after the reservoirs fell out of use (even breached and abandoned reservoirs still retain some moisture and thus still have water table effects).[20] Although platforms for water lifting devices are not uncommon in the region, in no case are such devices still in use. It may be, then, that many of these features date to the period between the seventeenth and twentieth centuries, when population densities in this region were low, electric pumps not yet in use, and the large, interconnected Daroji Valley chain of reservoirs was no longer fully functional.

Although many, if not most of the reservoir-associated wells in the Daroji Valley appear to post-date their associated reservoirs, it is also clear that reservoirs were expected to have wells. A text of AD 1385, Padmananka's *Padmaraja Purana,* describes a reservoir as follows, "The tank, besides the (strong and lengthy) bund, had strongly built stone sluices, *sluice wells,* canals, and channels. The tank was full with water and the irrigated lands below it had well grown standing crops, while the gardens had varieties of fruit-bearing trees" (Kotraiah 1995b: 9, emphasis added).

Although these are not in evidence today, nor are there any clear archaeological indications of them, literary texts mention water-lifting devices that were used with reservoirs. Water lifting devices are not unknown in this area, but in my experience these are always associated with either wells or canals. Ramps and pulleys for cattle-assisted water hauling from wells are the most common kind of lifting device, but one also occasionally sees a kind of Persian wheel device with pots attached to a rotor and a lever system also using (now plastic or metal) vessels. These days much lifting of water is facilitated by electric pumps and hoses. Besides cattle-ramps on wells, the two kinds lifting technologies, wheels and levers, clearly existed in the Vijayanagara period. A text written around the middle of the fifteenth century by Lakkanadandesha, a resident of Vijayanagara, and purporting to describe the court of Bijjala III, the Kalachuri king of Kalyana, notes (Kotraiah 1995c: 7), "... there were a number of tanks and ponds fitted with water-lifting contrivances called *eta* and *ratala*". *Eta, etam, etapadam,* and *peri-etam* are all names for lever-based water-lifting devices while *rahattaghadia,* and *rate-gadige* are chains or wheels of pots, a form of the Persian wheel (Kotraiah 1995a: 198, 202). The lack of association between these devices and reservoirs today speaks to the declining importance of reservoirs, and especially to their replacement in dry areas with bore wells and electric pumps.

In the driest upland areas, reservoirs sometimes occur in linked systems with agricultural terraces, in a kind of inverse relationship to the terrace-reservoir (upstream-downstream) symbiosis described above where terraces served to protect reservoir watersheds. In this case (reservoir-terrace; upstream-downstream), reservoirs collected runoff from precipitous, rocky slopes and either redistributed the water to terraced fields below or simply protected those fields from excess water flow and erosion. The reservoir is thus located at the head of the system, in areas where the low, simple terraces built by Vijayanagara agriculturalists would not have been stable. Figure 49 illustrates VMS-133/226, one reservoir-terrace system located to the south of the city in a dry upland area north of Papinayakanahalli. This reservoir is seriously breached, so its sluice arrangements are not clear, but it is evident that water released from the reservoir flowed down a cultivated slope defined by terrace walls to a large flat area below. The close relationship between terraces and reservoirs is further illustrated by the fact that VMS-133/126 is itself upstream from the Halla *kere* (VMS-190), a very large reservoir, so that one might consider both of the reservoirs and all of the terraces to be part of one very large system. The interrelation of facilities in the Vijayanagara region makes it clear just how difficult it is to understand the spatial structure of past agriculture without taking into account entire landscapes and the whole range of facilities.

Forms of Cultivation, Kinds of Reservoirs

As I have suggested, Vijayanagara reservoirs, although constructed and laid out in consistent ways, constituted quite a diverse set of facilities. Varying in water source, size, reliability, and integration with other features, they were able

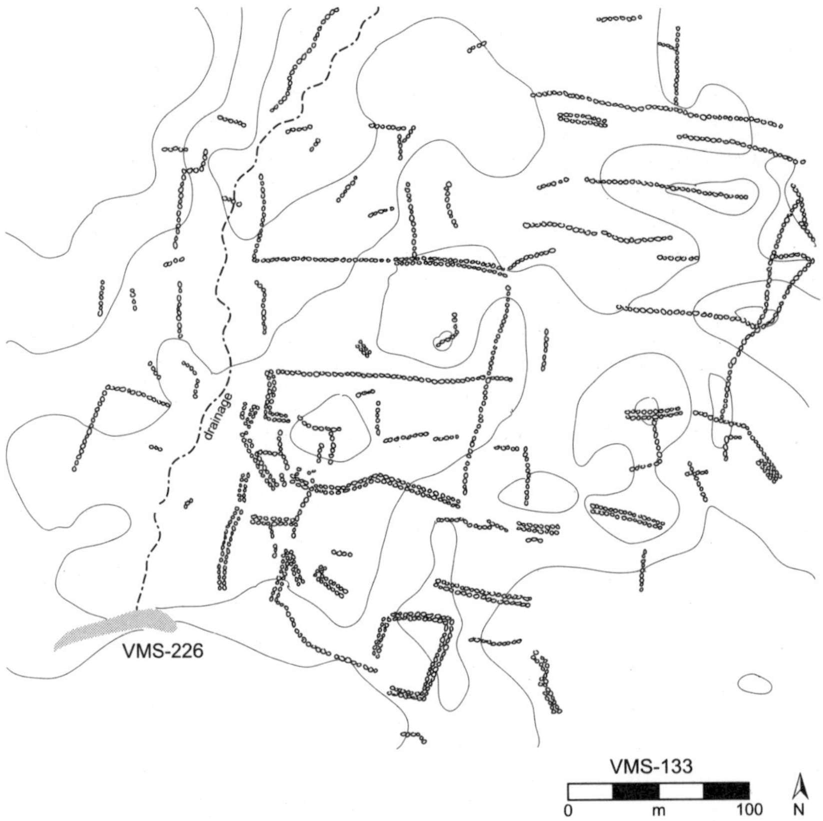

Figure 49. VMS-133/226, reservoir-terrace system in the watershed of Halla *kere*.

Figure 50. 16th-century Raya *kere*, sluice 1, southwest of Hospet.

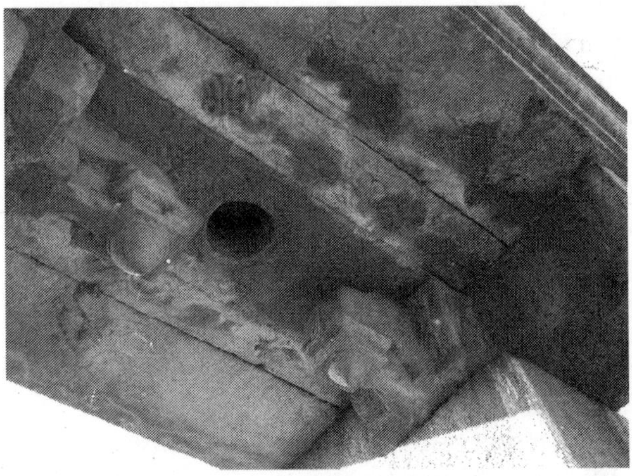

Figure 51. Detail of Raya *kere*, sluice 1, with lotus design.

to support cultivation in all the four traditional categories. The great majority of Vijayanagara reservoirs are filled by seasonal runoff, and support primarily wet-cum-dry cultivation. Such reservoirs usually contain water only during the monsoon and for a few months afterwards, though there are some that retain small permanent pools. Runoff-fed reservoirs vary greatly in size and in water-holding capacity, depending on the size and nature of their catchments. Most very small reservoirs are runoff-fed, but the Daroji *kere*, the largest reservoir in the entire district, was also supplied entirely by runoff, both from upstream reservoirs in the main valley chain (Chapter 7) and from some reliable streams coming down from the Sandur Hills. Wet-cum-dry cultivation under runoff-fed reservoirs allowed for quite flexible production strategies. In favorable settings and in wetter years, wet crops such as rice or vegetables could be grown after the monsoon. More often, however, wet-cum-dry cultivation allowed for the more secure production of dry crops such as sorghum and other millets. Trees are also often associated with reservoirs and useful trees may be planted on the embankment. However, only a few of the runoff-fed reservoirs in this region could have supported permanent orchards.

Some runoff-fed reservoirs belong in the category of dry cultivation, since they cannot support "wet" crops. Containment reservoirs all fall in this category. Although little or no water may collect on the surface, such facilities both slow and spread the flow of surface and subsurface water and soil down the slope. Cultivation is thus carried out in the bed of the facility rather than below it, a pattern evident from both structural features and sediment distributions. Abandoned or silted-in reservoirs may also be treated like containment reservoirs, with crops grown in the bed after the rainy season.

Wet or garden cultivation may be supported by the more reliable runoff-fed reservoirs, as the Avinamodugu *kere* does today, even given its greatly reduced capacity (Chapter 8). However, multicroppping of water-loving rice, vegetable, and tree crops was possible only under perennial irrigation – meaning, in this region, only where waters of the Tungabhadra could be tapped. As noted, the Daroji Valley has no recourse to canal irrigation and the only two system reservoirs in the Vijayanagara region are the early Vijayanagara Kamalapuram *kere*, which is still in use, and the Sangapuram *kere*, no longer in use. In the latter case, the production capacity of the land under the reservoir bed was apparently too valuable to lose and the canal which supplied the reservoir now simply waters all the fields directly, the reservoir being perhaps deliberately breached.

It is too simple, however, to match cultivation forms with reservoir forms. Although it would be very convenient to do so, given that we have a great deal of information on physical residues of agricultural actions, we must realize that agricultural practice was both flexible and situational. A more reasonable account of past agriculture, then, will be phrased in terms of ranges of action, where broad physical parameters set close limits on what farmers may do, but do not entirely determine them. On the one hand, the existence of a reservoir allowed farmers' strategies of production to be significantly more flexible than they would be under a rainfall regime. On the other hand, participating in the use and perhaps maintenance and management of a major reservoir and its *ayacut* (area irrigated) also enmeshed farmers in complex social and political relationships and obligations, relationships that both enhanced agricultural productivity and, perhaps, limited options such as mobility.

Reservoir Construction: The Anantarajasagar Inscription and Portuguese Accounts

Although I discussed the organization of reservoir construction in a general way in Chapter 2, the review of the morphology and function of reservoirs in this chapter can now set the stage for a reintegration of organizational, cultural, and technical concerns. In this light it is worth discussing an unusually detailed inscription describing the construction of the Anantarajasagar reservoir, east/southeast of the Daroji Valley, now in Cuddapah district, Andhra Pradesh. This reservoir was built in AD 1369, early in the

Vijayanagara period and covers an area of some 41.4 square kilometers. The embankment is 1,372 meters long, 45.7 meters wide, and 10 meters high. The reservoir dams the Maldev River which, although somewhat more substantial than the *nullahs* feeding the Daroji *kere*, is a small stream, not a river on the scale of the Tungabhadra. Note that this reservoir is actually shorter than the Daroji Valley reservoirs VMS-1015 and VMS-1019 (Chapter 6).

The inscription both details the number of laborers involved in the construction of the facility and prescribes desirable and undesirable qualities for reservoirs in general. These qualities include not only attributes of the landscape, water supply, and arable soils, but also political considerations, including concern for the availability of skilled workers, and, of course, patronage. Although the numbers in the inscription are probably conventional or at the very least rounded – 1,000 laborers over a two-year period – the order of magnitude is probably reasonably accurate. Randhawa (1980: 99) summarizes the inscription's prescription of desirable qualities or conditions for reservoir construction:

1. A rightous king, wealthy, happy, and desirous of aquiring fame.
2. A person well-versed in the pathas *shastras* (texts on hydrology).
3. Hard soil in the bed of the tank.
4. A river with sweet water with a course of about 38.6 kilometers [3 *yojanas*].
5. Two projecting portions of hills.
6. Between these projecting portions of hills a dam built of compact stone, not too long, but firm.
7. Two extremities of hills should be devoid of fruit-bearing trees.
8. Bed of tank extensive and deep.
9. A quarry nearby with long and straight stones.
10. Fertile, low and level land in neighborhood to be irrigated.
11. A watercourse with strong eddies in the mountain region.
12. Masons skilled in the art of tank construction.

Features to be avoided are listed in a similar fashion (Randhawa 1980: 99):

1. Oozing of water from the dam.
2. Saline soil.
3. Location of the site at a boundary of two kingdoms.
4. High ground in the middle of the tank.
5. Scanty water supply and too extensive an area to be irrigated.
6. Too little land to be irrigated and excessive supply of water.

It is also worth mentioning one other textual description of reservoir construction, this by the Portuguese trader Domingo Paes who visited the city of Vijayanagara, possibly several times, between AD 1520 and 1522, during the reign of its most famous king, Krishnadeva Raya. Paes is discussing the construction of a reservoir near Hospet, very probably the one now known as Raya *kere* (king's reservoir), the embankment of which is "only" 1,100 meters long but is very high (28 meters) and steep (Figure 42). Paes writes (Sewell 1900: 244-5):

> In order to make this tank the said king broke down a hill which enclosed the ground occupied by the said tank. In the tank I saw so many people at work that there must have been fifteen or twenty thousand men, looking like ants, so that you could not see the ground on which they walked so many there were; this tank the king portioned out among his captains, each of whom had the duty of seeing that people placed under him did their work and that the tank was finished and brought to completion.

Curiously, this reservoir is not mentioned in any known inscription, but its two sluice gates are undoubtedly from the sixteenth century (Figures 50 and 51). Although they are only single and not double sluices, these are also among the most elaborately decorated sluices in the entire region, so perhaps its royal associations are accurate. The mention of "captains" may indeed refer to *nayakas* who are often reservoir patrons: kings, as noted, being less often associated with reservoir construction (Morrison and Lycett 1994, 1997). The Raya *kere* is somewhat notorious, since it no longer holds any water to speak of and yet does not appear to be breached. Both Paes and another Portuguese visitor, Nuniz (who may have borrowed his account from Paes), describe in some detail the tribulations associated with this reservoir. Apparently it failed to work properly – Paes claims that it burst two or three times, which seems likely given its position but which utterly fails to account for its present lack of water – until sacrifices of "the blood of men and horses and buffaloes" were made as recommended by an unspecified god via some Brahmins (Sewell 1900: 245). That the reservoir was not functional in the 1870s is evident from the district manual (Kelsall 1872: 16-17). In any case, even this brief excursion into written descriptions of reservoir construction serves to remind us that both technical and social considerations played a part in reservoir irrigation and that these were never viewed as fully distinct realms.

RESERVOIRS AS MONUMENTS

Although I have already alluded to this identification several times, it is worth reiterating that reservoirs may quite legitimately be seen, not only as monumental constructions by virtue of their size, visibility, and labor requirements, but also a monuments in that they were meant to be seen and to be prominent, to make statements about the world and about their builders (Morrison and Lycett 1994). Reservoirs not only watered people, animals, and plants, they were part of how the agricultural landscape came to be known and named, many villages being christened or rechristened after the names of their reservoir. Textual references to reservoirs often focus on their impounded water, as discussed below, but they may also extol the length and strength of the *bund*, the number and variety of sluices and channels, and in at least one case, the reservoir is likened to the spur of a mountain. This allusion is made in an early inscription of AD 150 or 152 describing the construction and reconstruction of the well-known Sudarshan lake, near Girnar in Gujarat (Kotraiah 1995a: 6).

Reservoirs, often associated with inscriptions and sometimes with donor portraits, commemorated past action, and even today there are local traditions about the construction history of most reservoirs, many of them directly evoking ideas of a glorious past in the Vijayanagara period. This region now receives a large number of tourists annually, mostly from within India but including many international visitors. Thus, the Vijayanagara empire is still very much present in the area, with the so-called "Hampi ruins" the primary attraction for tourists and the Virupaksha temple and several other Vijayanagara-era shrines the major draw for pilgrims. Tourists and pilgrims do not visit reservoirs; in spite of this, there exist many stories about the histories of reservoirs. Some are quite sophisticated while at other times there seems to be no more than a vague sense that a particular facility is "old". This perception of reservoirs as part of a glorious cultural heritage, a heritage worth remembering, was evident to me when I received a visit one day from an officer of the local irrigation department, who roared up across the fields on his scooter, subordinate riding pillion. Although I had meet several irrigation officials, I had not meet these two and they proceeded to question me about my actions, having heard that someone was going around to old reservoirs. We were standing next to a rather unimpressive and clearly defunct reservoir in the Daroji Valley, miles from any village. Once it was established that I indeed had permission from both the central and state governments and that I was interested only in old reservoirs, the officer's concern that I was stealing the irrigation secrets of Karnataka began to fade and be replaced by pride in his region's noted past, a past so worthwhile it would draw a foreigner from the distant United States.[21] Once we established that I was not interested in taking something but, in his words,"studying ancient glories", he was satisfied.

Reservoirs also quite clearly recreate the world of humans, plants, animals, and gods. They do this most directly by collecting and storing water and watering the land, creating landscapes that may be seen as lotus ponds, beautiful green fields, and cool, shady retreats. They water herds of auspicious cows, as well as less auspicious pigs, goats, sheep, and buffalo. Several abandoned reservoirs in the survey area, and most notably one remnant embankment in a canal-irrigated area to the west of the city of Vijayanagara, have been transformed into graveyards. In these canal-irrigated zones, dry, protected land is at a premium. Several Hindu communities as well as Muslims and Christians bury the dead rather than cremate and there are numerous burial grounds in the area. The transformation of a defunct reservoir embankment into a graveyard of course changes the character of the monument dramatically, but it is also possible to see reservoirs as being more than agricultural even while they are in active use. Thus, even if reservoirs are considered solely as physical features of the landscape, they clearly operated in realms quite distinct from that of agricultural production. Aside from the other uses of reservoir-collected sediment (brick making, construction) and water (stock watering, domestic use, recreation) and of reservoir-associated products such as fish, flowers, and trees (growing in or on the embankment), reservoirs transformed transportation routes[22] and defensive systems and stood as prominent, visible reminders of personal charity, religious devotion, and proper behavior – as *dharmic* markers on the landscape.[23]

Reservoirs as Oceans: Or, The Origin of Life in the Waters

The connection between reservoirs, which ideally will have large expanses of water, and oceans is not difficult to comprehend. As noted, the names of some reservoirs themselves draw this connection; Dharmasagara, for example, the "ocean of *dharma*". At times, the ocean is metaphorically present without there being any actual reservoir – the name of the Vijayanagara-period village of Bukkasagara (VMS-101), not evidently associated with any reservoir, may be translated as "ocean of Bukka". In contemporary (Vijayanagara era) perceptions of agricultural landscapes, literary texts often purported to describe some past city or region, doing so in highly conventionalized terms. These conventional descriptions also draw comparisons between the (glorious and positive) places and people depicted and the world of the gods (cf. Duncan 1990). For example, The *Shivatattvachintamani*, written around AD 1450 by a minister of Devaraya II about a minister in the court of the Kalachura rulers of Kalyani describes the city as follows (Kotraiah 1995c: 5):

> As one approached that (grand) city, on the outskirts of the city itself one could see a beautiful and pleasing pleasure-garden. It had a number of trees, bearing large bunches of fragrant flowers on account of which they were haunted by swarms of bees. It had cool pleasure resorts (buildings) with ponds (probably in the centre).[24] There was a big tank with groups of water-birds and swans playing there merrily. That beautiful garden was comparable to that of the one of the gods, the chariot of the Spring (*chaitra-ratha*), or the one of the god Indra. It had trees and plants bearing well ripened fruits such as sweet pomegranate, sweet oranges (*madalam*), dates . . . [a long list of fruits follows] . . . and on account of their dense growth in that garden, the rays of the sun were not able to reach the ground below.

The imagery is of course lavish; not only is this Kalyan beautiful and prosperous and its king and people of good character, but the gardens of the place bring to mind those of the gods. This is a very well-established literary convention in south India so that we may assume that the comparisons between specific monuments and heavenly attributes are always close at hand. And in the case of oceans and water, the scope for comparison is powerful.

Oceans, of course, have a special salience in South Asian cosmologies, all of life having ultimately emerged from the waters. Coomaraswamy (1993: 98), citing Hume's translation of the Upanishads, mentions the following passages, "in the beginning this world was just water", "all this world is woven, warp and woof, on water", and, in the words of Brahman, "the waters, verily, indeed, are my world". In Hindu cosmology, the origins of the world begin with the cosmic ocean, the ocean of milk upon which floats Vishnu, asleep on the coils of the great cosmic serpent Sesha, also known as Ananta (endless). Vishnu awakes and creates the universe. From his navel (the procreative center) arises a lotus from which "appears the creator god Brahma, who then manifests the universe which is maintained by Vishnu and then destroyed by Shiva: Brahma is enfolded by the lotus which withdraws into

Vishnu's navel who, finally, falls asleep once more.[25] Vishnu is married to Lakshmi and Shri, who form a single being, though they were originally distinct goddesses." (Flood 1992:115; and see Zimmer 1974). Similar accounts are told by Buddhists and Jains (cf. Flood 1992; Duncan 1990). By the Middle periods, Vishnu was generally viewed as having ten specific forms or incarnations (*avatara*), among them the fish, the tortoise, the boar, Narasimha (the man-lion), the dwarf, Parashurama (Rama with the axe), Rama, Krishna, Buddha, and Kalki. Several of these *avataras* figure in a further account of the cosmic ocean (Flood 1992: 116):

> The *Matsya Purana* tells how the first man, Manu, is saved from a cosmic deluge by the Fish. The Tortoise places himself at the bottom of the ocean of milk as the support for the mountain Mandara, which is then used as a stick by the gods and demons to churn the cosmic ocean, from which various desired, and undesired, objects emerge, including the nectar of immortality (*amrta*). The Boar rescues the Earth, personified as a Goddess, from the bottom of the cosmic ocean and brings her to the surface where he spreads her out, piles up mountains, and divides her into seven continents.

In general, these seems little doubt that evocations of oceans in the names of reservoirs and in their literary descriptions are intended to bring to mind the ocean of milk, and though texts also make less specific comparisons to the pleasure-gardens and lakes of the gods, the cosmic ocean is probably always kept in mind to some extent whenever metaphors of oceans are invoked (and cf. Duncan 1990: 97-101)

Puranic cosmologies are matched by geographies which accord much significance to oceans.[26] With Mount Meru at its center, the world (at least the part containing India) is surrounded by concentric rings of, first, salt oceans, then seven other lands and six further types of ocean (for a total of seven) containing sugar cane juice, wine, ghee (clarified butter), buttermilk, and, finally, milk (Flood 1992: 112). As noted in Chapter 1, the *Rayavacakamu*, a seventeenth-century Telugu text ostensibly about the great Vijayanagara king Krishnadeva Raya (Wagoner 1993: 90) includes among a list of things the king should do: "bear on his sturdy shoulders the entire circle of the earth, which is surrounded by the seven oceans of salt, sugar, alcohol, ghee, curds, milk, and pure water". So it is that the earth itself rests on the back of the waters which surround it, just as a lotus rests on the waters of a lake or reservoir. The aquatic lotus, in fact, has a special kind of dual signification, representing both the waters and the earth; as representatives of the earth, lotus flowers often provide support for buildings (for example, as mouldings, represented in fluted designs of leaves or petals), columns (as bases), and even gods (as seats, for example of Lakshmi who usually sits on a lotus) (Coomaraswamy 1993: 155).[27] Although figures of Lakshmi are important, lotuses figures somewhat less prominently in reservoir decoration.[28] However, there certainly were (and in some cases, are) actual lotuses living in many reservoirs. The name of the village of Kamalapuram (lotus village), though common, almost certainly refers to the Kamalapuram *kere* and its aquatic vegetation and, less directly, to the wealth and abundance created by this facility.

At this point, we must digress slightly to consider some aspects of what Coomaraswamy calls the "water cosmology", and especially the special relationships he describes between water and trees and between water and vegetation more generally. In his study of the complex history of *yakshas*, a distinctive and somewhat elusive class of deities who may be most closely translated into English as "spirits", though although described as "tutelary deities, patron saints, and Guardian Angels", Coomaraswamy (1993: 15, 54) describes their close association with trees and water and hence with wealth and life itself. Coomaraswamy notes that *yakshas* and *yakkini* (or *yakshi*, female *yakshas*) may dwell in particular trees and, in particular, *yakkini* or, in Coomaraswamy's translation (1993: 83), dryads, are worshiped by women who desire children.[29] More than simply tree dwellers, however, these spirits are the unseen sources or roots of particular trees and in their associations with various Vedic and other deities, *yakshas* and *yakkini* are more generally, "the invisible spirit that indwells and manifests itself in the tree of life. . . . For just as the World-tree is the Brahman in a likeness . . . so can any designated tree be regarded as the visible form of its indwelling *yaksha*" (Coomaraswamy 1993: 11). Although the historical connections of *yakshas* with other named dieties are very complex, as Coomaraswamy lays out in some detail, they are associated with gods such as Kubera,[30] who resides on Mount Kailasa[31] where he has many lakes, gardens, parks and other landscape elements also celebrated in Middle period texts where earthly landscapes are indeed often explicitly compared to those of the gods.

Yakshas do not live only in trees, they also have various other possible homes (Coomaraswamy 1993: 62), "The haunt or abode (*bhavana*) of a *yaksha* . . . may be outside a city, in a grove or park, on a mountain or at a *ghat*, by a tank, at the gates of a city or within a city, or even within the palace precincts." Note that many of these haunts are either associated with trees (groves and parks), water (reservoirs and *ghats*, or steps, which typically lead down to rivers though one assumes they could also be steps leading to canals or reservoirs), or gates and doors (outside a city, at the gates of a city). Reservoirs are, of course, associated with water (of which more below), but they are also places with many trees, steps, and "gates".

Yakshas, as noted, are powerfully associated with water, some even control the rains. *Nagas* (serpent dieties) are also water-dieties who are said to control the waters, but who are acually less powerful and more withholding (from a human point of view) than *yakshas* who control (Coomaraswamy 1993: 98), "that essence (*rasa*) in the waters which is one with the sap in the trees . . . and with the seed in living beings". Water, of course, is the source of all life – plants having risen from the primeval waters, and from plants all other life including gods, humans, and cattle (Coomaraswamy 1993: 110). Though I have greatly simplified Coomarswamy's detailed analysis, the special connections between *yakshas*, water, plants, reproduction, and, ultimately, life itself, should by now be clear. What remains to be considered are the physical and representational aspects of these relationships, aspects which should be amenable to archaeological investigation.

We can begin by noting that "dryads" are often represented as beautiful women standing on *yakshas*, elephants, *makaras*, fish-tailed elephants, or occasionally, lotuses (Coomaraswamy 1993: 83). These various "vehicles" for these goddesses are all water-associated; *makaras* are mythical beasts looking something like crocodiles and like crocodiles, they are aquatic in habitat. Coomaraswamy notes (1993: 87), "The dryad types with *makara* vehicles . . . bear an intimate relation, not amounting to identity, with the figures of the river-goddesses Ganga and Yamuna, with *makara* and tortoise vehicles placed at the doorway of many northern medieval temples." Many Vijayanagara gates, for example the massive gateway supporting the entrance tower (*gopuram*) over the sixteenth-century Krishna temple in the city, are flanked by such "dryads" embraced by vines who stand on *makaras* spouting vegetation from their mouths.[32] The significance of this vegetation is discussed below, but I draw attention here the association of these goddesses with doorways, including temple doorways.[33]

Makaras, then, are themselves symbols of the waters and "the essence in the waters, the principle of life" (Coomaraswamy 1993: 142); their mouths are the source of the masses of meandering vegetation which are among the most common decorative motifs on temples, sculptures, and mouldings.[34] This vegetation motif is more than simply decorative. It is instead powerfully meaningful, as Coomaraswamy argues (1993: 98, emphasis added): "the 'Plant Style' *is the iconography of the Water Cosmology*". These plants are not simply generic, they are representations of lotus plants, whose underwater rhizomes contain multiple nodes from which separate stalks containing leaves or flowers rise up to the water's surface. These nodes are sometimes depicted realistically, though they may also be highly stylized. *Makaras* themselves also vary in their degree of "realism", if a mythological beast can be said to be realistically depicted. They are very common decorative elements, occurring not only in sculpture, but also as *makara-torana*. These are ornamental arches made in the rough shape of a (full-face) *makara*, sometimes complexly carved with a *makara* face and sometimes just exhibiting the general *makara* outline without any internal detail. Tellingly, *torana* refers to a gateway; one of the definitions of *makara-torana* offered by Sircar (1966: 193) is "gateway with figures of crocodiles". *Makara-torana* are common in Vijayanagara temple architecture and appear on Vijayanagara sluice gates as decorative elements on mouldings. In this, one sees no particular difference between mouldings used in temples and those on sluices. While it would be satisfying to be able to say that *makara* occur more often on reservoirs than they do elsewhere, this would not be correct. Reservoirs tend to have simpler mouldings and fewer sculptures than do temples and so they certainly have fewer representatives of the waters – *makara, yakshas,* conches, aquatic animals, brimming vessels, even *nagas* – than do temples. I would suggest, however, that water and vegetation imagery had a powerful resonance in association with reservoirs and other bodies of water.

Another being associated with water imagery is, surprisingly enough, the elephant, mentioned already as an aspect of the Gajalakshmi (elephant Lakshmi) motif – Lakshmi flanked by elephants, usually with raised trunks forming a kind of arch or gate over her. This connection between Lakshmi and elephants is long-standing as is the notion of elephants as watery beings. Elephants are quintessentially the mounts of kings and maintenance of elephants is both a prerogative and duty of kings, elephants having a special attraction to their relatives, the clouds, which bring the critical monsoon rains. We can begin explaining some of these associations, perhaps, by noting one of the accounts of the emergence of Airavata, the divine, multi-trunked elephant that would become the mount of Indra, king of the gods (Zimmer 1974: 104-5). Although Airavata figures in more than one cosmogenic account, several texts link his origin and that of his consort, Abhramu, to the story of the churning of the milky ocean.[35] Zimmer (1974: 105-6) explains:

> After the gods and titans had labored at their task for a thousand years, a curious assortment of personifications and symbols began to arise out of the milk of the universe. Among the early figures were the goddess Lotus, and Airavata, the milk-white elephant. Finally appeared the physician of the gods bearing the Amrita, the elixir of immortality in a milk-white bowl.
>
> A special value is attached to the so-called "white elephants" – albinos showing light or rosy spots – because they suggest the origin of their anscestor from the Universal Milk. They are endowed to a high degree with the peculiar magic virtue of the elephant, the virtue, that is to say, of producing clouds.

Zimmer goes on to note (1974: 106) that Abhramu means "she who knits the clouds", pointing out that in this mythic time, elephants had wings and could roam the sky, just like clouds. A group of high-flying elephants fell foul of a powerful ascetic and were grounded, leaving them wingless but still apparently attractive to the monsoon-bearing clouds. Zimmer (1974: 108-9) concludes, "Thus the worship of the white elephant . . . bestows on man all those earthly blessings which the goddess Lotus, Shri-Lakshmi, Fortune and Prosperity, the Mother Earth, fertile and abundant with water and riches, has in store." The elephant is thus known both as *Shri-Gaja,* elephant of Shri-Lakshmi, and as *Megha,* "cloud". It is "a rain cloud walking on earth" (Zimmer 1974: 109). Keeping elephants, then, may be seen as kingly in many ways. Essential to Middle period military strategies, key symbols of soveriegnty, power, and deep pockets, elephants, especially white elephants, were kept for the benefit of the king's subjects and the productivity of the land. Costly royal herds, in this view, extend their benefits broadly (Figure 52).

Elephant iconography is further interlocked with watery themes through the association of elephant with *nagas. Nagas* (snakes) are, as noted, watery, underground, treasure-guarding creatures, who, like *yakshas,* are associated with trees. As Sutherland (1991: 39) explains:

> The essential substance that links yakshas, nagas, and trees is water. The *naga*'s connection with the waters stems, on the one hand, from inhabitation by snakes of the moist underworld and, on the other hand, from the twisting forms of snakes that are homologous to winding rivers. The rivers contain fertile waters that (like snakes) flee the destructive heat of the sun and go

> underground to withhold their fructifying waters . . . *nagas* and trees are thought also to *contain* the life-supporting liquid they symbolize. The watery essence is manifest in trees, as sap and in *nagas* as venom.

Venom was one of the first substances to have appeared in the churning of the cosmic ocean. Zimmer (1974: 63) notes that *nagas* often serve as door-guardians on both Buddhist and Hindu shrines; although they are common on and near south Indian temples, they generally do not flank temple doorways in our region.

How, then, do *nagas* and elephants come to be associated? Not all elephants flew freely through the sky – we must introduce here the *dig-gajas,* the elephants of the directions (Sutherland 1991: 40; Zimmer 1974: 105) who hold up the universe, as does the serpent Sesha, Vishnu's bed while sleeping on the milky ocean, indeed a part of Vishnu himself. *Nagas* are thought to look like elephant trunks and indeed there exist elephant-deities also, confusingly, known as *nagas* (Sutherland 1991: 40). The four (or eight) *lokapalas,*[36] "world guardians" have *dig-gajas* as their vehicles or mounts; these direction-guarding elephants have themselves come to be seen as the *lokapalas,* protectors of territory and sacred spaces (Sutherland 1991: 67) who, in Buddhist shrines, are often sculpted on door frames as door-guardians.

I close this brief review of the iconography of water and plants – keeping in mind some of the ramifying associations of these with the life force, cosmogenesis, other watery essences, human reproduction, gates, steps, and doorways, and the personal devotion of women – with consideration of the *purna kumbha* or *purna kalasha,* the "vase of plenty". According to Coomaraswamy (1993: 161) this vessel, generally spewing forth (lotus) vegetation, is the commonest of auspicous symbols, a "life symbol" associated with fertility and fruitfullness; indeed such vessels continue to be potent symbols in contemporary ritual practice.

The earliest examples of the *purna kalasha* are found in Buddhist sculpture of the Early Historic period where the vessel is associated with the goddess Lakshmi. The vessel in question is a globular jar, its body enclosed by a ribbon or band (Coomaraswamy 1993: 162), containing a never-failing source of water. Coomarswamy (1993: 161) notes that the full vessel is carried as a symbol by some divinities, particularly *nagas* and river-goddesses. Pairs of *purna kalasha* are often placed at entrances with pairs of (carved) vessels flanking temple doorways, one at the base of each door jamb. These vessel forms are also employed as capitals and as supports for pilasters, the pot-and-column design being quite common on the exterior of Vijayanagara temples (see Figure 46). *Kalashas* also occur as the uppermost elements on temple towers, as "pot finials". Wagoner (2000 personal communication; and see Davis 1997) explains, "In essence, the *kalasha* . . . is a symbolic representation of the waters of life, which it holds in ritual contexts. These *kalashas* are the most important ritual object in temple consecration rites; the power of the various dieties are invoked into the waters that are placed in the actual pots, and then these waters are used to lustrate the temple and thus infuse it with both the water of life and the concentrated essence of the dieties. Placing the symbolic metal or stone *kalasha* on top of the temple spire is one of the most important ritual acts in the consecration, equal in importance to the *prana* (or *pratishtha,* 'instilling of the life-breath') performed for the image in the sanctum."

In the context of this analysis, I mention two reservoirs from the western Daroji Valley, both capped by a pair of pot-finials exhibiting the requisite enclosing band and containing, instead of luxurient lotus meanders, something that looks very like a ripe coconut but which is ribbed, not unlike the finials on urban structures in the Vijayanagara "courtly style" (Michell 1992, see Chapter 7 for a fuller discussion). The salience of an unending source of water for a reservoir seems clear; note also the association of *kalasha* with doorways and gates, here sluice gates. Figure 70 illustrates the southern sluice from VMS-1003; note that in addition to the pot-finials, the central arched figures on the moulding are *makara-torana,* albeit very simple ones. It may not be too much of a stretch to suggest a further connection between the water in the *kalasha,* the water of life, and the water in the reservoir itself,

Figure 52. Base of shrine atop Kamalapura *kere*, with elephant frieze.

Figure 53. Kurugodu *kere*, southern sluice, with domed superstructure.

Figure 54. Temple immediately below Kurugodu *kere*; domed superstructure matching sluice.

recalling the origin of life in the waters. In this vein, we can consider an earlier inscription (Kotraiah 1995a: 10) describing the king Rajendra Chola pouring pots of Ganga (Ganges) water into the reservoir he constructed to commemorate a victorious march up to the Ganges. This reservoir was named *Jalamaya sthamba*, the "water pillar of victory", and the water in that reservoir was henceforth known as the Chola-Ganga. The Chola king also had a temple constructed at same time and had the nearby village (re?)named Gangaikonda-Cholapuram.

Basic issues of cosmology, life, reproduction, and abundance, then, find their iconography in symbols of water and vegetation, incorporating symbols and personages as diverse as *yakshas*, river-goddesses, *makara*, and other aquatic animals including snakes, conch-shells, trees, lotuses (and by extension all vegetation), and even brimming water vessels. All of these images are in some sense divine, many have persistent associations with doors, gates, and openings, and many have relevance for reservoir iconography, a point elaborated in the following section. The ninth-twelfth century (and certainly pre-AD 1484) text, the *Mayamata*, a "treatise on dwelling" (Dagens 1985: 58) makes a series of prescriptions for the correct foundation deposits of different kinds of structures: "In the case of a reservoir, well, tank, pond, or bridge there should be disposed, to the north or to the east, in a hole the size of two cupped hands, a bowl and a fish as well as a frog, a crab, a snake, and a *makara* in gold."

RESERVOIRS AS TEMPLES

In the discussion of sluice gates, above, I began to make the argument that sluices and temple doorways have a series of direct morphological, iconographic, and meaningful links. Not only *are* sluice gates doors in a quite literal sense – water doors – patrolling and marking the openings between the inside and outside of the reservoir, but water itself and its evocations in concrete imagery (*kalasha, yakshi, makara*) are also consistently associated with doors, gates, and openings, as noted above. Non-reservoir doors and gates decorated with these motifs bring to mind, then, water, trees, and life itself, all qualities and landscape elements concretely associated with reservoirs. Reservoir sluice gates are not like just any doorway, however. They appear most like temple doorways, especially those doors leading into the sanctum itself or the antechamber in front of it. Like those doors, sluices often have a central carved figure of Lakshmi, Gajalakshmi, or, somewhat less often, Ganesha and rarely, Sita with Hanuman and Sugriva.[37] This similarity is weakened by the fact that the most common over-door motif in temples is the lotus while I know of no reservoir sluices with centrally carved lotuses. Perhaps the water or even the aquatic vegetation which was (ideally) visible through the sluice "door" was enough itself enough of a watery symbol? Or, and this seems perhaps more likely, this association, while striking, fails to grasp all of the intricacies and variations of meaning encoded in Vijayanagara constructions.

If there is a connection between doors/ openings and sluice gates, then there is an equally compelling association between doors/ sluice gates and temples. I have already noted that door-like motifs (two upright jambs supporting a lintel, often capped with moulding sequences) representing entire buildings, motifs that look remarkably like sluices, were used in temple decoration and sculpture to "stand for" entire temples or other structures. As such, it is possible to suggest that not only were sluices meant to invoke temples and temple doorways, or even that these references may have been reflexive so that reservoirs came to mind when viewing temples, but further that reservoirs were in fact seen as *being* something like temples themselves with the sluice "standing for" an entire shrine and having the great advantage of being, like the earth, surrounded by the "ocean". Like temples, too, some elaborate sluices had brick and plaster superstructures; one fourteenth- to fifteenth-century temple near Kurugodu, on the Bellary Plain, even has an elaborate domed superstructure that precisely mirrors the form of a small temple nearby (Figures 53 and 54).

The Halla *kere* (VMS-190), mentioned above, is a reservoir with masonry deliberately made into a striped pattern of alternating reddish and whitish bands. Although the red-and-white stripes one sees on temples tend to run up and down, the overall visual effect is striking and is surely meant to make the reservoir look like a temple or perhaps more convincingly, a temple tank. Here we might recall the semantic ambiguity represented by the use of the term "tank" to refer to all water-containing features, an ambiguity that I rejected at the outset of this work. However, if we re-invoke this ambiguity, and if we agree that sluices evoke temples and specifically temple doorways, then surely reservoirs evoke temple tanks and more broadly and metaphorically (and perhaps even less immediately for most people), the cosmic ocean. If reservoirs are something like temples, then, it is the sluice which stands for the shrine, a contention strengthened by the present-day practice of bringing sluice gates under worship, even ones with no obvious "religious" attributes like sculptures.[38] I should note that formal shrines on reservoir embankments are also not uncommon, as are unconstructed tree shrines. If sluices are the shrines – perhaps only doors to the shrine – then it may be the water itself which forms the primary focus of devotion. Finally, to conclude this perhaps overgrown comparison, I mention the fact that Vijayanagara temple tanks typically surround a small central pavilion, generally built of four columns which support a roof. The later, sixteenth-century double sluices look quite similar to these little pavilions, even to the use of decorative brackets with pendant "banana-flower" designs. These later sluices look even more like temples than simpler, two-column ones, and are perhaps meant to elaborate on this relationship.

I close with some social perspective on this extended excursion into the metaphors and potential meanings of reservoirs, sluices, water, and plants. I have discussed the ways in which reservoirs, as physical features and objects of human engineering skill and labor, worked and how they lay on the landscape and by both being and working, transformed it. Like all human creations and apprehensions, however, reservoirs and their elements also encoded a variety of meanings and evoked a variety of responses. Although we cannot fully explicate those, largely because of our dependence on texts, which represent only a limited perspective, it is possible to point to a rich field of signification involving the origins of the universe and the waters, the life-force, vegetation, and, critically, abundance and wealth. Water, however, is not simply primeval and life-giving. It is also a powerful field of dispute and in South Asia, as elsewhere, control of water has long been a weapon of the strong against the weak. Not only was water valued and controlled for irrigation and even sport, but water sources were also controlled and segregated to produce and maintain social hierarchies. Here water is much more than simply an economic good – though it is that – but is instead a polysemic signifier of issues of purity and power as well as prosperity and abundance. Water is ritually powerful, aesthetically important, evocative of key religious themes and, certainly, a scarce physical substance critical for production and indeed life itself for humans, livestock, and plants. In the environment of the semi-arid interior of southern India, water was infinitely important. We might finally recall some of the themes of ecological change and anthropogenic landscape transformation discussed in Chapters 1 and 2 in closing with a comment (Schroeder 1993: xv) by the editor of Coomaraswamy's *Yakshas*: "The domains of the *yakshas*, trees and the waters, face a material crisis marked by deforestation, pollution, and the disappearance of cultures and species. Water seen only as H_2O may be water denatured."

NOTES

1. Areas of elite residence and administration are also often associated with tanks; there is not necessarily a clear separation between the use of tanks for ritual ablutions and, for example, for pleasure or simply cleanliness. Although I separate temple tanks and reservoirs here, the following chapters should make clear the close association between reservoirs and temples.
2. Kannada usage, too, contains some flexibility and variability in the naming of water storage and collection facilities. Although the term *kere* is the most common and consistently used term referring to reservoirs in Vijayanagara-period

documents, inscriptions may also use several other terms. Kotraiah (1995a: 198-202; definitions in parentheses are his) glosses these as follows: *cheruvu* (tank, reservoir for irrigation); *ere* (tank/reservoir [this is the Tamil term, in Kannada usage it refers primarily to the embankment]); *gundu* (small pond of water used for irrigation); *jalasaya* (tank or reservoir), *kanya-kere* or *kanyagere* (virgin tank; one built for the first time); *kere, katte, kumte, kattai, kola* [or *kolla*, which generally refers to a cistern], *kolam* (tank/reservoir of different sizes); *madaga* (tank); *nadi-tataka* (tank fed by water from a river canal); *orateya-kere* (tank with springs of water); *orateya-kunda* (spring well/small pond); *samudra, sandra, sarovara* (tank/reservoir with vast sheet of water for irrigation [these terms indicate oceans or seas]); *sasasi* (lake, reservoir).

3. The indiscriminate use of the term "tank" seems to be largely a British usage. Francis Buchanan, on his trip across southern India in 1800 noted, "The inhabitants here distinguish also two kinds of tanks. The first is the *Eray* [*eri*, Tamil], which is formed by throwing a mound, or bank, across a valley, or hollow ground; so that the rain water collects in the upper part of the valley, and is let out on the lower part by sluices, for the purposes of cultivation. The other kind of tank is the *Culam* [*kolam*, Kannada], which is formed by digging out the earth; and is destined for supplying the inhabitants with water for domestic purposes." (Buchanan 1988 [1807]: 11-12). Although his terminology here seems to reflect language differences more than formal variation, he is correct in suggesting local typological differentiation.
4. Buchanan (1988[1807]: 49) notes a similar kind of distinction among reservoirs, "I observed no watered land [in a region of southern Karnataka]. There are, indeed, some small reservoirs; but the water contained in these, is destined merely to supply the cattle with drink. A small reservoir of this kind in the Karnataca language [Kannada] is called Cuttay [*katte*], as the large ones for watering land are called Carays [*kere*(s)]. They are both formed exactly in the same manner, by building a mound or dam, of earth and stone, across a hollow ground. Large reservoirs, or Carays, might no doubt be formed everywhere in a hilly country; but where there is not a sufficient expanse of level land with a good soil for the cultivation of rice, the expense of such works would far exceed the profits." Some of the various Kannada names for reservoirs (*kere, katte, kumte, kattai, kola, kolam*, see Kotraiah 1995: 200) are, indeed, sensitive to size.
5. Occupational specialists engaged in reservoir construction (*uppara, vadda*) are often said to be "diggers" of tanks, although from the physical remains themselves, it is clear that this digging was primarily for the tons and tons of fill required to make the earthen embankment. The engineers (*tantrapala, jalasutrada*; Kotraiah 1995a: 202) were clearly differentiated from laborers. In the early nineteenth century, Buchanan (1807: 78) noted the existence of "Uparu" a right-hand caste of "persons who dig tanks, and build rough walls".
6. The notion that particular places or plots "belonged" to particular facilities is clear from the inscriptional record. Just as land belonged to specific villages (notwithstanding the fact that people from other places might own or work it), agricultural land belonged to specific reservoirs, canals, or other facilities. That this concept was broader than simply the land watered by the facility in question is clear from a number of cases in which, for example, donations of land belonging to a canal include dry land as well as irrigated land.
7. Lotus leaves are large and flat; a twelfth-century Kannada text describes a royal meal in which various pickles were served on a lotus leaf instead of the more usual banana leaf (Achaya 1998: 92).
8. This clay concentration is itself a resource of some importance. Reservoir-bed sediments are often used in brick making, with some brickyards even located in dry reservoir beds.
9. The term *mahajanas* refers to members of a local (village) assembly or council; sometimes these are understood to be Brahmins, especially in earlier contexts. Later, the term seems to have come to refer to merchants or merchant associations. Without knowing the precise situation of this village, it would probably be impossible to say who the *mahajanas* were, but it may be presumed that they consisted of the locally dominant (adult male) landholders.
10. In fact, the most common kind of disturbance of abandoned reservoirs is the mining of the embankment for fill. Often, the corpus of the *bund* has been dragged away and spread out across local fields by farmers in search of fresh soil. Such excavation takes a great deal of effort as earthen embankments are usually highly compacted; at its most extreme, fill-robbing leaves almost nothing of a reservoir behind but a masonry shell and sluice gates.

11. Or *persist*, but it is very difficult to completely eradicate a reservoir and we have recorded many remnant facilities that were clearly replaced by other forms of irrigation. Thus, I think it is safe to suggest that our observations do reflect a general pattern.
12. The Kamalapuram *kere* is itself quite long, *c.* 1,750 meters, illustrating the lack of a consistent correlation between sluice monumentality and reservoir size (except that monumental sluices never occur on small reservoirs); sluice scale on large reservoirs appears to be chronologically sensitive (see, especially VMS-1015, Chapter 6, for an example of this).
13. Not everyone agrees that these represent makara heads; Michell (1995: 196, 273) argues that the so-called *kirtha-mukhas* or monster-masks, represent heads of yalis, another mythical beast.
14. Why sixteenth-century sluices are often so highly elaborated is an interesting question. Surely some of this trend, which follows that of temple elaboration quite closely, stems from the political implications of endowing and repairing reservoirs and increasing competition for legitimacy in the sixteenth century. The morphological as well as symbolic and institutional connections between temples and reservoirs (below) seem to keep pace.
15. Sita is the wife of Rama, hero of the *Ramayana* epic. Sugriva and Hanuman are two royal brothers, both monkeys, who helped Rama to rescue Sita when she was captured by a demon. As noted, the kingdom of the monkeys, Kishkindha, is traditionally associated with the Vijayanagara region and some of the events of the *Ramayana* are said to have taken place here. Note that VMS-1015, sluice 1, in the main valley also has this sculptural program.
16. In three dimensions, the doorway becomes a small four-columned structure, a *mandapa* which although not necessarily limited to temple architecture, does make up the basic structural building block of the temple.
17. Later documents clarify the dangers of concentrated monsoon runoff (Kelsall 1872: 76): "On May 6, 1851 [well before the usual onset of the rains], a storm swept through the district in the direction of north-west to southeast, entering the district in the Hospett taluq. The storm was accompanied by torrents of rain which produced a general inundation and destroyed, or otherwise injured, all the communications of the country and all the works of irrigation within its influence. Several of the finest tanks in the district were completely destroyed as reservoirs. The bunds of these works that had stood the usual rain of centuries and that might have challenged the whole of India to produce their like in strength and careful construction, were over-topped by the waters which broke through them, leaving large chasms from 10 to 420 yards in length. Daroji tank sustained two breaches, on 160 and the other 80 yards in length. . . . The total number of tanks breached or seriously damaged amounted to 253. . . ."
18. "In order, however, that when there is plenty of rain, the tank may be completely filled, a row of stone pillars is placed on the top of the sluice; and, the water rising to a level with their base, a temporary wall is formed of mud, sticks, and straw, placed between the pillars, so as to confine the water until it rises as high as the top of the bank. People watch this night and day, in order to break down the temporary bank, should any additional rain endanger the whole." (Buchanan 1988[1807]: 4). This kind of technology was also used on other dams. The anicut for the Turtha canal, a long wall or *dam* of masonry in the river bed that channeled water into the canal, was also fitted with upright posts (iron bars) for holding up a temporary enhancement of the dam.
19. Wells used for irrigation (*bavi*) tend to be differentiated from step wells (*koneri, nada-bavi*) and from temple wells (*okkarane-bavi, pushkarani*).
20. It is not always possible to date a well by construction style alone. Like other structures, very simple construction styles are not necessarily temporally sensitive. However, there are numerous formal well designs from the Vijayanagara period we have documented elsewhere in the study area but not in the Daroji Valley. Most of the apparently post-Vijayanagara wells in the Daroji Valley also seem to pre-date the twentieth century (when quarrying technology changed, making it straightforward to distinguish recently quarried rock). This suggests a particular trajectory of use in which, with the decline of labor-intensive regular maintenance of a reservoir, patterns of exploitation shifted with local residents capturing some of the water captured by the facility in newly-dug wells, using the smaller seasonal pools still gathering in the deepest part of the reservoir (it is not uncommon to find a single sluice still maintained while all the others are

silted in), and using parts of the reservoir bed for dry farming.

21. He actually accused me of this. It was difficult not to laugh, standing next to an eroded and breached reservoir; if I wanted to steal engineering secrets wouldn't I have selected facilities that *worked*?
22. Reservoir embankments are long, elevated, linear features in a landscape that they help make artificially moist. As such, they make excellent road beds and are almost always used as footpaths. Low-lying, watered fields are difficult to cross, especially in the rainy season or even after plowing when dirt clods slow down people on foot and can even create danger for horses. Large expanses of water in reservoir beds or even the mucky beds of dry-season reservoirs are significant barriers to movement.
23. Elevated reservoir embankments are like walls as much as they are like road beds. In some cases, reservoirs in the survey area were integrated into fortification walls. The Kamalapuram reservoir, VMS-231, carries a major road leading into the city and is part of the outer circuit of city walls with two bastions built onto the embankment. The eastern, smaller bastion faces out over the water and the western, larger bastion faces the irrigated land below the reservoir. The road at the west end of the Kamalapuram reservoir embankment also once had a masonry gateway where the "regular" outer city wall met the reservoir embankment.
24. This is not phrased very clearly, but the image invoked is not so much of the typical irrigation reservoir but instead of a temple tank with its central pavilion.
25. "When the divine life substance is about to put forth the universe, the cosmic waters grow a thousand-petalled lotus of pure gold, radiant as the sun. This is the door or gate, the opening or mouth, the womb of the universe." (Zimmer 1974: 90).
26. The Puranas are a diverse set of ancient texts detailing cosmologies, law codes, genealogies, and many other topics. They are believed to be codified oral traditions and although they were first written down in the Early Historic period, they also contain many later additions.
27. Lakshmi herself was directly born of the waters; both Lakshmi and the lotus are seen as sources of wealth and abundance as indeed are water sources such as reservoirs. Note that sculptures of Lakshmi are common over both temple doorways and reservoir sluices. In the *Rig Veda* (following Zimmer 1974: 91) Sri-Lakshmi's epithets include "lotus-born", "lotus-eyed", "decked in lotuses", and "lotus-colored". She has two sons, "Mud (*kardama*) and Moisture (*ciklita*), personifications of the ingedients of rich soil." (Zimmer 1974: 91).
28. Major exceptions include the Daroji reservoir and the Raya *kere* (Figure 51).
29. *Yaksha* worship is part of a broader *bhakti*, or devotional tradition that was extremely important in the Middle periods. *Yaksha* shrines include stone tables or altars where offerings that may include alcohol and meat are given (Coomaraswamy 1993: 62, 77). In his analysis Coomaraswamy notes (1993: 76, 78-9) that women worshiping at such shrines often prayed for daughters, a significant point in a devotional landscape where sons are so often desired and valued. It is noteworthy, then, that many reservoirs in the study area not only have sluices which are converted to active shrines, but that they also often support large trees which shelter women's shrines containing icons of fertility and, in some cases, evidence of blood sacrifice. Although as I discuss below, there are few overt references to *yakshas* in reservoir iconography, their (in some sense ongoing) presence seems indisputable.
30. Significantly, Kubera is known as a giver of wealth and is often associated with Lakshmi, the goddess of wealth and abundance.
31. This northern mountain is also, of course, the abode of Shiva (and see Sutherland 1991).
32. Or "creepers", whose "embrace" is seen as erotic.
33. This discussion has thus far failed to highlight another important aspect of water symbolism and imagery—the importance of rivers as sources of auspiciousness and fertility (see Feldhaus 1995: 3-4). Rivers are specially associated with women, both human and divine, and river water is often worshipped as a goddess (recall the Pampa *tirtha*), its water sometimes carried to distant locations for ritual purposes (the most noteworthy example of this being, of course, the movement of Ganga water). However, Feldhaus notes a case (1995: 32-3) in contemporary Maharashtra in which reservoir water is substituted for river water; she also notes that worship is offered to river water on the occasion of dam construction in order to placate it and prevent it from doing harm (1995: 45). Rivers, she notes (1995: 22), are often understood to "flow invisibly or in 'hidden' (*gupta*) form, between the various spots where

water can be seen". Sacred associations, then, need not be restricted to huge perennial streams but might also apply to smaller drainages, many of which are called "rivers". Vijayanagara reservoirs were certainly understood to be damming rivers and in that sense, reservoirs may also be seen as (parts of) rivers. Feldhaus notes the further association between rivers and cows (1995: 45) explaining that rivers "are often architecturally arranged so as to be shown emerging from the mouth of a stone cow's head (*gayamukh*)", often in association with a temple tank at river-source shrines. We have recorded cow-head drainage spouts on Vijayanagara shrines in the intensive survey area, but there are also significant textual references to reservoirs named "cow's mouth" (Shulman 1985: 67), suggesting reservoir as river source which, metaphorically, seems right if we consider the many irrigation channels coming out from below the single 'source' in the bed.

34. Other sources of this vegetation are the navels and mouths of *yakshas*, the jaws of other fish-like animals, a conch, or a "brimming vessel". These vessels or pots are discussed below but it should be noted that conches, *makaras*, pots, and fish-like creatures all represent the waters.
35. The *Mahabharata*, *Vishnu Purana*, and *Matsya Purana*; see Zimmer (1974: 105) for details.
36. These are guardians of the directions, one of whom is Kubera, ruler of the *yakshas*. Kubera himself is called (Sutherland 1991: 67), *nara-vahana*, or "one whose mount is a man".
37. Many, if not all sluices also appear to have once been plastered and whitewashed, just as temple columns typically are.
38. Signs of contemporary worship include sluices painted with red and white stripes and adorned with plaster and whitewash—all amendments made to shrines and temples —as well as nearby oil lamps, painted symbols, and/or offerings of flowers, cloth bundles, money, incense, or other things.

Chapter Five

THE WESTERN DAROJI VALLEY

> . . . the king made a grant of land of the village Nirugunda in Vikkiga 70, a subdivision of Kogali 500, to the 300 Brahmanas coming from the Dravidian lands and fully versed in the books of divers Vedic schools. . . . On the second date, the same king made a grant of the same village and the village of Krishnapallika to the same Brahmanas, 500 in number. . . . (Patil and Patil 1997: 124, copper-plate inscription from Nilagunda dated AD 1087 and AD 1123)
>
> . . . while Tribhuvanamalla Raya-Pandya was ruling Nolambavadi 32000 and Kaniyakallu 300, the 300 *Mahajanas* of Nirggunda in Kogali-*nadu*, the 500 *Bananjigas* and the *Nanadesis* presented the land and tolls for the worship of Svayambhu Bhimesvara situated to the north of the village of Nirggunda, in the "Old Ruins" (*haleyahalu*). A similar gift was made on the second date, by the gardeners, oil-mongers, and others. Another grant of garden land was made on the third date. (Patil and Patil 1997: 126, lithic inscription set up in Bhimesvara temple, dated AD 1079, 1136, and 1174).
>
> Records the death of Kallaganga, the Muliga of Nirggunda on the occasion when Mareyal[v]a, son of Chayandirasa, fought in Banavasi-*nadu* to rescue the cows of Nirggunda. (Patil and Patil 1997: 127, inscription on hero stone in same temple)

This chapter begins discussion of the Daroji Valley itself. From the more general consideration of the first three chapters we move now to a closer look at this specific locality and its transformations over the last five millennia. The western end of the Daroji Valley constitutes a distinct watershed and contains a coherent system of interlinked reservoirs of the Vijayanagara period. As discussed in the following chapter, the village of Papinayakanahalli can be seen as the pivot of the valley, dividing the western valley from the main valley. The western system is situated in a region with a long history of land use; there is abundant archaeological material from at least the Early Neolithic (*c.* 2400 BC) including several ash-mounds as well as excavated remains of a small settlement (VMS-110). That this area continued to be an important locus of settlement is clear from the traces of Iron Age, Early Historic, and what are probably Early Middle period settlements as well. It is difficult to say if this occupational history was continuous or not, but it is clear that the nature and organization of land use in this area underwent radical restructuring over the last four millennia. The bulk of this chapter is devoted to the obtrusive record of Vijayanagara-period land use, but this record is itself only partly explicable without reference to earlier alterations of the landscape and to the continued salience of particular places in local cultural geographies.

The western valley, a funnel-shaped watershed about 8 kilometers long that begins upstream on the east in the relatively constricted and level west end of the Daroji Valley, unfolds to the west to become an expansive plain of black sandy soil, only occasionally broken by small granitic boulder outcrops (Figure 55). This plain is now much modified by canal and railroad construction as well as by the sprawling town of Hospet. However, it is clear that this broad level area (the flaring mouth of the funnel, if we can imagine water flowing from the narrow to the wide end of this funnel) where runoff from the east is slowly dispersed, was one of the primary zones of agricultural production supporting Hospet, officially "established" in the sixteenth century as *Tirumaladeviyara-Pattana,* and its

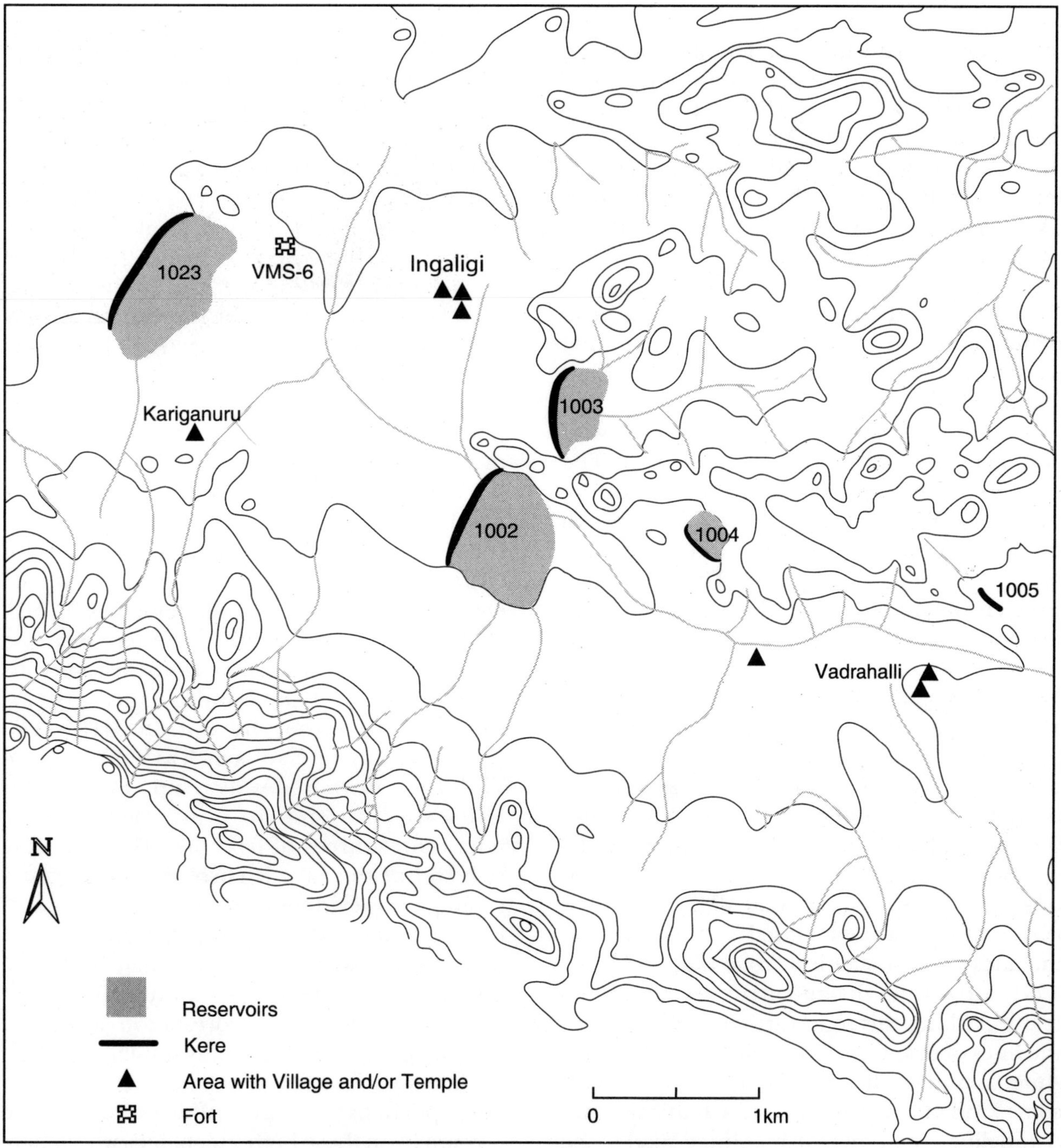

Figure 55. Western Daroji Valley, overall map.

environs.[1] There is, however, reason to believe that settlement there predated its official founding, as discussed below.

The western Daroji reservoir system consists of a rather loose chain of facilities that ends on the southwest with a rise in ground level toward Hospet and the smaller sixteenth-century settlement of Sankalapura. The land watered by the last reservoir in this system, VMS-1023, slopes down toward the north and this drainage route leads right to the Vijayanagara town of Anantasayanagudi, named for its impressive temple dedicated to the reclining Vishnu (Anantasayana, lying on the serpent Ananta, see Chapter 4). Originally known as Sale-Tirumala-Maharayapura (Patil and Patil 1995: xxi), both the town and temple (named Ananta-padmanabha in the dedicatory inscription) were established in 1524 (Patil and Patil 1995: 120-1).[2]

The western valley, then, is connected with Hospet by proximity rather than drainage. The road to Hospet now climbs a hill out of the valley near the modern town of Kariganaru, a railroad loading point for iron and manganese products from the Sandur Hills. The major road from Hospet to the city of Vijayanagara runs to the northeast through the small settlements of Anantasayanagudi, Kondanayakanahalli, and Mallapannagudi. Both Anantasayanagudi and Mallapannagudi contain large Vijayanagara temples, and at least Mallapannagudi was originally walled. That there was a clear northern route between the Daroji Valley and the open plain in which this string of settlements was located is clear from the location of several features, including VMS-6, a walled fortification and associated settlement that includes an 800 meter long road wall, and VMS-1001, a roadside shrine (there are additional features along this road further north). Given the lines of drainage connecting the valley with Anantasayanagudi, it may be that there was also some kind of route running north this way and paralleling the more clearly defined road to the east.

The western Daroji Valley, then, must be seen not only as a major watershed and a highly constructed agricultural zone supporting nearby Hospet and its neighbors, but also as the entrance from the densely settled plains on the west to the constricted passageway of the Daroji Valley. As we will see, the latter saw its major expansion of settlement only in the sixteenth century or Late Vijayanagara period. Nevertheless, the Daroji Valley must have been an important route of east-west movement that avoided the congestion and obstacles of the city to the north, a geographic role it also apparently filled as early as the Neolithic.

The southern edge of the western valley is defined by the metamorphic Sandur Hills, which rise to some 1000 meters (*c.* 3300 feet) in this area. The Sandur Hills are now pock-marked by the scars of mining and have been largely denuded of woody vegetation. Historical records from the nineteenth century describe these hills as being densely wooded (e.g. Kelsall 1872), as discussed above. Palaeobotanical data suggest that the contemporary treeless character of the hills was prefigured by a similar state of deforestation in the Vijayanagara period (Morrison 1995a). The Sandur Hills send significant quantities of runoff into the valley. However, this runoff is largely contained within entrenched stream channels or *nullahs*. Runoff velocities in such *nullahs* can be very high and there were no attempts to capture *nullah* flows in reservoirs near the base of the Sandur Hills. Instead, stream flow from the Sandur Hills was channeled into reservoirs such as VMS-1002 and VMS-1023 further downstream. The Sandur Hills are also rich in minerals and were important sources of iron ore. That the iron-rich soil of the hills is currently eroding at a rapid pace is evident from the red silt deposits in reservoirs and *nullahs*; pre-twentieth century silt deposits can also be seen in several reservoirs. If indeed the Sandur Hills experienced an episode of deforestation during the Vijayanagara period that was similar to that of the late twentieth century, then both the danger and (perhaps) the potential of runoff and erosion from these high, steep, hills would have been great. Mass wasting of soils would have posed significant problems of reservoir siltation. At the same time, erosion can be seen as a kind of soil renewal that deepened and enriched valley sediments. At present, there is limited indication of large-scale erosion off of the Sandur Hills prior to this century while evidence for erosion from the northern granitic hills is more compelling.

The northern edge of the western valley is marked by much lower hills of granitic outcrops cut through with basaltic dykes. These hills form a series of low ranges with numerous internal drainage basins. The only woody taxa these hills now consistently support are xerophytes such as *Euphorbia caducifolia* and *E. antiquoruum* as well as scrubby *Acacias* and other leguminous shrubs. Grasses constitute the other major form of vegetation on the granitic hills. This depauperate vegetation is maintained in the face of intense pressure caused by regular firing (to clear brush, promote sprouting grasses for grazing animals, and make wood collection of large thorny plants easier), grazing, firewood collection, and agricultural clearing. The extent to which large scale erosion from these now-rocky slopes may have taken place is an important question and one with significant implications for the life history of the Daroji reservoir systems. Unlike the Sandur Hills, these lower and less monolithic granitic hills sent down smaller, less destructive seasonal runoff flows that could easily be contained behind the embankments of small reservoirs. For that reason, we see a concentration of both reservoirs and settlement along the northern edge of the western valley, a pattern echoed to the east in the main valley.

In this Chapter, I describe the interconnected reservoirs of the western Daroji system, linking them to other cultural features that, with them, help define the landscape of the western valley. Although this and the following chapter are loosely organized by time, it should be noted that this scheme is less evident in the experience of the landscape itself and indeed, as should become clear, certain places show complex and accretional occupational histories that can only be understood in terms of place rather than period. Here, however, I have imposed a general chronological scheme which makes description of the valley landscape somewhat easier to follow although I have not attempted to subdivide, for example, the Vijayanagara period in this narrative structure. Within the bounds of this framework is a secondary one, in which we follow the path of runoff as it flows from east to west down the slopes of hills and along the valley floor.

SETTLEMENT AND LAND USE IN THE WESTERN VALLEY

A number of features make it clear that the western valley saw a complex and long-term history of land use and that it was periodically the locus of several small-scale settlements. Many of these are only approximately dated, which limits our interpretations. Nevertheless, it is possible to hazard a rough sequence of habitation and of major patterns of land use that this region sustained. I do not suggest that there exists any particular analytical utility in considering this region as a unit of settlement or as a meaningful division of space for periods other than the Vijayanagara period. Even in Vijayanagara times, one could make the case that only the loose interconnection of the four western valley reservoirs provides a justification for positing a western valley system as such. Keeping that in mind, we can review what evidence there is on the long-term history of the western valley.

Herders and Dry Farmers: The Southern Neolithic

We begin our consideration of human use of the western valley in the Neolithic period (3000-1000 BC). There are several locations with evidence of use during the Neolithic in the western valley and, as discussed in following chapters, there is reason to believe that the entire Daroji Valley formed an important corridor of movement and locus of use at this time. In the intensively surveyed area to the north of the Daroji Valley, we identified only a few isolated artifacts, most in obviously secondary contexts, that could be assigned to the Paleolithic (cf. Lycett 1991), suggesting that Paleolithic use of this broad region was not intensive.[3] We have, at present, no indication of Paleolithic use of the western valley. The Mesolithic period in southern India is poorly defined (see Morrison 1999 for a discussion), and here I reserve the term Mesolithic to refer to materials from that long period between the early Holocene and the Neolithic. As discussed below, there is likely to be Mesolithic occupation of the western valley, although our evidence is scanty. In the Neolithic, all of the major loci of use are situated in or near VMS-110, a habitation site located on the edge of (the Vijayanagara-period) reservoir VMS-1004.

VMS-110 in the Neolithic

VMS-110 was first recorded in 1988; in 1997 we returned to carry out test excavations in the reservoir and in the slag scatter we originally believed to be associated with the reservoir. Surface materials indicated that a small settlement with a Neolithic component existed on the top and near the base of the granitic hills east/southeast of the site where VMS-1004 would later be situated; subsequent study indicated Neolithic ashmounds and artifacts both on this outcrop and to the north of the valley containing VMS-110. Although our excavations were limited, it was possible to obtain charcoal from midden contexts; radiocarbon dates from VMS-110 are given in Table 5.1.

Unfortunately, the base of the Neolithic deposits at VMS-110 was not encountered as excavation had to be discontinued before sterile soil was reached. Thus, it is probable that this area was occupied even earlier than our earliest dates and it is possible that Mesolithic materials underlie the VMS-110 Neolithic deposits, as they do, for example, at Sanganakallu, 55 kilometers to the southeast (Ansari and Nagaraja Rao 1969; see Figure 8). Neolithic deposits are distinguished on the basis of a suite of distinctive ceramic wares and forms, including micaceous types, that are clearly different from the overlying Black-and-Red Wares (BRW) and other Iron Age ceramics. In addition to ceramics, Neolithic deposits contain both flake and blade tools of fine-grained cryptocrystalline raw materials as well as of locally available basalt.

The eroded remains of three vitrified ash concentrations surrounded by a scatter of artifacts some 90 meters in diameter lie atop the granite hill at the northern end of a level terrace (*c.* 120 by 900 meters) just east/northeast of the VMS-110 midden area. The westernmost ashmound is the largest, approximately 10 meters across, and is located on the edge of the terrace looking down over the valley. The other two ash accumulations are smaller and located in the middle of the terrace; each is 6 to 8 meters in diameter. The concentration of artifacts is dense in some areas (6 to 25 sherds/square meter) and sparse (1 to 5 sherds/square meter) in others. Lithic artifacts consist primarily of flaked basalt, but we did note one small brown chert blade core.[4] With the exception of one piece of iron slag, the rest of the artifacts were ceramics, the latter mostly heavily comminuted and including slipped red wares, black wares, and Black-and-Red ware. There were no Neolithic ceramics on the surface. This is not the only location we have recorded with Iron Age/Early Historic ceramics in association with dense ashy deposits, so it is apparent that either activities producing ashmound deposits persisted after the Neolithic period or that the same places were consistently reused. Note that no Russet-Coated Painted Ware (RCPW) was noted on this hill; it is thus possible that this is a locus of Iron Age settlement (or Neolithic and Iron Age) that was

Table 5.1: VMS-110 Radiocarbon Dates

Lab. Number	Level (depth, cm bsd A)	Calibrated 2σ range	Uncalibrated	Period
Beta-115793	level 3 (33)	BC 175-AD 75	2040+/-50 BP	Early Historic
Beta-115794	level 4 (32)	BC 370-100	2180+/-40 BP	Early Historic
Beta-131371	level 5 (41-51)	BC 80-AD 120	1980+/-50 BP	Early Historic
Beta-131370	level 7 (61.5-70.5)	BC 2340-2035	3780+/-50 BP	Neolithic
Beta-124327	level 8 (79)	BC 2455-2175	3850+/-40 BP	Neolithic
Beta-124328	level 13 (120-30)	BC 2465-2205	3880+/-40 BP	Neolithic

not much used in the Early Historic. However, given that RCPW is always a rare ceramic type, this interpretation should not by given much weight. A pecked bull figure in the side of a small boulder overlooking the valley west of the outcrop may also have been made at this time (Figure 56). A second eroded ash mound lies over the granitic hill north of VMS-110, as discussed below.

The surface distribution of ceramics in the valley indicates that Neolithic ceramics occur across about 1 hectare of the valley's surface. This is difficult to translate into settlement area, since we do not know whether or not these materials represent repeated but intermittent occupations or a more permanent presence in the area. Further, valley colluviation and siltation associated with the later reservoir, VMS-1004, have undoubtedly blanketed the distributions of these earlier materials. From our limited excavations in what appear to be midden contexts at the base of the outcrop, we can say that the depth of cultural deposition was substantial, but at present we cannot evaluate potential mobility patterns. It seem likely that Neolithic inhabitants of the western valley grazed animals, especially cows, here, planted some dry fields of millet and other crops, and gathered and hunted wild plants and animals. Our small-scale excavations and surface studies also suggest that *after* the Early Neolithic this small valley saw either intermittent use or, perhaps was continuously but lightly used by groups practicing variable degrees of mobility and/or spatially complex and differentiated patterns of land use. Thus, simply because this particular place on the landscape was not "occupied" at a particular time (in the sense of materially obtrusive, permanent habitation) does not mean that it was not *used* as part of a round that may have involved herding and the collecting of plants, wood, clays, or other materials.

Unfortunately, botanical preservation was poor and although flotation samples for macrobotanical analysis were processed, we did not recover charred plant materials. Faunal analysis indicates both the importance of domesticated cattle and of sheep and goat, as well as the presence of domesticated pigs (*Sus*). A limited range of wild animal taxa are also present, including a few bivalves that must have been obtained from the Tungabhadra River.

Ashmound VMS-1078

North of this small protected valley (the valley that would eventually contain reservoir VMS-1004), a second ashmound (32 meters in diameter), also highly eroded, lies in the middle of the long, level valley that would later form part of the watershed of VMS-1003. On the surface near this ashmound there are now only a few quartzite flakes and no ceramics, but both the degree of disturbance (the vitrified ash has apparently been mined; the feature is something like a doughnut-shaped hole rather than a mound. Further disturbance is indicated by the remnants of a brick-making operation that lie just east of the ashmound) and the probable heavy colluviation of this valley might have erased any surface artifact record here. That this area was a locus of intensive occupation during the Neolithic and perhaps before is indicated not only by the ashmounds and occupational debris, but also by consistent reports of microliths in the hills all around this area (Balasubrahmanyam, personal communication). These microliths may or may not represent actual microlithic blade technology (cf. Lycett and Morrison 1989), but they are sufficiently distinct from later lithic artifacts to suggest a widespread use of the western valley landscape by early Holocene farmers, foragers, and herders.

Iron Age and Early Historic: Megaliths, Villages, and Iron Production

As focused as the remains of Neolithic occupation are in this small area and in other pockets within the larger region, they are much less intrusive than the transformations wrought during the Iron Age and the following Early Historic period. The Iron Age, as noted, is often associated with megalithic mortuary monuments, but there is some likelihood that such remains were actually built over a very long period of time, perhaps even into the Early Middle period (Lycett and Morrison 1998; and see Wagoner 1995). The radiocarbon dates from VMS-110 make it clear that there was a major hiatus – between 2000 and about 400 BC – in either the presence or intensity of occupation (or both) in this small valley. Nevertheless, there are many megalithic monuments (discussed below) all around VMS-110 and, no doubt, in other parts of the Daroji Valley as well. Certainly some of these could date to the Iron Age, notwithstanding the radiocarbon dates from VMS-110, but it seems more parsimonious to accept the growing body of evidence that megalithic monuments were constructed over a very long span of time and to associate these features with the Early Historic occupation of VMS-110. Thus, we have no secure basis for suggesting an Iron Age (here conceived narrowly as a time period) occupation of VMS-110, nor indeed, of the Daroji Valley. Clearly, however, archaeological bases for distinguishing this long period of time are weak and it is likely that this region was at least intermittently occupied during this time.

As discussed in previous Chapters, the Early Historic was a period of dramatic change in the south. During this long period, the Daroji Valley seems to have been a secondary area of occupation, a zone of specialized activities away from the main corridor of settlement along the Tungabhadra River to the north (Lycett and Morrison 1998). The evidence from VMS-110 makes it clear that at least one of these specialized activities was the smelting of iron ores from the nearby Sandur Hills.

VMS-110 in the Early Historic

During the Early Historic, VMS-110 was an industrial location and small associated settlement geared toward iron production. Iron-rich nodules were taken from a nearby annual stream deriving from the Sandur hills. We have identified specific areas (Figure 57) where ore was broken into chunks and roasted; there appear to have been multiple smelting locales with a technology of small, ephemeral furnaces similar to that described by Gogte for Iron Age Naikund (1982). This smelting activity led to the deposition of a massive pile of slag and other iron production by-products (Figure 58); this slag would eventually form the embankment of reservoir VMS-1004.

The scale of iron production at VMS-110 certainly verged on the industrial. Later Vijayanagara iron-working (both smelting and smithing) was, in contrast, carried out on a much smaller scale – notwithstanding the much larger regional population – and seems to have been a mobile, perhaps seasonal activity (Lycett 1994). The location of VMS-110 near an iron ore source is perhaps not surprising. What is surprising is the degree to which production must have been oriented toward more distant settlements, at least those clustered along the banks of the Tungabhadra some 8 kilometers to the north, and perhaps well beyond that. Determining the networks of exchange through which those iron objects moved remains an important avenue of future research. That the inhabitants of VMS-110 had at least some connection to the larger world of south India is attested to by the presence of an "imitation" Rouletted Ware (RW) sherd, determined by XRF analysis to have been manufactured far to the south, in the present-day state of Tamil Nadu (Gogte, personal communication). Other ceramics such as BRW and RCPW appear to have been locally manufactured.

Again, the size of the Early Historic settlement at VMS-110 is difficult to determine. The surface ceramic scatter is somewhat larger than 1 hectare, giving a very rough indication. Like the Neolithic occupation, there are no structural remains present on the surface. Our excavations also yielded a number of ceramic, bone, shell, and carnelian beads, similar to those found in other settlements of this broad period. The faunal material is remarkably similar to that of the Neolithic deposits. As in the Neolithic levels, flotation yielded no botanical remains. Even though, as noted above, rice became more common in southern India during this period, it was unlikely to have ever been grown in the vicinity of VMS-110 prior to the expansion of irrigation facilities into this area.

Evidence of human modification extends well beyond the small valley containing excavated midden deposits and industrial

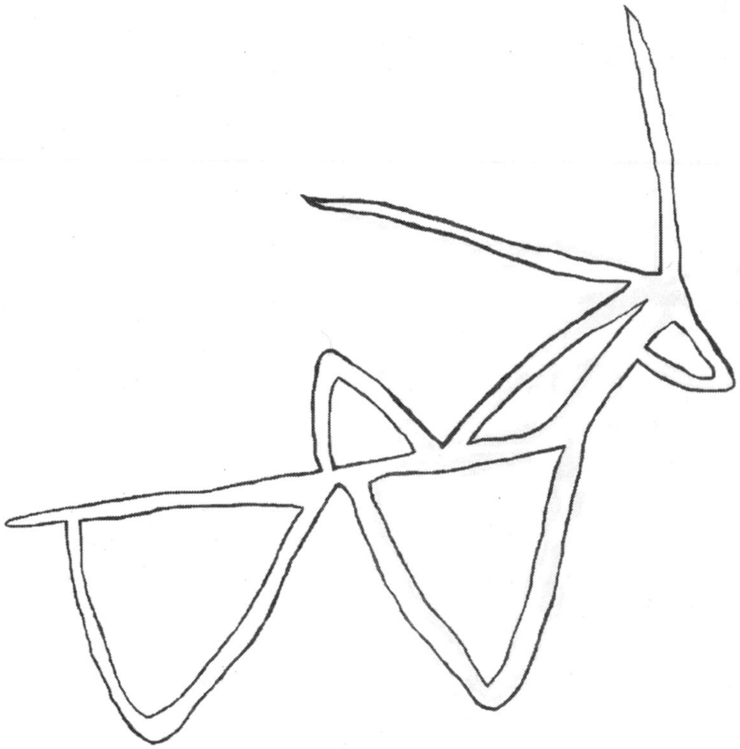

Figure 56. Pecked bull from VMS-110.

Figure 57. VMS-110, surface collection crew at work.

Figure 58. Tapped slag from VMS-110.

smelting debris. This evidence includes both artifacts and features, the latter including (in addition to the ashmounds discussed above) several passage-chamber megaliths or cairns; numerous stone circles, some enclosing slab-lined cists; rock bruisings and petroglyphs; rows of pecked cupules; crack features; and a long masonry wall running down the outcrop to the east of the settlement and iron processing area (cf. Lycett and Morrison 1998). Beyond the valley itself, there are at least three areas with significant concentrations of features: the granitic hills north of the valley; the ashmound lying just over these hills to the north (VMS-1078, above); and the slopes and hilltop of the outcrop east/northeast of the valley. The latter has been divided into two separate sections, the features on the hill slope, described below, and the terrace area which also contains remnant ashmounds, described above. The hills bordering the valley on the north also merit closer examination, but even a cursory analysis indicates tens of stone circles built up on the rocky talus slope. These circles tend to blend in with the boulder-strewn slope, but they are nonetheless anthropogenic features. Some circles intersect, sharing sections of their stone borders. There are no clear cists within the circles, but these may be obscured by colluviation.

Hillside Megaliths and Other Features East/Northeast of VMS-110

Pastoral groups regularly move through this area on a seasonal basis. While we were excavating in December 1997, there was a pastoral camp located on the upper terrace of the outcrop east/north-east of the Early Historic settlement and industrial areas of VMS-110; a few weeks later it shifted to the level area south of reservoir VMS-1004. Because of this form of contemporary land use, there are several ephemeral hearths and stone alignments in this area which, however, can be clearly distinguished from the chipped-stone construction of earlier megaliths. Down the slope of this outcrop runs a massively-built wall, *c.* 2 meters wide, consisting of both piled and roughly coursed cobbles, never more than 1.5 meters high (Figure 59). Many wall elements are unmodified, but many are also chipped, indicating an Iron Age/Early Historic construction date. Near its western end (the wall runs southwest-northeast but I shall discuss it as if it ran east-west) at the base of the outcrop are at least four stone cist-circles.[5] The fact that every day several tractor-driven carts are loaded up with boulders from this very area suggests that very many more have been destroyed. Next to this concentration of small cist-circles is a large, dark-colored boulder with several pecked designs. These designs are often found in association with megalithic monuments, but it is not known what they represent. Moving up the rocky slope and following the wall almost to the top of the outcrop, one encounters first a dilapidated, east-west oriented passage-chamber tomb (2.5 by 1.5 meters) lying just south of the south face of the wall and near it, a second, parallel passage-chamber tomb in even worse condition (Figure 60). There are several petroglyphs nearby and a boulder in between the two megaliths shows signs of pecking (Figure 61). The location of these megaliths is unusual in that they are on a slope and are, in a sense, subordinated to the wall rather than having a lofty central position on a level hilltop.

At the top of the hill near the end of the wall – a location with an excellent view of the small residential valley as well as of the Daroji Valley to the south – a large horizontal boulder touches the wall's south face. On it is are two intersecting rows of small, round, pecked cupules (2 centimeters in diameter, also common near megalithic mortuary complexes) forming a cross shape. Up here, the wall has up to 6 courses preserved; its eastern end touches a jutting ridge of dark-colored dolerite which forms a natural barrier.

Following this same outcrop further north, there is an area with few artifacts but several "crack features", natural cracks in the exposed rock that have been filled in with cobbles, boulders, and sometimes chipped stones. A sparse, low density artifact scatter consisting of recent sherds, Vijayanagara earthenware ceramics, and lithics (including a few schist

Figure 59. Wall on outcrop north-east of VMS-110.

Figure 60. Wall with dilapidated passage chamber megalith.

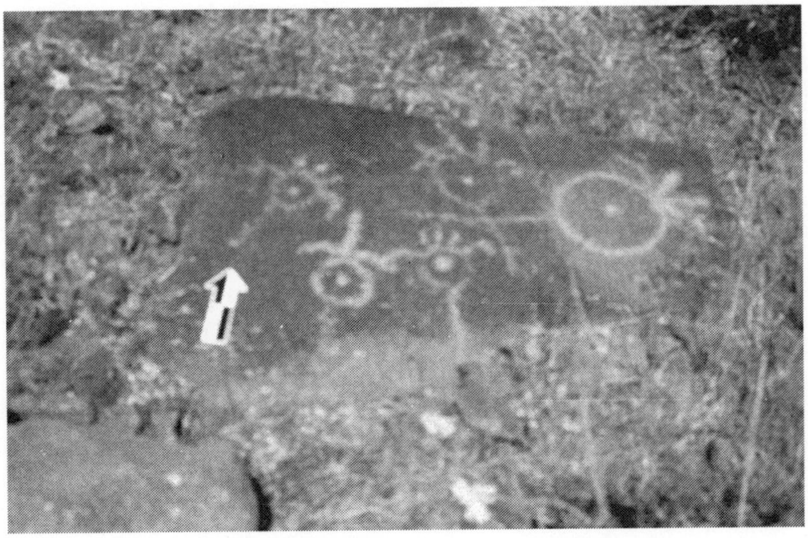

Figure 61. Boulder with pecked designs.

flakes) lies scattered across the outcrop, testimony to the consistent movement across and use of this hillock.

The area at the northern end of this same outcrop and on its level top is the location of the three highly eroded, vitreous ash deposits (ashmound material) and the brown chert blade core, both of which appear to pre-date the Early Historic. As noted, the ceramic assemblage was entirely Iron Age and/or Early Historic. It should, however, be noted that we conducted no collections or excavations in this area and there is, therefore, much more to learn about the use life of this terrace.

Summing up the evidence for Iron Age use of the western valley, we have only megaliths, themselves of broad temporal provenience, to suggest that people lived and worked in this area. It is likely, however, that there was at least occasional exploitation of this region for grazing and collecting in the five hundred years between the end of the Neolithic and the beginning of the Early Historic.[6] In the latter period, the celebrated Ashokan edicts appeared in areas just north (Koppal), northeast (Udegolam and Nittur), and southeast (Brahmagiri) of the Daroji Valley and the corridor along the Tungabhadra River supported several large settlements and numerous mortuary complexes (Lycett and Morrison 1998; Sinopoli and Morrison in press). It has been suggested that the reason the Mauryan polity took an interest in this remote part of the interior (and hence the reason that Ashokan edicts exist here) was for its mineral riches, including gold near Maski (where there is also an edict) and the famous Kolar gold fields. If this is correct, it may also be the case that Sandur iron ores and iron products were among the material desired by the northern state. In the Early Historic, the western valley was home to the specialized smelting site of VMS-110. This and the small Iron Age/Early Historic ceramic scatter near the embankment of reservoir VMS-1023 are the only material traces of Early Historic use of the western valley, a pattern that differs significantly from the following Middle periods, when this region became primarily agricultural and residential.

The Early Middle Period: Small Villages and Runoff Farming

During the Early Middle Period (AD 500 to 1300), the western valley was only sparsely occupied and, further, the pattern of use shifted from iron production to agriculture, herding, and smaller-scale iron and copper working. This general pattern is clear from both textual and archaeological sources. The latter are restricted to what is probably a twelfth to thirteenth-century settlement underneath the southern end of reservoir VMS-1003, just south of a major breach (noted above). This settlement has been massively displaced by the reservoir and, at this end, the reservoir embankment consists entirely of cultural fill. The latter contains a very high density of earthenware ceramics with rim morphologies similar, but not identical to Vijayanagara rim forms (cf. Sinopoli 1986, 1993); unlike Early Historic types, they are primarily unslipped. Slipped and/or polished wares are either black or red; there are evidently no Black-and-Red Wares nor are there any painted ceramics. This kind of assemblage – dominated by unslipped earthenwares but containing a substantial minority of slipped black wares and slipped red wares – is consistent with the assemblage from the twelfth to thirteenth century town of Haneya (Morrison 2005), located on the other side of the outcrop from the older settlements of Brahmagiri excavated by Wheeler (1947). Nevertheless, either some Iron Age/Early Historic occupation or the reuse of Iron Age/Early Historic materials, perhaps from VMS-110 just over the hill, is indicated by the presence of a slab with a pecked motif characteristic megalithic mortuary contexts that is reintegrated into the waste weir of the reservoir. Finally, the presence of two hero stones strongly suggests an Early Middle period date and thus at present the preponderance of evidence points to the Early Middle Period.

The fill of the embankment of VMS-1003 also contains a large amount of charcoal, fractured and splintered mammalian long bone fragments, ash, and indicators of iron production. The latter include slag and tuyere fragments, indicating the smelting of ores as at nearby

VMS-110. However, the scale of production here is quite modest, much more in line with the small production locales of the later Vijayanagara period than with the specialized workshop of VMS-110. Other kinds of production are indicated by a (single) copper crucible with adhering slag and an unfired, decorated clay spindle whorl (indicating textile production). One ash deposit, in particular, is very large and may be related to either industrial production or domestic activity. None of this evidence suggests large-scale, industrial production and it seem more likely that this was a small agricultural village which produced several of the kinds of materials required for tools, vessels, and clothing.

Near the southern end of VMS-1003 are several walls built of small boulders that appear to be – at least in part – recent. A broken hero stone has been (re)set in one room defined by these walls. As noted, hero stones are common in the Early Middle period and more rare (though not unknown) during the Vijayanagara period. Although this one may not be *in situ*, it is also not unreasonable to think that it has not been moved very far (they are very heavy). The sculpture, of a woman following a horse and rider, is without the multiple vertical panels that one sees in some hero stones in this area. It may be that some of the walls in this area are actually remnants of the settlement that have been built on to.

Inscriptional evidence is also useful in locating areas of Early Middle period settlement in the western valley. Although most of the architecture and inscriptions from Hospet come from the sixteenth century and later, one damaged and incomplete inscription dating to the twelfth century (Patil and Patil 1995: 121), refers to the Kalachurya king Bijjaladeva (see Table 5.2).

VIJAYANAGARA OCCUPATION IN THE WESTERN VALLEY

The evidence for Vijayanagara use of the western valley is clearer than that of earlier periods. As described above, this part of the Daroji Valley supported a loosely integrated chain of runoff-fed reservoirs, a chain that began near the town of Papinayakanahalli on the east (Chapter 6) and ended near the modern town of Hospet, itself officially established in the sixteenth century. The western valley has very little inscriptional information, although there is more information from Hospet itself (Table 5.2).

Unfortunately, none of the reservoirs in the western valley can be precisely dated. The sluices of reservoirs VMS-1002 and 1003, in spite of their early-appearing moulding sequences, seem in other respects (size, proportion, presence of decorative elaboration) to follow sixteenth-century sluice idioms. I have suggested that these finial-capped sluices may be deliberately archaic (cf. Michell 1994; 1985a: 276), and if this is correct then they may indeed date to the sixteenth century. However, it is also possible that they are early, as their mouldings suggest, and are simply unusually monumental. Both sets of sluices are probably contemporaneous, but beyond this there is little certainty.

In the western valley there are at least three habitation areas that appear to date from the Vijayanagara period and to have continued to be occupied for some time. These include VMS-6, a fortified hilltop with associated habitation debris, an area now abandoned and perhaps used and occupied only in the sixteenth and/or seventeenth century; Ingaligi, with its remains of seventeenth century (?) fortification in and around the still-occupied village; and Sankalapura, established by AD 1513 and still occupied today.

In addition to these three areas of concentrated structural remains, there is evidence of at least two major roadways. The first runs north-south through an opening in the Hampi-Daroji Hills and is indicated by the alignment of VMS-6 and an 800 meter long road wall[7] just north and east of this settlement, a small shrine (VMS-1001), a temple (VMS-375), a step-well and road wall[8] (VMS-374) near this temple, and the walled town of Mallapannagudi.

There is an inscription (Gopal 1985a: 186-7) in Mallapannagudi, on a slab in front of the temple that may refer to this north-south road. The inscription is in Kannada, dates to AD 1412 (Patil and Patil 1995: 123), and describes the

Table 5.2: Inscriptions of the Western Valley and Hospet (all periods)

Location	*Context*	*Date*	*Summary*	*References*
Sankalapura (western valley)	on a stone slab in the village	AD 1513, Tuesday, 20 September	records that king Krishnadeva Raya made a gift of the village of Sankapura to the temple Kota-Vinayaka situated on the east side of the Deveri road in Vijayanagara	Patil and Patil 1997, no. 450; *ARE* 1895-6 no. 398 of 1896; *EI* IV, pp. 266-9; *SII*, V, no. 1353
Hospet	on a stone slab in the Sannaki Virabhadrasvami temple	Twelfth century	damaged and incomplete. Records titles of king Bijjaladeva	Patil and Patil 1997, no. 419; *ARIE*, 1980-1, no. B 122.
Hospet	on a slab in the same temple as above	AD 1531, Monday, 11 September	Notes that Kampadevarasa-Anna (a donor) and the Nanadesha merchants agreed to pay one *kasu* per load of paddy and 2 *panas* (a coin) on every marriage for the service of the god Gaureshvara at Tirumaladevi-ammana-pattana.[9]	Patil and Patil 1997, no. 420; *ARSIE* 1912-23, no. 679 of 1922; *SII*, IX ii, no. 539.
Hospet	on a slab set up in town (not *in situ*?)	AD 1536, Saturday, 3 April	Abbaraja Timmapa, agent of the minister (*pradhana*) Tirumalaraja, made a gift of the cess (*mulavisa*) for the service of the god[10] Tiruvengalanatha in Tirumaladevi-yarapattana with the consent of the merchants (*shettipattanasvami*) of Tirumaladeviyarapattana, Varadajammanapattana and Krishnapura.[11] The text mentions Bisilhalli pass.	Patil and Patil 1997, no. 421, *ARSIE* 1922-3, no. 682 of 1922; *SII*, IX ii, no. 573.
Hospet	on a slab built into the wall of a mosque in town	(Hijri 1210); reign of Tipu Sultan	Ghafoor Khan, a person of high lineage, had the mosque built.	Patil and Patil 1996, no. 422; *ARSIE* 1922-3, no. 680 of 1922.
Jambunatha-nahalli[12]	on the pillars of a mandapa on the path leading up to the Jambunatha	AD 1549, Saturday, 28 December	Documents a gift of four *padis* of rice per day for offerings to the god Hanumantadeva on the Jambukeshvara hill. This rice was to come from the provision made for the service of god Anantasayana.[13]	Patil and Patil 1997:120, no. 415; Filliozat and Filliozat 1988:14; *ARE* 1903-4, no. 23 of 1904; *SII*, IX, no. 635; XVII, no. 24.

construction and endowment of a roofed well with a grove around it. This may refer to the beautiful octagonal walk-in well now on the western edge of the village, although there is also an inscription on this structure itself indicating that it was built in AD 1485 (Patil and Patil 1995: 123). Such wells and associated structures were often set up on main roads for the benefit of travelers and it may be that the present well replaced an earlier one. This earlier well (Patil 1995: 123, and see Gopal 1985a: 187) is said to be located at a junction of the roads, "leading to Bisilahalli-Kanuve and Badavaliya-Kanuve".[14] Mallapannagudi itself sits on a major east-west road that connects Hospet with the city of Vijayanagara; the other road mentioned may be the one running south into the Daroji Valley (there is no evidence for a northern road). Unfortunately, it is not possible to match the names of the roads with contemporary place names, so if this inscription does refer to a Mallapannagudi-Ingaligi road, then it would suggest that the place-name Ingaligi is more recent than the fifteenth century.

The second road in the western valley runs approximately east-west, part of the major route that once extended the length of the Daroji Valley. As discussed in Chapter 6, this route would have connected Hospet with Daroji and the Bellary plains east of Daroji; it could have provided a kind of by-pass to the dense urban landscape to the north. In general, the dominant northwest-southeast trend of the Hampi-Daroji Hills served to funnel moment across the landscape into certain well-defined courses. The Daroji Valley would have been one of the most important east-west routes south of the city, especially given the major barrier created by the Sandur Hills on the south. Even today, the rail line linking Bellary and Hospet runs through the Daroji Valley, as does a paved road.

The western valley system integrates only five reservoirs. In contrast to the main valley system where flow relationships are mostly direct (excess discharge from reservoir A flows into B which flows into C and so on), here three of the upstream reservoirs discharge overflow into the main drainage system of the valley rather than into another reservoir located immediately downstream. Thus, it seems that physically, this system was less tightly integrated than the main valley system, where disruptions in one link – excessive siltation, a breach, or even irresponsible use of water – would have had significant consequences down the line, especially where such a disruption involved a large reservoir. Sluice morphology is also more diverse in the western valley, and may indicate a greater temporal range in construction dates. If this is the case, then the lower level of reservoir integration may relate, in part, to construction history.

Also unlike the main valley system, the western valley system did not have a large reservoir at its terminus. Although VMS-1023 is certainly substantial, it is not in a position to collect all the runoff from the valley, as the Daroji reservoir does and, in fact, it may never have received any benefit from reservoirs to the east. The Daroji reservoir, at least in its present configuration, post-dates many of the other reservoirs in the main valley and its construction had a major effect on agriculture in the eastern valley, not only by watering fields below and allowing the expansion of Daroji town, but also inundating agricultural land upstream and thus reshaping the distribution of productive land. One consequence of the looseness of the western valley system was that it never saw the kinds of radical restructuring of configurations of water, land, and even routes of movement that the main valley experienced. Instead, there seems to have been a kind of gradual filling-in process, with new reservoirs constructed over perhaps a hundred-year period. In part because of the nature of topography and runoff in the western valley, but also as a consequence of the small number of reservoirs, new facilities would not have had major effects on the operation of older ones. The looseness of the western valley system also reflects the lower concentration of population there.

Reservoir VMS-1005

This small reservoir (Figure 62) is the first in the western valley system and lies northeast of the village of Vadrahalli. The embankment spans a deep, narrow valley in a northwest-southeast oriented spur of the Hampi-Daroji Hills. The granite here is heavily shot through with veins of basalt. The bed of the reservoir is blanketed by a luxuriant growth of thick, dark grass; the ground slopes up quite steeply to the north. Downstream from (south of) the reservoir is a narrow (25 to 30 meters wide) gorge which runs approximately 60 meters to the south before discharging its seasonal supply of water into the broad Daroji Valley. Soils in this area are coarse, red-brown and sandy. Lush irrigated vegetable fields, coconut palms, and several large trees grow downstream from the reservoir, but these are watered by (recent) electric pumps. VMS-1005 is relatively short (72 meters long by 16 meters wide) but is quite high (4 meters) for its length. Both the *bund*

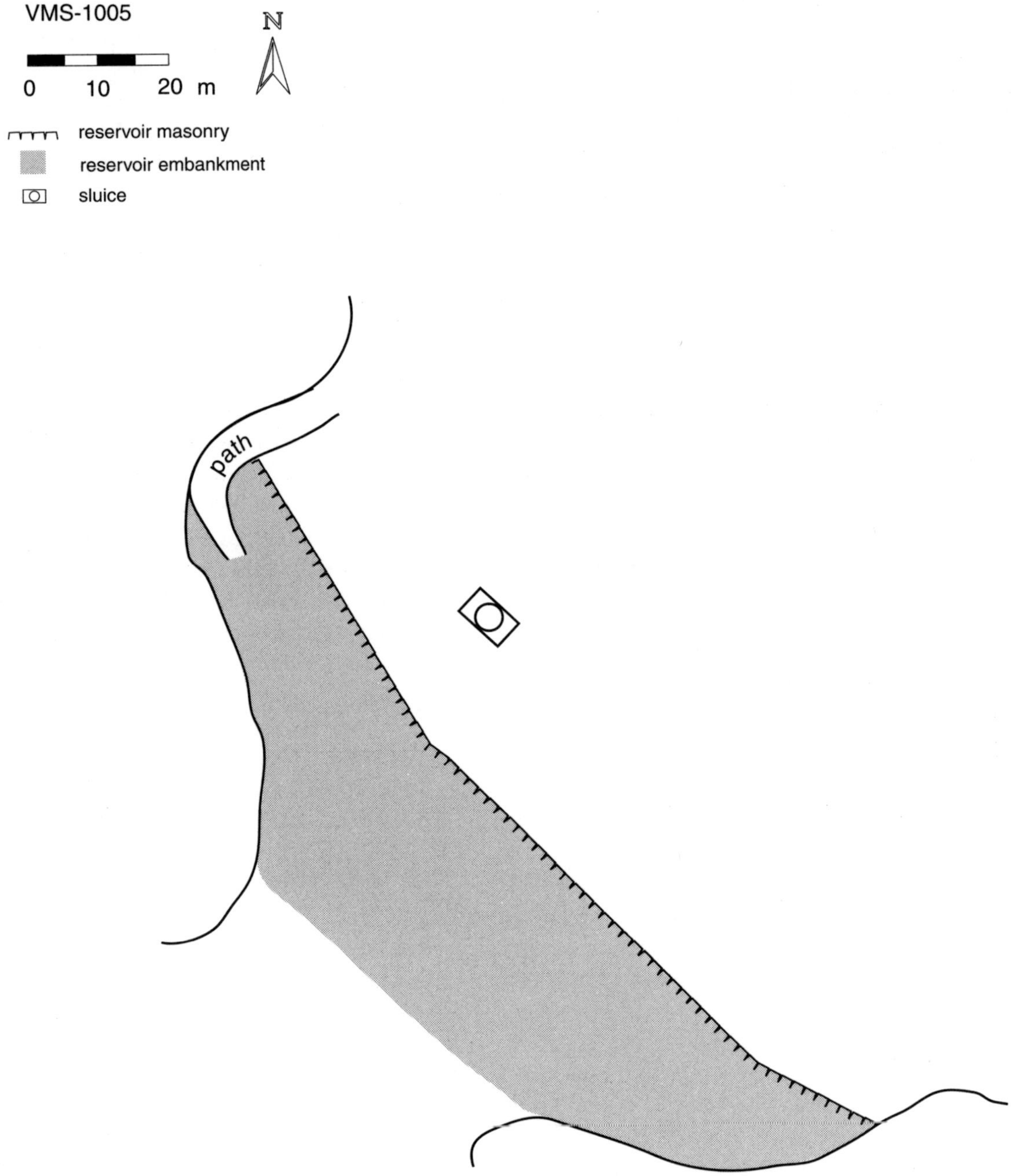

Figure 62. Plan of reservoir VMS-1005.

morphology and the topography of this steep-sided valley suggest that although the watershed of this facility was not large, runoff velocity could be significant. The embankment has not, however, been breached although the reservoir is clearly no longer in use.

Construction

The earthen embankment is faced with masonry on the northern side. Its 13 masonry courses are stepped out at a rather steeply pitched angle. The masonry consists of split and approximately rectangular medium-sized boulders. Courses are regularly laid and well-fit, with only a few chinking stones used. Near sluice 1 the steep pitch of the masonry is reduced and the height of the embankment declines to 9 masonry courses. The west end of the reservoir abuts a low granitic outcrop; several gaps in the outcrop have been crudely stopped up with piles of boulders, openings which could have served as informal waste weirs when water levels were high.

Sluices and Outlets

The single sluice consists of two square dressed uprights made of a fine grained granite marbled with veins of basalt. The center cross-bar is *in situ* although all of the upper elements are missing. Immediately in front of (north of) the sluice is the tunnel opening, visible beneath the two long horizontal slabs that extend north, one from each upright. There is no indication of an outlet on the south side. Any excess flow from this reservoir would have joined a small seasonal drainage eventually dammed by VMS-1002.

Reservoir VMS-1004

VMS-1004 (Figure 63) spans a small valley tucked into the northern hills that define the main Daroji Valley. This sinuous reservoir blocks off an opening between two outcrops, creating an enclosed bed that was probably used both for planting as well as for the impoundment of water. As discussed above, this reservoir was cut out of the side of a large mound of cultural debris, mostly iron slag, remnants of a settlement that was first established during the Neolithic (if not sooner) and then reoccupied as both settlement and industrial site in the Early Historic period. The mound supplied the bulk usually provided by an earthen embankment and had the effect of creating a large area of high ground south of (downstream from) the bed of the reservoir. Thus, water distributed from this facility was conveyed down a deeply incised channel southwest of the reservoir embankment to a small, lower area of level fields. It seems unlikely that there was ever any excess flow out of this reservoir that could have made it way down the valley, but it is at least possible. Such flow would have led directly into VMS-1002 to the west.

The bed of the reservoir is now cultivated with dry-farmed crops such as millets and oilseeds. No water appears to pool up after the monsoons, but the clay-rich sediments near the embankment were very wet in December 1997. There is one sluice, now defunct, over a tunnel which is still operating. The high ground level south of ("downstream" from) the embankment makes the embankment difficult to see from the south. Thus, unlike many other reservoirs which are striking, elevated features on the landscape, VMS-1004 appears from the main valley as merely a small swale and its extent can only be appreciated from vantage points in the surrounding hills.

The area of impoundment north of the embankment measures 250 meters north-south by 600 meters east-west. The ground surface immediately south of the embankment is 1 to 2 meters higher than that to the north, so that the top of the embankment is flush with the southern ground surface. Excavations show that this reservoir has at least 1 meter of accumulated silt in its bed. These accumulated sediments consist of regular patterns of specific grain sizes, with clay sediments accumulated in a band closest to the embankment, silt-sized sediment further out, followed by silt/sand mixtures, and finally sand which would have been deposited around the edges of the water. This pattern is entirely consistent with the flow of runoff into the reservoir from three sides and gradual slowing of that runoff as it approaches

Figure 63. Overview of reservoir VMS-1004, looking west.

Figure 64. VMS-1004, detail of tunnel outlet below reservoir.

the embankment. Sediment grain sizes are distributed in similar belts in other reservoirs as well, allowing flow patterns of runoff to be traced with some accuracy. This pattern of sediment deposition also illustrates what may be the most serious long-term threat to the operation of any runoff-fed reservoir – the danger of excessive siltation and loss of water holding capacity. The total length of the embankment is 160 meter, assuming that it originally stretched across to the eastern outcrop.

Construction

The embankment (the slag mound, as noted above) is faced with masonry on its north side. This masonry consists of medium-sized unmodified and rounded small boulders, irregularly coursed. The masonry courses are slightly stepped out, but the overall slope of the masonry face is very steep. Up to 9 courses of masonry are visible, with the height of the embankment varying greatly. It is highest (*c.* 2.5 meters) at the western end and becomes lower (1.5 meters) as it approaches the outcrop that marks the eastern end of the facility. Near this eastern end, outcropping boulders form a natural embankment 5 to 6 meters high. There is a small gap between these boulders and the high basaltic outcrop on the east, but this gap is not blocked in any way. There may have been a waste weir here, but it seems more likely that this gap simply represents disturbance of the ground surface, as a cart track passes through this opening. The western end of the reservoir merges almost imperceptibly with a natural granitic ridge.

Outlets and Sluices

There is only one sluice, located near the west end of the embankment. The sluice now consists of one broken upright, made from a dressed granite slab of rectangular cross-section. Some plaster still adheres to an inner face. The upright (1.5 meters high) is broken at the notch for the center cross-bar. No other sluice elements are present. The opening for the tunnel can be seen south of the sluice. The sides of the tunnel are formed by slabs set on edge; these are capped by a third slab. The floor of the tunnel is not now visible; it is 0.2 meter wide at the opening, widening to *c.* 0.35 meter further in. No brickwork is present.

Circa 20 meters south of the sluice, to the south of the embankment, is the outlet (Figure 64), oriented north-south, from which a modern irrigation channel flows. The outlet and the channel are lower than the surrounding fields by up to 1.3 meters. The outlet tunnel is constructed in a fashion similar to that on the inlet side, with walls and roof of long granite slabs. However, this southern end of the tunnel has two additional edge-set slabs on either side of the tunnel walls. These additional side slabs extend east-west, forming a well-defined end of the tunnel. The roof slab is wide enough to cover all the side slabs. A brick and plaster covering is visible over the tunnel at this end, and some angular rubble is also plastered into this construction. The floor of the tunnel is also exposed and is well-constructed of horizontal quarried slabs, oriented east-west. The brick-and-plaster covering ends (it is clear that was the original termination of the covering as the plaster forms a lip) about 2.5 meters before the tunnel itself does. The upper surface of the roof slab is finely-dressed at its exposed south end, also indicating that this was the original outlet point.

Reservoir VMS-1002

This reservoir, once very large, has been heavily disturbed and is breached by a seasonally active erosion channel (Figure 65). It lies in the lowest part of the valley floor and captures runoff from both sides of the valley, the highest reservoir in the western system to do so. The southern end of the reservoir is now obscured under the paved Hospet-Daroji road, tracks of the Southern Railway, and numerous open-cast iron ore mines. VMS-1002 received some runoff from a narrow outcrop to the north, but most of its water derives from the south and east, tapping at least six seasonal drainages from the Sandur Hills as well as any excess capacity from

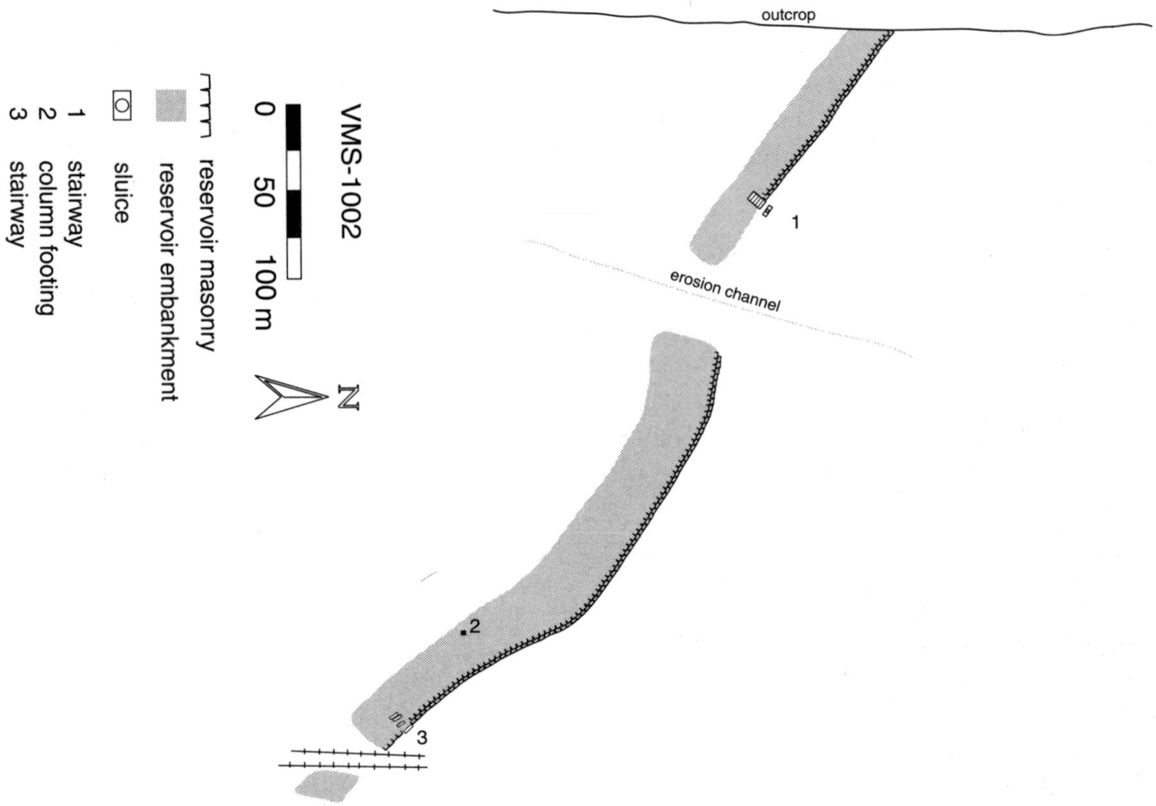

Figure 65. Plan of VMS-1002.

VMS-1004, upstream and to the east. The potential area watered by this reservoir is quite large, consisting of a broad, level plain of a sandy red loam now planted with dry crops and supporting grasses, scrubby *Euphorbias, Acacias,* and other thorn bushes. No water is now impounded behind this reservoir. Although its original extent is difficult to estimate, the embankment of this reservoir was at least 750 meters long, *c.* 28 meters wide, and 5 meters high.

Construction

At its northern end, where it joins an outcrop, the earthen embankment of VMS-1002 is very low (about 3 meters), gaining height rapidly to attain an elevation of 4 to 5 meters above ground level along its northern portion. The east face of the embankment is faced with masonry derived from metamorphic rocks of the Sandur Hills. The masonry consists of elements of varied sizes and shapes, from small to large unmodified, split, quarried, or dressed boulders (Figure 66). A somewhat unusual feature of the masonry is that it is set directly over the earthen embankment rather than on a rubble foundation course. Up to 8 irregular masonry courses are preserved near sluice 1. North of sluice 1, each masonry course is stepped out slightly, creating the typical stair-step form of Vijayanagara reservoirs. However, to the south of sluice 1, the courses of masonry become quite widely separated so that they form wide terraces along the eastern face of the embankment. Each terrace is composed of up to three courses of masonry and is between 1 and 2 meters wide. In this area south of sluice 1, the reservoir has been breached by a substantial stream, now deeply incised. Here the embankment rises to a height of approximately 7 meters and the exposed fill of the embankment (sterile red soil) has been robbed in and near the breach. Further south, near sluice 2, the masonry is badly disturbed, but it is clear that the height of the embankment decreases to *c.* 3.5 meters.

Outlets and Sluices

Two sluice gates are preserved, although the severe disturbance at the southern end of the reservoir and the probable extension of the embankment even further south makes it likely that VMS-1002 originally had 3 or even 4 sluices.

Sluice 1 (Figure 67) is the northernmost sluice, an imposing feature standing some 10 meters high. This large and well-constructed sluice consists of two square uprights joined by two lower cross-bars. The lintel consist of a three-part moulding. The lower moulding is two-stepped with an angled bevel and four corner quarter medallions. Separated from this by an inset vertical face is an upper moulding of the same type but with central half medallions as well as corner quarter medallions. Capping this moulding are a pair of finials consisting of a globular element with an upper rim and a lower band (the latter, however, not around its middle) atop a square base topped with a ridged and pointed element. The finial thus bears some resemblance to the *purnakalasa* or "auspicious pot" motif of a coconut in a globular jar.

This moulding configuration is unusual in several respects. First, although angled bevel moulding sequences of the type seen here are quite common in the early and middle parts of the Vijayanagara period (fourteenth and fifteenth centuries), none are as large as this one. This size difference is also expressed proportionally, with the sluices of VMS-1002 having proportions more akin to the slender and lofty sluices of the later Vijayanagara period (sixteenth century) than to the low and solid sluices found earlier. As noted, reservoir size does not necessarily translate into sluice size although it docs havc an effect on the number of sluices. The second interesting feature of this sluice is its finials, elements found to my knowledge only here and on the nearby VMS-1003. Although other angled bevel sluices in the study area have such embellishments as carved gods, goddesses, and donor portraits, none are as large and slender as this, nor do any bear finials of any kind.

West of sluice 1, a staircase of 15 steps led down to the water. The steps are built of long (3 meters) quarried slabs set into the embankment. The railings on each side of the staircase are formed of square and rectangular blocks of stone. The base of the stairway extends

Figure 66. Reservoir embankment, VMS-1002.

Figure 67. Sluice 1, VMS-1002, with pot finials.

out slightly to the east of the actual embankment (and thus down into the water itself, were there any). On the downstream (west) side of the reservoir near sluice 1, soil has been robbed from the embankment and the original outlet is not visible. However, there is a linear alignment of raised earth running eastwest opposite the sluice; this is probably the course of the tunnel that runs under the embankment. The solid construction of the tunnel underneath has probably prevented the excavation of soil from this area. Several chunks of plaster lie atop the embankment near sluice 1. Although there is no clear structural association for this plaster, a pecked column footing on a square granite block also lying on top of the embankment suggests that there may have been some kind of structure on the embankment here. A few recent graves have been dug into the embankment in this area.

Sluice 2 is much more poorly preserved and deeply silted in than is sluice 1 (*c.* 0.5 meter as compared to almost no siltation near sluice 1), although it seems to have originally been of similar height and proportions. Although its lower cross-bars are no longer visible, its construction seems similar to sluice 1. The lintel consists of the same sequence of mouldings but without the finials. The stone of this sluice is very rough and crudely carved, although traces of plaster on the southern upright suggest that these defects were less visible in the past; if there were brick-and-plaster finials here matching those on the sluice to the north, there is now no trace of them. Opposite the sluice is a slumped staircase, now somewhat difficult to distinguish from the masonry of the embankment. However, the presence of several long granite slabs suggests that it was much like the one opposite the northern sluice. A few Vijayanagara-type bricks, probably tunnel elements, are eroding out of the embankment west of sluice 2 but given the poor condition of the reservoir in this area, it is not possible to locate the tunnel outlet either east or west of the embankment.

Reservoir VMS-1003

Standing some 3 meters high, this long reservoir spans a broad, level valley ringed by outcrops (Figures 68 and 69). This east-west oriented valley collects runoff from the hills that surround it on the north, south, and east. The valley is tucked into the rocky hills; the collection and dispersal of runoff from this isolated valley benefitted fields in the broad level plain also watered by VMS-1002. These fields lie east of the settlement of Ingaligi (VMS-1040), which may have been occupied during the Vijayanagara period (below). The southern end of this reservoir cuts through an abandoned Early Middle period settlement; further east, up the valley, is a Neolithic ash mound (VMS-1078). The overall dimensions of the reservoir embankment are 465 meters long by 10 meters wide.

Construction

The reservoir is faced with up to 12 courses of stepped masonry on its upstream (east) side. Masonry courses are constructed from large unmodified granite and basaltic boulders, heavily water stained. The masonry is stepped back at a rather steep angle. Some masonry also faces the downstream (west) side of the embankment, stabilizing the earthen embankment. Here, as elsewhere, the downstream masonry is built near the base of the embankment and is only a few courses high.

One interesting feature of this reservoir is that it was constructed of at least three distinct arcs of masonry-faced earthen embankment. Unlike many reservoirs that simply curve in one direction, this reservoir consists of several separate curved sections joined together, giving it a wavy appearance in plan view. These sections do not, however, appear to have been constructed at different times, as the masonry at the intersections of the curved segments is consistently the same as the rest of the masonry and no join points or breaks can be discerned. At one location, the upper 4 to 5 courses of masonry appear to have been recently repaired.

Outlets and Sluices

Approximately 370 meters from the northern end of the reservoir is a well-built sluice (Figure 70) at the base of a staircase leading down from

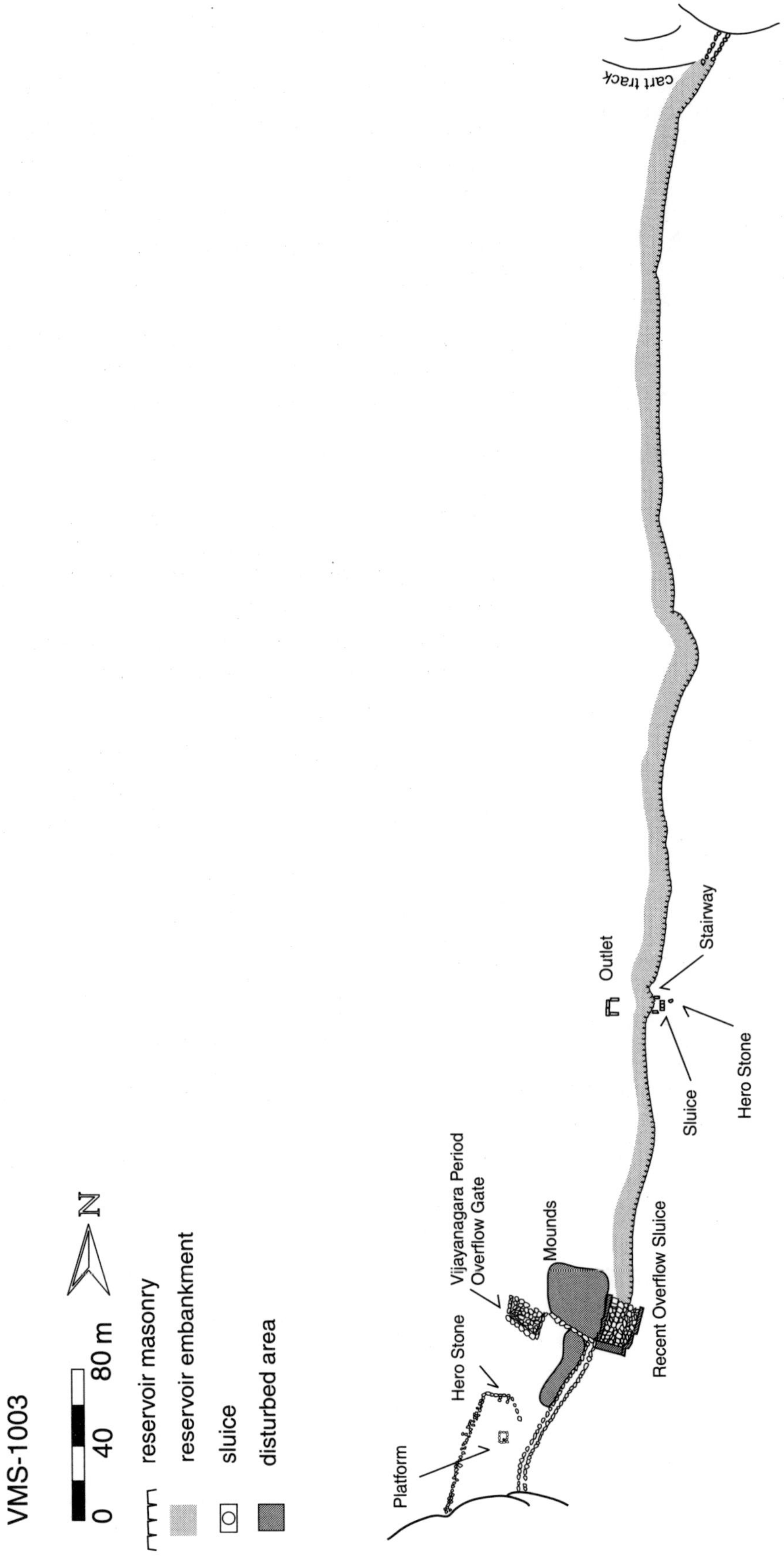

Figure 68. VMS-1003, plan.

Figure 69. VMS-1003, overview.

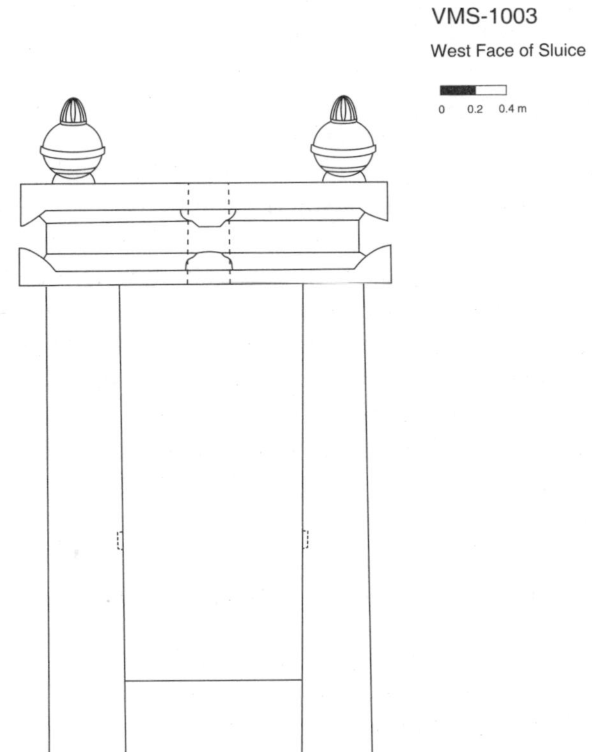

Figure 70. VMS-1003, elevation of sluice.

Figure 71. Hero stone in bed of VMS-1003.

the embankment to the east. The staircase is wide, about 5 meters, and is built of long dressed granite slabs. The stairs extend out beyond the embankment, nearly touching the sluice gate. The sides of the staircase are defined by simple balustrades of stacked blocks. Both stair and sluice are now heavily overgrown.

The sluice itself is of moderate size, 3.5 to 4 meters high. All its elements are well shaped and dressed. The uprights are square in section. The outlet has been covered over with silt (5 to 10 centimeters deep), but the upright backing slab on the west side of the sluice is visible. The lower cross-bar is missing, although there are square notches in the uprights where it was originally set. The lintel consists of a three-part moulding sequence containing lower and upper mouldings of the two-stepped with angled bevel type, each with central medallions (in a rough *makara-torana* shape) and corner quarter medallions. Like most three-part mouldings, these are separated by an unadorned granite slab that creates an inset vertical face between the mouldings. Atop the lintel are two finials, each resembling the "auspicious pot" motif (above). That is, atop a square base is a globular jar enclosed within a central band or ribbon, capped by a ribbed bud-like element, presumably a coconut. The overall form of this sluice is similar to those of VMS-1004, directly to the south, although it is much smaller in scale. The sluices of both VMS-1003 and 1004 are much larger, however, than most sluices with this moulding sequence, as noted above, and both are decorated with finials.

Near the southern end of the reservoir is sluice 2, an original *kodi* or overflow sluice. As discussed in Chapter 3, *kodi* are barriers that prevent water from flowing over the embankment when water levels are low, but which are lower than the embankment itself, allowing water to escape when reservoir levels are high. Formal waste weirs such as this one are generally well-reinforced with horizontally laid (and sometimes cemented) stone "aprons", protection against the erosive effects of flowing water which often forces a breach when it runs over less well-reinforced reservoir embankments. This overflow sluice is well defined by east-west walls on both sides. It is paved with rounded, well-worn boulders laid flat. The apron is 5 meters wide (east-west) and 15 meters long. One slab, evidently reused, has a weathered, pecked symbol of a type commonly associated with megalithic mortuary sites.

Associated Features

Lying in the reservoir bed *c.* 3 meters north-east of sluice 1 is a large slab with a carving of a male hero figure (Figure 71). He has a mustache, a round cap with a tassel (?) and is wearing a *dhoti* pulled up closely around his waist. Slung over his right shoulder is a sword hanging from a scabbard. His right arm is aloft and he is holding some small unidentified object in his right hand. His left hand hangs at his side; it is holding a large club. The sculpture is incomplete.

Near the southern edge of the reservoir is a wide (*c.* 25 meters) breach. In the sections of the breach are numerous ash layers, some artifact-rich, discussed above. Thus, it is clear that this end of the embankment was constructed of cultural debris, probably midden deposits from an Early Middle period settlement, already abandoned. This is rare, as most reservoirs are constructed out of sterile soil. Sluice 2 lies approximately 35 meters south of the breach. In this area the reservoir is in poor condition (it is only about 1 meter high here) and has been disturbed by a sugar cane field.

At the southern end of the breach an entirely new section of reservoir embankment has been constructed that runs to the east to meet one of the outcrops that defines the south side of the broad valley dammed by this facility. The fill of this newer embankment has been cut into and is built of artifact-rich fill and wall fragments from the pre-existing Early Middle period settlement.

The Walled Settlement of Ingaligi, VMS-1040

The occupied village of Ingaligi (Figure 72) lies to the west of reservoirs VMS-1002 and 1003 in a broad level area now covered with dry fields once supported by those facilities. These days Ingaligi is an out-of-the way place, situated not

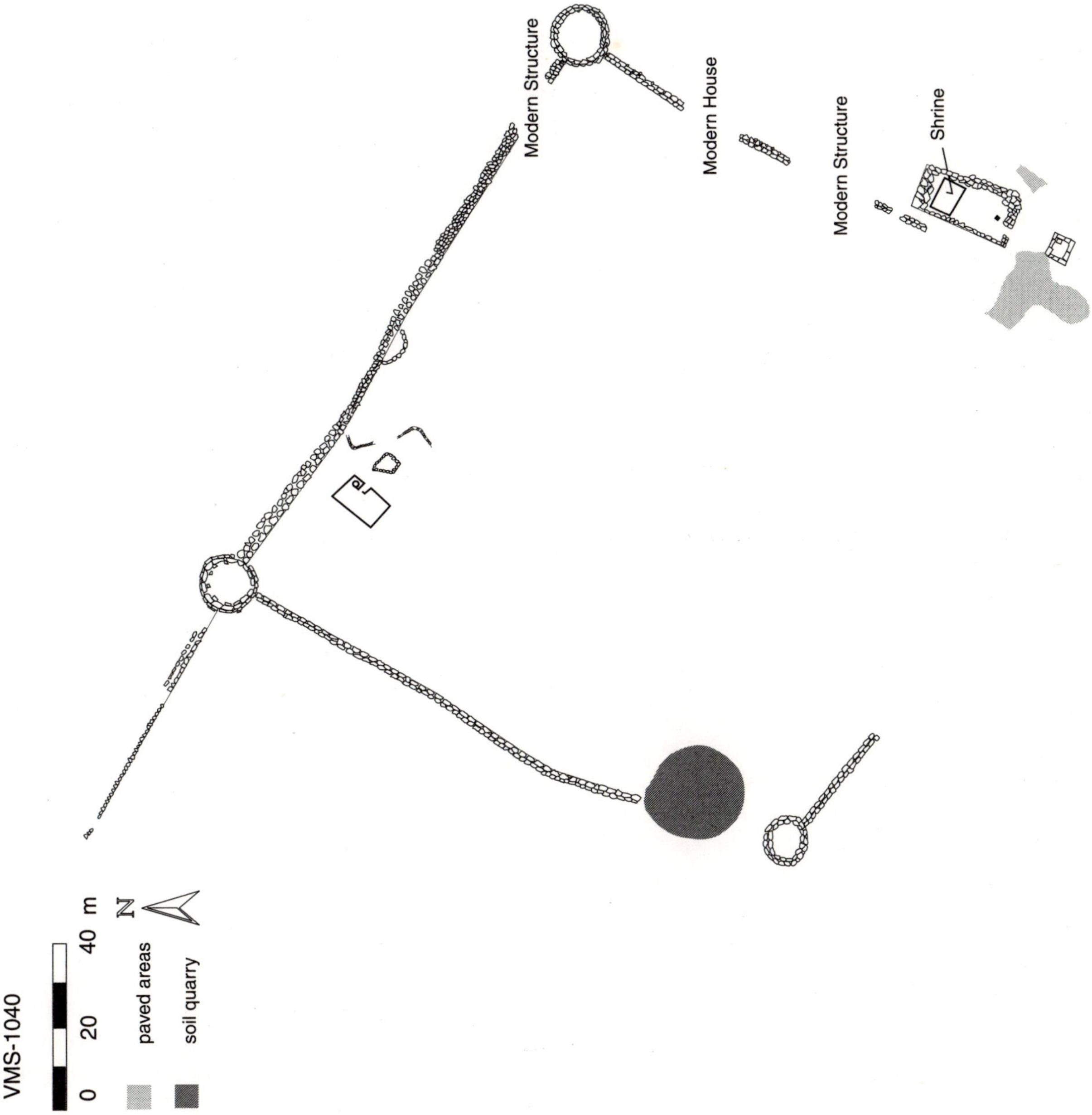

Figure 72. Map of Ingaligi, VMS-1040, with fort walls.

on the main east-west road through the valley but on a small road spur. The village itself consists almost entirely of recent structures but the whole is surrounded by a substantial set of fortification walls, VMS-1040. The construction date of these walls is unclear; they may date to the Vijayanagara period or somewhat later. The round bastions associated with the walls are sometimes said to be characteristic of "late" (i.e. seventeenth and eighteenth century) forts, but in fact there is a great deal of variation in form and formality of construction throughout the Middle period and into the Colonial period. My best guess is that the existing walls were built in the Nayaka or immediate post-Vijayanagara period, but it is also very likely that Ingaligi was first occupied during the Vijayanagara period when VMS-1002 and 1003 were built. Indeed, it may be that the older settlement under VMS-1003 is "old Ingaligi", following a pattern of village reconstruction and expansion common in the region where a named settlement may physically shift and even be abandoned for some time while retaining its same identity.

The Ingaligi fortification is approximately square. The walls are constructed of unmodified and split boulders; the two wall faces are separated by a rubble and earth core. At their maximum height, the fortification walls now reach 12 courses high (nearly 3 meters). Bastions (9 meters in diameter) are integral to the walls. There is no bastion in the southeast. Recent buildings encroach on the wall in various places (some are obviously made out of wall elements); this disturbance may account for the lack of a southeast corner bastion. However, there is a plastered entranceway into the village in this corner now; some well-worn cobblestones suggest that this entrance is not recent. Thus, there may have originally been a gate or other entrance at the southeast corner. Just east of the southeast corner is a walled enclosure 15 meters on a side. A few of the stones that make up these walls have Vijayanagara-style quarry marks, which although common on Vijayanagara-period structures, may also be indicative of quarrying techniques as late as the nineteenth century. In our experience thus far, however, when such marks occur on dated structures, those were invariably built between the fourteenth to sixteenth century. Nevertheless, is possible that such quarry marks may also be found on Nayaka-period masonry. Inside this enclosure is a recent temple with, however, what appears to be a Vijayanagara-period lamp column, topped by a moulding element with corner quarter medallions.

Ingaligi is a living settlement, part of what makes it difficult to trace its long history. That it was present in the late nineteenth century is indicated by Kelsall in his 1872 *Manual of the Bellary District.* Describing the roads of Hospet *taluk* (an administrative unit below that of the district), he notes (1872: 15), "The Bellary-Dharwar road enters the taluq near Ingligay and passes through Hospett." Ingaligi is also present on maps and documents (e.g. Government of Mysore 1969: 395) throughout the twentieth century, suggesting an unbroken occupation.

Roadside Fort and Settlement, VMS-6

Perched atop an isolated granite outcrop along the road leading up from the Daroji Valley toward Mallapannagudi is a small Late or post-Vijayanagara fort (Figure 73). A walled settlement is nestled up against the base of the outcrop on its northern and eastern sides. In addition to the fort and settlement, there is a large step well on the east side of the road, near VMS-1000, and approximately 50 meters east of the settlement. A somewhat isolated, smaller rock-cut well is located in a heavily disturbed area immediately north of the settlement.

Fortification

Built onto the crest and northern slopes of the high granitic hill is a heavily-walled enclosure whose walls incorporate 5 round bastions. Like similar structures, this fort is somewhat irregular in plan, following the contours of the hill and incorporating large boulders into its walls and foundations. Within these constraints, however, the basic square plan is evident, a plan so stereotypical that the Survey of India uses it as the generic map symbol for a fort. The total enclosed area is 1,130 square meters. The granite and basalt hill slopes down from

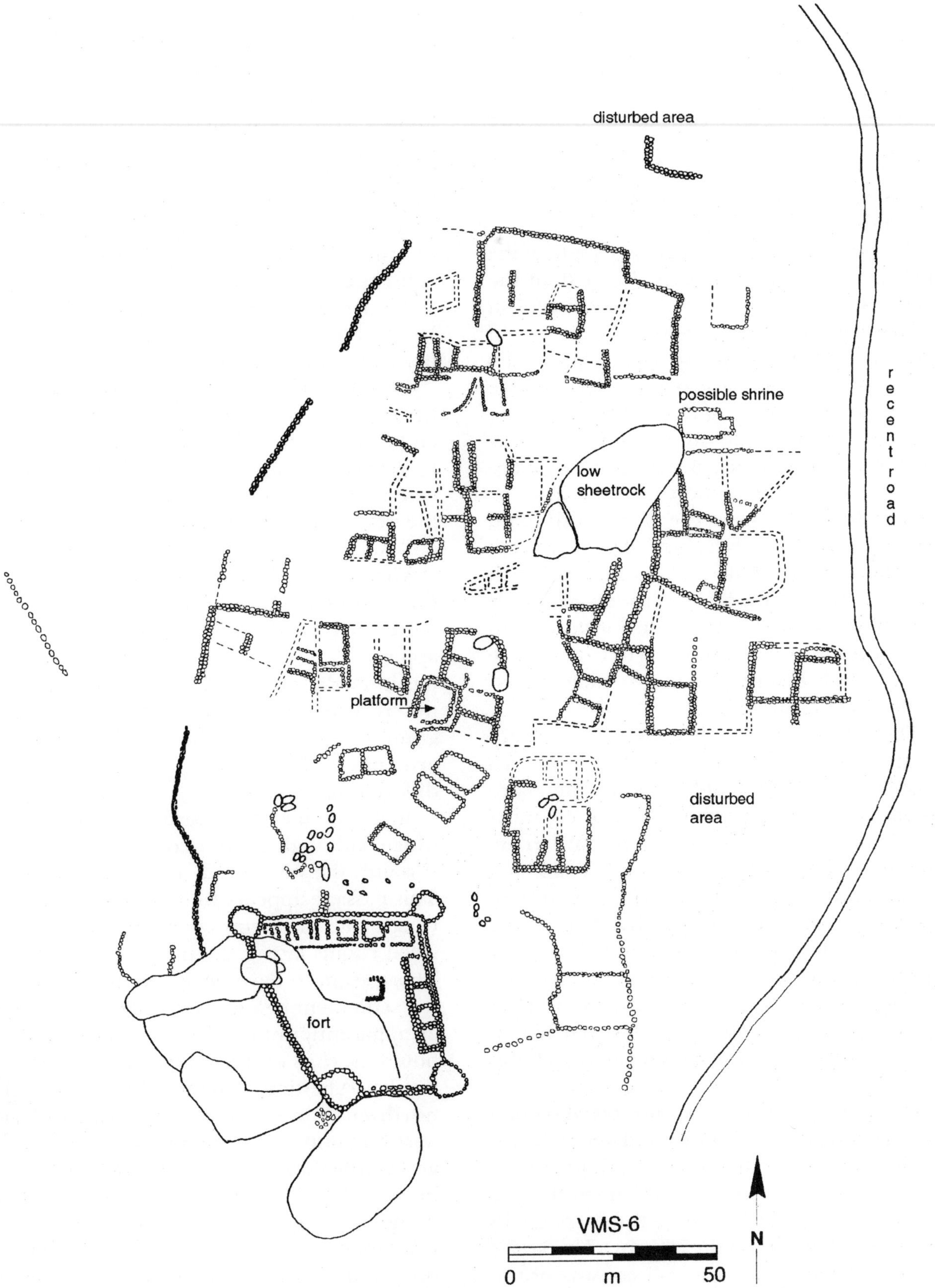

Figure 73. VMS-6, overview.

southwest to northeast, so that the western walls and bastions occupy the highest ground – the top of the southwest bastion is approximately 12 meters higher than the northeast bastion. The central part of the enclosure is built on what may be fill and consists of a sloping earthen surface with scattered boulders. This area includes possible foundations of 1 to 2 rooms. Several small rooms abut the north and east enclosure walls.

The northeast corner and eastern side of the enclosure are 1 to 2.5 meters lower than the central area. This side of the fort consists of an area of fairly level artifact-rich fill, the top of which is only 0.8 meter below the top of the north and east walls; the ground surface outside those walls is 2 to 3 meters lower than the interior surface. Along the interior of the east wall are foundations of 5 or 6 contiguous rooms. The masonry construction of these interior rooms, in contrast to the outer walls and bastions, is comparatively insubstantial. Except for some double-faced walls abutting the north fort wall, most of the interior rooms have only foundation walls a single course wide (0.3 to 0.4 meter); these small structures were presumably brought to full height with rammed earth or wattle-and-daub.

The exterior enclosure walls of the fort are all similarly constructed, consisting of two masonry faces with a rubble and earthen core containing a high concentration of ceramics and iron slag. The masonry is built from medium-sized and large unmodified and split boulders with abundant small chinking stones. In all cases the walls abut, rather than being bonded with, the bastions they adjoin. The south enclosure wall (1.5 meters wide) runs up a steep slope from the southeast to the high southwest bastion. Although this wall is now about 1 meter high, wall fall suggests that it was once higher.

Except for a short, poorly-preserved section of wall between the northwest and west bastions, the long western wall of the fort is higher than either the east or north walls in both base elevation and wall height (3.9 meters on its exterior, 2.7 meters on the interior). Unlike the other fort walls, the west wall consists of two distinct sections, the lower foundation courses creating a solid base for the upper courses. These may represent distinct construction episodes, but it is equally likely that the greater height of this wall necessitated this two-part construction. Viewed from the exterior, the lower 2.9 meters of the wall are made of large, regularly-coursed split and unmodified basalt boulders. This lower section does not appear to include an earthen core; three courses (1 meter) of this lower section are visible from the interior. The upper portion of the wall consists of 5 to 6 courses of small to medium-sized, irregularly-coursed granite boulders. Unlike the lower portion of the wall, the upper portion incorporates an artifact-rich earthen core.

Like the south wall, the north wall also climbs the ridge, sloping gently upward to its western end. The north wall survives to a height of up to 2.4 meters (up to 9 courses visible on the exterior); the ground surface inside the fort on the west is much lower relative to the surviving wall heights than it is on the east.

Viewed from the exterior, the east wall of the fort is preserved up to seven courses (*c.* 2.15 meters). Like the rest of the fort, this wall appears to have been built of whatever stone was immediately available; the division of this outcrop between darker basalt and lighter granite has resulted in the northern and southern ends of the east wall being constructed of different material.

In the middle of the north wall is an opening which, although in poor condition, was almost certainly the sole entrance into the enclosure. This passage appears to have been flanked by rough gate platforms consisting of two three-sided rooms facing the passage on each side. There seem to have been several routes from the settlement below up to the fort. One path, an apparently unmodified route between large boulders, runs west from the gateway, past the northwest bastion, and then slopes moderately northward down to an area just inside the western limits of the settlement. A second wide and gently sloping path leads down to the east between large boulders, passing the northeast bastion. Finally, immediately north of the gate is a small, steep, and narrow track leading directly down to the settlement. The latter may have been used as a kind of short cut when goods were not being transported up or down.

The five bastions (6.5 to 8 meters in diameter) are all approximately round, consisting of an outer masonry facing and a solid earthen core. The double-faced masonry is built up of irregular courses of medium to large split and unmodified granite and basalt boulders. Chinking stones are abundant. That some masonry has been lost is clear from the fact that the packed earthen cores are generally about a meter higher than the top of the masonry; both the southeast and northeast bastions have crumbled on their exterior sides. These two bastions now rise to a maximum height of *c.* 2.1 and 2.7 meters, respectively. Although occupying the highest ground, the southwest and west bastions (the latter is built atop a large boulder and is the only one not on a corner) are actually the shortest (*c.* 1.8 and 1.3 meters, respectively). The northwest bastion is the tallest and best preserved of the five, surviving to a maximum height of *c.* 6.1 meters. This bastion was constructed on a gentler slope than the others and also has a projecting footing consisting of three to four courses of large split and unmodified boulders.

Settlement and Well

The walled settlement lies at the base of the outcrop supporting the fort and covers an area of 135 by 130 meters or a little more than 1 hectare. There are at least five large, irregular blocks of masonry-walled structures, each probably representing several individual, agglutinated houses. It is difficult to say whether or not this was a specialized military location, occupied primarily or solely by soldiers, or whether it was a village with its own small fort. The fort itself has some resemblance to both the Ingaligi and Papinayakanahalli forts, both of which are now on the edges of small, primarily agricultural villages and it may be that this was a similar village, associated with reservoir VMS-1023.

Walls in the settlement are generally constructed of small to medium cobbles and some split boulders, and usually have two faces separated by a narrow earthen core, the latter often artifact-rich, suggesting some remodeling of a previously-occupied place. The settlement has at least 50 rooms and a number of enclosed courtyards as well as a central round bastion, a small platform and some isolated rooms near the fort, walled areas (perhaps pens or corrals) in the southeast, and a possible shrine in the northeast. There are two or three east-west routes through the settlement and one larger, north-south path. The overall layout is quite irregular and many walls are abutting, suggesting accretional growth rather than a single episode of construction.

Beginning with the area near the fort, we may note a walled passage, lined with a single row of cobbles, that leads up to the fort. Near the foot of this passage and slightly northeast of it is a rectangular structure with cobble walls built over large boulders; unlike other rooms in the settlement, this has no central depression, suggesting a platform. Platforms often occur near roads and gates and may have been either commercial and/or administrative. This structure does not seem to be a shrine, the other kind of building commonly constructed on a platform.

East of the fort are several large walled areas, much larger than other rooms and probably either animal pens of some kind or else enclosures containing the haystacks and manure piles of individual households, common even in contemporary villages. The area to the east of these enclosures is heavily disturbed. North of the enclosure is a single compact, square block of rooms, none of which are obviously courtyards. North of this is a long, east-west oriented, agglutinated block of structures that seems to stretch all the way across the settlement. It is quite wide (more than 50 meters) at its eastern end and narrower at its western end. This irregular row of structures contains between four and six individual blocks of rooms. Some of these show a differentiation of room size that suggests internal courtyards, a pattern also evident today. Immediately north of one of the eastern blocks of rooms in this long row is an isolated structure which may be a small shrine. This structure is rectangular with a narrow projection on the east, a common shape for a small temple with an antechamber and sanctuary. There is, however, no image here nor does the deity face east, the normative direction for a shrine (we have, however, documented very many temples that do not conform to this rule). Built into this row of structures, near the middle of the settlement, is a heavily-walled bastion, 5 meters in diameter, built on a prominence that rises nearly 3 meters higher than the rest of the settlement. This round bastion has a double row of encircling masonry and commands an excellent view over the settlement.

North of the long, east-west row of structures are two additional structural complexes, perhaps representing two large houses, each with several room and courtyards. There is a disturbed area on the north end of the settlement which may have contained additional rooms. The whole settlement seems to have been walled, though only remnants of the enclosure walls survive on the west and north. These are built of small cobbles, just like the walls of the settlement itself and there is some possibility that they are not original, but have been set up by local farmers interested in clearing rocks from their fields. If this is the case, then the settlement may have originally been slightly larger.

The artifacts found on this settlement include a large number of earthenware ceramics, some of which appear to date to the Vijayanagara period and others which are clearly more recent. Iron slag was found in small quantities throughout the settlement, suggesting its use as fill material (cf. Morrison 1990). Several tuyere fragments were also found, indicating iron smelting or smithing; the majority of these were located in the northwest corner of the settlement. Other artifacts included glass fragments, pieces of ceramic water pipe, a ceramic oil lamp and incense burner, and an iron ring (0.10 meter diameter). Two block mortars, consistent with Vijayanagara forms, were also found, as were two cobble-lined pits. The reused columns and lintels in the well are the only evidence for formal architecture and there are no roof tiles (a sign of high-status structures, roof tiles being controlled by sumptuary laws), indicating simple thatched roofs.

Just west of the settlement, on the east side of the dirt road that apparently follows the route of the older road, is a large Vijayanagara step well (40 by 20 meters), square with a west-facing staircase leading down to the water (Figure 74). The masonry sides of the well are built of 37 alternating courses of granite blocks and slabs (some with Vijayanagara-style quarry marks), the upper courses gradually stepped back. This masonry incorporates some reused lintels and columns. The well is somewhat overgrown and the northern side is partially collapsed. On its south side a platform extends out from the side of the well. The platform is 16 courses high (i.e. beginning near the middle of the exposed south wall) and *c.* 2 by 2 meters, making a solid base for the two long granite slabs (1.5 meters long by 0.5 meter wide) whose narrower ends extend out over the water and which would have supported water-lifting devices.

From the west side of the well emerges a long, walled passageway that encloses at least 37 steps down to the base of the well, where is still water, now heavily overgrown with vegetation. The steps are built of long granite slabs 1 to 1.4 meters long, steps getting narrower as one descends. There is a landing five steps down from the top of the staircase. The west wall also contains several protruding slabs (1.5 meters long by 0.5 to 0.8 meter wide), much like the protruding slab steps one sometimes sees in reservoir embankments, that could have been used as steps when the water level was high.

At the top of the well there are small structures on both the north and south sides. The southern platform (3.5 by 3 meters) is enclosed within a double-faced wall built of two to three courses of cobbles and is elevated some 0.1 meter above the surrounding ground surface; it abuts the side of the well. The northern structure (3 by 3 meters) is defined only a single row and single course of cobbles; it is not elevated nor does it abut the well. There are several concentrations of highly comminuted earthenware sherds on each side of the well, including the overhanging platform.

The shape and construction features of the well clearly indicate its Vijayanagara-period affiliation. Note that it is located along the road as well as being adjacent to the settlement; as such, it may be that it predates the settlement

Figure 74. VMS-6, step well with fort in background.

Figure 75. VMS-1000, water channel.

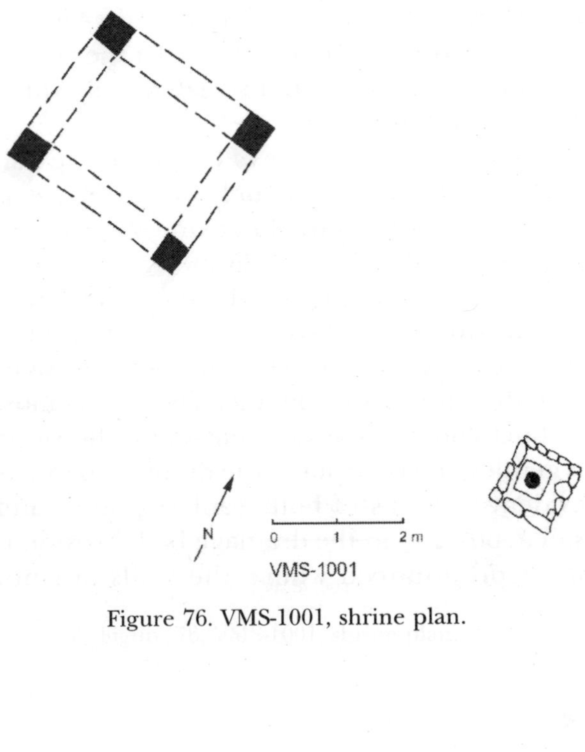

Figure 76. VMS-1001, shrine plan.

itself though certainly it would have been used by residents there as well.

On the whole, both the artifacts and architecture of VMS-6 suggest some Vijayanagara-period as well as later, post-Vijayanagara occupation. A small, contemporary shrine some 20 meters south of the fort is in active worship, as are two *naga* stones of uncertain age located in the northwest quadrant of the settlement. Post-Vijayanagara use may have significantly restructured the plan of the older settlement. However, unlike Ingaligi and Papinayakanahalli, this place, along the major Vijayanagara-period road leading north to Mallapannagudi, was abandoned. All of the forts in the Daroji Valley – VMS-6, Ingaligi, Papinayakanahalli, Daroji, and Toranagallu, are associated with opening or passes through the rocky Hampi-Daroji Hills. With the exception of Daroji, these all sit on isolated granitic outcrops in the valley itself rather than on the northern hills. In contrast, the fortifications of the Sandur Hills sit high atop those hills; there are no forts along its northern base.

Walled Drainage Channel, VMS-1000

VMS-1000 consists of wall segments that run along the edges of a large natural drainage channel, a feeder for the Kamalapuram Reservoir to the north that carries water from the Sandur hills. The 15 meters deep channel runs through a rocky gorge, its granite sides falling at moderate to steep inclines from the dry-farmed fields and rock-expanses above. To the west is the fort (VMS-6) and its associated well, which is linked to this feature.

Along the eastern edge of the gorge, the wall is distinct for approximately 30 meters. It is constructed with unmodified and split stones, forming a wall 0.75 to 1.25 meters wide with two faces separated by cobble fill. The wall would have reduced sediment inwash into the drainage as well as restricting access to the water by either animals or people. The wall is most distinct and well-constructed where the slope is gentlest. Erosion along the drainage banks is evident in terms of both bank exposure and soil deposition in the drainage bed. Erosion is most pronounced where the walls are not present, and where the slope into the canal is gentle. One the western side of drainage, near the fort and settlement, the "walls" are more substantial and are constructed by piling unmodified stones in a linear mound that is as wide as 2.5 meters in places. A total of about 80 meters of wall can now be traced along this gorge.

Another small drainage flows into the main drainage from the west-northwest; where the two waterways come together a series of quarried slabs form a paved passage for the water (Figure 75). The slabs are laid horizontally to create a flat surface *c.* 2 meters wide. The concentration of Vijayanagara earthenware ceramics is higher here, although overall artifact densities are low. The well that extends northwest/southeast from the slab pavement is different from many other Vijayanagara wells in that it is flanked by a kind of paved ramp formed by placing flat, unmodified stones along its mounded northern edge.

Shrine, VMS-1001

This small square shrine (2.5 by 2.5 meters, Figure 76) consists of 2 by 2 columns. The latter are square in cross-section, well-dressed but without any decoration. They carry plain rectangular capitals that in turn support granite roof beams and a flat roof of parallel slabs, oriented north-south. Inside this small shrine is an unusual and worn sculpture of a crouching, four-armed figure wearing a kind of loincloth – perhaps an ascetic? He is holding a drum in his uplifted right arm, suggesting an association with Shiva. This small *mandapa* has been recently modified by the addition of rubble walls. Facing the shrine to its east is a recently-built platform supporting a square sculpted block depicting two feet. This also appears to be recent. Although the shrine clearly dates to the Vijayanagara period, it cannot be assigned more precisely than that; we found no artifacts in association with this structure.

Reservoir, VMS-1023

West of VMS-1002 and VMS-1003, the western valley opens out as the northern granitic hills

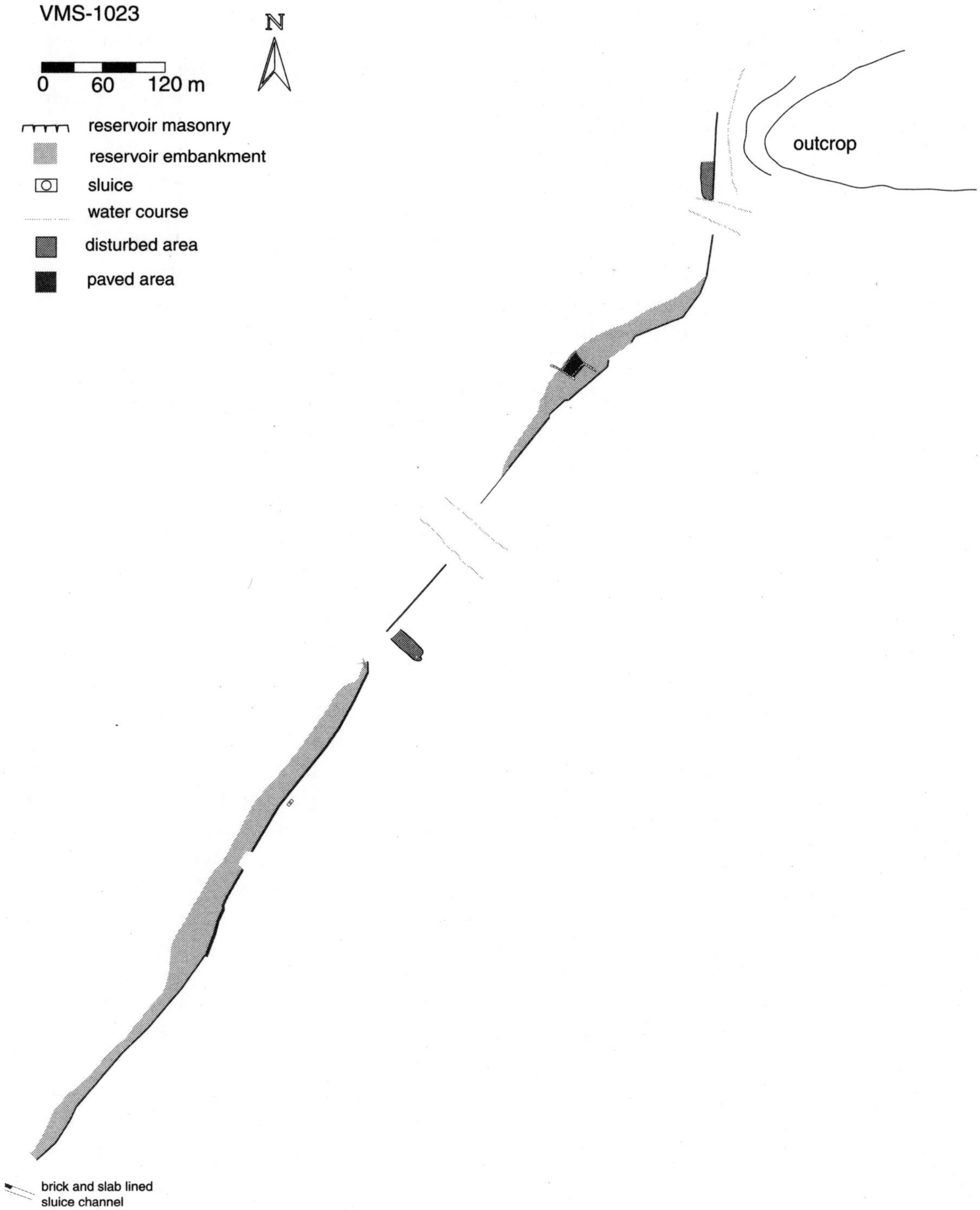

Figure 77. Reservoir, VMS-1023.

fall away, creating an open, less hilly corridor to the north. That this corridor was an important route of movement in from the south to the settlements west of Vijayanagara (Mallapannagudi, Kondanayakanahalli, Anantasayanagudi, Tirumaladeviyara-Pattana) is clear from the placement of VMS-6, a small fort and associated structures built on an isolated hilltop that guards this level area.

The southern end of this long embankment (Figure 77) has been completely destroyed by railroad tracks, which cover feature 1, a sluice channel. The northern end is also disturbed, and the original length of this reservoir was certainly greater than its present 860 meters. The embankment was at least 20 meters wide and the estimated area of water impoundment 1,000 by 325 meters. This reservoir draws water from a seasonal drainage channel coming down from the Sandur Hills; local topography suggests that overflow, if any, from VMS-1002 and VMS-1003 would have flowed to the north, just east of VMS-6, the hilltop fortification, rather than to the west and into VMS-1023. If this is correct, then VMS-1023, properly speaking, is not part of the western peripheral system, but is an independent reservoir. However, VMS-1023 hangs off the western end of the 500 meter contour which, despite minor but important variations, constitutes the base elevation of the entire Daroji Valley; as such, it provides a topographic counterpart to the Daroji reservoir, which sits at edge of the 500 meter contour at the eastern end of the valley. I thus include VMS-1023 here, even though it may never have received any effective overflow from reservoirs upstream. VMS-1002 and VMS-1003 seem to be associated with the settlement of Ingaligi, and VMS-1023 with the village of Sankalapura and perhaps also with the fort and associated settlement, VMS-6. Even if VMS-1023 never received any overflow from the reservoirs upstream, it was thus linked to them by patterns of association with nucleated settlements and by patterns of movement both downstream (west), along the strike of the Sandur Hills and toward the sixteenth settlement of Tirumaladeviyara-Pattana (Filliozat and Filliozat 1988: 13; contemporary Hospet), itself situated on the main route to points west (cf. Sewell 1900).

Construction

This reservoir is heavily disturbed, cut by railroad tracks on the south and breached in several places. At the southern end is feature 1, a sluice channel, marking the location of a former sluice gate. As sluice gates rarely occur at the extreme end of a reservoir, we may assume that any traces of the reservoir to the south have been obliterated by construction of the tracks. Dry fields straddle both sides and occur even on the top of the embankment here. The stepped masonry coursing on the east face of the embankment rises gradually to eight courses of medium-sized, unmodified boulders. The masonry is covered with a dense mat of thorny scrub and much of it has been robbed to build field walls. The original height of the embankment is unclear. Approximately 80 meters north of feature 2, a second sluice, this one with an existing gate, the embankment has been almost completely destroyed by stone and earth removal. Atop the embankment and about 200 meters from the present northern end is feature 3, a series of walls (single alignments of unmodified boulders) defining a rectangular area that encloses a pavement. Further fragments of paving lie to the west. This may be a formal overflow sluice. If so, then VMS-1023 and VMS-1003 are among the few reservoirs besides the Kamalapuram reservoir (VMS-231, Morrison 1995a) that have such formally constructed waste weirs. Alternately, and more likely, this walled rectangular area (walls extend beyond the rectangle, suggesting a feature that was previously more extensive) represents some other kind of feature, especially considering that ceramic densities are much higher in this area, which would not be expected of a waste weir.

The northern end of the embankment approaches a granitic outcrop. East of the northern end of the embankment is a deep, wide earthen channel that continues along the base of the outcrop for as much as 100 meters. This channel may divert water from the north into VMS-1023.

Outlets and Sluices

There are two and possibly three outlets through VMS-1023. Feature 1 is a remnant sluice channel 28 meters long, all that remains of a sluice gate and tunnel. The channel itself is wide, 1.5 meters wide, and 0.5 meter high. It is defined by granite slabs on all four sides; the entire slab-lined tunnel is capped with a long cover of bricks and mortar. At present, feature 1 is eroding out of the railway embankment, which has undoubtedly been partially constructed from the reservoir embankment itself.

Feature 2 is in better condition (Figure 78), consisting of an undecorated sluice gate some 8 meters east of the embankment about a third of the way up the length of the reservoir (from the south). No traces of a tunnel were recorded. The sluice itself is 2.5 meters high and is built of undressed, quarried granitic slabs. The entire sluice is set up on a low platform. The lower cross-bar, perforated for a stopper, is *in situ*, but the upper cross-bar is missing. A large quarried slab lies nearby, but its role in the operation of the sluice is unclear. There are traces of plaster on the eastern face of the southern upright. Remnants of white paint indicate recent ritual activity.

Feature 3 is the possible waste weir noted above. The paving stones consist of large, flat, unmodified boulders. As noted, the precise function of this feature is unclear, although it does seem likely that a facility of this size would have had at least three water outlets and that at least one of them would be located near its northern end. However, the high concentration of ceramics here appears to mitigate against the interpretation of this feature as a waste weir.

Associated Features

VMS-1024, a dense ceramic and lithic scatter 15 by 30 meters in size lies near the west face of the embankment of VMS-1023, approximately 60 meters south of feature 3. This scatter contains basalt flakes and sand-tempered redware ceramics that may date to the Iron Age or Early Historic period. As such, this scatter clearly predates the construction of the reservoir.

Sankalapura Village

This village, now something of a suburb of fast-growing Hospet, was clearly in existence in the early sixteenth century. In addition to the presence of several temples, there is an inscription (Patil and Patil 1995: 148) of 1513 which records the gift of that village by King Krishnadeva Raya to the temple of Kota-Vinayaka (Vinayaka in the fort, Patil and Patil 1995: 148).[15] A "kingly" figure sculpted on a column of sixteenth-century temple in Sankalapura may, in fact, be meant to represent Krishnadeva Raya (Figures 79 and 80).

The fort is said to be located by the east side of the Deveri road in Vijayanagara, which suggests this does not refer to VMS-6, which is located on the west side of the road and, in any case, was probably not conceived of as being in Vijayanagara. This is interesting, inasmuch as Sankalapura lies just below reservoir VMS-1023 and was undoubtedly associated with lands watered by this facility. Clearly, proximity alone did not determine how produce from a particular place would be assigned and this is simply one of many examples of the complex webs of produce rights (and consequent movement of agricultural products) that stretched across the Vijayanagara region, connecting sometimes-distant locations with one another.

NOTES

1. Our archaeological work has made it clear that the formal establishment of a settlement may not necessarily date its earliest structures; for example, it is clear that the Hospet area contained both structures and people prior to the sixteenth century (and see Kotraiah 1983). See also the inscriptions from Nilagunda, above. Nilagunda is located in one of the Early Middle period clusters of settlement to the west of Hospet; note that the village was (twice) given to Brahmins, even at a time when the largest temple was already located in an area of "old ruins". Note also the presence of a hero stone

Figure 78. Sluice F2, reservoir VMS-1023.

Figure 79. Kingly figures on 16th-century shrine, Sankalapura.

Figure 80. 16th-century shrine, Sankalapura.

and the importance of protection against cattle raiding.

2. The temple also contains inscriptions from 1549 and 1539 (Patil and Patil 1995: 20-1). Interestingly, the dedicatory inscription assigns (the revenues from) several villages in the Hastinavati-*valita* (an administrative division) for the support of worship and offerings in the temple. While the exact size and boundaries of this division are not definite, numerous inscriptions make it clear that it was located in the area around Kurugodu northeast of the main valley and extending at least as far west as Kurekuppa in the eastern part of the main valley. Kurugodu is more than 50 kilometers from Anantasayanagudi.
3. Although there are many Paleolithic sites in Karnataka and in southern India generally.
4. Very small blades are the basis of microlithic technology, common in the Mesolithic. However, blades continued to be produced in the Neolithic and it is not possible to say precisely when this blade core was manufactured.
5. Cist-circles are rings of (in this case) small, unmodified boulders (here 3 meters in diameter) enclosing a square or rectangular cist made of edge-set granite slabs, overlapping at the end. Excavated examples typically contain one or more burials (inhumations, secondary burials, and cremations are all known) as well as grave goods; the cist is usually deliberately – but not fully – covered over with earth.
6. Here I am, of course, using the period dates, even though radiocarbon evidence from VMS-110 seems to point to a primarily Early Neolithic use of the western valley. Obviously, we require much more chronological information than is presently available.
7. This wall is constructed of large cobbles and boulders, some split in half. It originally had two faces, though it has been somewhat disturbed by field clearing. At present, this long wall retains up to four courses, suggesting that this was quite a substantial feature.
8. This section also retains some worn cobbled road surface, indicating that at least this area near the temple was originally paved.
9. This is the name of the sixteenth-century settlement in Block S that filled in the area inside the outer city wall east of Kamalapuram and north of the Daroji Valley (Morrison 1995a). This settlement is near two very large temple complexes, the Pattabhirama temple (VMS-237) and VMS-142; note that donations moved almost 12 kilometers to the east and that this donation was recorded at a different temple than the one receiving the funds.
10. "For the portion of the divine food and the lamp-worship of the god . . ." (Filliozat and Filliozat 1988: 12).
11. All of these places are associated with major temple complexes, except perhaps the first. This is the name of a sixteenth-century town just west of and now underneath Hospet. The second is a variation on the name of the town described in footnote 7, while the third, Krishnapura, is the area associated with the great sixteenth-century Krishna temple, built by King Krishnadeva Raya to celebrate a military victory and to house an image of Krishna raided from that campaign. Note the close association of merchants with temple towns.
12. This sixteenth-century temple is located on a hill south of Hospet at the end of the western valley; it is still an important place of pilgrimage and worship (and see Balasubramanya 1991).
13. This would no doubt be from the great sixteenth-century temple to the reclining Vishnu (Anantashayana) at Anantasayanagudi, just east of Hospet along the main road leading into the city. There is a copy of this same inscription there (Patil 1997: 120, no. 415; Filliozat and Filliozat 1988: 14).
14. Note the mention of Bisilahalli pass in an inscription from Hospet (Patil and Patil 1997, no. 421) included in Table 5.2, above.
15. As noted, the gift of a village refers to the reassignment of revenues from that village.

Chapter Six

THE MAIN VALLEY: WEST

> This country wants water because it is very great and has few streams; they make lakes in which the water collects when it rains; and thereby maintain themselves. They maintain themselves by means of some in which there are springs better than others that have only the water from rain; for we find many quite dry, so that people go about walking in their beds, and dig holes to try and find enough water, even a little, for their maintenance. (Domingo Paes, Portuguese trader, written 1520-2; tr. Filliozat 1999: 61)

This chapter begins our consideration of the main part of the Daroji Valley, its construction as a human landscape, and the transformation of that landscape over time (Figure 81). In the western Daroji Valley we saw that relatively intensive if perhaps periodic use was made of the valley by Neolithic farmers and herders, people who marked specific places on the landscape through the creation of and additions to large and visible mounds of vitrified dung – ashmounds – and perhaps also through relatively more subtle markers such as rock-bruisings and painting. The places on the landscape so marked were apparently remembered or else their form resonated with later valley residents in some way, as a long period of apparent abandonment of the western valley, the entire Iron Age, was followed in the first few centuries BC (the Early Historic) by reoccupation of the precise location of this Neolithic settlement. This later use of the location of VMS-110 was, however, of a significantly different character. Although it is difficult to precisely characterize Neolithic VMS-110 – it was certainly a residential village or camp of a small group of people, perhaps families, though we cannot as yet say if it was occupied year-round or what relation it might have had to specialized procurement camps if it were indeed not such a place – Early Historic VMS-110 was certainly a very different kind of place, a specialized center of export-oriented iron smelting occupied by only a small group of people, probably the iron-workers themselves. What prompted these people to select this specific location is unclear; certainly both iron ore and quartzite were available here, but whether or not the superpositioning of settlement over a place (apparently) abandoned for two thousand years but with a continuing physical presence on the landscape was mere coincidence one cannot say.

Beyond this location, there is only scant evidence for use of the western valley during the Early Historic and succeeding Early Middle periods. The latter is marked only by a single remnant settlement, a settlement later razed to make the embankment fill of the sixteenth-century reservoir VMS-1003. This destruction not only makes it difficult to track agrarian practice in this period – fields in the vicinity of this isolated village probably relied on seasonal runoff from the small stream that would later be dammed to create reservoir VMS-1003 – but is in some sense also symbolic of the larger pattern of transformation in the valley itself that followed upon sixteenth-century agrarian and demographic expansion (Morrison 1995a), expansion coincident with the maximal extent of imperial control and with significant restructuring of regional settlement and land use well beyond the western valley. The western valley as whole, then, saw its most dramatic transformation during the latter part of the Vijayanagara period when an agrarian ecology involving the harnessing of monsoon runoff – the reservoir system – was established and when

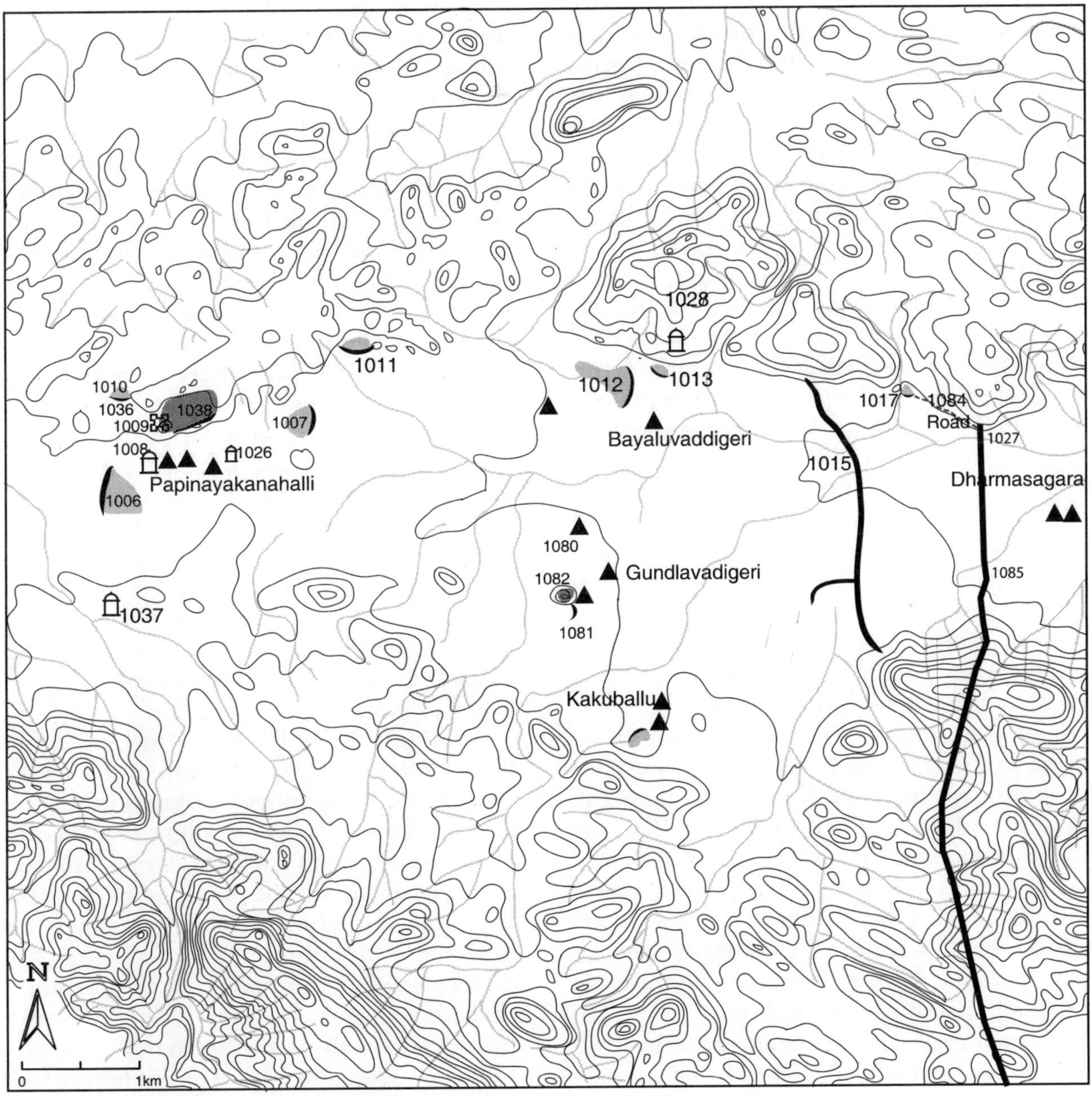

Figure 81. Map of the western part of the main Daroji Valley.

something close to the current configuration of rural villages was established. This pattern was again transformed during the succeeding centuries when villages armed and fortified themselves and reservoirs slowly silted in and were, one by one, abandoned.

The main valley is significantly larger than the western valley and its history is more complex. Like the western valley, observable anthropogenic landscape modification begins with the Southern Neolithic and, also like the western valley, the main valley bears the scars of repeated spatial restructurings; transformations of slope, runoff, sediment, transport routes, habitation foci, sacred places, vegetation, and spatial meanings that are complex, accretional, and ongoing. In this chapter, I continue the episodic characterization of time, blocking of large chunks of time into gross "periods". As crude as this practice is, this strategy may be justified by the present state of chronological work in this region and by the need to build comparisons across subregions. Although my analysis attempts to stretch and challenge our knowledge of landscape change in this part of southern India by considering very long expanses of time, it is also the case in the main valley, as elsewhere in the larger region, that any account of anthropogenic change must necessarily focus on the extraordinary expansion of reservoir irrigation during the Vijayanagara period, an expansion that changed the face of the valley in significant and enduring ways. Like the western valley, then, the main valley was dramatically (and irrevocably) transformed in the sixteenth century or Late Vijayanagara period, but unlike it, the main valley also bears the traces of a longer Vijayanagara-period history of settlement and rural land use. To this complex, local history we now turn.

The main valley proper begins near the town of Papinayakanahalli (Figure 81). What is now a rather quiet rural village was once the pivot of the Daroji Valley, a hinge at once hydrological – this is the place where the west-flowing watershed of the western valley and the east-flowing watershed of the main valley met – and, during the Vijayanagara period, social and ritual, this being the location of the valley's largest and most ornate temple complex and the place with the largest number of formal shrines.[1] For the centuries the Vijayanagara reservoirs were in use, a "period" of variable length and one continuing in some cases into the present, the distinction between the west and main valley, a distinction made on the basis of watersheds, is not merely of hydrological importance. Instead, the connectivity and interrelation of reservoir groups ensured that those using reservoirs and the lands in and below them were themselves linked in relations of interdependence and cooperation. Grouped reservoirs are, in some sense, the physical residues of shifting human social and political relationships; the physical looseness of the western valley reservoir system and its apparently shallow time depth contrasts with the main valley where reservoirs were more closely fit together and where there is a longer history of reservoir use, with evidence for at least one major reconfiguration of this agrarian landscape within the Vijayanagara period. Papinayakanahalli stands at the head of the main valley system and is served by no fewer than three reservoirs, all of them of considerable size. The settlement history of Papinayakanahalli is discussed below, but it may be noted here that its span of occupation extends from at least the sixteenth century up to the present.

Although the only clear evidence for pre-fourteenth century occupation of the western part of the main valley comes from the area around Kakuballu where there is a reported Neolithic ashmound, a locus of rock bruisings, and a hero stone, the presence of Neolithic, Iron Age, and Early Historic artifacts and habitations in both the western valley and the eastern part of the main valley (Chapter 7) suggests that this area must also have been in use during the three and a half millennia prior to the Vijayanagara period, if not longer.[2] The absence of Early Middle period settlements or structures in the western half of the main valley is notable and, in this respect, similar to the pattern of the western valley.

The fourteenth and fifteenth-century main valley was shaped by the same geological and hydrological factors as were later periods but the configurations of reservoirs, villages, and roads took a significantly different form than they would in the sixteenth century. The ancestral village of present-day Bayaluvaddigeri seems to have been positioned as a kind of node between a major trans-valley reservoir (VMS-1016) and a key transportation route leading to several northern settlements and, ultimately, the capital city itself.[3] With the construction of VMS-1015, a larger trans-valley reservoir, in the early sixteenth century and, perhaps somewhat later, VMS-1019, the Daroji reservoir, the landscape of the main valley was significantly transformed. Fields were submerged, reducing the area under some reservoirs and significantly affecting their associated settlements. Roads had to be realigned to accommodate new realities on the ground. The construction of very large reservoirs required considerable financial resources, and equally important, serious political clout. Obviously, the restructured landscape of the early sixteenth-century reflects, then, not only a new physical reality, but also a restructured political landscape, one which we can glimpse only dimly.

THE MAIN VALLEY UNITED AND DIVIDED

The main valley is *c.* 40 kilometers long and 1.5 to 6 kilometers wide. On the west, the valley is broad and open, narrowing as its runs gently downhill to the east; it then opens up again to accommodate its juncture with the broad Avinamodugu valley. The main valley extends east from Papinayakanahalli past the two successive trans-valley reservoirs and ends at the range of hills that separates the valley from the broad Bellary plains to the east. These hills, strongly fortified with a series of walls, are linked by the massive embankment of the Daroji reservoir, the culmination of the main valley system. In contrast to the western valley, the southern edge of the western half of the main valley is not formed solely by the steep escarpment of the metamorphic Sandur Hills. Here instead are several smaller granitic "foothill ranges" which fall between the valley floor and the Sandur Hills themselves. One might expect, then, there to be some reservoirs near the southern edge of this part of the main valley. Although I have not located any such facilities – the small reservoir near Kakuballu is recent – this area remains incompletely studied and the possibility must be entertained that I have overlooked some indications of settlement in this area.

The main valley constitutes a coherent hydrological unit and, as such, I reserve discussion of its irrigation history for the end of the following chapter. However, the valley is also bisected by a massive Vijayanagara-period fortification wall, VMS-1085, running all the way across the valley and even up into the Sandur Hills, a feature which effectively divided the valley in two parts and which funneled traffic through two small gateways, radically restructuring movement through the main valley. This wall, discussed in more detail later in this chapter, is used to divide discussion of the main valley into two chapters. As I discuss both here and in Chapter 7, chronological shifts in settlement and agricultural production in the main valley followed, to some extent, the spatial restructuring created by the construction of VMS-1085; thus this division also tracks change through time in the human landscape. This chapter describes the reservoirs and other cultural features of the main valley up to the early sixteenth-century trans-valley reservoir (VMS-1015) and what is, arguably, its protective fortification, VMS-1085. Chapter 7 considers the valley below VMS-1085, including the earlier trans-valley reservoir (VMS-1016), the Daroji reservoir, and associated villages, temples, and fortifications.

Routes of Movement out of the Main Valley

The valley as a whole is oriented roughly east-west; it served as a major corridor of movement through the region as early as the Neolithic. During the Vijayanagara period, the valley was also served by a major east-west road, traces of which (VMS-1084) remain in the western part of the main valley. The western Daroji Valley is smaller and relatively more open than the main valley, but even the latter had several routes running north to the city of Vijayanagara. Within the valley as a whole, Papinayakanahalli's position is pivotal, not only as its hydrological "continental divide", but also in terms of its location astride a route through the rocky granitic uplands that linked the Daroji Valley with Vijayanagara to the north.[4] A road, recently paved along part of its length, now connects Papinayakanahalli with Kamalapuram to the north. It is quite clear that this route was also in use during the Vijayanagara period, as there are numerous features lined up along its course (Morrison in press a). In this dry, rocky area north of the northern hills of the Daroji Valley, these features include a small containment reservoir and a well that may have provided water to travelers passing this way (Morrison 1995a). Further north, the road passes to the west of the large Halla *kere* (VMS-190), running directly past an impressive elevated temple (VMS-7) on its way to Kamalapuram and a gate in the outer city wall.

This well-defined roadway from Papinayakanahalli to the city of Vijayanagara was not, however, the only road to lead from the western part of the main valley to the city. Bayaluvaddigeri, which I will suggest was somewhat eclipsed by the sixteenth-century restructuring of the main valley, lay near the southern end of a second road running north from the Daroji Valley near the twin reservoirs VMS-1012 and 1013. This road linked the Valley with the walled Vijayanagara-period settlement VMS-365 and from there, to a road leading northwest toward the city of Vijayanagara. Quite a few structures on and near this road date to the first half of the Vijayanagara period (Sinopoli and Morrison 2006b), suggesting the importance of this route and this region early in the period. At least one reservoir near Bayaluvaddigeri, VMS-1012, appears to date to the fourteenth or fifteenth century. If the expansion of Papinayakanahalli is primarily a sixteenth-century (and later) phenomenon, as appears to be the case, it also seems likely that the growth of Papinayakanahalli owes its genesis both to the construction of a new trans-valley reservoir and to the decline of Bayaluvaddigeri, events which are undoubtedly connected.

Finally, there seems to have been a third north-south road out of the valley, this one emerging from a narrow pass through the Hampi-Daroji Hills into the main valley just east of Dharmasagara. This natural pass supports a dirt track today and the position of the Vijayanagara-period temple VMS-1032 near this road suggests the existence of an earlier route as well. It is, however, worth noting that this southwest-northeast oriented path brings one out of the valley at a point quite distant from the city of Vijayanagara, the place where the narrow Nallapur Valley (in Block T of the VMS survey area, see Morrison 1995a) emerges onto the broad Bellary plain. The constricted Nallapur Valley is a kind of reduced mirror-image of the Daroji Valley, running parallel to it on the north. The place where the Nallapur Valley opened onto the Bellary plain was certainly seen as a strategic and potentially vulnerable entrance to the city's hinterland, as indicated by the presence of a hilltop fort just south of this entrance (VMS-1060, see Brubaker 2003 for a description). The much narrower opening to the Nallapur Valley is mirrored on the south by the eastern entrance to the Daroji Valley, now mostly blocked by the Daroji reservoir itself and also guarded by a hilltop fort (Doravati fort, Chapter 7).

SETTLEMENT AND LAND USE IN THE WESTERN SECTION OF THE MAIN VALLEY

Neolithic to Early Historic

At present, the earliest evidence for human use of the western part of the main valley consists of Neolithic ashmound material reported by Foote (1916: 94) from the saddle and base of the small hill adjacent to the village of Kakuballu. Foote also located Neolithic-age artifacts from the top of the hill. I have not relocated this ashmound (nor has it been noted by other scholars since Foote) and thus cannot comment on it or its associated artifacts.

Not recorded by Foote were two concentrations of rock-bruisings, VMS-1083. As landscape features, rock-bruisings have a rather limited distribution. They take advantage of color differences between the darker, patinated exterior of granite or basalt boulders and their relatively lighter unweathered bodies. The pecking and pounding – accurately and rather poetically described in the literature as bruising – that creates the lighter-colored image removes some of the patinated lithic cortex and leaves behind a kind of negative-image. These figures are usually clustered; sometimes occurring in long rows or fields of small boulders. They range in size from about 0.10 meter to more than a meter; one such image near VMS-110 has some remnants of red pigment suggesting that they may have been colored in and thus may not differ so much from painted images (the latter typically red, white, or yellow) with which they are sometimes associated. Even if they were originally colored, rock-bruisings would not have been highly visible features nor are individual features very large. As such, they share certain visual and scalar characteristics with some of the more subtle megalithic features (cairns, stone circles, crack features, alignments) they are often found associated with.

The larger group of rock-bruisings consists of approximately 40 pecked and pounded images, light against the darker rock, in a style consistent with those associated with megalithic memorial complexes. This group sits atop a small pointed hillock of dark-colored rounded boulders, an eroded dyke, rising from the granitic outcrop south of Kakuballu. On this prominence overlooking the main valley, the majority of images are the enigmatic figures we have whimsically termed "popsicle stick" or "antennae-head" anthropomorphs although we have in fact no sense of what these images might represent. These typically consist of a circle above a vertical line, the circle often surmounted by three radiating lines (our so-called "antennae", though we are in no way asserting that this is what they represent). These figures vary somewhat in form and often occur in groups; although we have seen imitations of these forms in recent graffiti, their consistent association with certain kinds of megalithic features makes it clear that they are associated with those features. In addition to these figures, VMS-1083 also contains pecked human figures, a cobra, a buffalo with long horns, and a bull. The latter is humped and has triangles for legs – identical in style to the pecked bull near VMS-110. The human figures, stick figures with outstretched arms and three large fingers, are also similar in style to rock-bruisings and paintings we recorded near megaliths north of the Tungabhadra River. The most interesting image in this group (Figure 82) is a complex geometric design identical to some contemporary *rangoli* patterns pecked into the top of a small flat boulder. This design, *c.* 0.3 by 0.3 meter, is deeply patinated and sits adjacent to a much less heavily patinated (though still far from fresh) and more shallowly pecked "antennae head" figure. There is a second locus of rock bruisings atop the outcrop to the southwest consisting entirely of "popsicle-stick" figures.

It is difficult to date these features. Conventional wisdom places them in the Neolithic, which may be correct. Obviously, this would also (potentially) imply that some of the megalithic features they are spatially associated with may be contemporaneous. It seems equally likely that these figures were made during the Iron Age and/or Early Historic periods when painted images also came into vogue and even perhaps replaced rock-bruising. At present, realistically, we can only place these images some time between the Neolithic and the Early Historic. At Kakuballu we did not find unequivocal evidence for megaliths nor were there artifacts associated with the rock-bruisings.

The evidence from both the west and the main valley make it clear that the entire valley was in active use during the Neolithic and may have been an important corridor at that time. The nature of land use in the Iron Age and Early Historic is much less clear but it may be fair to say that human use of the western part of the main valley was much less intensive and perhaps less regular than it was in the Neolithic.

The Early Middle Period

In the western part of the main valley we have no evidence for permanent settlement after the Neolithic and prior to the Vijayanagara period. As discussed in Chapter 5, there appears to be a remnant Early Middle period village underneath reservoir VMS-1003 in the western valley and, as Chapter 7 will detail, there is a

Figure 82. VMS-1083, "Rangoli" design rock bruising near Kakuballu.

Figure 83. Kakuballu village, sculpture.

rich record of Early Middle habitation near Daroji. The western part of the main valley lies between these settlement loci and it seems probable that this region was used for grazing and collecting, if not for agriculture. The only material evidence that may come from this period (but which may also date to the Vijayanagara period) are two hero stones. The first is a three-panel Shaivite hero stone (Figure 32) lying near the side of the road west of Dharmasagara; this slab disappeared in the early 1990s. The other memorial is a hero/*sati* stone set up on a recent platform in the village of Kakuballu. The man, who has a side hair-bun, stands with a sword held aloft in his right hand, his left hand held up behind the sword. Standing next to him, on his left, is a smaller woman, also with a side hair-bun and a raised right hand, a posture thought to be associated with *sati* memorials. In this hand she is holding an unknown lobed object; her left hand hangs by her side. A smaller figure, possibly a girl, is shown in profile to her left. A small bident is carved to the right of the man and a sun and a moon flank a central medallion over the two figures. This sculpture consists of a single panel carved into a large granite slab (1.25 meters high). A sculpted Bhairava image, somewhat idiosyncratically styled, is also located in the village and is, like the hero/*sati* stone, in worship. This image may date to the Vijayanagara period (Figure 83).

Vijayanagara Period

During the Vijayanagara period, both historical and material evidence indicate the presence of two distinct clusters or foci of settlement in this part of the main valley (Figure 81). The first and earlier cluster is centered around Bayaluvaddigeri and the road leading north toward the city of Vijayanagara that emerges into the Daroji Valley just west of that village. Bayaluvaddigeri, like Papinayakanahalli, the focus of the later cluster of features, is served by several reservoirs and there is evidence that Bayaluvaddigeri itself was occupied some time during the Vijayanagara period. Furthermore, Bayaluvaddigeri sits some 5.5 kilometers west of the earlier trans-valley reservoir, VMS-1016, far enough back from its water-spread to have avoided potential flooding or waterlogging. The settlement deriving the primary benefit from VMS-1016 would, however, have been VMS-109. This early cluster may date to the fourteenth and/or fifteenth century. The second and later cluster of settlement in the western part of the main valley was focused around Papinayakanahalli and appears to date to the sixteenth and seventeenth centuries. Papinayakanahalli lies 5.7 kilometers west of the early sixteenth-century trans-valley reservoir, VMS-1015. However, as in the earlier settlement configuration, another village, Dharmasagara, and not Papinayakanahalli was in position to farm the lands watered by that huge reservoir. I suggest that the massive fortification wall dividing the main valley into two parts (VMS-1085) was built in the Late Vijayanagara period in conjunction with VMS-1015 and that it served, in part, to protect the rich fields watered by this massive reservoir.

The following discussion is organized spatially rather than chronologically, beginning with the western end of the main valley. This description continues into the next chapter where I sketch an overview of the land use history of the main valley as a whole, including the important area around the Daroji reservoir. At the end of Chapter 7, I will attempt to untangle the complex history of the main valley; however, in the following sections we encounter the valley as a contemporary observer would, with material constructed at disparate times jostling together, overlapping, and as it always would have been, existing in various states of use, repair, and abandonment.

Restricting ourselves for the moment to the western part of the main valley and its two temporally-distinct clusters of settlements and other features, as noted, the western, Papinayakanahalli cluster appears to be later but as there is also substantial temporal overlap between these two clusters (Bayaluvaddigeri was never abandoned), I thus follow topography rather than my postulated chronology. The first cluster of structures related to Vijayanagara-period occupation of the main valley that we encounter is that centered in and around Papinayakanahalli. Papinayakanahalli is close to five reservoirs and lies at the foot of a low pass through the outcrops toward the city of Vijayanagara. The contemporary village lies just adjacent to a Vijayanagara-period temple and a small fort; two other shrines are found nearby. Of those structures that can be dated, all appear to have been constructed in the sixteenth or seventeenth centuries. Note that the larger temple complex is (nominally) Vaishnavite and is located in the village while the two smaller, Shaivite shrines sit outside. A third Shaivite shrine lies south of the village, but this is an Early Vijayanagara structure.

Of the eleven inscriptions located in the main valley, five are associated with the Papinayakanahalli cluster (Table 6.1)

The first two are found in the Ankalamma temple, VMS-1008, on the western edge of Papinayakanahalli. The third is the inscription of AD 1519 built into reservoir VMS-1015 discussed above, and the fourth is a short but as-yet-untranslated inscription on the foundation of the shrine VMS-1026, just east of Papinayakanahalli. One of the Papinayakanahalli inscriptions, dated to AD 1532, describes a sale of land near Nidugula (also known as Apinayakapura) for the support of a particular ritual service for the goddess Ankalamma of the temple (Patil and Patil 1995: 147; Gopal 1985: 189). The land in question is described as part of a *sarvamanya-agrahara,* a tax-free settlement of Brahmins (Patil and Patil 1995: 147). The second inscription is dated AD 1742 and describes the grant of the village Madinayakanahalli as tax-free gift to an individual (Patil and Patil 1995: 147; Gopal 1985: 190). The Bayaluvaddigeri inscription dates to the mid-fifteenth century, a period with few inscriptions overall. It is not clear if the Annalapura of the text refers to Bayaluvaddigeri itself or to some other place.

Fort, VMS-1009

This small fort (Figure 84) is built atop an outcrop north of the village of Papinayakanahalli. The outcrop is part of the northern hill range that borders the Daroji Valley, but it extends further south and is slightly higher here than are adjacent formations. This outcrop, further, is situated some 100 meters

Table 6.1: Inscriptions from the main valley, western half, Vijayanagara period

Location	*Context*	*Date*	*Summary*	*References*
Papinayakanahalli	on a column in the Ankalamma temple, VMS-1008	AD 1532, Thursday 1 August	refers to a sale deed of land at Nidugula, also known as Apinayakapura, a *sarvamanya-agrahara* for the *amritapadi* services of the goddess Arugondala Ankalamma. The land was sold by the sons of Talari Timmi-nayaka.	Patil and Patil 1997, no. 446; *ARSIE,* 1922-3, no. 744 of 1922; *SII,* XVI, no. 99.
Papinayakanahalli	on a slab set up in the village	AD 1742, Monday, 19 April	records the gift of the village Madinayakanahalli as *umbali* to Kaviraja's great-grandson.	Patil and Patil 1997, no. 447; *ARSIE* 1922-3, no. 745 of 1922; *SII,* IX ii, no. 699
VMS-1015	built into a reservoir embankment	AD 1519, exact date not yet calculated	see above	this volume.
VMS-1026	basement of a shrine	unknown	not yet recorded or translated.	None.
Bayaluvaddigeri	slab set up in recent Anjaneya temple	15th century on paleographic grounds	refers to the place Annalapura constructed by Hittala Bagila Mallaraja in the name of Annaladevi, queen of Devaraya II.[5]	Govinda 2000: 70-1.

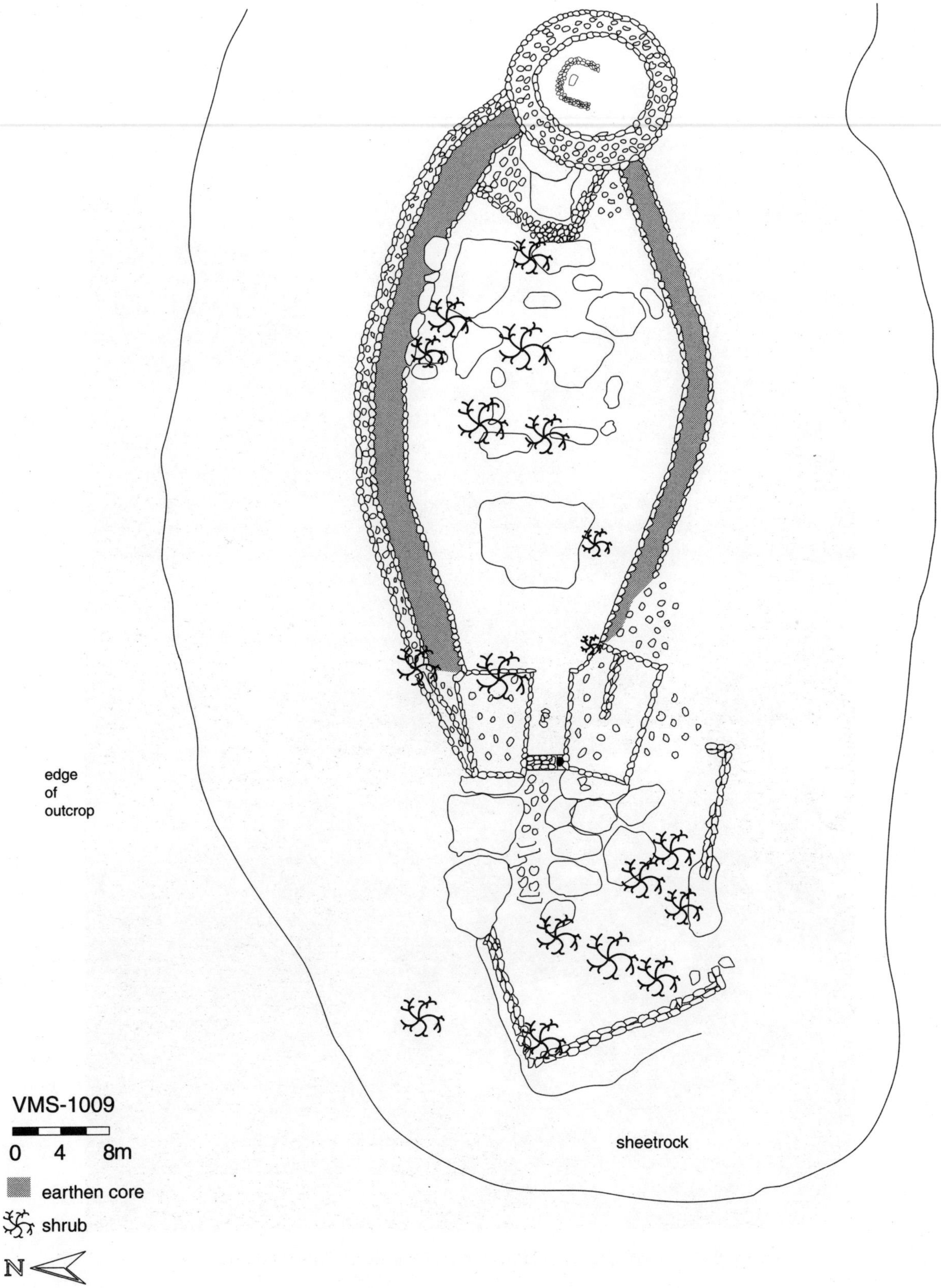

Figure 84. Plan of fort near Papinayakahalli, VMS-1009.

Figure 85. Gateway of fort, VMS-1009, looking over VMS-1008 and valley.

or so to the east of the narrow pass in these northern hills that is spanned by the reservoir VMS-1010 and leading north to the city of Vijayanagara. It is well situated, then, to oversee this road connecting the main valley with the city. The dry fields around the base of the outcrop contain a sparse scatter of earthenware ceramics, as does the earthen fill in the fort walls, suggesting that the construction of the fort postdates the inception of Vijayanagara-period settlement in the region. As fill dirt is rarely moved very long distances, we may further suggest that the occupation of Papinayakanahalli itself predates the construction of the fort.

The fortifications themselves are relatively small, 60 meters northsouth by 20 meters east-west. If we allow a scant 2 square meters per person, this structure could contain a maximum of 45 people. The commanding view from the fort is from the top of a large circular bastion some 6 meters high on its northern end. This earth-filled bastion is solid, 9 meters in diameter with a 1.4 to 2.0 meters wide walls. The lower courses include several very large (1 to 2 meters long) natural rectangular blocks as well as smaller angular cobbles and medium-sized split and unmodified cobbles. The construction materials are primarily granite from the northern hills, but the structure also includes some quartzite elements of varying sizes, presumably from veins in the granite. A small number of metamorphic rocks from the Sandur Hills are also present. Coursing is extremely haphazard, with chinking stones stuck in between larger elements. Atop the bastion is a small (2.4 meters diameter) east-facing, C-shaped wall, apparently recent. This 1 meter high shelter is wrapped around a white-painted angular rock, a shrine, but not one in active worship.

From the top of this bastion one can see over the northern hills to the valley containing Blocks S and T of the intensive survey area (Morrison 1995a). To the west, the valley and pass containing VMS-1010 is clearly visible. It is, however, the view over the main Daroji Valley itself – to the south, east, and west – that is the most striking. On the south, the doorway of the fort (Figure 85) directly faces the temple complex VMS-1008. The actual entrance to the fort is on the east, the side facing the village and also the most common direction for temples to face.

To the south of the high bastion, on a slightly lower terrace (2 to 3 meters lower) is an oval-shaped ring of walls that abuts the bastion. These walls are similarly constructed (two masonry faces with earthen cores) and although they abut the bastion, they appear to be contemporaneous with it. Like the bastion, the walls also incorporate some natural outcropping boulders. Within this ring of walls and near its northern end is a small footing wall that stabilizes the bastion. The ground inside the ring of walls is sloping and uneven, containing several large boulders, suggesting that there was no consistent or intensive use of this space. Artifact densities in this walled area are consistent with those of the walls and may be eroded from the wall fill. The western wall faces the most gentle slope of the outcrop, and is wider than the eastern wall which is protected by a steeper rock face. The western wall is constructed of two abutting parts, each consisting of masonry faces separated by a earthen core. The total width of this double wall is *c.* 3 meters.

On the southern end of the ring of walls are two roughly rectangular flat-topped bastions or high gate platforms. These appear to be bonded to the enclosure walls and define a narrow, north-south (1.8 meter wide) passageway that provides the only entrance to the upper walled area and the high bastion. The passage slopes down to the south and is somewhat silted in, perhaps with soil that once made the upper terrace more level.

The southern end of the passage contains a low doorway that faces the temple complex. The doorway is built out of 4 columns, each roughly dressed, square with octagonal insets. The columns defining the sides of the door are 1 meter apart while the paired columns of each side are separated by a gap of 0.7 meter. The columns are capped by long, quarried lintel slabs which are in turn covered by north-south oriented slabs over which smaller cobbles have been piled in the fashion of the other masonry of this structure. This doorway is now very low, *c.* 0.9 meter and is partially blocked. The original height of the door columns was, however, only 1.36 meters, so it would have been necessary for most people entering the fort to stoop over.

The passageway outside (to the south of) the door is quite steep and narrow, hemmed in by large boulders. Some small cobbles have spilled down this path, but there are still indications of steps. No more than one person at a time could have come up this path.

Some 8 meters lower than the doorway is a second walled terrace that slopes down slightly to the south. This terrace is contained by 1 meter-wide masonry walls similar to those found elsewhere in the fort. The entrance to this level was at a point just north of the southeast corner of this terrace, abutting a large boulder. A huge *Euphorbia* grows in this gap now, obscuring any details, but the opening is certainly no more than about a meter wide. Below this opening is a relatively steep expanse of sheetrock, some 50 to 60 meters long that defines the base of the outcrop.

The precise date of this fort cannot be securely established. The door columns are consistent with Vijayanagara construction forms, quarry marks, and stone dressing. They are apparently integral to the construction of the fort, so that if they are not re-used, this would suggest that the fort was built some time during the Vijayanagara period. However, and although this is less secure, the form of the bastions and details of the wall construction may indicate that the fort was built in the latter sixteenth or seventeenth century, perhaps later, possibly around the same time as VMS-6. The ceramics are consistent with Vijayanagara-period forms, but as noted, many of them occur in the context of wall fill and thus predate the construction of the fort to some extent.

Temple Complex, VMS-1008

This ornate temple complex (Figure 86) dedicated to the goddess Arugondala Ankalamma is situated in the village of Papinayakanahalli, at the foot of the fort. The temple complex appears to have been built in the fifteenth or early sixteenth century. It is not particularly remarkable, being in some sense a "classic" Vijayanagara temple complex; what is remarkable is its location in the Daroji Valley. This is by far the most elaborate structure in the entire valley, with the possible exception of the reservoirs themselves, and speaks to the centrality of Papinayakanahalli.

The east-facing shrine is contained within well-built *prakara* (enclosure) walls. Entry to the complex is through a formal gateway on the east side (Figure 87). Outside the gate, the road leading up to the temple (and some of the village streets to the south) is paved with large, rectangular, well-worn granite slabs. In the steps up from the street level to the level of the gate passage are several reworked elements, including an elephant balustrade and a large slab with a carved horse and hero figure. These are well worn, suggesting that they have been in place for some time.

The entrance gate itself is flanked by two platforms, each with 4 by 2 columns set on a three-part basement moulding (lower and upper mouldings are two-stepped with angled bevels and simple rectangular elements at the corners). The eastern, outer face of the gate is walled off with large horizontal slabs. On the northern platform, near the top, two rearing horses with male riders holding spears aloft are carved across two of these horizontal slabs. The opening of the gate is through a stone doorframe. This door has the goddess Lakshmi flanked by elephants (Gajalakshmi) carved over the lintel, and door guardians on either side. These are somewhat unusual; on the north is an Anjaneya Hanuman door guardian and on the south, a rather rustic-looking Garuda.[6] The gate platforms are quite plain on the interior, constructed of dressed blocks and slabs rather than a moulding sequence. The interior, west-facing sides of the platforms again are set on mouldings, which here have corner quarter medallions. The gate columns facing the passage are square in cross-section, with octagonal insets; those on the exterior are rough rectangular slabs. Simple cross-shaped capitols top these columns. The platforms are roofed over by a network of ceiling slabs topped by long roof slabs. The roof has simple angled eaves only on the east side.

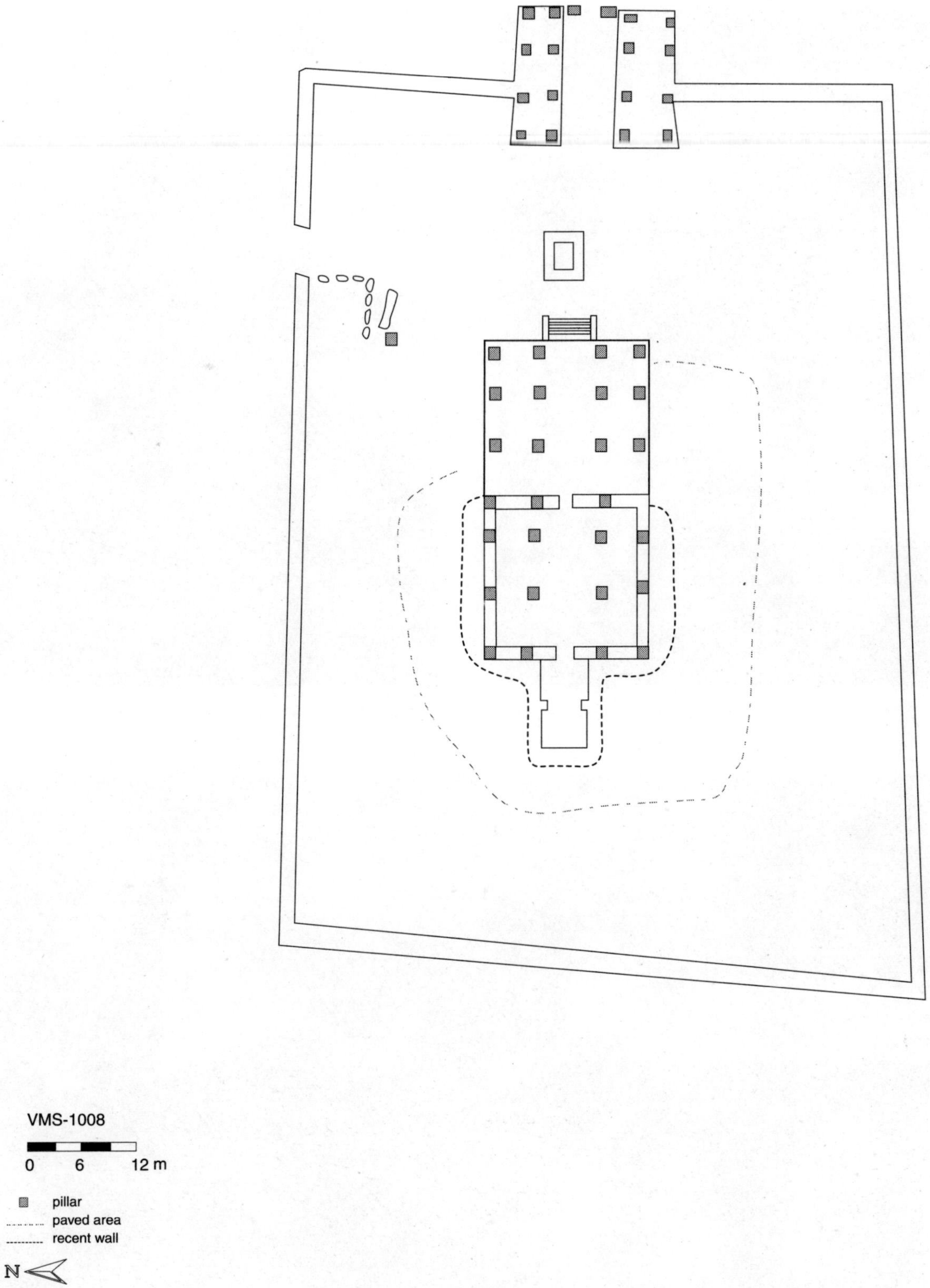

Figure 86. Plan of Ankalamma temple, Papinayakahalli, VMS-1008.

Figure 87. Entrance to Ankalamma temple, VMS-1008.

Figure 88. Superstructure of Ankalamma temple, VMS-1008.

Figure 89. Main shrine, Ankalamma temple, VMS-1008.

Carved on one of the interior columns of the north gate platform is a large tree, atop which is a seated monkey. There are a few etched game boards on the platforms.[7] The gate passage is paved, as is the inner part of the courtyard around the temple, but the level of this paving has certainly been raised. There is no superstructure on the gate.

Just inside the gate, facing the temple, is a modern lamp post and platform. The temple itself (Figures 88 and 89) consists of several distinct sections or rooms, all aligned along an east-west axis. The direction of entry is from east to west, moving from larger, more open spaces, to smaller, more enclosed spaces and from more accessible spaces to less accessible, increasingly sacred spaces. Typically, the outer, more open rooms are also more ornately decorated, with the sanctuary (where the deity resides) usually being undecorated. This temple has an outer (open) porch (*mandapa*), followed by an inner (walled) *mandapa*, an antechamber (*antarala*), and a sanctuary (*garbhagriha*).

The 4 by 4 columned porch on the east side of the temple is raised on a simple basement of 3 courses of slabs and blocks (the inner course being inset) rather than a moulding sequence. The low porch is reached via a small three-step staircase on its east side. The steps are flanked by balustrades with curving elements, but no animal depictions. The paving slabs of the porch have been recently replaced. The porch columns are square in section, with octagonal insets but unlike those of the gateway, those in the center are topped by rectangular capitals with cropped lower corners. On the edges of the platform, the capitals also have scroll-like elements and carved pipal-leaf decorations. Roof construction, like that of the gateway, consists of a lattice of granite roof beams that support a roof of long horizontal slabs. Simple angled eaves carried on protruding roof beams extend out from the porch on the south, east, and north. The top of the porch is capped by recent roof material. Several new plaster figures sit atop the porch and some recent plaster lions sit on the corners.

Entrance to the walled porch is through a door flanked by two recently-made Vaishnavite door guardians. The door frame is painted but appears to be undecorated. The walled porch consists of 4 by 4 columns of the same type as the outer porch. This room is walled in with long horizontal slabs. All the exterior walls have been covered over with a thick abutment of painted rubble and cement. This enclosed *mandapa* has a central ceiling of rotated squares.

The square antechamber is entirely plain, constructed of long slabs without adornment of any kind. Beyond the antechamber is a slightly smaller square sanctuary, also without decoration. The image inside the sanctuary appears to be recent. The *shikhara* (superstructure over the sanctuary and antechamber) is heavily plastered and painted but is clearly Vijayanagara in design. There are two main levels of niches and plaster figures topped by a two-part roof sequence. The whole is four-sided and while it does not resemble Early Vijayanagara *shikharas,* it is relatively simple and may be either fifteenth or sixteenth century.

The outer *prakara* wall of the temple is well-constructed of 4 to 5 courses of long, horizontal, dressed slabs. Although this wall has been extensively rebuilt, it is clear that it was quite a formally made structure. Some of these slabs are carved on the exterior with large fish and turtles, aquatic motifs often found on temple enclosure walls and temple tanks.[8] In addition to the eastern gateway, there is a small opening in the wall on the north side, near the eastern end. VMS-1008, known even today as the Ankalamma temple, is still in active worship. Although the central deity is the goddess, this temple also has a few Vaishnavite images and we thus might consider it at least nominally Vaishnavite. As I discuss in Chapter 7, there are very few Vaishnavite shrines or images in the Daroji Valley, a pattern which contrasts sharply with the region closer to the city of Vijayanagara.

Shrine and Step Well, VMS-1039

VMS-1039 consists of a small shrine associated with two step wells (Figure 90), one of which seems to be associated with it. These lie just to the north of the bed of reservoir VMS-1038 and just east of the fort, VMS-1009. Papinayakanahalli is less than 100 meters to the south.

Figure 90. Step well associated with shrine, VMS-1039.

Figure 91. Overview of reservoir, VMS-1010.

Figure 92. Sluice, reservoir, VMS 1010.

Like other structures in this area, the shrine and the rectangular well date to the Vijayanagara period.

The east-facing shrine is built over sheetrock. It sits on a low (0.2 meter) Vijayanagara-period platform built of well-fit square blocks, smaller than the more recent platform that surrounds it. The structure consists of an antechamber and a sanctuary, each two by two columns. The entire shrine is not more than 6 by 3 meters. Despite its small size, the walls are quite substantial, more than 1 meter wide and built of two faces of horizontal slabs connected by rubble fill. The front (east-facing) columns of the antechamber are somewhat unusual, rectangular in section with cruciform insets on the front, tapering toward the top. The antechamber has a ceiling of rotated squares with a central lotus medallion. A Vijayanagara-period Nandi sits inside the antechamber. The door to the sanctuary is flanked by pilasters; miniature columns which emerge out of large pots (*kalasha*). The sanctuary houses a *lingam.* In front of the structure are two *naga* stones and a broken Ganesha image. Traces of an old enclosure wall some 15 meters east-west by 9 meters north-south surround the shrine on the north, south, and west.

Approximately 25 meters to the south-east of the shrine is a square step well, apparently contemporaneous with the shrine. The north, south, and west sides of this 7 by 7 meters well are built of up to 7 courses of medium-sized rectangular blocks. The eastern side of the well is formed by outcropping rock. On the north side is a 1.5 meters wide stairway, now partly collapsed. Immediately northwest of this well are the remains of a double-faced wall. Some 10 meters to the north is a second, circular well. This more recent well is 4 meters in diameter, faced with up to 12 courses of small-medium angular stones.

As noted, this shrine sits within the bed of reservoir VMS-1039 and although heavy siltation into this facility has ensured that the shrine is now in no danger of flooding, presumably it was at one time seasonally surrounded by water. Its stepwell would also have been covered, though in the dry season this well could have taken advantage of the elevated water table created by the reservoir.

Shrine, VMS-1026

Both this shrine and VMS-1037 lie some distance outside Papinayakanahalli. VMS-1026 is a small, walled-in *mandapa* resembling a large granite box. It lies just north of the paved road and is east of the village in a dry-farmed field. This shrine is still in active worship although the majority of the structure was built during the Vijayanagara period. The basement is well-constructed of dressed slabs, a single course high. Built upon it is the platform floor which is also made of dressed slabs, each approximately 1 meter in length. The *mandapa* itself consists of 2 by 2 columns. Each corner column is joined by a wall built from long, horizontal slabs, three per side, each slab approximately 0.5 meter high. On the north exterior wall of the shrine there is an (untranslated) inscription on the lowest wall slab as well as a curved drain outlet (*pranala*) from the image basin.[9] The drain protrudes 0.5 meter. The east-facing doorway is defined by three granite slabs. There is a raised relief carving of rectangles around the doorway and a lotus on the lintel. Lying against the south side of the door is a slab with a relief of a *nagamma* (goddess with snake body). A single step leads up into the shrine which contains an original image basin. The latter now supports a recent image, apparently a *lingam.* To the north, resting against the image basin, is the fragment of a hero stone depicting a man on horseback, sword in hand.[10] The ceiling has three levels of rotated squares, creating a kind of truncated dome over the shrine. The flat roof is of Vijayanagara-style concrete; there may have been a more elaborate superstructure on the roof at one time.

Reservoir, VMS-1010

This reservoir (Figures 91, 92, and 93) lies to the northwest of the town of Papinayakanahalli and is located just west of the road that connects Papinayakanahalli with Vijayanagara via Kamalapuram. The road, which cuts through the eastern end of the reservoir embankment,

Figure 93. Reservoir, VMS-1010, plan.

runs through a narrow valley that opens into the main Daroji Valley at about the location of VMS-1010. The embankment may have once joined the outcrop on the east, an area that has also been subjected to recent quarrying. If this were the case, then VMS-1010 would have formed a barrier to movement along what was clearly an important Vijayanagara-era transportation route. There is no indication of a road running over the outcrops on either side,[11] so unless this reservoir predates the road, which is possible, it seems likely that the *bund* was never much longer than it is now and that the Vijayanagara road passed along the east side of this facility, just as the paved road does today.

VMS-1010 is well-sited to capture runoff from the long valley to its north, a watershed dominated by low granitic hills and with very little soil development and only sparse xerophytic vegetation. That the bed of the reservoir is partly silted-in is clear from the differential height of the embankment relative to the surrounding ground level – 1.5 meters on the north, in the bed, and *c.* 2 meters on the south. The reservoir no longer holds water but dry fields are planted in it every few years. The total length of the embankment is 125 meters; it is 10 meters wide at its broadest point.

Construction

The earthen embankment, quite straight in plan, is faced with stepped masonry on its north side. The latter is composed of up to seven courses of irregularly shaped unmodified and split boulders of a pink-gray granite. There is no masonry on the southern side of the embankment.

Sluices and Outlets

VMS-1010 has two outlets, a formal sluice near the eastern end and a waste weir near the western end. The sluice tunnel is still open and water still flows through it. When I first visited it in 1988, the sluice gate consisted only of two uprights – plain rectangular granite slabs, roughly dressed (Figure 92). Although the upper surfaces of these rather short uprights were uneven, they did not appear to be broken. No lintel elements were present, but there was a makeshift cross "bar" built of two sub-square blocks, each with a central hole, stacked atop one another and wedged in between the uprights with rubble. Neither was cut to fit the space it now occupies. The northern half of both perforated blocks had been broken off; the holes were closed off by a rectangular slab, set on edge, also wedged between the uprights. This makeshift cross-bar disappeared in 1996, signaling the end of efforts to regulate water flow through the tunnel.

The tunnel itself is still in use, as noted. Silt has been cleared out from around the sluice and in the tunnel; about .5 meter of silt has accumulated above the level of the tunnel near the sluice. The tunnel outlet is clearly visible on the south side of the reservoir. The tunnel itself is made in the usual way of upright slab sides, a slab floor, and a slab roof, all covered over with cement. The outlet emerges near a recent grave and there is no maintained water-course here below the reservoir, suggesting that the volume of water flowing through the tunnel must not be very great.

Near the western end of the reservoir is the waste weir. Like the composite sluice cross-bar, this appears to be a later adaptation to changes in the reservoir. This weir is really just a breach in the embankment filled in with piles of rubble and cobbles, leading to a well-defined water course that runs through a small outcrop and ends up in a dry-farmed field. The latter has been fallow nearly constantly for the twenty years I have passed this reservoir.

Associated Features

A sun, moon, and *lingam* have been pecked into a boulder near the western end of the embankment. Approximately 40 meters south of the reservoir embankment is a partly silted-in Vijayanagara step well and near that, a modern shrine with a Vijayanagara-era *Nandi* sculpture in it. The well is rectangular, 7 by 5 meters, and is constructed of small unmodified and split boulders and angular cobbles. Ten courses are visible above the water line, but some of the upper courses have been disturbed and may have been removed. The sides of

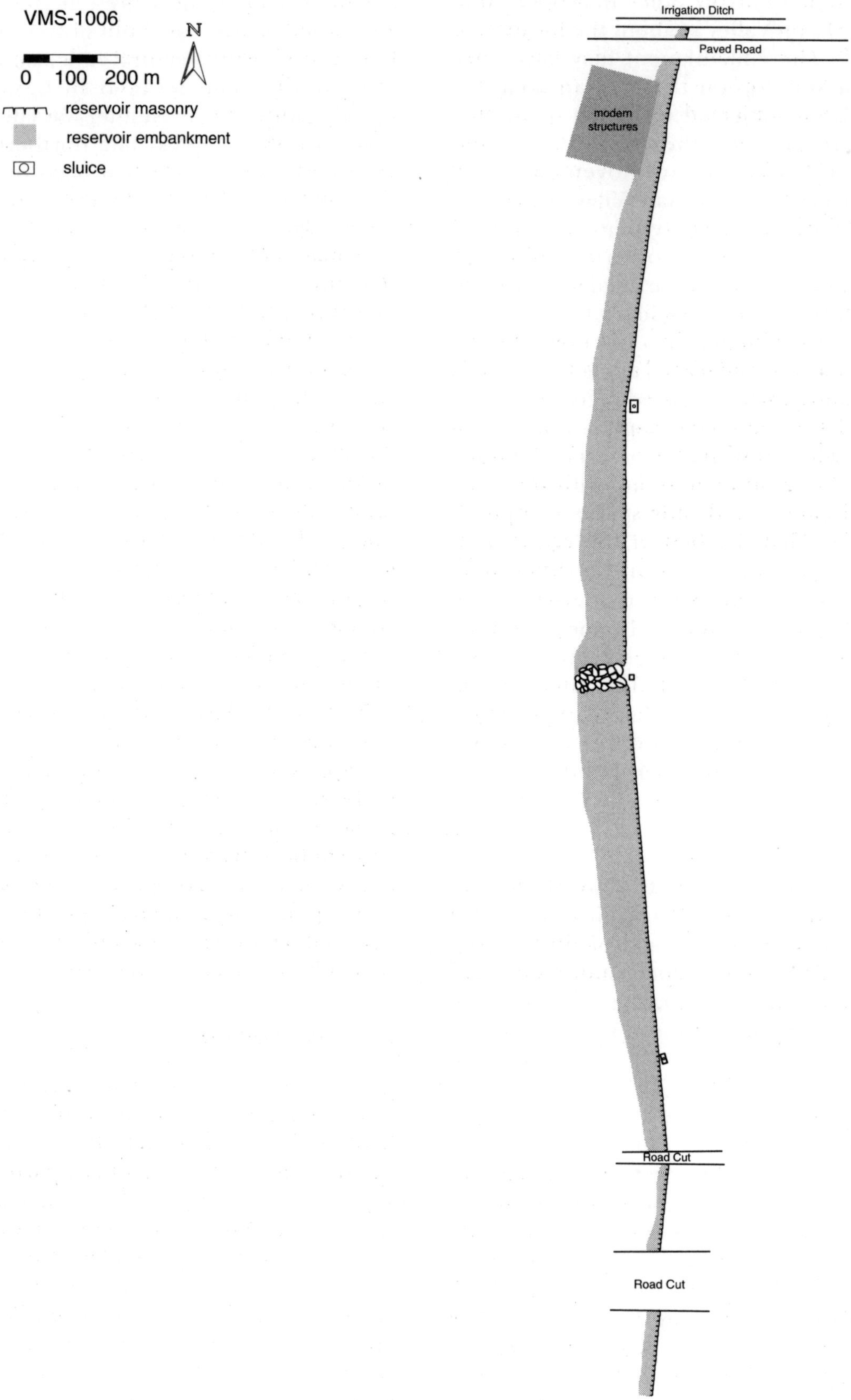

Figure 94. Plan of reservoir, VMS-1006.

the well step in only twice, each step having four courses of vertical masonry above it. Construction is rather haphazard and informal; there is no staircase, for example. This is one of the few wells in the Daroji Valley that can be assigned to the Vijayanagara period. Significantly, it is associated with both a road and a settlement, and was thus probably not solely or even primarily agricultural.

Reservoir, VMS-1006

This reservoir (Figure 94) is located just to the south of Papinayakanahalli and is part of a cluster of reservoirs that surrounds the village on three sides. Papinayakanahalli was probably occupied during the Vijayanagara period, in about the same location as the contemporary village. This correspondence is suggested by the presence of a Vijayanagara temple (VMS-1008) and a fortification (VMS-1009), in and just north of the village, respectively. VMS-1006 collects runoff from the east, north, and south. As such, it taps an east-to-west flow of water, the opposite of most reservoirs in the main valley system. It is included in this chapter chiefly by virtue of its propinquity to Papinayakanahalli and should be considered an isolated reservoir rather than part of the main valley system of grouped reservoirs.

The embankment is quite disturbed near its northern end, where there is a modern house. Similarly, its southern end lies south of a railroad line which cuts through the *bund.* The total present length of the reservoir is 680 meters, but its original extent is unclear. The embankment is between 8 and 25 meters wide.

Construction

The earthen embankment is relatively low, about 3 meters, (possibly the result of a significant accumulation of colluvial fill) and is faced with masonry on the east side. Perhaps the most striking feature of this reservoir is the large size of the elements used in the evenly-coursed masonry facing (up to 3.5 by 4 meters). Opposite the southern sluice, 6 courses of masonry have been preserved, although large trees have partially displaced this masonry. The embankment is damaged near the second, northern sluice gate, but a few meters to the north its condition improves and at least eight courses remain. Fields below (west of) the reservoir are currently dry-farmed and are generally fallow except near the northern end of the feature where a well and electric pump support a field of coconut palms. Above (east of) the reservoir, the land is dry farmed. North of sluice gate 1, a breach in the embankment has been blocked with stones robbed from the masonry revetement.

Outlets and Sluices

There are two sluice gates. Sluice 1 (Figure 95), on the south, is the better preserved and consists of two well-cut, unadorned uprights, square in section. Upper elements are absent, although the center cross-bar is present. All elements are of a dark, fine-grained granite. The sluice stands *c.* 3 meters high with uprights situated 1.8 meters apart. East of the sluice are four slabs lining the outlet to the tunnel which is 0.6 meter wide.

Sluice gate 2 stands 4 to 4.5 meters high and currently consists of two dressed uprights, 1.8 meters apart, square in section, which taper slightly toward the top. No upper elements remain. Square notches for the center crosspiece are located *c.* 2.5 meters from the top of the uprights. The center crossbeam has fallen onto the ground in front of the sluice. A small chunk of Vijayanagara-style concrete lies adjacent to the northern upright. Three stepped slabs overlain with concrete are located *c.* 25 meters north of the second sluice in the field below the embankment; these may form part of the covering of the tunnel.

Associated Features

A badly damaged upright column sits in the bed of the reservoir. The roughly cut, *c.* 2 meters-high column is square in section with two inset octagonal bands. Since no cross-bar niches are visible, it is doubtful that this element served as a sluice gate. It appears instead to have come from a Vijayanagara temple.

East of VMS-1006 are several small gravel-

Figure 95. Sluice 1, reservoir, VMS-1006.

Figure 96. Gravel mulched field below VMS-1006, detail.

Figure 97. VMS-1038, reservoir overview, with VMS-1009 in the background.

mulched fields, not all contiguous (Figure 96). These are dry-farmed fields densely mulched with small pebbles of uniform size. Although the soil in this part of the valley is naturally quite gravelly, such fields have an extremely high density of gravel and are not natural features. The gravel often extends right up to masonry field boundaries; piles of size-sorted gravel are also often found around the edges of the fields. Gravel-mulching helps retain water in the soil and retard evaporation. Gravel mulches are still employed occasionally in the area, so it is impossible to say how old these gravel expanses might be. However, there are some gravel-mulched fields north of the Daroji Valley (in Block S of the VMS survey area, Morrison 1995a) that are associated with Vijayanagara-period terrace systems. Even these, however, could represent reuse of older field areas. There is no evidence for the manuring of gravel-mulched fields in any period.

Reservoir, VMS-1038

Immediately north and somewhat east of the village of Papinayakanahalli lies VMS-1038, which collects runoff from the barren granitic hills to its immediate north (Figure 97). The fort, VMS-1009, is situated some 300 meters west of this reservoir and given that Papinayaka-nahalli covers most of the land potentially irrigated by it, this facility may have primarily served to impound water for the fort and the village. Although the base of the reservoir clearly dates to the Vijayanagara period, it has been extensively modified and now retains a small pond used year-round for watering livestock and washing clothes. The reservoir embankment is 440 meters long, 10 meters wide, and 2 meters high.

Construction

The embankment is faced with masonry on the north side, the side that retains runoff from the hills to the north. There appear to be two distinct episodes of construction with newer masonry (and perhaps embankment fill) sitting atop the older. Earlier construction is indicated by the lowest 3 masonry courses of the entire embankment, and the lower 6 courses on its eastern end. The extreme eastern end of the reservoir, with its all-original masonry, is cut-off from the rest of the facility by a recent dirt road. The lower stepped masonry courses are built of medium-sized unmodified boulders and a few long slabs with Vijayanagara-style quarry marks. The upper, later, masonry is slightly offset from the lower and although it, too, consists of unmodified boulders, the mode of construction is clearly different. At the western end of the embankment are 9 additional courses of newer masonry. There is also some masonry facing on the southern, downstream side of the *bund*; these 8 courses appear to have been recently constructed and are identical in form and style to the upper courses on the north side of the embankment.

Outlets and Sluices

VMS-1038 has only one sluice, clearly recent. It is entirely nonfunctional at present.

Associated Features

VMS-1039, a small Vijayanagara-period shrine and associated step well (Figure 90) is located 60 meters northeast of the reservoir embankment in the bed of the facility. The fact that this temple and step well are so close to the embankment suggests either that there was never very much water contained behind this feature, notwithstanding its length, or, more probably, that the shrine was periodically surrounded by water and was semi-submerged at least part of the year. This again brings to mind a temple tank with its central pavilion and, more broadly, evokes images of the encircling ocean. The doors to the sanctuary, as described earlier in this chapter, are flanked by pilasters consisting of *purna-kalasha* supporting slender columns. This kind of water imagery is, it should be noted, common on all temples and not only those in reservoir beds. However, the placement of a shrine in a reservoir bed – a kind of temple tank arrangement – is both striking and unusual, most reservoir-side temples sitting atop embankments.

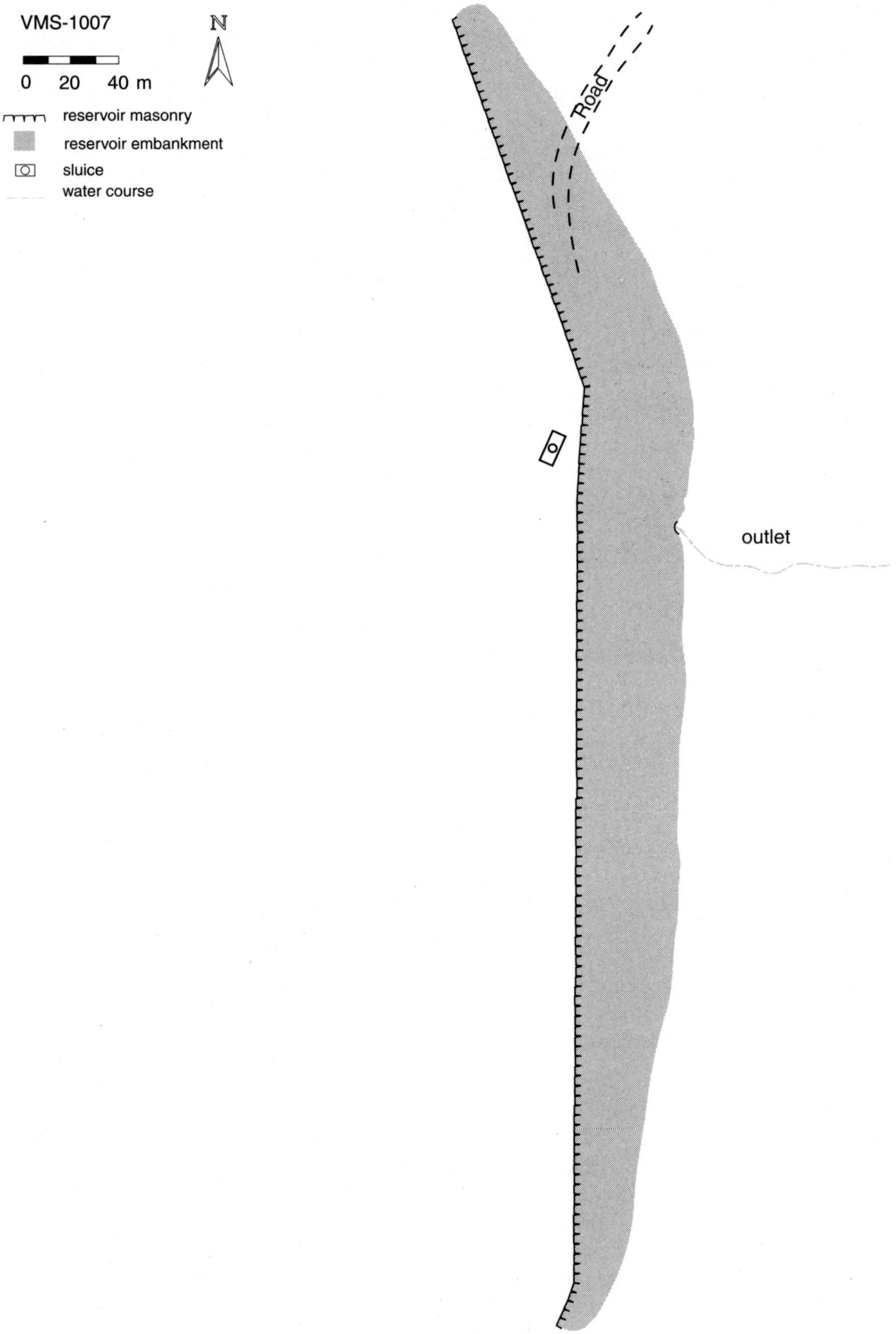

Figure 98. Plan of reservoir, VMS-1007.

Reservoir, VMS-1007

This high, wide reservoir (Figure 98) is part of the cluster of reservoirs around the village of Papinayakanahalli. Now, it lies just north of the paved road running through the valley. The embankment is 290 meters long, reaches a height of 4 meters and has a maximum width of 30 meters. It collects runoff from the outcrop to the immediate north and west; although the land slopes gently up to the north of this facility, the embankment does not extend all the way to the outcrop on this end. This reservoir is the highest facility capturing west-to-east runoff, the predominant direction of water flow in the main valley, and is thus at the head of the main valley system.

Construction

At its northern end, the embankment is in poor condition and sections of it have been dug away. At this end, there are only 3 courses of masonry present on the western, upstream side, but within 40 meters, the embankment becomes much higher with 9 courses of stepped masonry. Most of the masonry is uncut, consisting of medium to large stones but some are split and most are approximately rectangular. Although irregularly coursed, the masonry is stepped out quite evenly.

Outlets and Sluices

Ninety meters from its northern end, the embankment curves and there, where it achieves its maximum height, is the single sluice. There are no formal stairs opposite the sluice, just 12 irregular courses of masonry. Very little remains of the sluice itself. There is one upright which is broken at the point where the notch for the central cross-piece occurs (*c.* 1.5 meters above the ground surface). The upright is roughly shaped and approximately square in section.

The tunnel that carries water under the embankment is still functional. Several horizontal slabs near the sluice appear to be displaced parts of the tunnel facing. The soil covering the tunnel has slumped on the east side, leaving a gaping hole. The 0.50 by 0.50 meter tunnel is lined with tightly-fitted square slabs abutted by large, squarish bricks. The bricks do not cover the tunnel completely as they usually do; instead the cap has been supplemented with angular cobbles. The masonry of the embankment begins about 1.5 meters above the tunnel's roof slab.

Associated Features

East of the embankment of VMS-1007 is a square well constructed of tabular granite elements, 9.5 by 9 meters and 6.5 meters deep, fitted with a ramp (Figure 99). This type of well is designed to have animal traction lift water from the well. Irrigation carried out this way is known as *kavalai* irrigation. A pair of bullocks is backed up the ramp, water is collected in buckets or other containers hitched to the team who are then led down the ramp pulling the buckets. In some of these ramped cattle traction wells there are ingenious channels and chutes for the dispersal of water into gardens near the well; in these structures the water is immediately released into the channels at the top of the ramp (Morrison 1995a). The roughly-coursed masonry on the sides of this well is built up in five levels or steps, each step consisting of 5 to 6 courses of tabular stones. On the south side of the well is a staircase of protruding slabs. There is a small chute at the top of the well on the east side for sending water down from the top of the ramp.

On the north side of the well is a 7.5 by 7.5 meters platform with an overhang that extends out over the well. This platform is built of three long slabs, the center perforated by six small holes. The extending platform runs into a low earthen platform about one meter higher than the ground surface and bounded by masonry walls of small square blocks. In the center of the upper surface of the platform is a small (1 by 1 meter) central square plastered surface. The remnants of a water channel defined by edge-set slabs and a long elevated earthen mound extend from the western edge of the platform. There is a sparse to moderate ceramic density in the vicinity of the well. The construction style of this well suggests that it postdates the construction of the reservoir.

Figure 99. Step well associated with reservoir, VMS-1007.

Figure 100. Overview of Shiva temple, VMS-1037.

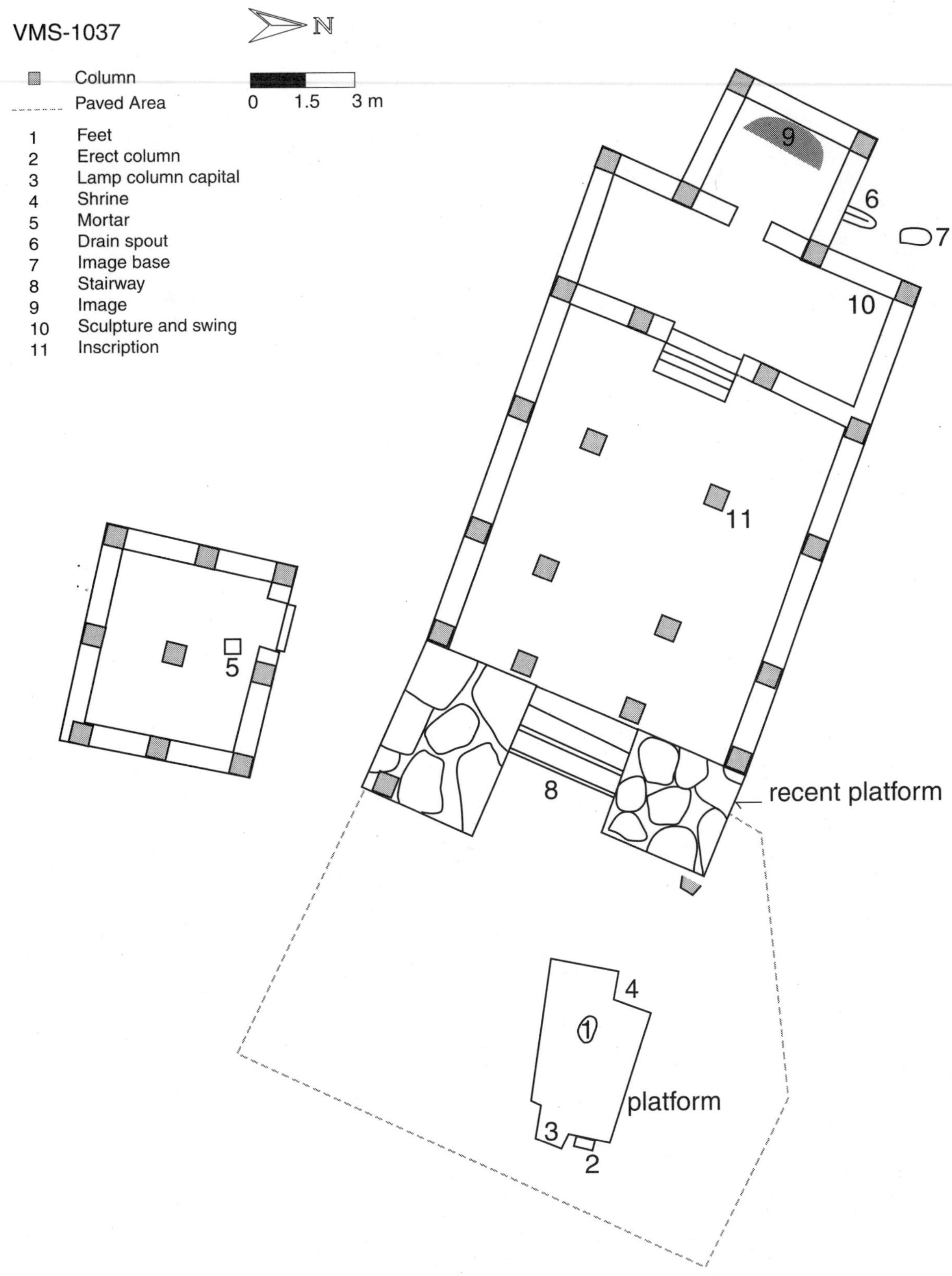

Figure 101. Plan of Shiva temple, VMS-1037.

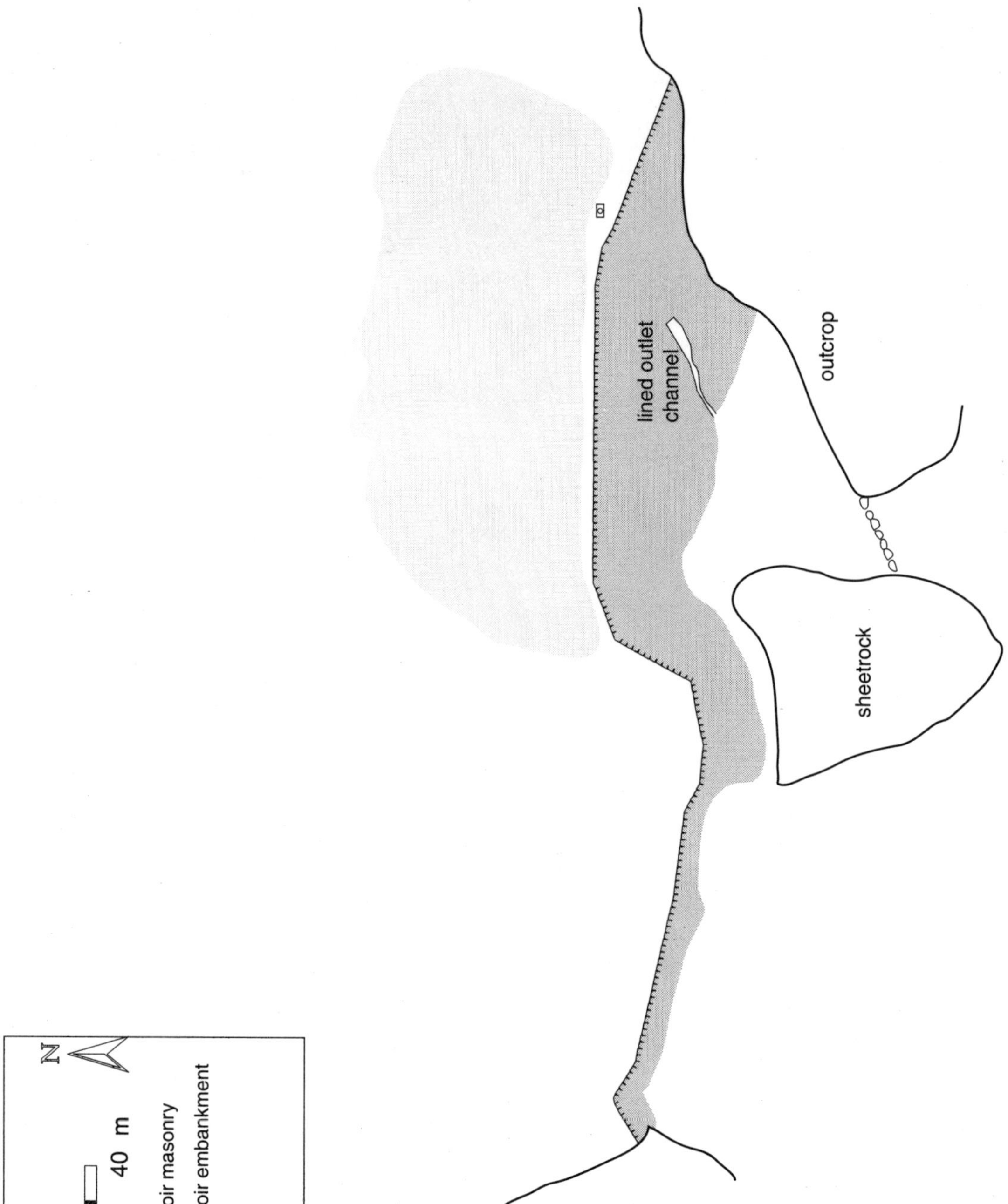

Figure 102. Plan of reservoir, VMS-1011.

Shiva Temple, VMS-1037

This small Vijayanagara-period temple complex consists of an east-facing temple and an associated *mandapa* (Figures 100 and 101). The Shiva temple begins on the east with an outer porch of 4 by 4 columns. These appear to be unsculpted, although there could be sculptures under the heavy layers of paint. The columns themselves are one of the most common Vijayanagara forms – square in section with two inset octagonal bands. Capitals are rectangular with inset bevels on the long end. Although the porch is walled, the walls are heavily plastered and construction details cannot be discerned. The capitals carry stone beams which in turn carry long ceiling slabs; in the ceiling is a central lotus medallion. The flooring is recent.

Beyond the outer porch is another one, 2 columns deep by 4 wide. The entry into this space is flanked by Shaivite door guardians (*dvarapala*), whose inner arms hold maces toward the ground and outer arms have raised palms. A small Hanuman and a *naga* are carved on the wall on the south side of the door.

The antechamber (*antarala*) follows; its floor is some 0.6 meter higher than the inner porch and it is approached up a stairway of three stairs. Columns in the antechamber are tapering squares with rectangular capitals. A small sculpture of Shiva in one of his terrifying incarnations (Virabhadra) is in the antechamber.

The sanctuary (*garbhagriha*) is a small room of 2 by 2 columns. The sanctuary, too, is protected by fierce door guardians, these standing with their hands folded in front of them in worship. A tiered ceiling of rotated squares surrounding a central lotus medallion protects the (recent) image that is in worship within this space. A drain projects out the wall to the north, and an old image base lies nearby. Outside and above the sanctuary, the superstructure (*shikhara)* is *c.* 2 meters high. It is relatively simply sculpted, and probably dates to the late fourteenth or fifteenth century. The roof has projecting eaves and a low brick parapet.

Approximately 5 meters east of the temple is a low platform (3 by 2 meters) with a pair of sculpted feet in the center and the displaced capital of a lamp column at the eastern end.

Southeast of the temple is a walled 3 by 2 columned hall (*mandapa*). These columns are simple, square in section with rectangular capitals. This small *mandapa* is walled with long rectangular slabs spanning the gaps between columns; it is entered through a door on the north. The structure carries a flat roof with a small brick parapet. It may have once have been larger as the west wall is quite rough and may have been damaged by the removal of part of the structure. The whole compound is enclosed with a recent wall; there is no evidence for an earlier wall. Note that this Early Vijayanagara shrine is more than 1 kilometer south of Papinayakanahalli. It is possible that the north-south road running past VMS-1010 was not yet extant in this earlier period and that the main east-west road ran further south than it does today, passing by VMS-1037.

Reservoir, VMS-1011

This reservoir is built up against an outcropping ridge at the northern edge of the main valley, opposite a small valley (Figure 102). Water is collected from the north and then distributed the fields south of (below) the reservoir. The fields below this reservoir are currently planted in cotton and are contiguous to fields below VMS-1007. The total length of the reservoir is 190 meters, its maximal width is 30 meters. This facility still retains water; at the height of the dry season, a small pool 95 by 35 meters still remained up against the *bund,* near the sluice (Figure 103).

Construction

VMS-1011 is still in use and is maintained; it appears to be relatively deep, indicating sustained removal of accumulated silt deposits. Further, the reservoir bed does not support any aquatic vegetation, which often grows in unmaintained (or poorly maintained) reservoirs that still hold water. The embankment is well-constructed and in good repair. It is sinuous in plan and is widest at its eastern end (*c.* 30 meters), where it extends onto the shallow lower slope of an abutting outcrop. The north face of the embankment is faced with masonry. The latter consists of stepped-out, regularly coursed, medium-sized unshaped and split blocks, interspersed with many chinking stones. The masonry is well-preserved on the western end of the reservoir, but parts of the embankment have been cut away. Some steeper masonry toward the western end of the embankment may represent a repaired section. Occasional protruding slabs set in the masonry facing form steps arranged in well-spaced diagonal alignments. Thirteen courses of masonry have preserved opposite the single sluice at the eastern end of the embankment.

Outlets and Sluices

The sluice (Figure 104) consists of two dressed uprights, square in section, capped by a lintel with a rather unusual three-part moulding sequence. Unlike most mouldings, where wider elements on top and bottom sandwich a smaller central element, here the middle element is the widest. The lintel begins with an inverted moulding, two-stepped with angled bevel. Atop this is a slightly larger moulding slab with a lower step followed by a sub-rounded bevel. Four large rectangles stand out from the bevel. This central element is capped by an inverted moulding, one-stepped with an angled bevel. In all cases, the angled bevels have sub-rounded corners which could almost be called convex; however, the bevels between the decorative rectangles are flat. Although there is a lower cross-piece, it is not pegged in (there are no holes for it and it is just wedged into place), suggesting that this element has been moved and that its original slot may be below the present ground level of the bed. If this is the case, then some silt inwash has certainly accumulated since the sluice was constructed, perhaps as much as two meters. The stopper slab – the edge-set slab that joins the uprights and which is usually is found underground or partly underground – is extremely rough and is probably not original.

The tunnel, which is open, may also have been reworked and/or repaired as it is significantly less formal than the sluice gate. It is unclear whether the masonry south of the sluice gate has been reset to make a new tunnel. The tunnel outlet is visible and apparently functional. Its base is lined for about 10 to 13 meters with rough masonry. The sides and capping stones are not visible. Flowing out from the tunnel is a water channel that winds its way through a 10 to 20 meters wide gap between the eastern outcrop and a large, low outcrop of sheetrock. The channel flows down a relatively steep gradient into the dry fields below which is partly broken by a wall, one course high and one element wide.

Associated Features

As noted, there is at least one and probably several cross walls built in the area below the reservoir. These walls would have helped slow the flow of water into the lower-lying fields to the south. There is a moderate density scatter of Vijayanagara earthenware ceramics in the fields below the reservoir, an unusually high density for this kind of context.[12]

Bayaluvaddigeri Village

With Bayaluvaddigeri we begin consideration of a part of the second (earlier) settlement cluster isolable in the western part of the main valley. Although the village of Bayaluvaddigeri is still occupied, there are indications of earlier settlement here. The architecture of the village is mixed, consisting of concrete, cinder block, thatch, and masonry. The dry-laid masonry structures are substantial and at least one is surrounded by a high wall, almost the width of a fortification. These structures are unlike either Vijayanagara or seventeenth-century architecture; they may date to the nineteenth or early twentieth centuries. However, there is more unequivocal evidence of an older period – a small hero stone sits in the main village square. This is a simple sculpture (Figure 105) which probably dates to the Early Middle period. In front of the recent Anjaneya temple is a fifteenth-century inscription referring to the construction of a place, "Annalapura", named after the queen of Devaraya II. As noted, it is

Figure 103. Reservoir, VMS-1011, overview.

Figure 104. Sluice, VMS-1011.

Figure 105. Hero stone in Bayaluvaddigeri.

not clear if this is Bayaluvaddigeri itself or some other settlement. Although this lithic inscription is not built into any structure and, as such, could have been moved from elsewhere, it is large and heavy and may well point to the existence of Bayaluvaddigeri by the fifteenth century, an interpretation consistent with larger archaeological patterns. Whether or not Bayaluvaddigeri was actually founded at this time is, even if we assume identity between it and Annalapura, an open question. As noted, archaeological evidence makes it clear that many places in the region which were officially "founded" at one time or another actually existed as occupied places long before and thus we might only say that if this inscription does refer to its present location, then it suggest that this place was established during or before the fifteenth century.

In the small enclosure of the recent Virabhadra temple is a large sculpted Gajalakshmi on a triangular granite block; this may have originally been placed over a gateway; in any case, it certainly came from a substantial structure. Both this sculpture and the granite lamp post in front of the temple date to the Vijayanagara period. From this admittedly imperfect evidence we might suggest that Bayaluvaddigeri was established in the Early or Middle Vijayanagara period and was occupied more or less continuously to the present.

Census data from the nineteenth and twentieth centuries round out this picture somewhat. In 1871, the village of "Vaddigeri" in the Kamalapuram sub-region is listed as having 1,081 residents and 3,463 acres of land (Government of India 1874). In the 1901 census, "Bylu Vaddigeri" is recorded as having 169 houses and 671 residents, a substantial decrease. In 1903 and 1904, the Archaeological Survey of Madras and Coorg recorded "Bylmadigiri" as having five temples; four are noted to be modern while the fifth is described as (1904: 79-80):

> Virabhadrasvami temple, with a lingam of that name measuring 4½' × 1½' sculptured on a slab. A Ganesa, 3' high, the image of Lakshmi 1½' high, a statue of a small bull and three *nagarkals* are all in the temple. Outside the temple is a slab about 3' × 2' with the figures of Gajalakshmi and two elephants carved on it. There is another slab here, 3' high 1½' broad with old Telugu or Kanarese inscriptions. Toward the east of this temple, at a distance of about 50 feet, is a slab under a tree with the figure of Virappa sculpted on it.

Unlike several other villages in the region, then, there have been few substantial changes to the layout and content of Bayaluvaddigeri in the last hundred years.

Temple, Terrace, and Steps, VMS-1028

Atop the outcrop between VMS-1012 and 1013 and not far from Bayaluvaddigeri is a small temple with a simple superstructure (Figure 106). Except for two older columns, the temple appears to be entirely recent. The temple is built on a flatter part of the sheetrock, but artificial terracing has been required to make a large enough level area for the structure. The fill of this terrace includes gravel made from breaking up granite and basalt and contains a high density of earthenware ceramics (Vijayanagara period and later). A cistern in the sheetrock has been made by cutting out and enlarging a natural depression. On the southern edge of the terrace is a 2.5 meters diameter circular structure formed of irregularly coursed rubble walls 0.6 meter high. Although it is almost certainly recent, this masonry ring is reminiscent of round structures in the royal center of the city of Vijayanagara (enclosures X and XI; Fritz, Michell, and Nagaraja Rao 1985). These have been suggested to be grain storage features and indeed are similar to features at Badami and Chitradurga from earlier and later time periods, respectively. This, too, may be a storage facility – or, more precisely, a footing for a storage facility built of ephemeral materials. The southern terrace wall is 1.5 meters wide and, unlike all the other features on this terrace, appears to be old. There is also a masonry staircase built up onto the outcrop which may also be original. Thus, there is good reason to believe that this terrace was built in the Vijayanagara period, and even that it supported a small temple. Although most of what now remains on the terrace is more recent, the idea that an older temple was located here is supported by the 1903-4 report

Figure 106. VMS-1028, temple and steps above Bayaluvaddigeri.

Figure 107. Overview of VMS-1012.

of the Archaeological Survey (1904:79), "Field No. 1—Hill Block No. XIII.—(1) About a hundred yards north-east of field No. 45, is a very ancient Isvara temple on the slopes of a hill, with a lingam and statue of a small bull. South of this, is a small rough-built Udasalamma temple. Toward the south-east of this, is a flat rock wheron foot marks are cut."[13]

Reservoir, VMS-1012

VMS-1012 is paired with reservoir VMS-1013 (Figures 107 and 108), both of which water a small area just north of the village of Bayaluvaddigeri. VMS-1012 lies on the edge of the village; recent changes to this facility have been substantial. Both reservoirs are still in use by Bayaluvaddigeri residents, who use the water for agriculture and some domestic activities.

This reservoir captures runoff from nearby outcrops and from an ephemeral drainage emerging from a gap in the northern Hampi-Daroji Hills. This gap forms a valley nearly 1 kilometer wide that carries the confluence of several tiny *nullahs* that come together to fill VMS-1012. In addition to the Papinayakanahalli gap, this opening formed another (perhaps less well-traveled) route to the north from the Daroji Valley. This route leads directly to the walled Vijayanagara-period settlement VMS-365 and from there to a roadway that runs southeast-northwest toward the city of Vijayanagara. The course of the road is constrained by a more than 2 kilometers-long fortification wall, VMS-347, although there is no indication of a prepared road surface (Morrison in press a; Sinopoli and Morrison 2006b). Associated with the walled settlement is a large reservoir (300 meters long by 20 meters wide), VMS-349, which has a simple sluice without mouldings. Just west of this settlement and on the other side of a large outcrop is a smaller reservoir, VMS-1014, probably also associated with the Vijayanagara-era village.

VMS-1012 contains some water (and aquatic vegetation) even in the dry season, with a pool of 100 by 50 meters recorded one February. The fields below the reservoir appear to support rice and vegetables, at least occasionally, indicating a relatively abundant water supply. However, these same fields are uncultivated in the dry season, suggesting that this supply is not adequate for year-round cropping. The bed of the reservoir appears to have silted up considerably. The embankment is narrow, only about 10 to 12 meters. It is 370 meters long and approximately 3 meters high at its southern end (slightly lower on the north). Thorn scrub, succulent field borders, grasses, and some deciduous trees surround both the reservoir and the village of Bayaluvaddigeri.

Construction

The earthen embankment is faced with masonry on its upstream, western side. This masonry does not appear to be original; it is sloped rather than stepped and the masonry courses, of small and medium unmodified cobbles, are haphazard. There are a number of protruding stones incorporated into the embankment wall. Again, these do not appear to be original. There is also some masonry facing along the base of the embankment on the eastern, downstream side.

Outlets and Sluices

There is one simple sluice (Figures 109 and 110), nearly 3 meters high, which may date to the fourteenth or fifteenth century. The uprights are undressed slabs, rectangular in section. The upper cross-bar is a slab with a very flat, two-stepped with angled bevel lower moulding with a central half medallion (on either side) and four corner quarter medallions. The undecorated central slab, which covers the lower moulding, is much too small for the lower moulding, suggesting that it was either broken and then squared off, or that it is a replacement. There is no trace of an upper moulding. About 2 meters below the upper cross-bar are the square peg holes that once seated the lower cross-bar, now missing.

The tunnel near the sluice has evidently been totally reworked and is now blocked with a large irregular stone. An upright slab has been cemented to the east side of the sluice uprights; the original is probably buried as this edge-set slab actually extends *above* the holes which once

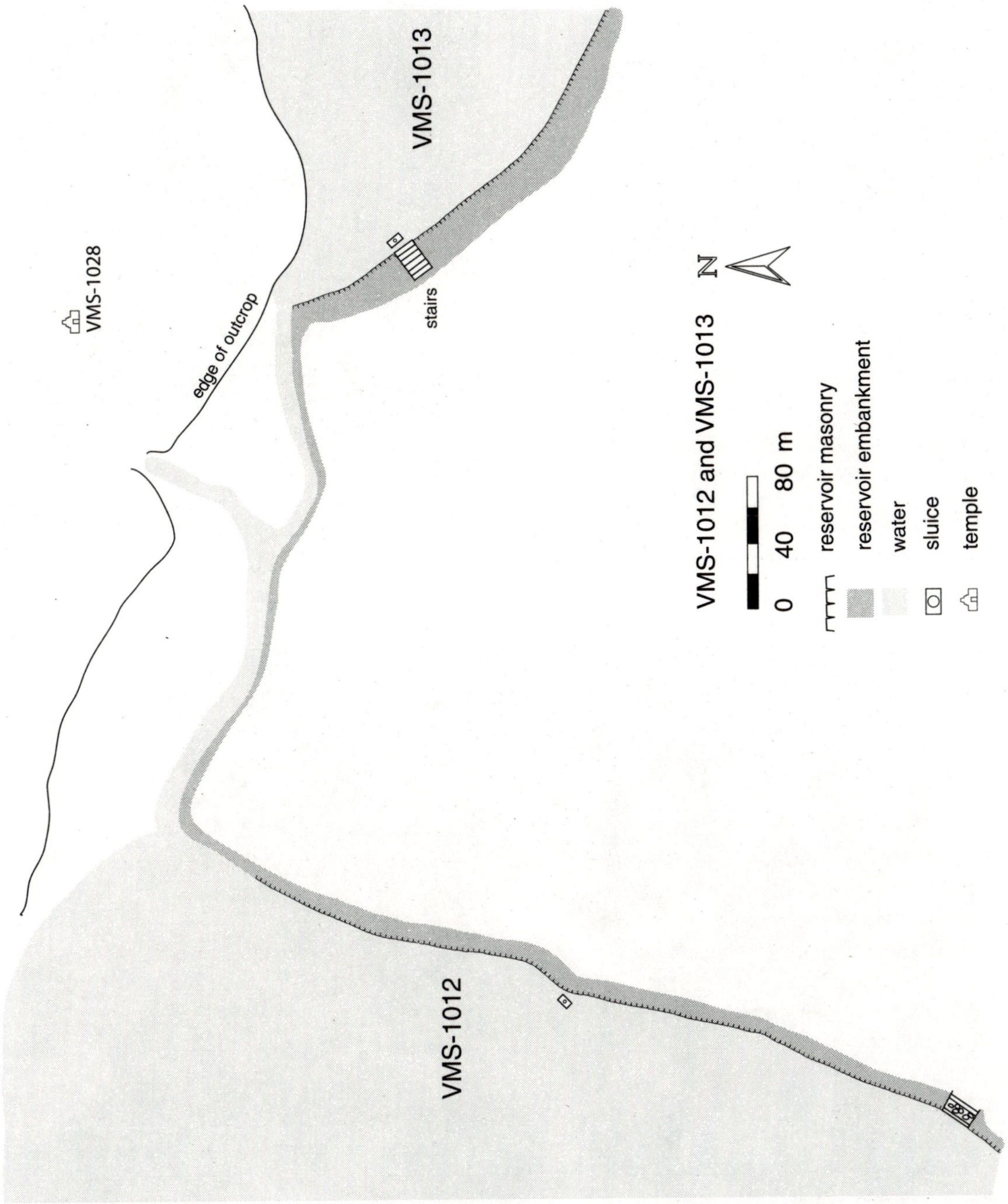
VMS-1012 and VMS-1013
0 40 80 m
reservoir masonry
reservoir embankment
water
sluice
temple
N
VMS-1028
edge of outcrop
stairs
VMS-1013
VMS-1012

Figure 109. VMS-1012, sluice overview.

Figure 111. VMS-1013, sluice overview.

Figure 110. VMS-1012, sluice detail.

seated the lower cross-bar. The tunnel opening here has been extensively reworked and a new cement and plaster platform has been built around the base of the sluice gate.

Near the southern end of the embankment is a waste weir or *kodi*, entirely recent. This 15 meter wide feature is built of masonry and cement, forming a low, flat spillway in the embankment for the safe release of excess water.

Associated Features

A dirt road, possibly recent, runs parallel to and just east of the embankment.

Reservoir, VMS-1013

VMS-1013 is a small reservoir just north of Bayaluvaddigeri linked to VMS-1012 by an unlined, sandy water channel bounded by a low earthen embankment (Figure 108). This reservoir sits just south of a large sheet-rock outcrop; a small valley in the outcrop contains an erosion channel draining into the bed of the reservoir from the northeast. This facility holds some water even in the dry season. Several large outcropping boulders in the bed are water-stained and must be seasonally submerged. The water-holding area is constrained by sheetrock on the north. The embankment is low, reaching its maximum height of 3 meters near the sluice. It is 210 meters long but only 10 to 12 meters wide.

Construction

The embankment is faced with masonry on its (north)eastern side. The southern end has only 5 courses of masonry, but at its northern end the stepped masonry rises to 13 courses. Here the masonry elements are unusually small and the courses are closely packed with chinking stones. Some of the stones have been split but none are more elaborately shaped. The stepped masonry is very steep in this section, making it difficult to get up and down, but some protruding slabs are periodically integrated into the embankment here, forming steps down to the water.

Outlets and Sluices

There is one sluice, of the Vijayanagara period (Figure 111). This 4 meter high sluice consists of two well-dressed uprights capped by an incomplete three-part moulding. The latter begins with a lower moulding – two-stepped with a convex bevel, medallions in the shape of *makara-torana* (two on each long axis and one on each short axis), and corner quarter medallions. The lower moulding is capped by a slab with incised upper and lower grooves. The upper moulding is missing.

About 3 meters below the lintel are the square insets meant to seat the lower cross-bar. The latter is, however, not *in situ*; it has fallen a few centimeters below its seating notches but remains wedged in between the uprights. Although most lower cross-bars are built from a single shaped granite slab, this one has cement knobs which would have been slotted into the seating notches. Below the lower cross-bar is an edge-set slab with a square notch cut into the bottom. There has been some attempt to rework the tunnel with cemented rubble; the cement-knobbed lower cross-bar may also be recent. Lying near the sluice is what appears to be a (granite) cross-piece. Although one might assume that this is the original element, it is 0.96 meter long while the opening between the uprights is only 0.92 meter wide. Clearly, whatever happened here, there has been a history of attempts to fit and refit the lower cross-bar. Several long stone slabs, probably coverings from the tunnel, also lie in the reservoir bed north of the sluice.

The sluice was recorded in 1988. By 1996, the sluice had disappeared, replaced by a recently-constructed shrine.

Associated Features

There are two features of note near VMS-1013; a terrace containing a temple (VMS-1028) and a well. The latter lies *in* the bed of the reservoir, about 30 meters north of the embankment near its center. This small square well (5 by 5 meters) is constructed of up to 10 courses of tabular granite with a few quarried rectangular blocks also used in the construction. Tabular granite is often used in twentieth-century construction. One large stone slab extends over the well on its north side; such slabs are used to support ropes for raising water. The well is in poor condition but still holds water. There is a possible stairway/entrance in the southwest corner.

That this well post-dates the reservoir is clear. However, it is also possible to see from the variable silt levels in the reservoir bed not only that there was significant siltation into the bed of VMS-1013, but also that the northern half of the bed was cleaned out before the well was constructed. It appears that siltation became so severe that silt inwash reached almost to the top of embankment, as it still does along the southern portion of the bed. Silt removal in the northern part of the bed may have taken place *in order* to excavate the well, the prospect of clearing the entire reservoir perhaps seen as not worth the effort. The location of the well in the reservoir bed suggests an attempt to squeeze some water out of the raised water table created by the reservoir, and the propinquity of Bayaluvaddigeri suggests that at least some of this demand for water was for domestic use rather than solely for agriculture and stock watering.

Gundlavaddigeri Village and Fort, VMS-1082

North and east of Gundlavaddigeri village and north of reservoir VMS-1080 is a square step well possibly built during the Vijayanagara period. This well, 25 by 25 meters, is now dry and disused. It is about 8 meters deep with trees growing in the bottom. The sides of the well are also heavily overgrown but they appear to be some combination of exposed earth and rock-cut sections. Only on the west where there is a possible entrance is there any masonry – 4 courses of medium-sized split boulders, somewhat irregularly coursed. Around the well are some fragmented earthenware ceramics and a piece of iron slag. This well, which could date from any time between about the fourteenth and nineteenth centuries, may have been located along a road leading down from the main route through the valley toward Gundlavaddigeri.

The village itself is still occupied; in 1871 it had an occupation of 334 in an area of 2,502 acres.[14] By 1901, the population had dropped to 253; 131 of these are listed as landowners, certainly small farmer-proprietors. The temple in the village is recent although some of the domestic architecture is older, perhaps nineteenth or early twentieth-century. The village sits at the base of a small inselberg that carries a fort, VMS-1082. This outcrop also constitutes a watershed for one of the small reservoirs associated with Gundlavaddigeri (VMS-1081).

The outcrop bearing the fort is not very large but it is steep and there are few easy ways to climb it. The easiest route is on the southern side where an informal path, now much used by cows, leads to the top of the hill. The fortified top of the outcrop is not completely enclosed within walls; only the less steep sections leading up the uneven terrace atop the granitic hill are hidden behind heavy double-faced walls built of a varied assortment of material – cobbles, small, medium-sized, and large unmodified and split boulders. The path on the south side may not be the original route up to the fort as it is blocked by a low, wide (1.5 meters) wall with no apparent opening. On the eastern edge of the outcrop overlooking the village is a round, solid bastion *c.* 10 meters in diameter and about 3 meters high perched atop some large boulders (Figure 112). This structure is abutted by fortification walls and is similar to other bastions in the area, including those at VMS-6, Ingaligi, Papinayakanahalli, and Buvanahalli. The masonry includes irregularly-shaped quarried blocks with "Vijayanagara-style" quarry marks, roughly coursed and loosely fitted with abundant small chinking stones.

The interior of the fort has a very uneven surface and there has clearly been no attempt to level it. Artifact densities are low, with only a few earthenware fragments noted. Although some of these could be recent, there is at least one rim sherd with a characteristic Vijayanagara form. In the most level part of the fortified terrace are several rubble walls defining at least one large rectangular structure with two 5 by 5 meter rooms. Like other similar "refuge" forts in this area, this structure does not seem to have

Figure 112. Gundlavaddigeri fort with small bastion on rock.

Figure 113. Stairs, VMS-1080.

been intensively used and may have been reserved for emergencies. Again, these structures are difficult to date; there is some reason to see them as being from the Vijayanagara period but perhaps more reason to place them in the late sixteenth or seventeenth centuries when individual settlements required protection during periods of government decentralization. Virtually every village in the Daroji Valley with evidence of precolonial occupation was either fortified or adjacent to its own small fort; if some of these individual fortifications do indeed date from the later sixteenth century (after the fall of the city in AD 1565) it may suggest that, as would be likely, some of the larger, integrated systems of defense built during the Vijayanagara period (the massive fortification walls with restricted gates, for example) were no longer maintained and staffed and each settlement had to make its own arrangements.

Reservoir, VMS-1080

North and east of the village of Gundlavaddigeri is a heavily disturbed reservoir. Curiously, this facility, now almost entirely reworked and clearly long-defunct, has masonry on its eastern side, suggesting that it collected water from a modest, localized topographic rise, a slight swell so minor that it does not even register on the Survey of India topographic map with its 20 meters contours. This runoff runs from the northeast to the southwest, opposite the major direction of main valley runoff flow. Thus, VMS-1080 is not connected in any way to the rest of the reservoirs in the main valley and should be considered an isolated facility. The area around this reservoir is currently dry-farmed. Although much of the earthen embankment has been spread into the fields to the west and the masonry facing is actively being removed and reworked, there is still at least 200 meters of *bund* left. The original width is difficult to estimate as is the date of construction. The latter probably lies within the Vijayanagara period but it is not possible to be more precise than this.

Construction

Masonry still remains in only a few places on the embankment and even there it shows signs of reworking. There are only 4 courses of stepped masonry in any one location; at one spot there are 9 masonry courses but the upper 6 are sloped rather than stepped, indicating a later repair. The masonry consists of medium-sized split and unmodified granite boulders with some roughly shaped square blocks. Most of the masonry has been removed and piled up along the southern end of the embankment where it forms a wide wall atop the low bund. The wall then turns ninety degrees to the west where it has been made into a sloping revetement of horizontally-laid boulders and blocks with numerous small, protruding blocks. This revetement protects the north side of a small channel from erosion and is clearly quite recent.

Outlets and Sluices

Although there are no extant sluice gates or other openings in the embankment, near the southern end of the bund, where masonry is piled up into the wall, there is a two meter wide staircase of flat granite slabs, possibly recent (Figure 113). There is some suggestion, however, that the original stepped masonry here was neatly squared off near the steps, suggesting that these steps may replace an older, original staircase. If this is correct, then this was probably the location of a sluice gate. There is a recently-built well just 10 meters east of the steps in what would have been the bed of the reservoir. Alternately, this could have been a containment reservoir, in which case there would be no outlets.

Reservoir, VMS-1081

Adjacent to the small isolated outcrop bearing the Gundlavaddigeri fort (VMS-1082) is a now-abandoned reservoir which once collected runoff from that small outcrop as well as from more generalized runoff from the valley floor to the west. This reservoir then, unlike VMS-1080, should be considered a part of the main valley system, albeit a small one. Although this reservoir, like VMS-1080 to the northeast, is also in poor condition, its original length (182 meters) height (about 3 meters), and width (more than 12 meters) can be estimated. This facility lies near the southwest edge of the village and is surrounded by dry-farmed fields. From the exposed section in the larger breach (below), it is clear that this reservoir is heavily silted-in, with more than 1 meter of accumulated sediment and possibly as much as 2 meters near the southern end of the *bund*. It is probable that both this reservoir and VMS-1080 were abandoned for this reason.

Construction

The west face of the earthen embankment is strengthened by up to 4 stepped masonry courses. These are made of unmodified medium-sized and large granite boulders; some of these stones have been removed from their original positions and piled up atop the bund to make a wide wall. In part, these newer walls (and the thorny vegetation growing on the embankment) serve to delineate field borders and to prevent animals from entering fields so defined. The earthen core of the *bund* is being spread into fields east of the reservoir.

The reservoir is breached in two places; one gap about 30 meters south of the northern end has been repaired but there is a larger, unrepaired breach 90 meters further south. An active erosion channel runs through this 12 meters wide opening which may have been the location of a sluice.

Outlets and Sluices

Although there is now no trace of any opening, the larger breach (above) may have been the location of a sluice or waste weir.

Reservoir, VMS-1015

This massive reservoir dams one of the narrowest parts of the main valley about 2 kilometers east of Bayaluvaddigeri. Spanning the entire width of the valley, the 9 meters high, 2,060 meters long reservoir embankment runs roughly northsouth, although it is somewhat curved in plan (Figure 114). The fill of the earthen embankment contains no visible artifacts. VMS-1015 dates to the early sixteenth century, although it appears to have several episodes of construction and is most likely to be a smaller fourteenth- or fifteenth-century reservoir that was greatly enlarged in the early fifteen hundreds. The earlier reservoir seems to have been as much as 950 meters long – very large indeed – but the sixteenth-century version of VMS-1015 represents an ambitious increase in scale. As discussed below, this facility was associated with the village of Dharmasagara, probably giving the latter its name – the "ocean of *dharma.*" In 1903-4 the Archaeological Survey (1904: 79) described a reservoir near Bayaluvaddigeri, "*Patacheruvu katta* – An ancient ruined tank bund with 3 or 4 fine sluices". This is probably not VMS-1012, which has only one sluice; instead it must refer to VMS-1015. If this is the case, then we can see that although the village retained the name Dharmasagara, the reservoir itself came to be known by another moniker.

The sixteenth-century construction of VMS-1015 is well established, based on both sluice architecture and an associated inscription (described below). The presence of an earlier component is based on sluice morphology and the geographic likelihood of a smaller reservoir being located in the northern half of the valley here, where two seasonal streams meet in a small declivity. At its maximal extent, VMS-1015 had four sluice gates.

In the main valley near VMS-1015, the valley floor slopes down from the Hampi-Daroji Hills toward the south before rising again to the Sandur Hills. The highest part of the valley floor is on the north, a fact which visually accentuated the loftiness of the Sandur Hills on the south. The embankment height also varies, being higher in the center where the valley floor is the lowest. The topography of the valley floor, then, suggests that traffic through the valley must have run primarily along the northern edge, a supposition supported by the position of settlements such as Bayaluvaddigeri and Dharmasagara and by the placement of temples along the northern edge of the valley. Clearly, the construction of a trans-valley reservoir would have blocked most existing roads and paths and it is reasonable to imagine that these would have been reconfigured somehow.

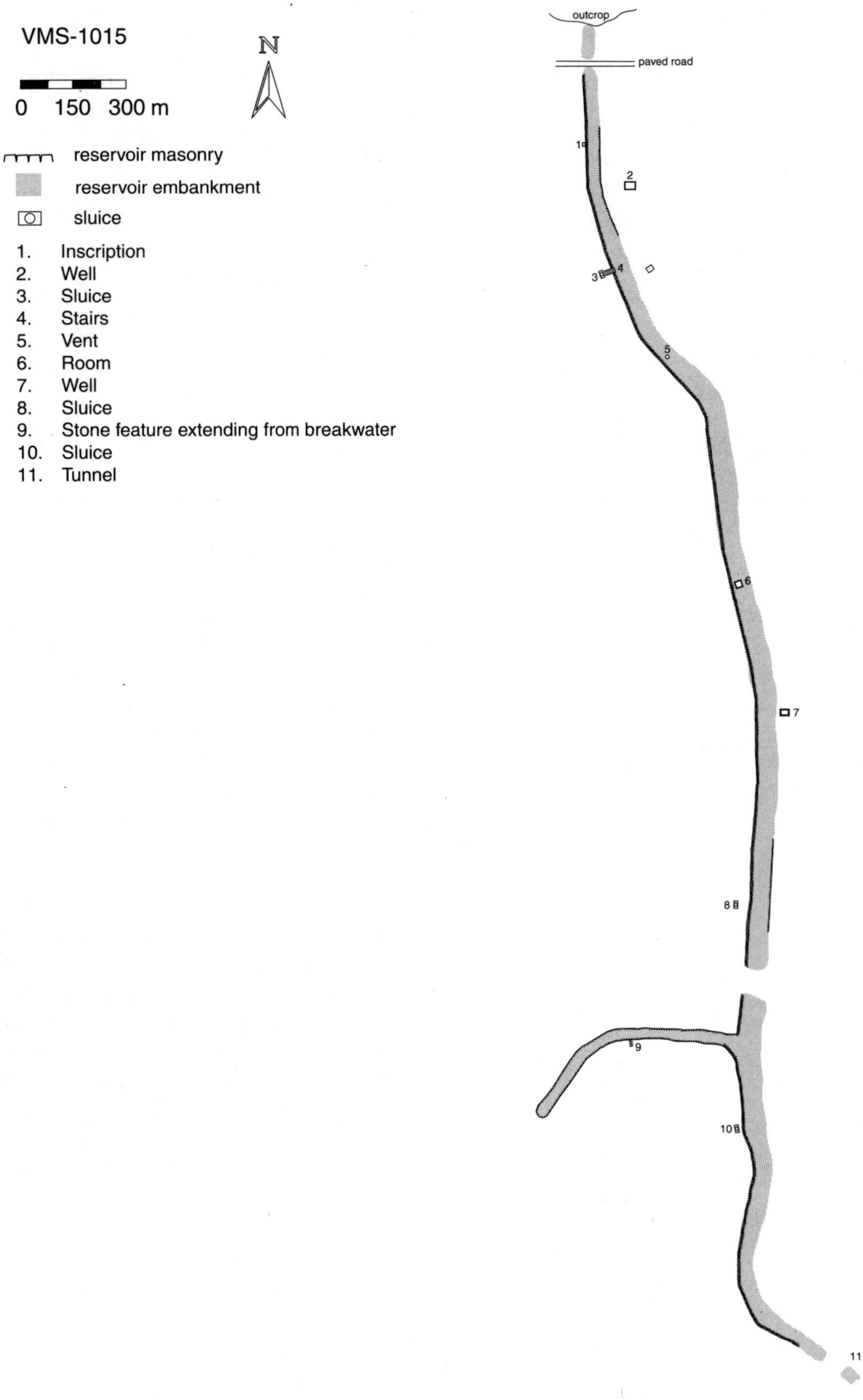

Figure 114. Plan view, VMS-1015.

Figure 115. Northernmost breach in VMS-1015.

Although there is no direct evidence in the form of road walls or a paved surface, it seems quite likely that after the construction of VMS-1015, traffic would have hugged the northern edge of the valley. The current paved road cuts right through VMS-1015 near its northern end.

As a trans-valley reservoir, this facility concentrates all the runoff from the main valley to this point. The force of this flow must be considerable. Although VMS-1015 is extremely high, it is not unusually wide, averaging about 30 meters in width. It does have a curving breakwater (described below) near its southern end, a somewhat exceptional feature that certainly owes its existence to the fast-moving runoff coming from the Sandur Hills.

VMS-1015 is no longer in use, having breached in six places. As discussed below, the older trans-valley reservoir, VMS-1016, is also seriously damaged, illustrating the risks of directly harvesting runoff from the Sandur Hills, a feat only the trans-valley reservoirs attempt. A few of the western valley facilities such as VMS-1002 and 1023 do tap into *nullahs* originating in the Sandur Hills, but only the trans-valley reservoirs (and VMS-1021, Chapter 7) actually touch the Sandur Hills. Although these hills constitute a reliable watershed, they also send down dangerously fast torrents in the rainy season, a situation that could only have been accentuated by Vijayanagara-period deforestation of the Sandur hills (Morrison 1995a). Such torrents posed both risks and an opportunities; clearly, trans-valley reservoirs required an accelerated maintenance schedule and an even greater than usual concentration and coordination of labor and resources for their maintenance.

The bed of the reservoir is now used for dry farming, as is its former *ayacut*, or area of irrigation. In a few places, bore wells fitted with electric pumps support the production of garden crops such as vegetables. The embankment is partially overgrown with thorny shrubs and trees; it is now used as a footpath.

Construction

Because of the great length of the embankment, this description begins at its northern end and moves toward the south. Just south of the paved road, near the northern end of the embankment, is the first breach, an impressive 10 to 12 meters wide gap where the embankment has been swept away (Figure 115). In this breach is a wall or footing built of small boulders, one course high, built perpendicular to the embankment. It is not clear whether this is a later addition or part of the original foundation of the *bund*. Just south of this breach and built *into* the western masonry, are two large protruding slabs, one of which contains a long inscription (described below). In this area, the western side of the embankment is faced with 10 courses of stepped masonry composed of medium to large unmodified and split boulders (Figure 116). The eastern side of the embankment is also faced with masonry, but here the stones are smaller and more irregularly coursed. This eastern masonry stops short of sluice 1 and does not continue beyond it.

About 200 meters south of the road, the embankment increases in height to an average of 18 courses of relatively smaller masonry, and contains another (uninscribed) protruding slab. In this high area is sluice 1 (Figure 117), which appears to be early. On the embankment just behind sluice 1 is a staircase composed of roughly cut slabs, some with Vijayanagara-style quarry marks. The steps are worn smooth from use. The 15 lower steps are in good condition, but the upper 10 to 15 are somewhat slumped. The sides the staircase are defined by long quarried slabs. There are some earthenware ceramics atop the embankment in this area, too fragmented to date. South of sluice 1 there is a round masonry and cement vent atop the embankment (described below).

The second breach occurs south of sluice 1. This gap is between 15 and 20 meters wide; its erosional channel is damp even in the dry season and it is clear that a substantial amount of water moves through this point. The third breach was caused by the construction of power lines and, again, is 15 to 20 meters wide. In between the third and fourth breaches is a small, square structure built atop the embankment (described below). Fifteen meters south of the third breach is a fourth, smaller breach. At this opening, the embankment is still

Figure 116. VMS-1015, embankment detail.

Figure 117. VMS-1015, sluice 1, overview.

in situ, but fill has eroded out to the east and even the west face is somewhat slumped. At this point, the embankment is much lower than it is further north, with 14 courses of medium-sized unmodified cobble masonry. The fifth breach is relatively minor and is the result of foot traffic. The embankment here is quite low, having only 6 courses of masonry. It may be that the southern end of the earlier, smaller version of this reservoir was somewhere around here, as the ends of an embankment are usually much lower than the middle.

South of this low area, the valley soil begins to grade from a mixed red and black to a pure red (*masab*) soil, tinted by the mineral-rich deposits of the Sandur Hills. The masonry also begins to change, from granite to the darker metamorphic rocks that make up the Sandur Hills. A sixth breach is found near sluice gate 2, where the embankment has 10 courses of stepped masonry. Just over 100 meters south of sluice 2, the railway line has blasted through the embankment, forming a 50 meters wide gap.

South of the rail line is a remarkable breakwater, a protruding curved embankment faced with masonry revetment on both sides. This feature is more than 400 meters long, itself the size of a substantial reservoir embankment. The masonry is stepped on both sides and rises to between 8 and 10 courses. The breakwater is 25 meters wide and 3 to 4 meters above the present ground surface. The style of the breakwater masonry is similar to that on the main embankment. Unfortunately, the junction between the two is somewhat disturbed, but they do appear to be continuous and contemporaneous. The breakwater is positioned to capture the flow from the confluence of two seasonal streams coming down from the Sandur Hills. As noted, it does not seem to be an earlier facility integrated into this one; instead it must serve to protect the main *bund* by capturing and slowing down water from these Sandur-derived *nullahs*.

South of the breakwater is sluice 3. Near the southern end of the embankment, where it rises to meet a rounded hill, a recent road runs through a 45 meters wide gap in the embankment. That this is an early breach and not the result of a recent intervention is suggested by the remains of an under-embankment tunnel, all that is left of the fourth sluice. Thus, we can count eight breaches in this huge reservoir, six of which seem to have been caused by flooding.

Sluices and Outlets

Sluice gate 1 (Figure 117), a modestly scaled, fourteenth- or fifteenth-century sluice is deeply buried, with its lower cross-bar just visible above the ground surface. The roughly dressed, rectangular uprights support an upper cross-bar with a three-part moulding sequence. The latter consists of a lower and upper moulding (two-stepped with angled bevel, with half medallions and corner quarter medallions) separated by an inset central slab. This slab contains a central carved panel facing the embankment. The panel depicts Sita flanked by Hanuman and Sugriva, both of whom face her respectfully with folded hands. This sluice is quite similar, down to the sculptures, to VMS-4, sluice 1, an early fifteenth-century facility.

Sluice gate 2 (Figures 118 and 119) is a huge double sluice approximately 6 to 7 meters high, built entirely of dressed granite elements. The construction of this sluice echoes that of temples in a different way than the usual "doorway" design of most sluice gates. In this sluice, the uprights are much like the columns of temples and other formal structures, even having capitals and a roof rather than a lintel. Rather than two uprights, this sluice has four, not unlike a two-by-two columned *mandapa*. Instead of the usual mouldings atop the uprights, it has cross-shaped brackets with pendant rectangles, capped by lintels with square projections and horizontally-laid ceiling slabs, just like a temple. Above these is a pitched roof made of large stone slabs; the roof slabs have shallow angled bevels.

The eastern set of uprights holds in a lower crossbar with a central hole, now about 3 meters above ground level. However, there is no corresponding hole in the roof. The western set of uprights does, however, have a perforated roof, indicating that water flow was sometimes controlled through this side. The entire sluice

Figure 118. VMS-1015, sluice 2, overview.

Figure 119. VMS-1015, sluice 2, detail.

Figure 120. VMS-1015, sluice 2, tunnel covering.

apparatus is set up on a low platform or plinth, which is also quite formal and constructed entirely of dressed slabs. The sides of this plinth are defined by a three-part stone basement on the north, west, and south. This consists of a simple horizontal slab, followed by an inset slab covered by an upper horizontal slab. This follows the form of a regular three-part moulding (three horizontal elements, the central one being recessed) and is similar to the basements of many stone structures in the city. The plinth is bisected by a slab-lined channel which leads from the reservoir bed through the sluice and into the tunnel.

Sluice 2 has a well-built tunnel (Figure 120) extending from the sluice platform and extending into the embankment. The tunnel itself is not visible, but its brick and plaster covering enters the embankment just above the lowest course of masonry facing. The tunnel and its covering are roughly triangular in cross-section. Significantly, the tunnel incorporates two internal steps *up* from the sluice area toward the embankment; water pressure would have forced the water to flow into the tunnel and upward.

Sluice 3, a large double sluice south of the breakwater, is similar to sluice 2, but is less massively constructed and more poorly preserved (Figure 121). The eastern set of uprights has an upper cross-bar with an off-center, incomplete hole, a pattern similar to that of sluice 2 where the eastern set of uprights would not have been functional under high water conditions. The lower cross-bar on the western set of uprights is made from a (reused) moulding slab (two-stepped with angled bevel and half medallions). This slab is not pegged into place and may be a later replacement. Like sluice 2, the four uprights of sluice 3 sit on a prepared foundation. Here, however, the basement is much less formal, consisting only of two east-west cement slabs joining together the paired uprights. There are no dressed slabs or moulding-type sequences, nor is there a platform. The tunnel is clearly visible running from the sluice into the embankment. It is slab-lined and covered with cemented bricks and then cobbles.

The fourth sluice is indicated only by the remains of its tunnel, now exposed in a breach. Embankments often breach near sluices and it is probable that this breach predates the road now passing through it. About 50 meters of the tunnel is exposed here. The tunnel passage is defined by quarried slabs on all sides; the opening is *c.* 1 meter wide and 0.5 meter high. The slabs forming the roof of the tunnel are capped with a layer of cement; the whole tunnel is then covered with a semi-circular sheath of brick and concrete.

Associated Features

There are several features associated with VMS-1015. From north to south, these include an inscription, a well, a vent, a square structure, a second well, and a stone wall extending from the breakwater. The inscription is discussed separately, below.

Approximately 150 meters north of sluice 1 is a rock-cut and partially masonry-lined well (Figure 122) some 25 meters east of the side of the embankment. Like most reservoir-side wells, then, it is placed below the embankment. The well is 5 meters deep. Its date of construction is unknown, but it may be post-Vijayanagara.

On top of the embankment, between the third and fourth breaches, is a 9 by 9 meters square structure built of one-course high walls of small to medium cobbles and rubble. There are no doorways, no wall fall (suggesting that the walls were never any higher), and no artifacts associated with this "room". It may be the base for a structure built of wattle-and-daub or some other ephemeral material.

About 350 meters north of sluice 2 and about 30 meters east of the *bund* is a 5 meters deep, masonry-lined, rock-cut well. The edges of the well are littered with plaster fragments. The masonry is constructed from thin slabs of metamorphic rocks, a shape not usually associated with Vijayanagara construction. The corners of the well are not quite square, but the west and probably the south sides of the well have stepped-out masonry walls, as do most Vijayanagara wells. It is not possible to assign a date to this well but, like the well to the north, it appears to post-date the sixteenth century.

Figure 121. VMS-1015, sluice 3.

Figure 122. VMS-1015, northern well.

Figure 123. VMS-1015, DAM staff recording inscription.

Inscription

The inscription (Figure 123) is incised into a granite slab, somewhat irregular in shape, built into the western masonry of the *bund*, about four courses down from the top. The slab is carved with a sculpture depicting a sun, moon, trident, and *lingam*, and has 17 lines of text. The text itself is in a somewhat "rustic" (that is to say, non-literary), sixteenth-century Telugu and refers to a grant of land beneath the Dharmasagara reservoir.[15] The following translation was provided by Phillip Wagoner:

1-3. Sri Ganadhipati. Obeisance to Srimat Ramanuja.

4-6. In the year 1439 of the Salivahana-Shaka era, being the cyclic year Ishara, on the seventh day of the bright fortnight of the month of Shravana, [?in the reign of?] Shi Virapratapa Shi Krishnarayalu.

7-11. This inscription [?indicates?] the grant of land under the Dharma-sagara tank ...?... which is controlled for a rent[16] [? by Shakapati-nayaka?].

12-15. Additionally, the wealthy merchants say that if anyone interferes in this matter, they will incur the five great sins and be reborn as an ass.

16-17. So saying, this is the inscription that the merchants set up. Sri.

The Shaka year 1439 corresponds approximately to AD 1519; this inscription also mentions the Vijayanagara king Krishnadeva Raya, who ruled between AD 1509 and 1529 (Stein 1989a). It is interesting to note that although the (irrigated) land under Dharmasagara *kere* seems to have yielded revenue (although this is not entirely clear) for a local *nayaka*, Shakapati-nayaka, the inscription itself was commissioned by a group of merchants. Presumably these merchants also had some financial stake in the land grant. It is somewhat unusual, although by no means unheard of, that the person or institution receiving the grant is not mentioned. Perhaps this was thought to be well-known and in no need of reiteration. Given the physical integration of this inscription into the *bund* masonry, it seems likely that the reconstruction and expansion of VMS-1015 was completed in or around AD 1519.

Reservoir, VMS-1017

This small reservoir (Figure 124) blocks the mouth of a narrow but deep valley in the granitic hills on the north side of the valley, a short distance east of VMS-1015. North of the reservoir is a recent concrete-and-stone dam; north of that is a Vijayanagara-period fortification wall (VMS-1079) that blocks movement through the valley. The reservoir is no longer in use and is deeply silted in as indicated, in part, by differences in ground level above and below the *bund*. North of the embankment, the bed of the reservoir is only 0.6 meter lower than the top of the embankment while on the south side the ground surface is more than 3 meters lower. Even more telling than this, however, is the original waste weir whose surface is now 1.5 to 2 meters *lower* than the reservoir bed. Generally, of course, the base of the *kodi* sits well above the bed of the reservoir. All this serves to indicate a sediment build-up of more than 2 and perhaps as much as 3 meters.

The fortification wall, although more than 300 meters to the north of VMS-1017, would certainly have interfered with some of the runoff flowing south from the sides of the narrow valley toward the main valley. The reservoir is small and could probably have filled in spite of this, but it is also possible, given the current state of this facility, that the reservoir had already fallen out of use by the time the wall was built. If this is right, then it may date to the Early Vijayanagara period; this is however mostly conjectural. The reservoir bed itself does not support a particularly luxuriant vegetation, only a few small thorn bushes and some low grasses. Even in the months right after the monsoons the bed is dry. The embankment is 69 meters long and 15 meters wide.

Construction

Both sides of the embankment are faced with masonry consisting of small to medium-sized unmodified and split boulders. There are only four courses on the northern, upstream side of the *bund*, but the stepped-out courses are quite regular. On the southern, downstream, side of the embankment, construction is more haphazard and the pitch of the masonry is steeper; this face is bowed out rather than really stepped. There is one flat, dressed rectangular slab lying parallel to the south side of the embankment. The masonry opposite this slab is stepped out whereas elsewhere it is nearly straight. This seems to be the location of a staircase leading up the embankment; an unusual position for a staircase. These generally lead down to the water and not up onto the embankment from below the facility. Here, however, the steep pitch of the southern masonry virtually requires this and it may be supposed that the usual approach to this small reservoir was from the main valley to the south.

Sluices and Outlets

There are no sluices but the western end of the embankment has an informal waste weir. There is a 4 meter wide gap between the embankment and a low outcrop that forms the western end of the dam; this gap is partly filled in with piled-up boulders.

Other Features

A very sparse scatter of Vijayanagara-period earthenware ceramics lies scattered in the plowed fields below the reservoir.

Fortification Wall Across a Small Northern Valley, VMS-1079

A long, narrow valley emerging from the north side of the main valley just east of the trans-valley reservoir, VMS-1015, presents a potential, if not easy, route to the north through the rocky hills. This possibility is blocked by VMS-1079, a massively-built fortification wall, more than 350 meters long and up to 5 meters wide that stretches across the valley. The wall is built of two faces of cobbles and boulders which sandwich a cobble and boulder core. Up against this, an additional face was added onto the northern side of the wall, widening and strengthening it significantly. This third face occurs primarily in the low-lying parts of the valley where not only might human traffic be more likely, but the force of runoff through the valley would have been greater. Even now there is a stream running down the floor of the valley which carries water in the monsoon and immediate post-monsoon seasons; the wall is broken where this drainage runs through it. Perhaps there was some kind of opening here, either a gate or else a drainage feature that would have allowed water to reach reservoir VMS-1017 which lies about 300 meters downstream at the mouth of the valley.

Fortification Wall Across the Valley, VMS-1085

About 500 meters west of the village of Dharmasagara and a little more than 1 kilometer east of the embankment of the large sixteenth-century trans-valley reservoir, VMS-1015, a massively-built, formal fortification wall runs from the southern edge of the granitic hills that define the northern edge of the valley, across the floor of the main valley, up onto the metamorphic Sandur foothills. Amazingly, this wall runs all the way up to the top of the Sandur range, hugging the rugged terrain and turning sharply towards Hospet (R. Brubaker, personal communication). In all, this wall is more than 15 kilometers long, and averages 12 to 15 meters wide in the valley and 2 to 3 meters wide in the hills.

The construction of this wall across the valley floor is consistent with that of fortification walls surrounding the urban core and royal center of the city of Vijayanagara, with an outer face of well-fitted quarried and dressed grantic blocks built against an earthen core. These large blocks are primarily triangular in plan with a square or rectangular face – the tip of the triangle faces toward the interior of the wall. The inner (west) side of the wall is not faced with masonry, pattern we also see in some of the urban core walls. This formal construction stands in sharp contrast to the masonry style of most fortification walls outside the capital city and it seems probable that either the patronage arrangements and/or the craftspeople and laborers involved in building this huge barrier differed from those of most of the other fortifications and walls in this region and other outlying areas. This supposition is strengthened by the presence of a Vaishnavite temple (VMS-1027) interior and adjacent to this wall, not far from its northern gate. As noted, all of the other shrines and indeed the majority of religious images in the Daroji Valley are associated with either forms of Shiva or of the Goddess, figures with significant local appeal.[17] Vaishnavite shrines and temples, in contrast, have more "official" and elite connotations, with Late Vijayanagara emperors preferentially worshiping forms of Vishnu, supporting Vaishnavite sects, and endowing Vaishnavite temples. It seems significant, then, that the only Vaishnavite temple in the Daroji Valley is spatially associated with this formal fortification wall, a wall unlike any other this far away from the city itself.

We do not know, unfortunately, either the construction date or the conditions of construction of this wall. Given its form, undoubtedly high construction cost, and strategic location, I suggest that it was either built with official patronage – if not the king or one of his ministers then perhaps a local *nayaka* – or under official orders. The presence of this fortification points to the strategic importance of the Daroji Valley for the city and its leaders. The valley is ringed in by fortification walls and other barriers to movement, including reservoirs. Despite the sometimes precarious position of reservoir irrigation, the produce of this valley was undoubtedly an important factor in the overall food supply of the city, a role which makes the huge investment in irrigation facilities here somewhat more explicable.

It is not clear exactly how high VMS-1085 might have originally been. There are never more than about 3 courses of blocks preserved along its entire valley-floor course; only when the construction style changes to piled-up metamorphic boulders (Figure 125), as it does at the base of the Sandur foothills, is much more of the wall preserved.[18] It is possible that these well-cut blocks simply formed the base of a higher, plastered wall of rammed earth. There is one example of a wall like this in the royal center of the city and as all the beautifully cut, dry-laid masonry walls in the city were once covered with plaster, presumably no one would have been the wiser. It could also be the case that the wall has been systematically dismantled. If so, this was an extremely orderly process leaving no traces (stray blocks, chips of granite from block reduction) along the more than 2 kilometers of its valley-floor length, not the kind of record one expects from years of attack by local farmers but instead suggesting a well-planned and well-financed program of removal. There are many examples of rammed-earth superstructures in the region, suggesting that local conditions are generally favorable for their preservation and thus suggesting that this massive wall has seen some kind of deliberate destruction.[19]

There are two openings in VMS-1085 on the valley floor (Figure 126), not including the present-day course of the paved road through the valley which runs through a gap in the wall. The northern gate lies some 20 meters south of the outcrop that defines the northern edge of the valley. The wall continues up the side of the outcrop, restricting the flow of traffic to the 3 meter-wide gate passage itself. The southern edge of the latter is flanked on the exterior, eastern side by a large, low gate platform (7 by 4 meters). Gate platforms are almost always paired, one on each side of an entrance, so this solitary platform, built, unlike the wall itself, of unmodified boulders, is rather unusual. The gate passage itself is defined by two courses of very long, horizontally laid split boulders. There is a moderate-density scatter of Vijayanagara earthenware ceramics in the field to the east of this gate. The road that once went through the gate (VMS-1084, below) can be clearly traced to the west, but on the eastern side of the wall any trace of it has been obliterated by cultivation.

The southern opening in this long fortification wall is located in about the middle of the valley at about the same latitude as the village of Dharmasagara. This suggests not only that the wall is either contemporaneous with or post-dates the village, but also that the Dharmasagara villagers needed regular access

Figure 124. VMS-1017 and surroundings.

Figure 125. VMS-1085, wall on ridge; arrow shows wall crossing horizon.

Figure 126. VMS-1085/1027, wall running across valley.

to the area east of the wall, the area watered by VMS-1015, the massive sixteenth-century reservoir.[20] In fact, it may even be the case that the fortification was intended in large part to protect the rich, irrigated lands under this reservoir. As noted in the discussion of this facility, the construction of this huge reservoir would have radically altered routes of movement through the valley, pushing traffic up onto the edge of the northern outcrop. Road segment VMS-1084 runs, precisely as predicted, along the edge of this outcrop; although movement along the edge of the steeper Sandur foothills might have also been possible, the fact the wall extends all the way up the side of the first range of foothills and that there is no gate at this end suggests that movement was very tightly channeled through the two (perhaps three if the modern-day road has cut through an original opening) openings in the wall.

The mid-valley gate is wider, about 10 meters, but is in poorer condition than the northern gate. There are traces of a gate platform on the north side of the opening – again, on the exterior or eastern side of the wall. Both the placement and construction style of this wall, together with its association with the lone Vaishnavite shrine in the Daroji Valley, suggest its association with the city of Vijayanagara. The wall faces *outward* toward the east, protecting entrances to the city as well as the relatively built-up and more intensively farmed western main valley.[21] It is massively and formally constructed in the "urban style" of the Vijayanagara period, a mode of construction that would have required a great deal of labor and some specialized construction skills. Compared to the more informal fortification walls that ring the eastern end of the valley (Chapter 7) as well as the hilltop construction of VMS-1085, this valley-floor wall stands out. There is some possibility, even probability, that these walls were all constructed at different times, but as many different types of walls were built in and around the city during the Vijayanagara period, I doubt that chronology *per se* can account for the differences between this wall and others in the Daroji area. Its construction was certainly differently organized from these and, I suspect, was also differently financed and sponsored.

East-West Road Segment, VMS-1084

Running through the northern gate in the fortification wall described above is a 1.2 kilometers long road segment, part of the road that once ran the length of the valley (Figure 127). The visible remnants of this route begin just west of the gate where east-west road walls define a 9-meter wide road bed running along the base of the outcrop. These walls are better-preserved further west where they are built of dark-colored unmodified boulders, 3 to 4 courses high. Moving west, the road bed is elevated, built up onto the side of the outcrop and supported by earthen fill revetted with a wide (2 meters) double-faced wall on the south. The course of the road is slightly sinuous, perched partway up the outcrop and following its curving edge. The road is not very high, just above the dry-famed fields below. This section of road up on the edge on the outcrop ran over some of the naturally outcropping boulders whose surfaces are now quite worn; the gravelly surface of the outcrop apparently did not require surfacing as did the sections further west. In this area, the road begins to leave the outcrop, following a relatively straight course over the sandy ground and there are traces of a cobbled road surface in between the two road walls. Near its current western end the road surface has been plowed. In this area the fields south of the road are littered with patches of rubble; however, artifact densities are low and it is not clear what kind of structures there may have been here. The road remnant ends near the reservoir VMS-1017, a facility which captured runoff from the mouth of the small valley blocked up further north by the fortification wall VMS-1079. Although it seems probable that the road once ran along the embankment of this reservoir, the poor condition of the *bund* makes this proposition difficult to evaluate. Were the road to continue along its present course, it would rejoin the northern outcrop just east of the trans-valley reservoir VMS-1015; it almost certainly once extended as far east as Bayaluvaddigeri and

Figure 127. Roadway, VMS-1084; arrow points to road wall.

Figure 128. Shrine, VMS-1027.

perhaps even along the entire length of the valley.

Vaishnavite Shrine and Walled Enclosure, VMS-1027

East of the 'ocean of *dharma*' (VMS-1015), is VMS-1027, a small shrine built up against the western (interior) face of the massive fortification wall, VMS-1085. Several smaller walls have been built up against the fortification wall to form a substantial walled enclosure around the shrine. The shrine (Figure 128), which now sits on the northern edge of the paved road through the valley, consists of a Vijayanagara-period core almost entirely enclosed within recent whitewashed masonry walls. The original configuration seems to have been a small square sanctuary (presumably walled, but this is unclear given the heavy structural overlay), facing south toward the road and fronted by a porch. The porch may have originally had only two columns, or it may have had four, the outer two being entirely swallowed up in newer walls. It seems most likely that there were ever only two, standing on either side of the lotus-medallioned doorway into the sanctuary. There is no image in the sanctuary now and it has a ceiling of rotated squares.

The columns are square in section, each with two inset octagonal sections and sculptures enclosed in circular medallions. The most prominent of these is a kneeling Garuda figure on the interior of the western column, near the base. Garuda, the vehicle of Vishnu, faces the sanctuary, hands folded in worship. The newer floor material buries him up to his knees. Opposite Garuda, on the interior of the eastern column, are (from the lower panel up) Narasimha, a turtle, and a lion, all symbols of Vishnu. The western column also has a *hamsa* (a mythical goose) carved on its exterior sidc; all the rest of the sculptures are either geometric or floral. Unusually, there are no capitals atop the columns so they carry the granite roof beams directly. The ceiling is made of parallel granite slabs, obviously original, but the roof above it is all recent.

Besides sitting by the side of the road, this shrine was also placed just inside a Vijayanagara-period fortification wall that runs north from the edge of the road. This wall is most substantial on the east, where its eastern, outward face consists of large quarried blocks, some square, some rectangular, and some triangular. The points of the triangular blocks face into the wall; many of the massive fortification walls associated with the city have this kind of construction. Only one course of this wall remains and even that is broken in several places. Still, it is possible to trace the course of the wall because there is a long linear earthen mound that follows its course. The wall is about 6 meters wide – quite substantial – but there is no masonry facing on the interior, west side, a pattern that is seen, for example, on the outer circuit of city walls (Morrison 1995a). All this suggests a fortification wall meant to impede movement into the valley from the east. This north-south fortification extends only about 100 meters to the north, ending at a seasonal stream that lies about 100 meters south of the outcrops that mark the northern edge of the valley. This wall seems to have been the eastern, and by far best-constructed side of an enclosure, *c.* 150 meters east-west and 100 meters north-south. The north side of the enclosed area is marked by banked soil along the edge of the *nullah.* There is a fragment of masonry wall at the western end of this northern boundary; both the wall and the drainage curve sharply to the south so that the drainage crosses the road about 150 meters west of the shrine. In this area, the fragmentary wall is 1.2 meters wide and is solidly constructed of small boulders, some split in half, and cobbles. On its exterior, western face the wall is 3 courses high. There are sections of a southern enclosure wall about 25 meters long that now lie in a ditch along the side of the paved road. The wall seems to be built over a drain of long parallel slabs placed north-south (perpendicular to the road). The drain is capped a course of large (up to 2 meters long) rectangular blocks and slabs. Like the massively-built fortification wall to the east, these elements have numerous Vijayanagara-style quarry marks. This foundation is then capped by 3 to 4 courses of split boulders.

Inside this enclosure is a recent well and a

few scattered earthenware sherds. I noticed one piece of iron slag, but no other artifacts. It is not at all clear what the purpose of this enclosure was. The variable construction styles of the walls and especially the coincidence of the southern drain-cum-enclosure wall with the present road ditch suggests episodes of reconstruction, especially since most of the masonry of the massive eastern wall is now missing. I suspect that the major Vijayanagara-period fortification wall that extended across the valley was later partly dismantled and the enclosure built. The enclosure subsequently fell out of use although the temple continues to be actively maintained and monitored, even to the extent that visiting archaeologists are closely watched.

DISCUSSION: THE WESTERN PART OF THE MAIN VALLEY

Despite its isolation into its own chapter, the western part of the main valley should be considered in conjunction with the rest of the main valley. Although the only direct evidence for pre-Vijayanagara use of the western part of the main valley are some fragments of a Neolithic ashmound near Kakuballu and a few Early Middle period hero stones, the evidence of Vijayanagara occupation and use is both abundant and complex. I have begun to dissect the remains of the main valley into discrete clusters of features, what I have called the Bayaluvaddigeri cluster (earlier, further east) and the Papinayakanahalli cluster (later, further west). These clusters certainly, however, overlap in both time and space and I have allowed some of that ambiguity into the text by following the contemporary landscape of the valley rather than a reconstructed sequence of change. In the following chapter, I complete the description of the main valley, holding for Chapter 9 a general discussion of the basic patterns of land use this analysis reveals.

NOTES

1. Associated with the still-occupied village of Papinayakanahalli are a temple complex (VMS-1008), a smaller temple (VMS-1037), two shrines (VMS-1039 and VMS-1026), and a fort (VMS-1009).
2. The evidence for Iron Age habitation is equivocal, due in part to criteria for assigning dates to surface finds, as discussed in Chapter 2. It is not possible at present to rule out Iron Age use of the main valley and indeed, it seems likely that this region was used in some way at this time.
3. By trans-valley reservoir, I mean a reservoir whose embankment stretches all the way or almost all the way across the valley and which collects runoff from both the northern and southern sides of the valley. Note that only trans-valley reservoirs directly tap runoff from the Sandur Hills.
4. Papinayakanahalli today lies at the intersection of the important paved road that connects Hospet (the taluk headquarters) with Bellary (the district headquarters), and a dirt track (recently paved) that runs north to Kamalapuram and the tourist and pilgrimage areas of Vijayanagara and Hampi. A huge monumental gateway has recently been built at the intersection of these roads, mirroring one constructed for a cultural festival in Hampi built where the road to Hampi branches off from the Hospet-Kamalapuram road. Apparently, Papinayakanahalli is still viewed as a kind of gateway to the city of Vijayanagara.
5. Vijayanagara king Devaraya II ruled between AD 1422 and 1446 (Karashima 1984).
6. Note that both of these deities are Vaishnavite, Garuda being the vehicle of Vishnu. Neither of these manifestations are typically used as door guardians, but I assign them that role based on their position on the sides of the door frame.
7. Rock-etched game boards are common on gate platforms, forts, and other places where people spent long periods of time, including temples. Some of the games represented are still played today.
8. Aquatic creatures are appropriate denizens of *prakara* walls, as the temple itself can be seen as the earth surrounded by the cosmic ocean just outside the walls.
9. The *pranala* or water-chute generally exits the sanctuary on the north side (the normative direction for temples to face being east); it carries off fluids from the *abisheka* or ceremonial bathing of the image. Fluids may include water, ghee, coconut milk, cow's milk, etc.
10. This hero stone probably was sculpted some time in the Early Middle period. However, as it

is not *in situ*, it is difficult to draw any firm conclusion from this about pre-Vijayanagara land use in the western part of the main valley.

11. Such indications are not uncommon and include paths cleared of boulders, road walls, areas of worn sheetrock, cobbled surfaces, steps or ramps, and even elevated, constructed road bed.
12. See Lycett 1994. Artifact densities around agricultural features are generally extremely low and outside habitation areas and manured fields, ceramics most often occur in well-defined clusters of limited size. In the Daroji Valley, as in the intensive survey area to the north, there do not appear to be many field camps associated with agricultural activity (or if there were, they left little to no enduring trace). In contrast, we have many indications of small-scale and/or short-term encampments in the rocky uplands where grazing and collecting typically take place.
13. This must be the same location as Field No. 45 is noted to be on the southeast boundary of the village. The "very ancient" temple is described as a Shaivite (Isvara) temple with a less-formal goddess temple nearby.
14. In the census categories, there were 46 cultivators, 15 laborers, 84 women and children, 2 in government service, 1 learned, 3 in minor professions, 2 'dress' (tailors, etc.), 6 property (?), and 9 others (Government of India 1874: 249), a total accounting for 167 of the inhabitants.
15. I am deeply indebted to both Phillip Wagoner for supplying the transcription and translation and to the Karnataka Directorate of Archaeology and Museums, who took the impression of the inscription. Apologies to him for excluding the diacritics which he duly supplied.
16. The inscription specifically mentions *guttaku* or *guttige* tenure, a system of tax farming in which rights of tax collection are auctioned off to *guttedars*, or tax farmers. This kind of system saves a great deal of state infrastructure and effort and was widely employed in the empire. It is, however, interesting that this kind of indirect taxation would have been employed so close to the capital city where one might presume greater centralized control over revenue extraction.
17. As noted, we can extend a partial exemption to Hanuman images and the worship of Hanuman from consideration as an "orthodox" Vaishnavite deity. Hanuman can be legitimately seen as something of a local hero/god, being native to this place. The "traditional" birthplace of Hanuman is marked by a high granitic outcrop on the north bank of the Tungabhadra River not far from Vijayanagara city. Vijayanagara-period Hanuman representations are almost invariably in the heroic form known as Anjaneya; these images, something greater than life-sized, tend to be associated with gateways and entrances. Hanuman does appear in other forms on Vijayanagara architecture, usually Late period Vaishnavite temples. In this case he might appear in a worshipful posture, standing with folded hands, or may be depicted together with his brother Sugriva, Rama and Sita, all of whom, together with Hanuman, himself, are key figures in the *Ramayana* epic. As discussed above, this region is often represented locally as Kishkindha, the monkey-kingdom and ancestral home of Hanuman and his family.
18. Brubaker has recently documented the remarkable extent of VMS-1085. In its Sandur Hills incarnation, the wall is built of roughly-coursed cobbles with no differentiation between internal and external faces. Like some of the walls in the Sultanpur area (Chapter 7), VMS-1085 turns a sharp corner at the top of the hill in order to follow the ridge to the west. Brubaker suggests that the wall may serve more as a boundary marker than a fortification.
19. There are several historical references to the destruction of walls, moats, and other fortifications by the British. By the early twentieth century, municipalities had to obtain permission from the Archaeological Survey department before they pulled down any fortifications that were "old". Clearly, a fortification that blocked the entire Daroji Valley, an important route of movement and one that avoided the canal-irrigated fields to the north, would have been a significant impediment to the movement of troops and others. The wall is broken through by the railway line, but this alone cannot account for the wholesale destruction of this feature.
20. Recall that the association of land under this reservoir with the village of Dharmasagara was established by the inscription built into the reservoir *bund*.
21. That is, relative to the eastern part of the main valley and the Avinamodugu valley, Chapters 7 and 8.

Chapter Seven

THE MAIN VALLEY: EAST

> At Daraji there is a very fine lake and a b., to reach which it is necessary to go off the road and climb a steep incline. A tiger killed a man and woman here in 1878, and was hunted but escaped. The lake is 8 m. [miles] long and 1 m. broad and ought to be connected with the Tungabhadra r., in which case it would afford a never failing supply of water for irrigation. Snakes and scorpions are very numerous here. (Eastwick 1859: 347)

The eastern part of the main valley (Figure 129) is dominated by the massive Daroji reservoir, VMS-1019, the culmination of the main valley reservoir system. The area just upstream from the Daroji reservoir is now mostly uncultivated and uninhabited, with the exceptions of the villages of Kurekuppa (Vijayanagara-period Anantasetu) and Gadiganuru. This region was once more densely populated. The Daroji reservoir is supplied by three large seasonal streams: the Banuchandra Vanka on the north, flowing out of the main valley; the Nari Halla on the south, coming more directly down from the Sandur Hills; and the Kanigana Halla, flowing out of the Avinamodugu Valley (Chapter 8). All of these drainages were foci of settlement at one time; land use along the Banuchandra Vanka is considered in this chapter.

Unlike the western end of the main valley where Vijayanagara-period constructions dominate the contemporary landscape, the eastern end has good evidence for intensive land use during the Neolithic, Early Historic, and Early Middle periods as well. The broad Bellary plain to the east of the Daroji *kere* was a major focus of both pre- and post-Vijayanagara settlement, as noted in Chapter 2. This long-term record makes the landscape history of the eastern part of the main valley both complex and interesting; it is clear that both land use and the very shape and appearance of this area have changed radically over the last four millennia.

Of course, as elsewhere in this region, the actions of people during the Vijayanagara period left a powerful imprint on the eastern valley landscape. Both the Daroji reservoir and VMS-1016, the older trans-valley reservoir replaced by the sixteenth-century VMS-1015, had a substantial effect on drainage patterns, vegetation, soils, and transportation routes. Associated with VMS-1016 is a small, now-abandoned settlement, VMS-109, while further east is a complex palimpsest of abandoned settlements, including the villages of Pemmanahalli and Gonahala. The town of Kurekuppa is nestled at the base of an isolated granitic hill not far from the western edge of the Daroji reservoir. Kurekuppa, which also has a Neolithic ashmound, is associated with a badly-damaged reservoir, VMS-1018 and it is possible that both declined in importance following the expansion of the Daroji reservoir in the seventeenth century. There is some indication that the eastern part of the main valley has been overgrazed and degraded; the dominant vegetation now is a depauperate thorn scrub which has very little utility to local residents – it provides only a little forage and firewood and even these are sought elsewhere when the opportunity presents itself. This landscape contrasts with the well-tended fields of the western half of the main valley where soils are more well-developed and plant taxa more diverse. The eastern part of the valley is much wider than the western part; it has received less colluvial deposition and its

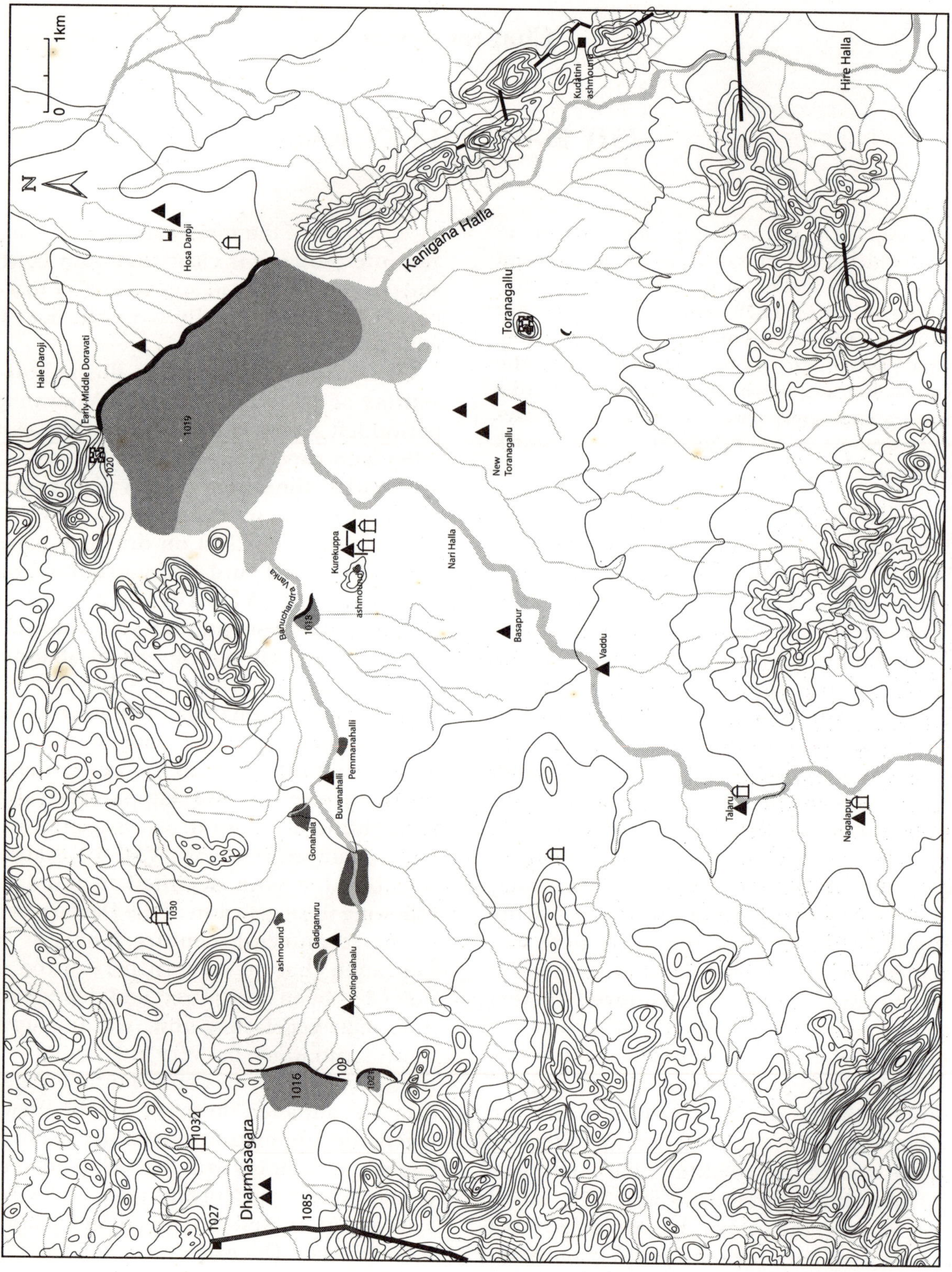

Figure 129. Map of eastern part of the main Daroji Valley.

watercourses are much more well-defined and deeply entrenched. In this chapter I first complete the description of the main valley and then discuss some of its overall historical contours and transformations.

SETTLEMENT AND LAND USE IN THE EASTERN PART OF THE MAIN VALLEY

As discussed in Chapter 6, the massively-built, formal fortification wall VMS-1085 divides the main valley in two. While all the well-dated structures of the western part of the main valley can be assigned to the Vijayanagara period, that is not the case for the eastern section. Here we have good evidence for intensive use of the main valley during the Neolithic, Early Historic, and Early Middle periods as well as the Vijayanagara period. As always, assessment of Iron Age occupation is problematic, and there is little unambiguous evidence for use of the eastern part of the main valley at this time. If this is correct, it would create a curious gap in what is otherwise a record of continuous occupation of this area from the beginning of agricultural communities in the south to the present, suggesting that much of this presumed gap may stem from problems of archaeological systematics rather than any actual abandonment of the region.

The Neolithic in the Daroji Corridor

Gadiganur Ashmound

In the eastern valley, north of the village of Gadiganuru and near the base of a steep escarpment there is an artifact scatter which surrounds the eroded remnants of two Neolithic ashmounds, VMS-1033 (Figure 130). First described in the 1903-4 Archaeological Survey of India report on the region,[1] these mounds were also noted by Foote (1916: 93) and Subbarao and later visited by Allchin (1963: 50) who described it as follows:

> There are two small ashmounds, neither of any great height, separated by about 200 yards. All round and between the mounds there is a scatter of stone artifacts and pottery ranging from Neolithic and Iron Age to early historic periods. It was difficult to find any well-sealed deposits, but such pottery as we found in association with the mound, or on exposed sections was of Neolithic A1 and A2 ware. . . . Very slight traces of a vallum of ash remain. The settlement area, which produced many stone axes and other typical finds of Neolithic date, as it had done earlier for Foote and Subbarao, makes it clear that the two ashmounds relate to a small Neolithic settlement at this site. . . .

When we visited this place almost forty years after Allchin's description was published, we found only one mound, some 40 by 65 meters and only about 3 meters high, and no trace of a "vallum of ash". This mound has been cut into on the west side; the exposed section clearly indicates two major layers of vitrified dung. The upper surface of the mound is flat. It currently supports a tree and a tree shrine. In the area around the ashmound is a moderate density of brown and gray plainware sherds, only a few of them micaceous. In this area and in the area to the east of the mound are also numerous red-slipped Neolithic sherds and a lithic assemblage consisting largely of smaller quartzite and larger basalt flakes. I was able to locate only one sherd that could possibly be called Black and Red Ware, a pattern which does not suggest a post-Neolithic date for this location, contrary to the findings cited above.[2] The question of the occupational history of the Gadiganur site thus remains open. Although the Gadiganur ashmound seemed to me to have been in use solely during the Southern Neolithic, the possibility that earlier researchers removed evidence of later use of this place, that subsequent disturbance has obscured it, or that our brief visit was insufficient to recover such evidence, must be entertained.

Kurukuppa Ashmound

In addition to the Gadiganuru ashmounds and settlement, Allchin also describes an eroded ashmound on the isolated granitic hill at Kurekuppa (1963: 51). This place, which later became a Vijayanagara *agrahara*, yielded Neolithic artifacts, including groundstone mortars and pestles that were actually embedded in the ash of the mound (Figure 131). Kurekuppa is now located near the

Figure 130. Gadiganur ashmound.

Figure 131. Kurekuppa ashmound.

western edge of the water-spread of the Daroji reservoir, off of the main road in an area now overrun with thorny scrub. Like several other parts of the eastern main valley, the area around Kurekuppa seems to be only erratically exploited, with the areas given over to thorn bushes not even suitable for grazing and only occasionally used for firewood. Although much more work on vegetation history remains to be done, it is tempting to see the contemporary degraded landscape of the eastern part of the main valley as, at least in part, artifactual.

The Kurekuppa ashmound site sits atop the granite inselberg west of the village; the ashmound is located in a small saddle between two boulder-strewn peaks on the northern edge of a large, somewhat sloping terrace. There is a small shrine currently under construction some 120 meters northeast of the ashmound, but the present disturbed state of this feature seems to significantly predate this construction. The vitrified dung-cinder deposits cover an area of approximately 30 by 10 meters and are mounded to a height of between 2 and 3 meters. The ashmound is in poor condition; at least half of it has been mined out and large blocks of cinder dung have been reused as structural elements in the numerous small walls atop the outcrop. The western 15 meters of the exposed face of the mound is constituted of a solid mass of vitrified cinder dung, while the eastern 15 meters is comprised of *in situ* cinder interdigitated with and fused to large granite cobbles and boulders, many of which appear to be in their original positions, suggesting that the dung making up this mound was originally piled on and around natural boulders before being fired. The magnitude of the disturbance makes the original size of the ashmound difficult to determine.

On an elevated terrace directly northwest of the ashmound is a linear alignment of medium-sized cobbles, only about 4 meters long. An elevated high point southeast of the ashmound contains a number of rock bruisings pecked into the exposed boulder faces, as does the slope down from the southern edge of the terrace. Artifacts are scattered all across the terrace, although the highest concentrations are in the area just south of the exposed face of the ashmound. Among the cultural material noted on the surface were flakes of red-brown chert, flakes and retouched flakes of quartzite, a polished basalt celt fragment, a granite anvil stone and large saddle quern, and a moderate concentration of Neolithic grey/pink micaceous ceramics.

There is some indication that the lofty outcrop now supporting Daroji Fort also had some Neolithic settlement. Bruce Foote (1914) reports stone celts from the base of the hill, tools which are traditionally seen as Neolithic (indeed, as neoliths) but which can date as late at the Early Historic. On the eastern slope of this same hill, I encountered a beautiful mustard-colored chert microblade, a microlith which could date to any time between the Mesolithic (also known as microlithic) and the Early Historic.[3] Despite the ambiguities in dating these isolated finds, it does seem likely that more systematic work on the Daroji Fort hill might result in the identification of Neolithic-period remains.

Kudatini Ashmound

A third ashmound site, and by far the most impressive, is the well-known ashmound and associated artifact scatter in the Kudatini pass (VMS-1035, Figure 19). This pass, at the eastern end of the Daroji Valley and near the mouth of the Avinamodugu Valley is now one of the few easy routes through the rather smooth, rounded hills defining the eastern end of the valley. Unlike the rocky, granitic hills to the north with their masses of exposed rock, these hills have some soil development and although they now support only grasses and *Euphorbia*, it seems probable that this vegetation assemblage is a product of wood-gathering and overgrazing and that the hills once maintained a slightly denser array of xerophytic vegetation. The Kudatini ashmound seems to be situated strategically in the pass, in a position to view and observe the area around it. From the ashmound, one can see the massive Bellary inselberg (Copper Mountain) to the east, and north of this the smaller granitic hills near Kupgal and Sanganakallu. To the west/northwest and back into the Daroji Valley, one can see the isolated hill associated with Kurekuppa, and Toranagallu at the mouth of the Avinamodugu Valley, though it is not possible to make out the location of the Gadiganur ashmound. The paved Hospet-Bellary road literally runs through the ashmound, the road having cut the mound. This road divides into two segments, one in each direction, to avoid totally destroying the mound, though it has been extensively damaged.

Perhaps because of its accessibility, Kudatini has been studied several times, the first possibly by Mackenzie in the late eighteenth century, but since then by Newbold (1836: 670-1, 1843: 129-36), Cole (1838: 130-3), Foote (1887b: 262-73), Longhurst (1916: 145-7), and Raymond and Bridget Allchin (Allchin 1963: 52-7). Although Longhurst supervised the initial highway department cut into the mound and the Allchins also worked with a fresh highway department section, none of this work was based on systematic excavation and there are no radiometric dates from the mound or surrounding areas. Although Kudatini is often presumed to be an isolated mound with no evidence of settlement, there is in fact an artifact scatter associated with the ash mound. Allchin notes (1963: 53) that they visited the mound on several occasions in 1957 and located no "finds" around it or on nearby slopes. This is consonant with the experiences of my first visit to the site. However, on subsequent visits in the later 1990s we were able to locate a moderately dense scatter of ceramics and lithics in the area around the ashmound. Still, this scatter may not indicate the presence of a permanent settlement and may represent the remains of repeated episodes of short-term occupation.

The overall size of the Kudatini mound in 1957 was reported by Allchin (1963: 53) as 150 by 100 feet (70.9 by 47.2 meters, though these figures are obviously estimates and the plan shows a mound only about 45 meters long. The road cut runs the length of the mound so even though this map has no direction indicated, it must be the west face of the mound). Although Newbold (1836) described the mound as being 45 feet (21 meters) high, Allchin (1963: 53) estimates it at 25-30 feet (12 to 14 meters); it is somewhat shorter than that now.

Allchin and Allchin (1963: 56-7, Figure 132) found Neolithic artifacts in association with the mound and in their numbered strata from the road-cut, but they also located, in the area above the exposed section they studied, 16 sherds of Neolithic (A_2) gray ware, one of "A_1 rusticated ware", five of a red-slipped brown ware they view as being "Upper Neolithic", and ". . . one tiny sherd . . . of a distinctive type of black-and-red ware, resembling the A_5 ware of Pilklihal and characteristic of the Upper Neolithic rather than the Lower. This ware is certainly not the typical B_1 Black-and-Red of the Iron Age, nor is it the later B_3 Black-and-Red of the Early Historic period." I have real doubts that this sherd dates to the Neolithic; it seems more probable that it was deposited later in the context of some ongoing use of this location (below). Allchin (1963: 57) summarizes their findings as follows:

> . . . the mound is situated on a lonely pass some distance from any trace of ancient or modern habitation. The base is a leveled area of moorum[4] upon which there is a dark earthy accumulation over which there are repeated layers of ash. Some of the less-vitrified layers show traces of bedding of between 2 in. and 4 in. in thickness, but these relate to deposition rather than burning. In the upper third of the section there are sandy earthy layers which show evidence of settlement.

In general, we may say that during the Neolithic the Daroji Valley was part of a broad zone of intensive settlement activity and ashmound construction and use especially focused around the granitic inselberg where the city of Bellary is located today. That area (Figure 8) contains a number of Neolithic settlements and ashmounds, including Kupgal, Sanganakallu, and Halakundi; a second cluster found to the north includes Sanavasapur, Lingadahalli, Kanchagara Bellagallu, Suguru, and Tekkalakota. Significantly, several of these places were major settlements; if not places occupied by large groups of people – though some of them probably were – then certainly places occupied and visited over and over again as mobile agro-pastoralists moved through the region. Clearly, none of the Daroji ashmound sites, while evidently places where a range of artifact types were deposited, were large, dense

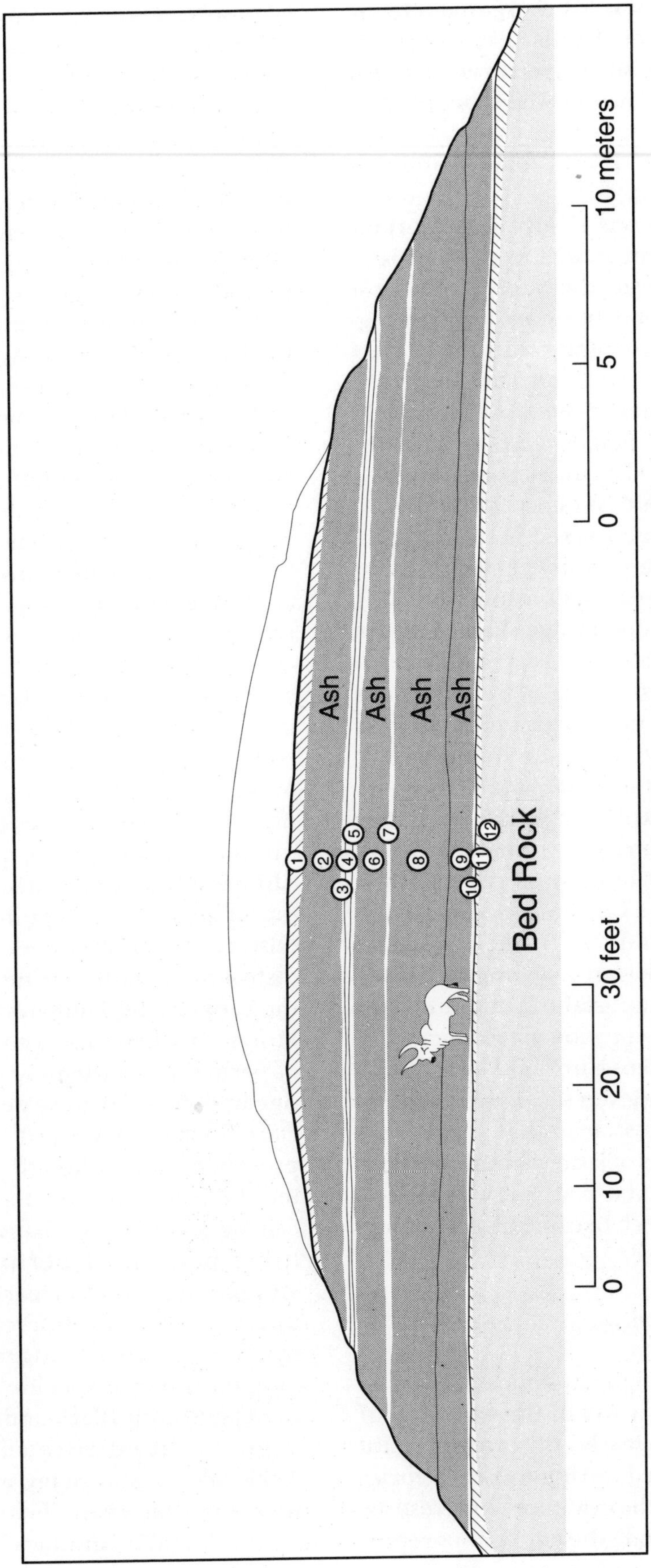

Figure 132. Kudatini ashmound, VMS-1035, based on Allchin 1963.

settlements of the size of Sanganakallu or even Kupgal. Many of the Daroji ashmounds probably represent strategic locations and places of special significance where people also involved with contemporaneous Bellary-area locations visited, lived, and made enduring memorials.

The Daroji Valley was clearly an important corridor of movement as well as place of residence and activity during the Neolithic. In most cases the places so distinctively marked by dung-burning fell out of use along with the artifact repertoire we associate with the Southern Neolithic and were not re-built or reoccupied. Nevertheless, these places were clearly not forgotten, as evidenced by the rich local legends that grew up around specific ashmounds, legends that sometimes linked the great epics with local history, for example the tradition that "Valighat" (VMS-26), a small ashmound near the south bank of the Tungabhadra, is the funeral pyre of Vali. Such oral accounts mirror in many respects the structure of local religious texts of the middle periods, texts which tell their own stories but do so using the framework of the "classics" such as the *Ramayana.* Even where localities are not explicitly linked to larger cultural themes, ashmounds remained places associated with past human or superhuman action as seen by the local attribution of the Gadiganur ashmounds as "ruined villages" recorded by the 1903-04 Archaeological Survey of India. It will be important in the future to untangle the internal chronological dimensions of Neolithic settlement and land use in this region; however, even given the present nascent state of research, it is clear that there were distinct spatial clusters of land use and coherent landscapes of marked and memorialized locations, some of which became places of long-term local importance.

Iron Age and Early Historic

At present we have only a few indicators of Iron Age and Early Historic use of the eastern part of the main valley; clearly, this area was not unoccupied or unused during these centuries but the sparseness of the evidence is interesting. These indicators include the ambiguous report of post-Neolithic (Iron Age and Early Historic) ceramics from Gadiganur ashmound, a report I was unable to substantiate. The second clue to post-Neolithic occupation of the eastern part of the main valley consists entirely of the loosely-dated artifacts found on and near the Daroji Fort hill, evidence which hardly suggests that the main valley was a major focus of interest after the Neolithic and before the Early Middle period. Much clearer is the recent evidence from Kudatini ashmound where recent road work revealed an Iron Age sarcophagus burial cut into the mound (Boivin 2004).

As discussed in Chapter 2, there was a major historical shift in economic strategies that roughly coincides with the end of the Southern Neolithic, a shift that involved reduced residential mobility, settlement aggregation, the introduction of new crops such as rice and, apparently, the use of seasonal inundation for crop watering rather than a sole dependence on rainfall. In addition to these economic changes, there were clearly also major shifts in ceramic technology, patterns of local and regional exchange, practices of memorial-making, and, almost certainly, religious practice. Some of these changes are manifest on the landscape in quite obvious ways. Although Neolithic artifacts and ashmounds are found all over our region, Iron Age and Early Historic materials are more restricted in their distribution, with a string of towns tethered to the banks of the Tungabhadra river (Lycett and Morrison 1998), apparently the primary locus of permanent settlement during both the Iron Age and Early Historic periods. In the western Daroji Valley, VMS-110 is a specialized iron-processing site; although this and several other loci of Iron Age and Early Historic artifacts can be found away from the river, the Neolithic pattern of peripatetic dry farmers and pastoralists was clearly replaced by something dramatically different. Nevertheless, the material record also suggests continuity in the long-term use of specific places – ashmounds associated with Black-and-Red Ware ceramics, deep stratified sites such as Brahmagiri, Tekkalakota, and many more – which should warn us that even these significant social, political, and economic changes took place in the context of an inhabited and meaningful landscape and, even if those meanings changed through time, as they surely must have, the same physical places continued to be used and remembered, in many cases up to the present.

Politically, it is also the case that our region was drawn in some way into a larger world during the Early Historic. While it seems unlikely that the Mauryan empire actually exercised much effective dominion over the residents of Doravati, it is the case that northern Karnataka is home to several clusters of Ashokan rock-edicts representing claims made by this distant polity over the people, places, and resources of this area. The eastern Daroji Valley lies within a large triangle created by three clusters of Ashokan edicts – to the northeast at Udegolam and Nittur, to the southeast at Brahmagiri, and to the northwest at Koppal (Morrison 1997a; Sugandhi 2003) – and must have been a place that was at least *en route* between these inscription clusters and their associated settlements.[5]

Early Middle Period

As discussed in Chapter 2, the Bellary plains just east of the Daroji Valley were home to a concentrated cluster of towns, forts, and temples in the Early Middle period, particularly from the tenth century onwards. Kudatini, Kurugodu, and Balakunde were all places of some importance, containing numerous temples, fortifications, and inscriptions. The western edge of this broad plain touches the eastern edge of the Daroji Valley, a boundary which, except for the artificial embankment of the Daroji reservoir, is marked by a northwest-southeast trending line of granitic hills. Most Early Middle period settlements on the Bellary plain are located at the base of granitic outcrops, here restricted to small but steep granitic inselbergs.[6] The settlements of Daroji/Doravati are no exception to this pattern, lying at the foot of the line of hills marking the eastern edge of the valley. Looming over Daroji/Doravati town is the fort which commands a magnificent view over both the Daroji Valley and the plains to the east. The village of Kurukuppa, now located to the west of the massive Daroji reservoir, also contains a small but well-made Chalukyan-style temple, indicating that the cluster of Early Middle period habitation at the eastern edge of the main valley, now divided by the water of the Daroji *kere*, was once more continuous, extending at least as far west as Gonahala.

In addition to Doravati itself, the Daroji Valley contains a cluster of Early Middle period settlements and temples strung along the upper researches of the Nari Halla. The Sandur Hills, too, contain a number of important Early Middle locations; both these and the Nari Halla settlements are briefly described in Chapter 8. The Banuchandra Vanka, too, had some streamside Early Middle period habitation, notably the

Table 7.1: Inscriptions from the main valley, eastern half, Early Middle periods

Location	*Context*	*Date*	*Summary*	*King*	*References*
Gonahalu	on a broken slab lying in front of the Shiva temple (now missing)	AD 1014	Documents the gift of taxes (*pannasu*) made to the god Mahakaladeva at Pampa[7] by the queen of Iriva-Nolamba-dhiraja, a member of the Pallava family and a subordinate of the king	Vikramaditya V, Chalukyas of Kalyan	Patil and Patil 1997, no. 423; *ARSIE* 1922-3 no. 722 of 1922; *SII* IX, no. 79.
Daroji	on a pilaster on the Ramalingesvara temple on the fort hill north of the reservoir.	AD 1105, Tuesday, 10 October	The *mahamandalesvara* [named] Kacharasa made a gift of land to the god Ramesvara in the fort of Doravati.		Patil and Patil 1997, no. 501; Patil 1996: *VPR* 1988-91, 245-6.

village of Gonahala, occupied from the early eleventh century up until the middle of the twentieth. Among the other settlements in the eastern part of the main valley, only VMS-109, the abandoned village associated with reservoir VMS-1016, may have an Early Middle period component. It seems somewhat more likely, however, that VMS-109 was occupied during the Early Vijayanagara period.

The Village of Gonahala

The 1978 Survey of India map marks the location of Gonahala with a small x, the symbol for an abandoned village, while the 1928 version shows it without this symbol. Gonahala is listed in an official government of Mysore list (1969: 395) of villages published in 1969, although it should be noted that abandoned villages generally continued to "exist" in an official sense as long as they had revenue-yielding land registered to them. In 1871, the village had 25 houses and a population of 174.[8] In 1903/04, when the Archaeological Survey of India visited the region, it is clear that Gonahala was still occupied. Their report describes two temples in "Gonahallu", one, presumably old, dedicated to Virabhadra. This temple, they notes, "has a very finely sculptured image of that name, but unfortunately broken into two pieces. There are is also an image of Ganesha 2 feet high sculptured on a slab". (1904: 79). The report goes on to note the existence of a Telugu inscription and several *nagakals.* The other temple in Gonahala they describe as modern, though it is noted to contain a 6 by 3-feet Hanuman; these large images generally date to the Vijayanagara period.

The inscription (in Kannada, not Telugu) noted by the ASI was published in 1922 (see above). This record was created in AD 1014, during the reign of Vikramaditya V, ruler of the Chalukyas of Kalyan. At this time, Gonahala was quite distant from the political center at Kalyan; the inscription was commissioned by a woman with claims to royalty, the queen of Iriva-Nolambadhiraja, a member of the Pallava family and a subordinate of the king. The inscription, which records a gift of taxes (*pannasu*) made to the god Mahakaladeva at Pampa, on the banks of the Tungabhadra, directly links this small and relatively insignificant village with the sacred pilgrimage center at Hampi, 21 kilometers to the north. This linkage is extremely interesting, especially given the relative weight of Early Middle settlement on the Bellary plain and not primarily along the Tungabhadra itself. That some of the links between the Daroji Valley and what would come to be the locus of the Vijayanagara capital itself are of such long-standing is something of a surprise. Clearly, however, the dedication of Gonahala to the god at the Pampa *tirtha* continued well past the Vijayanagara period, as indicated by a second inscription in modern characters, described below, which warns against the "misappropriation" of the village Gonahalu which belonged to the god Virupaksha. The land recorded as being under *inam* tenure in the 1871 census may indeed reflect the continued claim of the Virupaksha temple on the land of Gonahala; if so, it is a relationship of remarkable stability, especially when one considers the significant transformations of the Daroji Valley since the eleventh century. When the relationship between the Virupaksha temple and the village of Gonahala was first established, the latter was a mostly isolated settlement farming the streamside deposits of the Banchandra Vanka and presumably engaging in other activities such as herding, gathering, and small-scale iron production. As the Daroji Valley was filled in with villages in the fifteenth and sixteenth centuries, agricultural strategies and the landscape itself were transformed through the construction of large reservoirs. Gonahala is not near any reservoir, nor is it in an area of significant sixteenth-century occupation. The soils of the eastern part of the main valley today are degraded and the vegetation consists primarily of thorny scrub, not used even for grazing.

The area between the postulated location of Pemmanhalli (discussed below) and the former Gonahala is strewn with artifacts, a localized scatter with diffuse edges bleeding out toward Pemmanahalli. This scatter contains a large proportion of plaster, lightweight iron slag, black and red-slipped earthenware, and a large number of small cobbles. A diffuse scatter of earthenware continues east to what was clearly the core of the village, a cluster of three temples (Figure 133) surrounded by a very heavy concentration of artifacts. This core area has fragments of a substantial but informally built wall surrounding it, suggesting that it was walled and fortified.

The ceramic artifacts found in this place consist entirely of brown, black, and red earthenware; many have Vijayanagara rim forms. A single piece of coarseware (Sinopoli 1993) is also consistent with Vijayanagara-period occupation. In addition to the more generalized artifact scatter, there is a localized concentration of iron slag between the two northernmost shrines. Some of the slag is very light and may be from smithing rather than smelting, but there are definite indications of iron smelting as well, including furnace fragments, in this location. The only other artifact types were a single fragment of dark brown/black glass and a recent plastic bangle fragment. This assemblage is of considerable interest. Although we can be reasonably certain that Gonahala was occupied at a time when European and East Asian ceramics were widely available in southern India, for example, it seems that the inhabitants of this small village did not have significant access to such exotic goods. The links between Gonahala and the large, cosmopolitan city of Vijayanagara are clear, the links between this village and the larger post-Vijayanagara colonial world less so.

The northernmost of the shrines in Gonahala is a simple, plastered and painted one-room structure made of small blocks. This shrine appears to have been recently built; it contains an image of a goddess as well as some framed icons. Near this shrine is 10 by 10 meters rock-cut well which still holds some brackish water. Fifteen meters south of this small shrine is another recently-built structure, a south-facing Hanuman temple enclosed within fragmentary walls. This temple is probably the same one described by the Archaeological Survey and is still in worship. It faces the road, which now runs about 350 meters to the south but which may have run through the village when it was occupied. This temple has a sanctuary containing the large, Vijayanagara-period Anjaneya Hanuman; appended to the sanctuary is an open porch with wooden columns. The enclosing walls, as well as the lamp column and platform and the simply-made gate platforms that create an entrance into the temple on the southeast are all recent, dating to the nineteenth or early twentieth centuries.

The third temple, however, shows some evidence of the earlier occupational history of Gonahala. This shrine (Figure 134), also enclosed within walls, is in the southeastern part of the village and is mostly of recent construction (plastered and whitewashed small blocks) but incorporates a well-made stone door frame.[9] The door frame supports flanking door guardians, each with a pointed hat (typical of Vijayanagara kings) and a club – curiously, neither has any clear sectarian affiliation. Over the lintel is a carved Gajalakshmi. It is difficult to say precisely when this door frame was made. The door guardians are unlike most Vijayanagara-era *dvarapala* in that they are not clearly Vaishnavite or Shaivite, but the carving style is not inconsistent with a Vijayanagara-period date. The temple is built on a low platform much older than the structure itself; the presence of a single dressed slab in the platform near the north-facing door of the temple signals its Middle period construction. There is no inscription in evidence, but the enclosure around the temple does contain an extremely well-carved Ganesh, a more recent *lingam*, and a *nagakal* set up under a small tree.

To the northeast of the shrine and within its enclosing walls is a small but carefully-made keyhole-shaped step well, this probably from the Early Middle period. The well itself is 3 by 3 meters square and is entered through a 4 meters long staircase descending from the west, toward the temple. The well has been reworked and has been repaired with cobbles, but the original construction of well-dressed granite slabs, stepped back only once, is still evident. On the flat eastern side of the well is a large and beautifully-carved lotus medallion (Figures 135 and 136). This well is extremely well-made, of a quality not usually found in small villages,

Figure 133. Gonahala, overview of temples.

Figure 134. Gonahala, door to shrine 3.

Figure 135. Gonahala, Early Middle period step well.

Figure 136. Gonahala, lotus medallion on step well.

a pattern which reflects not only the generally higher level of craftsmanship in pre-Vijayanagara structures (many, but not all, Vijayanagara-period structures and sculptures were "mass produced", apparently focused on sheer quantity rather than quality), but which may also reflect the largesse of its well-off patron.

Gonahala has, then, a long and (until recently) apparently continuous occupation history as well as a long-standing relationship with the Virupaksha temple in Hampi. It was established by the beginning of the twelfth century, occupied through the Vijayanagara period and abandoned some time in the middle of the twentieth century.

Kurukuppa Shiva Temple, VMS-1090

This small but well-built, east-facing temple (Figure 137) lies at the end of a street paved with granite slabs. Remnants of a *prakara* wall lie near the shrine, which is now surrounded by village houses. Although it has paired Kannada and Sanskrit inscriptions from AD 1523 describing the construction of a temple in Kurekuppa dedicated to Virupaksha, this structure was clearly built much earlier, during the Early Middle period. Known today as the Pampa Maheshvara temple, this is clearly the shrine referred to in the inscriptions.[10] This apparently false foundation inscription is very interesting, especially given the tendency, noted above, to claim extra antiquity for new temples, even when that is spurious.[11] These two inscriptions are carved into the lower part of the 2 freestanding columns on the outer porch.

The temple consists of three parts – an outer porch, antechamber, and the sanctuary, divided into three side-by-side shrines. The outer porch (Figure 138) consists of 4 by 2 columns bounded by a waist-high railing of dressed slabs. The columns sit on bases made to look like three-part moulding sequences; they are square below a large, elaborate octagonal inset. Above the inset, they are round (lathe-turned) and are topped with both square and cruciform capitals. Both the flooring and superstructure are recent, but the latter is still supported by the original long roof slabs, which slope down slightly to the east. These support projecting stone eaves. One ceiling slab has a line of lotus medallions and small carved human figure (a donor?). The overall proportions of the porch and indeed of the temple as a whole – low and broad – are consistent with the local, Chalukyan style.

The walled antechamber is also 4 by 2 columns (but with a solid wall between it and the sanctuary) and is approximately the same size as the outer porch, with similar columns. The wall of the sanctuary contains three separate areas, two smaller flanking a larger, central chamber. In the north and south walls of the antechamber, near the eastern end, are two side shrines in ornate niches. The latter are 1.2 by 0.5 meters and are topped by medallions as well as, unusually, a carved representation of a temple tower or *gopuram*. A small *gopuram* – the stepped edge created by lines of quarry marks – also tops the door to the southernmost sanctuary. Both of the side shrines at this eastern end of the structure have elaborate doorways; the southern has small attached columnettes next to lines of foliage, lotuses, and even a stack of small lion images. There is no central image over this door, but it is carved with pendant lotus buds. Finally, on each side of the door to the southern sanctuary are Shaivite door guardians (and/or donors) inside ornate *makara-torana* frames (Figure 139). These consist of an image of Shiva wearing a tall, conical hat (with drum, trident, club, and one hand held up) flanked by 2 small women with loose hair (no hair buns). Inside this shrine is a small, perhaps Vijayanagara-period Garuda and a more recent Ganesha sitting on an older image base.

Although the door to the larger, central sanctuary has recently been partly covered with white tile, it was clearly always very plain, with only a single row of lotus designs way up near the ceiling. There is a large, possibly late, Nandi facing the main image, a (recent) Shiva *lingam*. The northern sanctuary has to most elaborate doorway. This is flanked by attached columnettes with elaborate foliage designs and dish-shaped capitals. Carved into the door frame is a Gajalakshmi; above this are 2 pendant banana flowers and 4 of the carved *gopuram*

Figure 137. Shiva temple, Kurekuppa.

Figure 138. Columns on porch, Kurekuppa Shiva temple.

Figure 139. Doorway to sanctuary, Kurekuppa Shiva temple.

images. Carved on the threshold are door guardians similar to those of the southern sanctuary, but without the flanking female figures. In the room, a recent Goddess image sits in an older image base next to a small Shiva image of uncertain age.

The temple as a whole sits on a very worn platform of solidly-fitted dressed granite slabs; the latter with a slightly rounded version of a two-stepped with angled bevel moulding. The temple basement is, however, quite elaborate though thickly whitewashed. In front of the temple is a low wall – perhaps a remnant of an elaborate *prakara* wall? (6 meters long by 2 meters wide) – made from a large three-part moulding. The lower part is two-stepped with angled bevel; above it is an inset section with lotuses inside diamonds, alternating with carved elephants. The upper beveled moulding (no step) has corner full-round medallions with lotuses carved on top. Sitting atop this wall are two very well-made lathe-turned columns unlike those inside the temple itself. The former are entirely round, quite slim, and may have been re-set from some other location.

As should be clear, this Shiva temple is still in worship. It appears to have a long, continuous occupation history from the Early Middle period to the present.[12] Given its sixteenth century (and present) identification with the Pampa *tirtha* and the Virupaksha temple, along with the fact this was an important locale in the Early Middle landscape, it seems probable that the Kurekuppa Shiva temple was originally connected with the Hampi area and with Pampa Maheshvara right from its construction.

Kurekuppa Village

The village of Kurekuppa, though occupied today, contains abundant clues to its more distant past. Scattered throughout the village are remnant walls and sculptural elements, including a hero stone (Figure 140) which may date to the Early Middle period. I discuss the evidence for Vijayanagara-period settlement below, including the remains of a Hanuman temple. Like the village of Gonahala, Kurekuppa was associated with the Pampa *tirtha*, though the precise nature of the connection is not clear. Possibly, this area was given in a land grant with reciprocal obligations to supply produce to the temple; given the later presence of a Brahmin settlement here, it may be that this was also the original composition of the village as well. Given the proximity of both Gonahala and Kurekuppa to the cluster of Early Middle period settlement around Kurugodu to the east, this connection to the rather distant Hampi region is interesting. Clearly, in this case links between specific temples, villages, and fields endured even as regional political contexts changed dramatically in the Vijayanagara period. As at Gonahala, there is no reservoir near Kurekuppa though the now badly-damaged VMS-1018, some 750 meters northwest of Kurekuppa may possibly have been constructed by the Early Middle period. It may be that, in addition to dry farming and grazing, the local residents used water from a reservoir now covered by the Daroji *kere* or perhaps took advantage of their location in between the Nari Halla and the Banuchandra Vanka, two of the larger seasonal streams in the valley. The latter seems likely given the more general pattern of location of Early Middle period villages along such streams; these streams are larger and more reliably moist at the eastern (downstream) end of the Daroji Valley.

About 35 meters down a slab-paved road east of the temple is a round bastion, now incorporated into occupied houses. Similar to others in the region, this solid structure is faced with masonry of unmodified and split boulders with some chinking stones. There are a few dressed blocks incorporated into the structure, which may date to the Vijayanagara period. Some 10 meters in diameter, the bastion is now about 8 meters high. Despite the mention of three other bastions surrounding the temple in 1904, there is now no evidence for these nor is there any evidence at present for a fortification wall around the village. If such a wall did once exist, it may have looked similar to that around Ingaligi, in the western Daroji Valley.

Opposite the Vijayanagara-period Hanuman temple (below), a large hero stone has been incorporated into a newer platform. Inside a

Figure 140. Kurekuppa village, hero stone, Hanuman temple.

Figure 141. Daroji fort Hill, overview.

single frame and beneath a carved sun and moon, the hero stone depicts two men on horseback headed toward the viewer's right. The leader has either a round hat or a hair bun; both men hold swords aloft on their right hands and the horses' reigns with their left hands. Their high status is attested by a small central figure of a man floating between the two and carrying a parasol. Lotus-like figures float to the left of each man's head. Also built into the platform are some *naga* stones and two Nandis of indeterminate age.

Daroji Fort, VMS-1020

The Daroji/Doravati Fort has been studied most closely by C.S. Patil, who published a detailed article (1996b) about its structures and inscriptions. The following discussion is based partly on this work. The fort at Daroji, now famous primarily for the bears that live there, sits high atop a steep-sided outcrop just north of the Daroji reservoir (Figure 141). As discussed above, it is not entirely clear when the first reservoir was built in the location of the present-day Daroji *kere*; there seems to have been a large reservoir here since at least the sixteenth century, but it is certainly possible that this was preceded by an Early Middle period facility. As discussed below, the Doravati Fort was associated with a settlement, also known as Doravati, at the base of the hill as well as with a second, much smaller reservoir that dams a small valley cut into the outcrop bearing the fort. Most of the land under this small reservoir is now submerged by the Daroji *kere*, this superpositioning strongly suggesting that the smaller facility predates the larger.

Daroji fort actually covers two separate hills, the southern of which lies adjacent to the Daroji *kere*. Access to the fort is restricted to the eastern side, not far from Hale Daroji, through the saddle separating the two hills. This route is narrow and steep and is blocked by two separate pairs of fortification walls, the lower built of small, rectangular quarried stones and dated by Patil (1996b: 244) to the seventeenth or eighteenth century, contemporaneous with the reconstruction of the Daroji *kere*. The upper walls are more massive, constructed of large split boulders dated by Patil (1996b: 244) to the thirteenth century or earlier. Both sets of walls have informal gates, not much more than openings in the walls. The route up to the twin hilltops also passes two water cisterns which collect runoff and rainfall from this rocky slope.

Between the two sets of walls is a path leading up the southern hill through a gate and to the Ramalingesvara temple, built in the early twelfth or late eleventh century (Figure 142). This three-part temple consists of an outer porch, a later addition (Patil 1996b: 245) to a shrine which originally consisted of a partially-enclosed antechamber (*antarala*) and a small, square sanctuary containing a natural *lingam* on a high base.[13] A carving of Gajalakshmi sits over the door to the sanctuary but there are no door guardians. The flat ceiling of the antechamber is carved with a large lotus; the columns are plain and square in section. According to Patil (1996b: 245), the superstructure has been renovated, but its stepped pyramidal shape and lithic construction suggests that this renovation was not recent. The exterior of this temple is relatively plain; atop a basement with a severely angled moulding sequence, rows of pilasters run around the wall of the antechamber. The sanctuary, as usual, is unadorned. The inscription associated with the Ramalingesvara temple is located here, on the exterior of the structure in between pilasters (Table 7.1). The inscription, dated to Tuesday November 12, AD 1105 (Patil and Patil 1997, no. 501), during the reign of the Chalukyas of Kalyan, notes that the officer (*mahamandaleshvara*) Kacharasa made a gift of land to the god Ramesvara in the fort of Doravati. This gift was meant both for the expenses of worship and for repair to the temple, suggesting that the latter predates it. This same officer is also mentioned in an inscription from Oruvyi dated AD 1148 (Patil and Patil 1997, no. 73) where he, along with others, is said to have constructed temples in Kurugodu, Kuttakanuru, and Hosa Kuttakanuru. Near the Ramalingeshvara temple is a natural cistern in the sheetrock which has been augmented by substantial masonry walls on the south and east.

Leaving the temple, the path up to the top

Figure 142. Ramalingeshvara temple, Daroji fort.

Figure 143. Daroji fort, upper enclosure.

of the southern hill passes through three more gates before it reaches the peak, enclosed by masonry walls and crowded with rubble-walled structures (Figure 143). The walls consist of small unmodified boulders and cobbles; round bastions are placed at intervals within the walls. This upper area also has a cistern. Patil (1996b: 244) notes the presence of a boulder with incised figures of a man shooting a tiger with a gun, a camel rider beating a drum, a horse rider holding a sword, an elephant with a howdah and flag, and a lion trampling an elephant. Many of these are common hero-stone motifs – the horse rider holding a sword for example – but these figures clearly do not all date to the Early Middle periods as guns were first adopted only the sixteenth century and were probably not common before the seventeenth. Patil (1996b: 247) suggests continuous use of Daroji Fort from the time of its first construction up until the eighteenth century (the British period, when independent rulers in this region, with the exception of the Raja of Sandur, were eliminated and forts brought under British control), and both the material evidence and the continuing use of the name Doravati suggest that he is correct.[14]

The hill to the north is itself defended by two lines of walls. On the north side these are built of large, horizontally-laid, trimmed boulders, while all of the others are constructed of small, trimmed boulders. Patil (1996b: 244) posits that the more cyclopean walls date to the thirteenth or fourteenth centuries and the smaller-stoned walls to the seventeenth or eighteenth centuries. The round bastions in this fortified area are similar to those on the southern hilltop. Also like the southern hilltop, the fortified apex of this hill is strewn with the collapsed rubble walls of numerous small rooms or structures as well as a natural cistern.

The Settlements of Doravati/Daroji

There has been a village or town named Doravati or Daroji from at least the late eleventh century onward and, as noted, material evidence hints at an even longer occupational history. As noted, today there are two Darojis, Hale or Old Daroji, still locally identified as Doravati, and Hosa or New Daroji. The physical remains of this shifting settlement are spread out over an area of about 3 kilometers and the complex archaeological palimpsest that this history has created is both cut into and partially covered by the reservoir itself. The 1903-4 Archaeological Survey of India report described no fewer than four ruined villages as well as two occupied villages (Bhatrahalli and Narasapuram) near Daroji, none of which still exist.[15] Because the occupational history of Doravati appears to be temporally continuous and because the material distribution of pre-Vijayanagara and Vijayanagara-period remains is also spatially continuous, the following descriptive sketch integrates description of both pre-Vijayanagara and later material.

The occupied village of Hale Daroji lies near the base of a low and isolated outcrop. Between this outcrop and the much higher fort-bearing outcrop to the west is an approximately linear but discontinuous spread of settlement debris covering an area of about 160 hectares. Most of this area seems to have been occupied during the Vijayanagara period. Beginning at its northern end, about a kilometer south of the village of Devalapuram, this complex and multilayered settlement area is bounded by a cluster of three small Vijayanagara-period shrines (Figure 144), simple square structures with rectangular columns decorated with octagonal insets. These shrines are still in worship and are heavily overlain with more recent masonry, plaster, and whitewash. From at least this point (the area to the north has not been systematically explored), there is a long road wall running toward the south, more or less paralleling the paved road. This double-faced wall is substantially built of large boulders; it is being dismantled by current residents. About 150 meters south of the shrine complex is an east-west cross wall (perhaps the northern wall of a defined settlement?) that intersects the north-south road wall. On the west, the cross-wall runs into the embankment of a small reservoir built at the foot of the outcrop. This reservoir, VMS-1086, is not part of the main valley system, but is isolated and thus is discussed here.

The embankment of VMS-1086 runs approximately north-south and is curved outwards toward the east, poised to capture the small but rapid flow of seasonal runoff from the high outcrop about 100 meters to the west. The earthen embankment is revetted with up to 9 courses of stepped masonry on its western face. Some of the masonry consists of split and quarried blocks though most elements are unmodified boulders. In late November of 2000, this facility was still holding some water. The embankment is 126 meters long and about 10 meters wide; the only outlet is a rough boulder-filled waste weir at its northern end. At its southern end is some kind of platform or structure; because this is being actively destroyed it is difficult to say more than this. The reservoir appears to date to the Vijayanagara period. The southern end of VMS-1086 segues into a second east-west wall which also joins the north-south road wall, thus creating a large enclosed area of about 250 meters north-south by 200 meters east-west, again perhaps some defined area of settlement. This second east-west wall, like the first, is around 1 meter wide and is variably built, with some sections having faces of small cobbles separated by an earthen core and others built entirely of small boulders, these occasionally split or quarried. Inside this enclosure, the ground is level and does not support much vegetation. There is a low density of comminuted ceramics, primarily brown earthenware with Vijayanagara rim forms.

South of the walled enclosure created by VMS-1086, the road wall and the two east-west cross walls, the long road wall continues but artifact densities drop off and there is a rock-strewn stretch without any clear remains of structures. In this interstitial area, I quite fortuitously came across the mustard-colored microlithic chert blade mentioned above.

Continuing south along the course of the road wall, evidence of structures again appears about 200 meters south of the walled enclosure. There is a (10 by 10 meters) square depression, probably a well, and several nearby boulders are scarred with Vijayanagara-style quarry marks. About 60 meters from the base of the outcrop – which has some soil development here and is not simply a granite dome but is more gently sloping – is a heavily eroded reservoir, VMS-1087. Like its counterpart to the north, this isolated facility captured runoff from the nearby hill and was not connected to any other reservoir. The earthen embankment lies about 60 meters away from the foot of the slope. It is heavily eroded and about 90 meters long. A few scattered boulders represent the few scraps of masonry that remain on its western face. The embankment is breached in its center and there are no indications of an original outlet.

Just to the west of (Hale) Daroji village, the evidence for intensive settlement picks up and from this point well to the south of the Daroji reservoir itself, the ground surface is littered with variable densities of ceramics and other artifacts (Figure 145). The northern boundary of this distribution is marked by an isolated upright granite boulder, strikingly tall and thin but evidently a natural feature. A small boulder at the foot of this upright has a pair of carved feet on it, suggesting a sacred role for the boulder itself. A block mortar lies nearby; to the south is an east-west running cobbled roadbed about 6 meters long. A column footing lies by the side of the road; all of this suggests a rather formal route, more like a temple street within an urban area than a rural roadway. This section of what we may call older Daroji does not seem to have been very densely settled; there are several small mounds but only a moderate density of black and brown earthenware ceramics. This area is used as a cemetery by the residents of Hale Daroji. Recent pits have exposed some of the subsurface deposits; these show no obvious structures but do reveal clustered trash deposits, including an ash concentration some 8 meters long by 1 meter thick. It may be that this area was used for cremations during the Vijayanagara-period and later occupations and that its present function as a burial ground represents some continuation of how this small area is marked and used.

The road wall which began far to the north near the three-shrine cluster continues though the areas just described and runs all the way south to a large bastion built on the foot of the fort-bearing outcrop, at a point just to the north

Figure 144. VMS-1086, looking to Hale Daroji.

Figure 145. Hale Daroji, settlement area, overview.

of the Daroji reservoir, a distance of some 4 kilometers. At no point is the wall very high and it seems to have merely served to define and direct the course of the road, marking off space in a fairly direct way but not in any sense serving as a fortification. As noted, the current paved road follows the course of the old road rather closely; according to older Survey of India maps, the former appears not to have changed course since the 1920s and, as the archaeological data outlined above suggest, perhaps not since the Vijayanagara period.

Just south of the present-day village of (Hale) Daroji, the scatter of artifacts and structures indicating the location of older Daroji widens out to the east. This area was marked on the 1928 Survey of India map as "Daroji (in ruins)" while contemporary Daroji is glossed simply as "Daroji". In that same map series (on the next sheet), what is known today as Hosa Daroji is also labeled "Daroji", giving the 1928 map *three separate locations for the same named place.* As noted, the 1903 Archaeological Survey described four ruined villages and two now-vanished occupied villages in the vicinity of Daroji (only a single occupied village was identified as such); three of these sites of "ruins" are unnamed while the fourth is known as Arlapuram. All this suggests not only a complicated occupational history, but also the possibility that the present palimpsest actually masks the presence of multiple named places, not all of which ought to conflated with that of Daroji, as I do here of necessity.

The settlement area south of Hosa Daroji (Daroji in ruins) has an artifact scatter of variable density. Little can be said about the composition of this assemblage other than its probable Vijayanagara-period associations because the entire area has been inundated with more recent trash; subsurface testing would be of great value here. In this area there are two Vijayanagara-period Hanuman temples, both of them dedicated to the heroic, striding form of Hanuman, Anjaneya, who was extremely popular in and around the city of Vijayanagara, found often at gateways. The northernmost of these two shrines, described below, incorporates some columns which may date to the twelfth or thirteenth centuries. An Early Middle period hero stone lies by the side of the road just south of the Hanuman temples and north of Hale Daroji. This three-paneled sculpture begins with a blank register in the lowest panel. The middle panel depicts a *lingam* in a *mandapa* (flanked by female *chauri* [fly-whisk] bearers and a tree and a snake); the upper panel shows the hero and two women, presumably his wives, sitting with folded hands while another man worships a *lingam.* Other scattered architectural elements that derive from Early Middle period structures include an ornate door jamb with a Shaivite door guardian (illustrated by Patil 1996b, plate 141), a lintel with a sculpture of Gajalakshmi and a door jamb with a Vaisnavite door guardian.

The long road wall continues south from this settlement area to the primary locus of Early Middle remains at the northern end of the Daroji reservoir. The wall joins a large round bastion against which a Jain *nisidi* stone is propped. This stone (illustrated by Patil 1996b, plate 142) may predate the Vijayanagara period. The bastion itself is built on the very edge of the outcrop, overlooking the road. It is 6 meters high and about 3 meters in diameter with a solid earthen core encased in rough masonry. Just south of the bastion, a dirt road runs west from the paved road toward the north end of the Daroji reservoir embankment, providing access to the Virabhadra temple on the hill. All along this dirt road and for about 300 meters south is further habitation debris, including artifacts, cobbles, bricks, ash, bone, and charcoal. The less-disturbed part of this settlement contains the remains of many small structures, probably wattle-and-daub or some other ephemeral material with rubble foundations. Altogether this now badly-damaged town is about 6 hectares, somewhat smaller than the area to the north which was the Vijayanagara-period locus of Doravati/Daroji. The northern end of Early Middle period Doravati, for this is what this material represents, lies at the base of the pass leading up the outcrop to Doravati Fort. The northern end of the Daroji reservoir embankment is itself constructed of artifact-laden, ashy settlement debris, a fact which not only indicates that this end (or perhaps all of) the reservoir post-dates the Early Middle period but which has also seriously disturbed the layout of the older settlement.

There is a very high density of ceramics, especially in the southern, disturbed part of Doravati (overlain by the reservoir embankment), where tractor tire marks criss-cross an expanse of freshly-bladed material lying atop the reservoir embankment. The ceramic assemblage includes red slipped and polished wares, polished and slipped black wares, and plain (unslipped) wares in black, brown, and red. Ceramics are wheel-made, some with elaborate rim forms. This assemblage is similar to that found on the Early Middle (twelfth-thirteenth century) town of Haneya near Brahmagiri. There were no ceramics from the Vijayanagara period in evidence when I documented this area, but closer research may show some overlay. Other ceramics include one piece of plain white porcelain, possibly European. Other artifacts noted in this fill include two black glass bangle fragments, the sawn-off lower end of a conch shell, a piece of iron slag, several mother-of-pearl fragments, one orange plastic bangle fragment (obviously recent), two pieces of a dressed basalt disk with a center hole (40 centimeters diameter and 6 thick), and a quartz core. Because of the poor condition of this settlement, it is difficult even to be certain of its original size. However, it is quite clear that before the Vijayanagara period, there was either no reservoir here or there were (at most) much smaller ones which left an open passage through the large gap now filled by the Daroji *kere*.[16] Doravati lay at the foot of the steep hill bearing the fort, right in the opening into and out of the Daroji Valley and at the edge of the densely settled Bellary plain.

Early Middle Doravati lay at the confluence of the three seasonal streams – the Banuchandra Vanka, Nari Halla, and Kanigana Halla – streams which would later make the Daroji reservoir one of the largest in the region. Like other villages and towns of the day, farmers and herders relied on water tables, rainfall and on the flows of these seasonal streams for watering produce and livestock, allowing a relatively dense population to inhabit and even thrive in this semi-arid landscape. The Early Middle period focus on the exploitation of streams and rivers and the lack of a developed infrastructure of reservoirs or canals meant that locational consideration differed from those of later, Vijayanagara settlements. Of course, topography and hydrology were not the only factors siting villages and towns; politics also played an important role. It is worth noting, however, that Doravati sits in a place equally well-suited to either a strategy of stream exploitation or to the construction of a large-scale reservoir, a fact which probably plays some part in its long and uninterrupted history. The organizational and social requirements and implications of each of these strategies differed enormously and it is thus the case that this long-term history of place – Doravati as a geographic entity has at this point some 900 years of history – also masks major changes in the structure, operation, and even appearance of the (material) place as well as significant changes in its political role and social composition. I do not intend to suggest that Doravati/Daroji endured as a focal place – a sanctified, fortified location – solely because of its physical advantages. Although these are indeed striking (it sits at a major confluence of streams, at the narrow entrance to a large valley, at the edge of a broad plain of rich black soil), it is also probable that its very occupational history and the material residues of that history made it into a spatial attractor quite apart from any strategic or economic advantages.

Vijayanagara Period

The eastern part of the main valley was used and occupied throughout the Vijayanagara period and, particularly with the construction of huge reservoirs VMS-1016/1021 and VMS-1019, the Daroji reservoir, the Vijayanagara period was the one in which the physical landscape of the valley was most radically transformed. The following discussion moves from west to east in this part of the valley, following the flow and runoff. Table 7.2 summarizes the known inscriptions from the eastern half of the main valley.

Table 7.2: Inscriptions from the main valley, eastern half, Vijayanagara & later periods

Location	*Context*	*Date*	*Summary*	*References*
Gonahalu	On a slab set up in front of the Shiva temple (now missing)	in modern characters	Warns against the misappropriation of the village Gonahalu which belongs to the god Virupakshadeva.	Patil and Patil 1997, no. 424; *ARSIE* 1922-3, no. 723 of 1922.
Kurekuppa (Kurikuppi)	on a column of a *mandapa* in the Isvara temple	AD 1523, Monday 20 April	Benkararasa (caste and family given) had a temple built for the god Virupaksha at Kuriyakuppe (surnamed) Anantasetu, an *agarahara* village in the Doravadi-*venthe* of the Hastinavati-*valita*. He also set up the (image of the) god Virupaksha in the temple and donated some *vrittis*[17] purchased from Basava-Dikshita for the god's service. The *mahajanas*[18] of the *agarahara* made a gift of garden land for the same purpose.	Patil and Patil 1997, no. 514; *ARSIE* 1922-3, no. 727 of 1922; *SII* IX ii, no. 514.
Kurekuppa (Kurikuppi)	on another column of the same mandapa as above.	AD 1523, Monday, 20 April	Copy of the Kannada inscription above in Sanskrit. Kuriyakuppe is called Anantasetu.	Patil and Patil 1997, no. 515; *ARSIE* 1922-3, no. 728 of 1922.
Daroji	on a slab set up on the reservoir embankment	none (Persian)	instructs that water in the reservoir is to be distributed to thirsty travelers in the name of Mohammed.	Patil and Patil 1997, no. 502; Patil 1996b: 246; *ARSIE* 1922-3, no. 726 of 1922
Daroji	built into the wall of a mosque	19th c. (Arabic)	extract from the Koran	Patil and Patil 1997, no. 503; Patil 1996b: 246.
Daroji	built into the wall of another mosque	19th c. (Persian)	notes that the mosque was built during the reign of Tipu Sultan	Patil and Patil 1997, no. 504; Patil 1996b: 246.

Dharmasagara Village

The village of Dharmasagara lies in about the same position where the sixteenth-century village was; this is clear from the lack of a discrete zone of older artifacts in the area. Evidently, the village has grown in size and now mostly covers earlier deposits. This pattern is relatively common in the region where, as we have seen, there is often remarkable continuity of settlement with place names serving to indicate enduring spatial identities if not precise locations on the landscape. This pattern may be particularly marked where structures are ephemeral and often rebuilt, common in villages of modest size and with residents of modest means. Granite buildings, especially temples which are rarely dismantled are among the most enduring structural elements, though as we shall see, a few temples recorded in the early 1900s are no longer present. No doubt today's cinder block and concrete will also remain on the landscape for a long time to come. In 1903-4, the Archaeological Survey made the following notation (1904: 80):

> *Field No. 154.*—The site of Dharmasagaram village. An ancient Hanumar [Hanuman] on the south, with an ancient image of that name 7' by 3' sculptured on a slab. There are two statues of Ganesa, one 3 feet and the other 2 feet high.

Figure 146. Gate complex in Dharmasagara village.

Figure 147. VMS-1016, overview of embankment.

> There are outside the temple several *nagarakals*. Toward the north-west of this temple, is a modern Basavara Gudi with an ancient statute of a bull.

As the description of VMS-1027 has illustrated, we can now suggest that Dharmasagara served as a kind of entrance into and out of Daroji Valley in the sixteenth century. It lay just outside VMS-1085, a substantial fortification wall entered through a gateway; the association of Hanuman shrines with fortified gateways and roads in the Vijayanagara region is a strong and consistent one.

Temple, VMS-1032

Recent construction almost completely encloses this small (4.2 by 4.75 meters) Vijayanagara-period shrine. The latter appears to have been a simple 2 by 2 column *mandapa* with a 2-column porch facing east. The porch columns are square in section with octagonal insets, the most common Vijayanagara form. The door into the small square sanctuary is also original; the granite lintel contains two square cut-outs and a central carved lotus. Two *naga* stones lean up against the doorway, flanking it like impromptu door guardians. The ceiling over the sanctuary is constructed of rotated squares, again a very common Vijayanagara form. The rest of the structure is either recent or is completely obscured by recent construction. In front of (east of) the shrine is a recently-built, whitewashed stone enclosure. Inside this enclosure is a small, sculpted Vijayanagara-period Nandi facing the shrine, in which there are several Shiva *lingams*.[19] A slab with a carved Nagamma (goddess with lower body of a snake) holding a snake in one hand lies propped up against the enclosure wall. This shrine is still in worship. The 1904 Archaeological Survey of India report (1904: 80) noted that there were traces of fortification walls on the tops of the hills near this temple.

Reservoirs in the Eastern Section of the Main Valley: The trans-Valley Reservoirs

Reservoir, VMS-1016

Like the later trans-valley reservoir, VMS-1016 is situated in a relatively narrow part of the main valley (Figure 147). Also similar to VMS-1015 is the great length of this facility and the presence of a breakwater (Figure 148). VMS-1016 collected runoff from both the north and south sides of the Daroji Valley and seems to have been linked in some way with reservoir VMS-1021 which is built at a more oblique angle, apparently in order to capture runoff from an entrenched, cliff-lined channel that comes down from the Sandur Hills. In some sense, then, this pair of reservoirs worked *in tandem* and it may be reasonable to see them as together constituting a single (compound) trans-valley facility. The settlement VMS-109 is spatially associated with these two reservoirs while both Gadiganuru and two now-abandoned settlements, Gonahala and Pemmanahalli, lie less than 2 kilometers away. The residents of these villages, too, may have farmed the fields watered by these reservoirs. Although I discuss the history of these settlements in more detail below, I should note here that not all of these places were occupied at the same time. It may be the case, in fact, that only VMS-109 and Gadiganura, perhaps sequentially, ever used this reservoir. The nearby village of Kotinganahalu is more recent.[20]

At present, the ends of the embankment do not abut outcrops; instead, the *bund* is nestled in the lowest part of the valley. This reservoir is, however, in extremely poor condition and it is thus difficult to know its original length; a conservative estimate is 720 meters although it may have been longer than this. The widest part of the embankment is about 20 meters wide. Long stretches of the embankment are actually significantly lower than the two meters noted on Survey of India topographic maps made in the 1970s. Because this reservoir is very large, it seems quite unlikely that the original height of the bund was only 2 meters – it is much more probable that there has been heavy siltation in the bed of this reservoir, perhaps as much as 3 or 4 meters of accumulation. Heavy siltation is a common reason for reservoir abandonment, and one may suggest that both siltation and breaching played a role in the demise of this facility. There may have been two or perhaps three sluice gates; at present there is definite indication of only one tunnel.

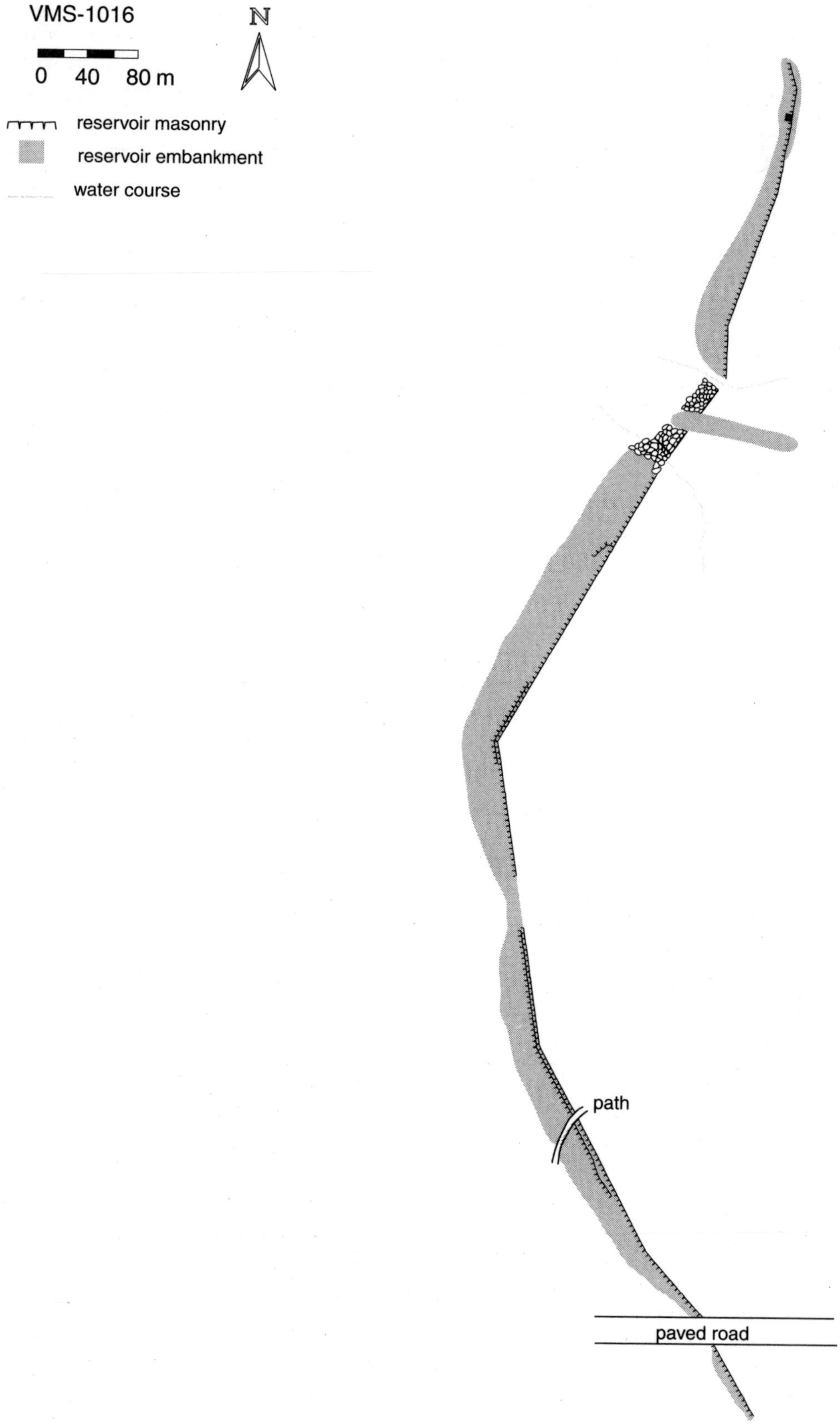

Figure 148. Reservoir VMS-1016, plan.

The area below the reservoir and to the north of the paved road is heavily eroded, dissected by deep channels. This eroded area extends some 80 meters to the east of the embankment and grades into dry fields. Above (west of) the embankment, the land is also degraded and is no longer under cultivation. This ground supports a luxuriant, impenetrable thicket of thorn bushes, as does much of the embankment. Although the facility has some obviously recent repairs, it is clearly not in use and unlike most other reservoirs, even abandoned ones, this facility sees almost no contemporary use. The bed is not used for dry farming, there is no well, there are no trees growing on the embankment, no path running along it, no graves, and no sluices converted to shrines.

Construction

The northern end of the *bund* is breached by the paved road that runs through the valley; this end of the reservoir is almost totally destroyed. A single course of masonry together with a small (approximately 0.2 meter high) rise in the ground surface indicates the course of the embankment at this end. The soil here is very sandy; the presence of an erosion channel indicates relatively rapid water flow through this area, pointing to the potential for destruction of the embankment. Even though it is sometimes only indicated by a north-south alignment of gravelly soil along the former course of the *bund,* it is, however, clear that there was an embankment here. The masonry on the western side of the embankment is preserved south of the paved road. Here there are 7 courses of irregular, medium-sized unshaped boulders of a coarse-grained granite with large quartzite inclusions. Many small, iron-rich cobbles from the Sandur Hills have also been used.

What appears at first to be a long wall running along the top of the embankment is probably just the uppermost course of stepped masonry. Many of the missing masonry elements (including some quarried blocks) appear to have been removed and piled up in the waste weir. The eastern side of the embankment is also severely eroded, and much of the fill has been robbed. There are scatters of pebbles along the western side of the embankment; these are probably foundation material for the missing courses of masonry. The embankment is widest near the center, narrowing at each end.

South of the road the reservoir is breached in three places. Two of these openings are actually just remnants of one larger gap that has been partly blocked with a newer waste weir. In this *kodi* is a breakwater, some 60 meters long, 12 meters wide, and 1.5 to 2 meters high. There are numerous fragments of plaster atop the breakwater, but no plastered features anywhere in evidence. The only other reservoir in the entire region that has a breakwater is VMS-1015, and this one, too, is situated nearer the southern than the northern end of the embankment, suggesting that runoff from the Sandur Hills was potentially much more destructive than runoff from the north. The embankment is somewhat lower to the south of the breakwater. The tracks of the Southern Railway run to the south of VMS-1016; if the latter extended further south, it has been destroyed by the rail line.

Outlets and Sluices

In the northern half of the embankment is a minor breach which is a likely location for a sluice gate. However, there is no positive indication of a sluice here.

Further south is a much larger breach in the *bund.* This aperture has been partly blocked with thousands of piled-up blocks, boulders, and cobbles which form a kind of pavement sloping down to the east. This pavement is faced on the west with upright slabs, some of which have been recently cut. Open, sandy drainage channels still exist north and south of this waste weir. The latter abuts the breakwater on both sides and is almost certainly a later repair. Some long granite slabs, perhaps original, lie proximate to these channels. The actual period of the repair cannot be precisely fixed, but it seems to have been in the twentieth century, based on quarrying technology used to make the freshly-cut slabs.

South of the waste weir, the matrix of the embankment has been extensively robbed. This sediment removal has exposed Vijayanagara-style concrete on the west side of the embankment. The concrete overlies a construction built of shallow, wide bricks (*c.* 15 by 8 by 2.5 centimeters, consistent with other Vijayanagara brick dimensions) and points to the existence of a tunnel (and presumably also a sluice) here. Immediately west of the tunnel is a (recent) field marker.

Associated Features

South of the waste weir a short rubble wall sits atop the embankment. This north-south wall is associated with a possible east-west wall; the two form a corner and thus a small room or structure atop the embankment. There is also a consistent, low- to medium-density scatter of Vijayanagara earthenware ceramics and lithics on and near the bund, and in the fields to the east of the embankment. This scatter may be associated with the settlement, VMS-109 (described below), which is adjacent to the reservoir near its southern end.

Reservoir, VMS-1021

This curved reservoir sits alone, sited without the benefit of adjacent outcrops. As noted, it works in tandem with the large trans-valley reservoir VMS-1016 to supply fields to the east of settlement VMS-109; the two facilities are in parallel positions in the system. VMS-1021 is supplied entirely by runoff from the Sandur hills, storing water from several small seasonal streams as well as a deeply-entrenched, cliff-lined channel that pours down off the hills in the rainy season. Perhaps for this reason, it is extremely poorly preserved and heavily silted-in. The embankment is 510 meters long and up to 30 meters wide. The southern end of the embankment is heavily disturbed; the *bund* was probably somewhat longer than it is today. The embankment now reaches a maximum height of 2.3 meters above the surrounding ground surface.

The bed of the reservoir is now a cotton field, watered by a well with an electric pump. The soils in this part of the valley are coarse, red, and sandy; in an exposed sediment profile below the reservoir, the upper .50 meter are a dark red-brown while the lower 1.5 meters consist of a coarse, rocky red soil with a high concentration of calcium carbonate (*kankar*) nodules.

Construction

Although the upstream masonry was clearly set on the western side of the embankment, the only traces of it are scatters of the gravel that once served as footings. This total lack of masonry is rare and suggests that elements may have been removed wholesale (as compared to the usual slow attrition of materials), perhaps for use on another reservoir.

Outlets and Sluices

In the middle of the low *bund* is a major, apparently deliberate breach through which water flow is controlled with a few well-placed slabs. Further south, approximately 80 meters from the southern end of the reservoir are two square uprights (0.33 by 0.30 meter and 0.36 by 0.36 meter) with Vijayanagara-style quarry marks, dressed on their interior faces and upper surfaces (Figure 149). These stubby uprights rise 0.56 and 0.53 meter above the bed of the reservoir – the top of the embankment is only about another meter higher – clearly indicating massive siltation into this reservoir. The tops of the uprights are not broken but are dressed to receive a lintel; the level of inwash into this facility is truly amazing and is matched only by that in VMS-1031, the Avinamodugu *kere* (Chapter 8). I estimate at least 2 and probably around 4 meters of sediment accumulation here. The absence of a breach in this area further supports this conclusion and there can be no doubt that this massive sediment inwash finally led to the abandonment of VMS-1021.

Associated Features

There is a deep (*c.* 15 meters), square, rock-cut well below (north-east of) the reservoir, which is now outfitted with an electric pump. The sides of this well are lined with masonry, its eastern side supporting an overhang with a large ramp. Like the well associated with VMS-1007, this ramp is for the use of animal traction in lifting water from the well. Although some cattle traction wells have channels for the dispersal of water; this particular example is more simple, and the water was presumably hauled down the ramp still in its container. The construction date of this well is unclear; its overall form reflects a persistent pre-electricity design while its specific masonry style suggests post-Vijayanagara construction. Its excellent condition, however, does suggests that it post-dates the reservoir, a pattern consistent with wells throughout the valley.

Settlement, VMS-109

VMS-109 is a small settlement nestled up against the southern edge of reservoir VMS-1019, just below the embankment. The presence of an abandoned settlement is indicated by an approximately 250 meters diameter scatter of earthenware ceramics, some expedient quartzite flakes, iron slag, and large chunks of plaster. There are no indications of masonry structures; if there were structures here they were probably wattle-and-daub or some other ephemeral material. There is an unusually high density of pebbles in the artifact scatter; these may be components of eroded mud brick or rammed earth walls. The presence of chipped stone tools is interesting. These tend to be simple flakes and cores, all made on low quality quartzite. The continued use of chipped stone on an informal basis well into the Middle period has been documented throughout south India (Morrison and Lycett 1989; Morrison 2006b); it may be associated with limited access to iron tools. The presence of iron slag might suggest some production of iron in or near this small settlement. This in itself is not surprising, given the nearness of the Sandur iron ore deposits. However, slag is widely distributed as a fill material even where there is no evidence for iron production – it is found in low concentrations across the Vijayanagara urban core, for example – and extensive slag scatters do not necessarily derive from proximate production locates. Even if we could locate evidence of nearby iron production, this would not in itself indicate that local people would have had access to all the metal tools they needed. Unfortunately, surface artifacts from VMS-109 were not collected and our understanding of this small settlement remains preliminary. Still is it certainly significant that VMS-109 has no formal architecture (temples, shrines, wells), no associated inscriptions, and no elite-associated artifacts. This may have been little more than a large cluster of houses or even a seasonal campsite. Its location adjacent to a large reservoir is, however, consistent with the possibility that this was a small permanent settlement.

Shaivite Temple, VMS-1030

Built into a natural rock overhang on the edge of a granite outcrop on the north side of the valley, this small Shaivite temple was built quite recently but it incorporates some Vijayanagara-period elements including a doorway and a Nandi sculpture. It may, thus, be a major reconstruction of a pre-existing shrine.[21] Most of the structures in this small complex are recent, including a large platform, an enclosure around the shrine, and a two-room temporary residence for visitors to the temple. New masonry steps lead up to the shrine on the lower part of the outcrop.

At the base of the outcrop where the stairs begin is a tree shrine consisting of several *naga* stones placed against a pipal tree (*Ficus religiosa*). As noted, both tree shrines and *naga* shrines are typically places of women's devotion. A 5 by 7-meters step well of recent construction has been built near the tree shrine. Further up the hill, the shrine itself sits under a granite overhang; water seeping from the rocks above flows down and drips off the edge of the 1.5 meters high rock. About 10 meters in front of the drip line is a recently-built platform and, nearby, a two-room lime-green painted cement structure, also recent. One of the rooms contains a small hearth, apparently used by visitors to the shrine.

The shrine itself is a simple rectangular structure built in the center of the overhang.

Figure 149. VMS-1021, tops of buried sluice.

Figure 150. Slab with carved Gajalakshmi, Gadiganuru village.

The granite doorway dates to the Vijayanagara period but the rest of the structure, built of small square blocks and heavily mortared, plastered, and painted in green, is recent. Shaivite door guardians stand in their usual locations at the base of the door jamb; the latter is cut into an octagonal shape above these fierce guardians. Inside the door, the shrine extends 7.5 meters into the back of the overhang where a Nandi faces a small *lingam*, the central image of the shrine. The cement floor is recent. An inscription above the doorway has a date of 1988. A crudely-shaped lamp column (2.8 meters high) painted with red and green horizontal stripes faces the shrine opposite the doorway.

East of the shrine is a short wall and west of it is a small (4.5 by 2.7 meters) concrete platform built into the overhang. In the center of this platform are three stone images; *lingam*, *nagakal*, and a small Hanuman. Near this platform are a block mortar, two incised tridents, and an incised game board.

The Village of Gadiganuru

Lying between the outer fortification of the eastern Daroji Valley and the inner fortification wall near Dharmasagara, this currently-occupied village clearly existed during the Vijayanagara period and seems to have a continuous occupational history since. In the late nineteenth century, Gadiganuru hosted a British bungalow (Kelsall 1872: 29), but this is no longer present and the village has little official infrastructure.[22]

The area to the west of the village has been heavily disturbed and is badly eroded; the entire area has been mined, perhaps for fill and the few thorny bushes that constitute the scrappy, denuded vegetation are artificially elevated on small mounds formed by the removal of sediment all around them. This area, about 155 meters east-west by 130 meters north-south, has very sandy sediments with abundant *kankar* (calcium carbonate) nodules; the surface is littered with high concentration of earthenware ceramics from the Vijayanagara period or later. There are no structures but a square, post-Vijayanagara well may indicate a seventeenth to nineteenth century date for the major occupation of this place. This is supported by the fact that the artifact assemblage includes shattered quartzite (possibly from industrial processes such as iron ore reduction or cement manufacturing) and some iron slag but no plastic, porcelain, glass, or contemporary graphite-coated earthenwares.[23] The ceramics are highly fragmented and not yet well-studied; some Vijayanagara rim forms do appear to the north, in between this area and the Neolithic ashmound on the northern edge of the valley. What this area represents is difficult to say with certainty. It could be the remains of a settlement, but it seems more probably to be a manufacturing location of some sort and a temporary encampment associated with that activity. This area is not unlike that found in the area east of Gadiganuru, discussed below.

In 1871, the village of Gadiganuru had a land area of 2,031 acres and a population of 1,227 within 262 houses (Government of India 1874). In 1903/4 there were still traces of fortification walls and a moat around the village (Archaeological Survey of India 1904: 79):

> The southern portion of the village lies within the fort walls and has three temple. Kalleśvara temple in the north-east corner appears to be very ancient. It has in it a *lingam* and a statue of a bull. . . . The fort walls on the north-east side, are destroyed, and only two bastions remain on the south side. There are traces of there having been a moat all around, which is now filled up, but is partly visible on the south side.

The Archaeological Survey report goes on to note that in addition to the "Kalleshvara temple", the village contained several modern temples and older sculptures of Gajalakshmi and a 6-feet (Anjaneya) Hanuman. These two sculptures, both of the Vijayanagara period, are now housed in the courtyard of a recent temple in the southern part of the village (Figure 150), as is a smaller Ganesh and a large number of *naga* stones. The Gajalakshmi could be a lintel element. Near this temple is a roofed gateway, built in the "classic" Vijayanagara form with flanking platforms. However, this particular example is made of cinder blocks and is entirely recent. One might suggest that it represents a re-construction of an older gate complex, which would be very interesting since even in 1903/4, this part of the village was no longer on the edge of the settlement and the defensive function of the gate, as such, would be entirely symbolic.

Habitation Debris Between Gadiganuru and Gonahala

East of Gadiganuru, the area near the road is disturbed and eroded but artifact-rich, just as it is west of the village. This extensive scatter of artifacts, pits, and disturbed ground extends, with some interruptions, all the way to the abandoned village of Pemmanahalli, nearly 3 kilometers to the east. About 1 kilometer east of Gadiganuru is a concentration of about 30 small, low mounds of reddish clay-rich sediment, all that remain of structures of rammed earth or wattle-and-daub, arranged, it seems, into clusters of structures rather than along straight roadways. These mounds cover an area of almost 500 meters east-west by nearly 300 meters north-south and lie scattered along the northern banks of the Banuchandra Vanka, an entrenched stream which, even in the dry season, carries some surface water in isolated pools ringed around with clumps of cattails (*Typha latifolia*). The mounds are smaller, about 10 by 10 meters, and approximately square near the eastern end of the settlement; on the west they are larger, as much as 30 by 25 meters (they are deflated and quite eroded, however, so that these measurements certainly overestimate the size of the original structure), and are more widely spaced. The soil in this part of the valley, even some distance from the stream, consists of a coarse alluvial brown sand, a backdrop which not only makes the reddish structures even more visible but which also explains the current scarcity of fields in this part of the valley.

Along the northern bank of the Banuchandra Vanka are also the remains of several highly eroded lime kilns, structures for processing *kankar* (calcium carbonate) nodules into lime. These are so heavily modified that there is little left but a linear smear, 40 by 6 meters, consisting of white, slaggy nodules, gravel, some iron ore, and a few eroded sherds. South of the stream is a dispersed scatter of iron slag and ore which includes both roasted ore and bloom but very little tapped slag, an assemblage which certainly derived from iron smelting but which may be re-deposited.

The structures are surrounded by a light scatter of artifacts approximately 300 meters east-west by 200 meters north-south which includes eroded black and brown earthenwares, a few scraps of rusted iron and various indicators of iron-smelting but no plastic, glass, or other indication of recent occupation. The few ceramic rims that I was able to locate appear to be relatively recent (that is, post-sixteenth century) but the ceramic scatter did not contain any graphite-rubbed earthenware. Near the eastern end of the settlement is a broken-up slab of (recent) concrete. This is, however, right under a power line and may have been built in connection with that feature. The somewhat curious layout of this settlement and its thin and rather depauperate scatter of artifacts that roughly follow the course of the road, might suggest a relatively short-term, perhaps specialized occupation such as a construction camp.[24]

Village of Gonahala

The settlement history of Gonahala, established some time in the Early Middle period, is discussed above. As noted, this small village on the banks of the Banuchandra Vanka was occupied during the Vijayanagara period and up until the middle of the twentieth century, when it was abandoned. Most of the construction in this place is either from the Early Middle period or the twentieth century; the only clearly Vijayanagara-period construction was a large Anjaneya Hanuman. As discussed above, Gonahala seems not to have been a place of great importance in the Vijayanagara-period Daroji Valley and is not associated with any reservoir. Although more paleoecological work remains to be done, as discussed below it seems probable that this eastern part of the Daroji Valley, in particular, saw significant land degradation and deforestation, processes beginning perhaps as early as the sixteenth century but continuing into the present.

Village of Pemmanahalli

A little less than a kilometer east of the contemporary village of Buvanahalli[25] are what may be the remnants of the abandoned village of Pemmanahalli, a place already devoid of permanent residents in 1871[26] but remembered as late as 1903/4.[27] At present, the erstwhile Pemmanahalli serves as the residence of a local *sadhu,* or holy man, who tends a shrine built around a large Vijayanagara-period Hanuman sculpture. Near the present-day road is a remnant bastion; only the eastern half of this earth-filled, round tower is still standing. Originally, it was about 10 meters in diameter. There are now up to 7 courses of masonry in place. These consist of small to large split and unmodified boulders, regularly coursed. As should be evident, these isolated bastions are relatively common in the nucleated villages of the region; sometimes they are associated with fortification walls while in other case no wall can be identified. It is difficult to say when most of these features were constructed and it seems likely that the basic form of the informal bastion stayed relatively stable for a long period of time. On the grounds of both construction and spatial association, I would suggest that bastions of this type were built from the fourteenth or fifteenth century right up until the latter part of the nineteenth century and may have been particularly important in the period of disruption following the collapse of Vijayanagara control over the countryside in the late sixteenth century.

Surrounding the bastion is an extensive scatter of artifacts, more than 70 by 70 meters. The assemblage includes plaster, iron slag, iron ore, and brown and gray earthenware ceramics but no glass or plastic. A boulder-lined walkway about 80 meters long has been constructed from the road north to the Hanuman shrine; in this walkway is an older *nagakal,* in worship. The Anjaneya Hanuman is set up on a recent platform. To Hanuman's west is a Vijayanagara-period step well, 8.5 by 8.5 meters with a 3 meters long entrance stair on the east. The well, which no longer contains water, is built of 14 courses of stepped masonry, mostly split pink granite boulders. There is a low wall built all around the well, but this is in very poor condition and in general, the ground surface here is heavily pitted and disturbed. The ceramics are entirely consistent with both Vijayanagara-period and slightly later materials; as noted, there is no evidence of recent occupation other than the presence of the *sadhu.*

The Village of Kurekuppa

Kurekuppa, established by the Early Middle period (above), is now a small village which, because of its location off the main road through the valley, is not much visited by strangers. As noted, the settlement lies at the base of a granitic inselberg containing a Neolithic ashmound and is less than 2 kilometers from the water-spread of the Daroji reservoir. Like all reservoirs, the water level in that facility varies so that this part of the bed is periodically ringed with mud and marshy vegetation. In the sixteenth century, Kurekuppa was an *agarahara* village known as Kuriyakuppe Anantasetu. As discussed above, this village contains a Chalukyan-style temple with, however, two "foundation" inscriptions from AD 1536 describing the patronage of an individual donor who (re?)established the image of the god Virupaksha in the temple and donated some land or produce rights to the temple. Members of the village assembly, here undoubtedly Brahmins, also donated land for the service of the god – perennially irrigated garden land. If this land were in the immediate vicinity of the village, then it was probably either watered by a well, by diverting some of the flow of the Nari Halla, or it may have been located under reservoir VMS-1018. However, there is no reason to believe that the land in question was contiguous to the settlement and it seems quite possible in question was under the Daroji *kere* itself, one of the most secure and reliable reservoirs in the entire region and thus one that would have supported garden land, even as it does today. Note that Kurekuppa was conceived as being in the Doravadi-*venthe* of the Hastinavati-*valita*, a clear indication of the continued salience of Doravati as a geographic (and administrative) category, even into the sixteenth century.

Hanuman Temple, Kurekuppa

Some 70 meters east and just slightly north of the Early Middle period Shiva temple is a newer shrine containing a Vijayanagara-period Anjaneya Hanuman. In the waist-high enclosure wall are reworked elements including a possible sluice cross-bar, a parapet section with three stone merlons, each containing a carved image, and a large triangular slab with a carved Gajalakshmi, perhaps once part of a door. About 15 meters northwest of this temple is a broken fragment of a Vijayanagara-period Anjaneya Hanuman with bared teeth, originally as much as 3 meters tall. All of these features match the description made in 1904 by the Archaeological Survey (1904: 78):

> (2) A modern Hanumar temple with the image of an ancient Hanumar 4 by 2 feet cut on a slab. Outside, and in front of the temple, is a rough stone with the image of Gajalakshmi and two elephants on either side. There are some *nagarkals* along with this. In front of the temple, there is a platform under a nim [Neem] tree, whereon is a slab 4 feet square, with three male figures sculptured thereon. There are besides two small bulls. Towards the east is an ancient well.
> (3) A modern Hanumar temple with the image of an ancient Hanumar 4 feet high.

The well mentioned by the ASI is clearly post-Vijayanagara, though its precise date of construction cannot be determined.

Reservoir, VMS-1018

This long reservoir is situated on a broad, nearly level plain some 750 meters north-west of the isolated hill marking the settlement of Kurekuppa. It has been heavily disturbed and is now completely non-functional. The embankment is sited in such a way as to suggest that it captured runoff from an older course of the Banuchandra Vanka, a seasonal stream originating out of the Sandur Hills that achieves considerable size near Gadiganuru and which also runs past the abandoned settlement of Gonahala. VMS-1018 is now cut by the Tungabhadra Right Bank High Level Canal, which has severed its western end. However, the decline of VMS-1018 may be considerably less recent, as it also sits near the edge of the waterspread of the Daroji reservoir (VMS-1019). The Banuchandra Vanka now flows directly into the latter.

The area around VMS-1018 is now under intensive wet rice cultivation, watered by the High Level canal. Field clearance for rice paddies can be extremely destructive; clearly field clearing and leveling have affected this reservoir as has the use of its embankment as a local road. Although this reservoir cannot be precisely dated, it seems probable that it pre-dates the proposed sixteenth-century construction of the Daroji reservoir. Given its position in the eastern portion of the main valley, an area not under cultivation even today and peppered with apparently pre-sixteenth century settlements and reservoirs, it may not be too much to suggest that VMS-1018 was built either in the thirteenth or perhaps even the twelfth century.

The total present length of this reservoir is 530 meters. It is only about 10 meters wide and its greatest present height is only 2 meters, suggesting considerable sediment infill. This supported by the height differential between the reservoir bed and the ground immediately below it, which varies from 0.25 meters to a little more than 0.6 meter. The original length of the embankment cannot be determined, given the fact that the eastern end of VMS-1018 is breached and that the western end is cut by the canal. However, at both ends the *bund* is lower and narrower near the disturbance, suggesting that only the extremities of the embankment have been destroyed.

Construction

The earthen embankment is oriented northwest-southeast and is faced with masonry on its southwest side. The latter consists of unmodified medium-sized and large boulders and is highly disturbed. Coursing is irregular and a maximum of 7 courses is preserved. The number of extant courses varies between 3 and 7, with the western sections near the High Level Canal being the highest. The downstream, northeast side of the bund is also defined by masonry, but this consists only of a few rows of small cobbles. The embankment is breached in two places, both apparently by swift-flowing runoff. The course of the road atop the embankment is scattered with small cobbles, some of which may have been footings for now-dismantled masonry.

Outlets and Sluices

Although there are no remaining sluice gates, the presence of two active water channels running under the embankment suggests the location of two tunnels and associated sluices. Although these features could be recent, it seems probable that they were placed to take advantage of existing tunnel locations. The first channel is located about 80 meters from the east end of the *bund*; it is not clear if this channel uses the tunnel masonry. The second place water passes through the embankment is about 150 meters from the east end of facility. Here it is clear that the reservoir has been modified, since a concrete pipe was laid under the embankment and subsequently covered with dirt. Two small blocks with Vijayanagara-style quarry marks lie along a field canal flowing north from this pipe; they could be derived either from the *bund* masonry or even from the sluice gate itself.

Associated Features

Atop the embankment and just west of the pipe is a recent shrine painted in red and white stripes. This shrine, built around a tree on the south side of the embankment, is constructed of roughly-cut slabs with Vijayanagara-style quarry marks.

Reservoir, VMS-1019

This is the monumental Daroji reservoir, the culmination of the main valley system (Figure 151). The embankment stretches from the granitic Hampi-Daroji Hills that define the northern edge of the valley to the long spur of the Sandur Hills that stretches up to define the Avinamodugu Valley, making the Daroji reservoir the endpoint of both main and the Avinamodugu valley reservoir systems. Prior to the construction of the Tungabhadra Dam, the Daroji *kere* was entirely runoff-fed, capturing the flow of runoff from three well-defined seasonal streams. From north to south these are the Banuchandra Vanka, the Nari Halla, and the Kanigana Halla. All of these derive, at least in part, from the Sandur Hills and all contain surface water for most, if not all of the year, though in the dry season water may be restricted to a few deeper pools. The volume of runoff into the Daroji reservoir would have thus always been substantial, as indicated also by the massive construction of the Daroji *bund*. Today, the water supply of the Daroji *kere* is supplemented by flow from the Tungabhadra Right Bank High Level Canal, which loops around the reservoir on its north, west, and south sides. This canal is, however, often dry and the input it provides is not (consistently) substantial. The Daroji reservoir contains water year-round in a pool more than 1.5 by 4 kilometers in size. In the rainy season, the water-spread expands to as much as 2 by 5 kilometers or 1,000 hectares. The reservoir is not very deep, never more than about 7 meters in the dry season, although water level rises substantially after the monsoons. In 1868/9, the Daroji *kere* was reported (Kelsall 1872: 16) to water a total of 1,639 acres (663.3 hectares) of agricultural land.

The land that is seasonally submerged by the reservoir is now covered with a grassy, marshy vegetation that supports a large bird population. West of this area, however, the ground surface is covered in a dense tangle of thorny shrubs but supports almost no other vegetation. The best lands watered by this facility are under perennial cultivation, mostly of rice, vegetables, and orchard crops; a complex network of earthen canals distributes water from the reservoir to these fields. The nearest population center today is the village of Hosa (new) Daroji which lies a little over a kilometer below the reservoir near its southern

Figure 151. Reservoir VMS-1019, Daroji *kere*, with bastion.

Figure 152. Reservoir VMS-1019, Daroji *kere*, with *kodi*.

end. Hale (old) Daroji, a smaller (occupied) village, lies 1.5 kilometers north of the north end of the reservoir near the base of the hills. Hosa Daroji does indeed seem to be new.[28] As noted, the settlement history of Doravati/Daroji is complex and specific loci of occupation shifted through time, sometimes building on locations with existing cultural remains and sometimes being established in places with less evidence for previous use. In any case, there seems to have been more or less continuous human use of this location from several thousand years BC to the present.

The present length of the embankment is 3.6 kilometers. It is an average of 12 meters high and more than 60 meters wide, by far the widest of any Vijayanagara reservoir in the region, although the sixteenth-century Raya *kere*, southwest of Hospet, is higher at 28 meters. As is typically the case, the ends of the reservoir curve back somewhat toward the water, containing it, though in general the embankment is remarkably straight. In plan, the *bund* has a large "kink" near the center, a kind of bulge extending to the west. This feature is explained partly by local topography; the reservoir is built into a small outcrop at this point. However, this is (or was) also a weaker section, for it is the location of the breach made by a flood in 1851 which completely destroyed the village of (Hosa) Daroji.

Construction

The northern end of the reservoir *bund* has several unusual construction features which suggest post-Vijayanagara construction. As discussed below, these features were probably reconstructed or repaired in the mid-nineteenth century; however, there may also be older antecedents to these structures. The far northern end has a waste weir or *kodi*, similar in form to that of the Kamalapuram reservoir, but built on a much grander scale. This spillway (Figure 152) is 80 meters long and consists of a low masonry wall near the water and a large stone apron or pavement below (east of) the wall. The water level in most winter months is very close to the top of this wall, so the *kodi* must actually flow many times throughout the year. Although both the wall and stone pavement are actively maintained and thus are generously cemented, the latter is built of flat boulders and quarried blocks, many with Vijayanagara-style quarry marks.[29] The northern end of the waste weir touches the base of the outcrops forming the north side of the valley. On the sheetrock and flat boulders that now lie just to the north of the spillway is a line of peg holes, possibly remnants of an earlier *kodi* arrangement, or else anchors for a supplemental temporary dam of brush or other moveable barrier. Elements in the waste weir are mostly quite water-worn.

South of the waste weir, the embankment takes the form of a curving, bastion-like feature (Figure 151) 60 meters in diameter that extends out into the reservoir. There is no earthen embankment behind the bastion. On the upstream, water-facing side, this structure is faced with regular courses of rectangular blocks each about 0.30 meter long. The courses are stepped out very slightly, only about 2 to 3 centimeters for each course, so that the overall effect is an almost-vertical face rather than the usual staircase-like arrangement of Vijayanagara reservoir masonry. Also unusual is the fact that this bastion-like feature is entirely plastered. Although this structure is currently being maintained – the interior face of the masonry (the east side, away from the water) has been cemented and painted – the plaster is obviously not new and in fact both the form of this bastion and its plaster are similar to certain kinds of courtly secular architecture in the city of Vijayanagara. This architectural style, formerly known as "Indo-Saracenic" but renamed by Michell (1992) the "Vijayanagara courtly style", clearly takes inspiration from both South Indian temple architecture and decorative motifs and from Deccani architectural and decorative programs associated with Islamic structures such as mosques and tombs. Michell (1992: 66-8) argues that this distinctive style was meant to convey a message of universality, of supraregional social and cultural affiliation in light of the capital's cosmopolitan population (and no doubt its rulers' aspirations of universal kingship).[30] It may seem to be a stretch to include this interesting plastered bastion-cum-reservoir embankment in Michell's courtly style category, particularly if its reconstruction does, indeed date to the nineteenth century as I will argue below, a time, it must be noted, when the area was under British colonial control and when the Vijayanagara empire did still exist in some nominal form. Beyond this, however, the idea of Vijayanagara had considerable local resonance and both this and the "traditional" role of legitimate rulers as caretakers of irrigation works certainly influenced British views of correct reservoir construction, views also colored by ideas about the activities of their predecessor, Tipu Sultan (below). However, as I discuss below, not only do we not know what the pre-British northern end of the reservoir looked like, but the sixteenth-century Daroji sluices also follow, within the functional constraints of their genre, some of the design characteristics of the courtly style and it thus seems reasonable to view this entire reservoir as an example of that design impulse, albeit one perhaps widely separated in time and political context from other examples.

The plastered bastion is both so striking and unusual that it merits some analysis. Early British observers viewed this structure – and, by extension, the entire reservoir – to be "Islamic" in style and hence supposed it to have been constructed by Tipu Sultan, the Muslim king of Mysore who ruled this area, with some interruptions, between AD 1782 and 1799, when he was defeated by the British army. Kelsall (1872: 16), for example, writes, "The Daroji tank was constructed under the government of Tippu Sultín. It is formed by damming up a gap in one of the minor ranges of hills with a bund three miles in length, and in some places 60 feet in height. The bund breached in the great storm at the close of 1851, and the greater part of the village was destroyed. It is rarely dry, though in the famine year of 1866 there was no water there for some time." (He also notes that excellent fish are caught here.) As Kelsall provides no source for this assertion, one can only guess why he attributed the reservoir to Tipu Sultan. There is a nineteenth-century inscription in a mosque in Daroji (Table 7.2) claiming that the mosque was built during the reign of (but not necessarily through the patronage of) Tipu Sultan (1782-99) and there is a Persian-language inscription on a slab lying atop the reservoir. Other than this, there is little reason to believe that Tipu Sultan or his government made many investments in this region, far to the north of Mysore, and even less evidence that the Daroji *kere* was in fact commissioned by him. As discussed above, it is most probable that this northern end of the Daroji reservoir – the waste weir and bastion – post-dates the rest of the facility which was almost certainly constructed all at once in what must have been an incredibly large-scale project. The chronology of the southern part of the reservoir is discussed below though we may say that it was built at some undetermined point late in the Vijayanagara period or shortly afterwards. The massive *kodi* and bastion seem to have been (re)built in the mid-nineteenth century; unfortunately we know nothing of what came before and whether the original construction included the bastion or not. As discussed above, the bastion and part of the northern end of the reservoir embankment cut through Early Middle period habitation deposits.

South of the bastion, the reservoir embankment takes on a more familiar form of a wide earthen embankment faced with masonry on its upstream, west face (Figure 153). The masonry consists of medium-sized unmodified and split boulders as well as some quarried blocks. There are an average of 28 to 30 courses of masonry, with very few projecting slabs and no formal staircases. Although some fill has been robbed from the eastern side of the embankment, it is clear that there was also a narrow masonry facing on this side, near the base. There are several sections here that show signs of patching. At one point a piece of reused center moulding from a rather elaborate structure – a protruding hexagon – is also incorporated into the embankment, suggesting a long history of repair and reconstruction. The northernmost 250 meters of the embankment (the earthen embankment itself begins south of the spillway and bastion) are built of a very ashy, artifact-rich material that was obviously scooped up from the remains of a settlement. Further south, the embankment is constructed of sterile sediment. At this point there are 24 courses of stepped masonry, here medium-sized to large boulders, both split and unmodified.

South of sluice 2, the masonry varies a great deal, with some sections of the stepped revetment built at a very acute angle and others at a very oblique one. There are several obvious repaired sections and several moulding fragments (mostly two-stepped with angled bevel) integrated into the masonry. Further south, where the bund begins to curve, it is clear that the entire embankment has been rebuilt. The lower part of the embankment is faced with shallowly-sloping stepped masonry, followed by a flat stone pavement, itself topped with a four course high wall. This broad bend is the location of an Irrigation Department observation tower and office which records the reconstruction of this large segment – the rebuilt section is at least several hundred meters long – on a plaque built into the wall of the building. The plaque reads: "This calingulah which was with the village of Darojee completely destroyed by a flood in 1851 was rebuilt in 1853 at a cost of Rs 40,000 (including other works)" and is signed with the names of the district collector, the civil engineer, and the maramut superintendent.[31]

Sluices and Outlets

There are, in addition to the broad waste weir described above, four other sluices associated with the Daroji reservoir. Unusually, all these sluices are identical, or virtually so, suggesting that they were built at the same time. All are quite large and formal, with all the granite elements carefully shaped and dressed. Sluice 1, the northernmost sluice (Figure 154), is not far from the plastered bastion. It has been fitted with new hardware and a long metal access ramp from the *bund.* The sluice sits about 25 meters away from the *bund.* Like the others, this is a monumentally-scaled, double sluice (8 to 9 meters above the current water level or about 13 or 14 meters total) covered by an elaborate roof. The sluice is supported by 4 dressed rectangular uprights, each capped with cruciform capitals with square cut-outs. Four horizontally-laid granite slabs laid atop the capitals take the part of the upper cross-bars; these massive supports are toothed and step out so that the eaves can rest on them. These slabs support a flat ceiling made of many parallel, horizontal granite slabs (Figure 155). This in turn supports a superstructure; a simple plastered "roof", attractively angled and made of both granite and mortared bricks (Figure 156). This form of construction combines typical Vijayanagara sluice construction – the doubled uprights have both lower and upper cross bars and are unusual only in their scale – with elements of Vijayanagara temple construction, including the capitals and the flat slab roof. The superstructure is, however, unique. Although some of the sluices of Raya *kere,* near Hospet, also have brick superstructures, these are in very poor condition and it is not possible to compare their form with the Daroji sluices. Unlike the Raya *kere* sluices, however, the Daroji sluices have no sculptures of deities although sluice 3 (below) does have a lotus medallion carved on the underside of the flat ceiling, just like a temple. All this should make clear that the Daroji sluices also form good example of Michell's "courtly style". The superstructure, in particular, has both the construction (plastered brick and mortar) and the "Islamic" look typical of such structures in the city, while the overall structure follows both established sluice forms and idioms of Vijayanagara temple architecture.

The lower cross-bars of sluice 1 are just visible above the water surface. Both are functional and are now fitted with metal rods. Although both the upper cross-bars/lintels are perforated, neither is now in use as water flow is regulated at the level of the lower cross-bar, suggesting that water levels may in the reservoir may be less variable now than they once were.

Sluice 2 (Figure 157) is only about 100 meters south of sluice 1. It is the shortest of all the sluices, rising only about 5 meters above the water. Its lower cross-bars are submerged, however, suggesting that this height differential is due only to the fact that sluice 2 sits in a deeper part of the reservoir bed and not that it was made on a different scale from the others. Like sluice 1, it is still in use and has been fitted

Figure 153. Embankment, VMS-1019.

Figure 154. VMS-1019, sluice 1, overview.

Figure 155. VMS-1019, sluice 1, detail.

Figure 156. VMS-1019, sluice 1, showing roof.

with recent metal hardware, a walkway, and a new cement staircase down the side of the embankment.

Sluices 3 and 4 are clustered at the southern end of the embankment just south of a small metamorphic outcrop that forms part of the embankment, much as 1 and 2 are clustered at the northern end.[32] Like sluice 1, sluice 3 is tall, about 9 meters above the water when last observed. Unlike the masonry of the repaired central section of the reservoir, which is rather unevenly and haphazardly built, the masonry near sluice 3 and south to the southern end of the embankment is very regular, built of evenly-laid steps of split boulders; it appears to be original. Sluice 3 is still in use and has been fitted with a metal walkway and control bars. The lower cross-bars were about 1.75 meters above the water level, again suggesting that the apparent height variation in the four sluices is only a consequence of sluice 2 being set into a low area in the reservoir bed – the degree of uniformity of construction is simply remarkable. Sluice 3 does, however, differ from its siblings in two interesting ways. First, the holes through which the control bars pass are square rather than round (the only example of this in the entire region). Second, there is a large, ornate lotus medallion – a feature commonly found on the ceilings of temples, usually in the porch or antechamber and almost never in the sanctuary – carved onto the flat ceiling of this roofed double sluice. The form and placement of this feature further emphasizes what I have suggested is a structural and iconographic argument being made by the morphologies of sluices for a parallel between Vijayanagara sluice gates and temple doorways, specifically the entrances to the *garbhagriha* or sanctuary itself. Needless to say, this feature does not in itself add to the case for patronage by Tipu Sultan, a Muslim, but neither does it necessarily refute it, as Tipu patronized many Hindu religious establishments (Brittlebank 1997). Other differences between Sluice 3 and the northern sluices include small variations in the structures supporting the roof (the four lintels are plain rectangles and instead of two square projections supporting the eaves, the latter rest on angled blocks sitting atop the capitals); like the lotus, these features are not visible from the bank.

Sluice 4 is again, virtually identical to the other sluices, but without a lotus medallion. Unlike the others, however, this sluice is no longer in use and has not been maintained, hence the plaster and whitewash covering its brick-and-plaster superstructure are almost completely gone. The lower cross bar is about .15 meter above the water surface, indicating that it sits a little higher than Sluice 3, a placement also evident from the remains of a very wide under-*bund* tunnel that runs from the embankment out to the sluice. One can walk along the top of the tunnel, which is 7 meters wide and runs about 20 meters out to the sluice; unusually, the tunnel seems to have been encased in masonry, the latter perhaps covering the more usual brick-and-mortar that generally encases the masonry-lined water passage. Sluice 4 is about 9 meters high and is located some 50 meters north of the southern end of the reservoir, a junction marked by first a low hill and then a much higher one. The railroad line cuts through the smaller hill and runs along the southern side of the reservoir.

Associated Features

At the northern end of the embankment and partway up the side of the outcrop containing the Doravati/Daroji fort, a flight of stairs (recently constructed but incorporating numerous older quarried blocks) leads to a south-facing Virabhadra temple built on a masonry-faced platform. The platform includes several large blocks with Vijayanagara-style quarry marks but it has clearly been reworked more recently. There are two small shrines on the platform, one quite recent but the other dating to the Vijayanagara period. The latter consists of a 4 by 2 columned *mandapa* built into a large boulder. The columns of the outer porch are later, but the columns of the inner porch are of the most common Vijayanagara form – square with octagonal insets. Carved onto the stone basement are depictions of a multi-headed *naga* and of a cow licking its flank.

Figure 157. VMS-1019, sluice 2.

Figure 158. Daroji reservoir, from Daroji fort.

The lamp column also dates to the Vijayanagara period; on its southern side is a sculpture of a female donor with a side hair bun. On the north, facing the sanctuary, are carvings of two female devotees. That this temple is (and was) a place of women's worship is clear; unfortunately there do not seem to be any inscriptions associated with either its initial construction or later expansion. The 1904 Archaeological Survey report (1904: 78) notes the presence on "Hill block No. 13" of an "ancient Ramalinga temple on the top of the hill with a *lingam* of the same in it. There are old Telugu and Kanarese inscriptions on two of the pillars of the temple. On the east, is a stone with foot marks cut thereon. Towards the north of this, is a well." If this is same structure, which seems probable, then the more recent remodeling must have destroyed or obliterated the inscription-bearing columns; there is no record of an inscription in published sources.

Atop the platform near the newer shrine is a small, badly-cut carved slab containing outlines of two *lingams* and a one-word inscription. This seems to be recent. On the boulders around to the west of the temples are two mortars and an inscribed game. The temples command a good view over the reservoir but the fort is not accessible from this point as the hill is too steep and rocky to climb in this area.

The Settlements of Doravati/Daroji

During the Vijayanagara period, the area around Daroji was known both as the Doravati-*venthe* and the Doravadi-Somalapura-*sime* (Patil 1996b: 243). Both of these terms refer to administrative divisions and thus illustrate larger-scale recognition of locally-salient place-names. As I mentioned in the discussion of Early Middle Doravati, above, the village of Hale Daroji lies at the foot of a small outcrop just north and east of the northern end of the Daroji reservoir (Figure 158). I suggested that the concentration of structures and artifacts just north of Hale Daroji was the remnant of a Vijayanagara-period settlement, now much obscured by recent trash-dumping. Here I describe some more features of that settlement, but I should point out first that Somalapuram is the name of a small village on the other side of the outcrop northeast of Hale Daroji. This Somalapuram may be the other half of the Doravadi-Somalapura-*sime.* Although Somalapuram is now just a small, out-of-the-way village on a dirt road, it is possible that the Vijayanagara town either actually extended all the way east to the present location of Somalapuram or that the latter, having maintained its own identity, later shifted somewhat away from Doravati. In either case, the location of Somalapuram and the use of the epithet Doravadi-Somalapura-*sime* for this region suggests that my identification of this northern settlement as Vijayanagara-period Doravati is correct.

As noted above, the Vijayanagara-period settlement contains two Hanuman temples. The northernmost temple appears to date to the Early Vijayanagara period; Patil (1996b: 245) suggests that twelfth- or thirteenth-century columns were reused in this structure. This south-facing temple although small, is elaborately carved, consisting of an outer, 4 by 3 columned porch and a small 2 by 2 columned sanctuary. The stone basement is decorated with a frieze of elephants. The outer, south-facing columns of the porch are low and stocky, square in section with complex octagonal insets and circular, disk-shaped capitals. Inside the (locked) sanctuary is a large slab carved with Anjaneya Hanuman. The sanctuary is enclosed within recent walls and there are no door guardians. Over the door to the sanctuary is a rather unusual, possibly secular sculpted panel. A central pavilion is flanked on each side by two women with Vijayanagara-style hair buns. The two nearest the structure are holding something on their heads while the other two have something draped over their arms. Inside the structure is a striding male figure with a conical hat, similar to those worn by Vijayanagara kings. Patil (1996b: 245) also makes this identification and suggests that two of the women are meant to depict queens. If so, this may be a donor portrait of some sort, though its placement is certainly unusual.

About 70 meters south of this temple is another south-facing, Early to Middle Vijayanagara-period temple. This one is somewhat more austere – its columns are also square with octagonal insets and disk-shaped capitals, but here the insets are simpler. The form of the building is identical to the northern shrine with a 3 by 4 columned covered *mandapa* abutting a square, 2 by 2 columned sanctuary. Inside the latter is a small carved sculpture of Anjaneya Hanuman; the sculpture is not from the Vijayanagara period and is quite possibly more recent. About 60 meters to the south is a small Vijayanagara-period boundary stone – a Nandi on a post with, unfortunately, no inscription.[33] A small chlorite sculpture of Krishna lying near the southern temple also dates to the Vijayanagara period (and see Patil 1996b: 245).

A quite substantial road wall runs south from the southern temple for about 100 meters along the paved road. The wall is constricted of split boulders set on edge, unmodified boulders, and a few quarried blocks. Near the present southern end of the road wall, perched on the side of the outcrop containing the fort, is a large, round bastion of quarried rectangular and square blocks. The bastion is solid, *c.* 25 to 30 meters in diameter and 10 meters high. This kind of feature is difficult to date, but given its location at the end of the Vijayanagara-era road wall it may have been built sometime between the fourteenth and sixteenth centuries.

It is possible to trace, then, the movement of Daroji from its Early Middle period location at the northern end of the reservoir *bund* to, during the Early Vijayanagara period, an area just to the north of Hale Daroji. The Vijayanagara town may have extended as far east as Somalapuram. At this same time, the Daroji reservoir was either built or expanded although it is not definite that the northern *kodi* and bastion were yet in place. In any event, the Early Middle period town was unoccupied by this time. The post-sixteenth-century history of Doravati is less clear. Hale Daroji may have once been on the southern edge of the Vijayanagara town; alternately, Hale Daroji may have been founded later, after the Vijayanagara town was already totally or largely abandoned. In either case, the identity as Doravati/Daroji was maintained. At some later time, Hosa (new) Daroji was established, presumably by residents of Hale Daroji, in the area under the reservoir and some distance to the south. Hosa Daroji is now the larger of the two and boasts several mosques as well as temples.

DISCUSSION: THE MAIN VALLEY

With the possible exception of reservoir VMS-1018 near Kurekuppa, all of the known reservoirs of the Daroji Valley were built during the Vijayanagara period, the majority of these in the sixteenth century. The eastern end of the valley, unlike the western end, was settled in the Early Middle period though these small villages were not densely packed and may have relied quite substantially on dry farming and stream-side inundation. The eastern end of the valley, too, has a highly degraded thorn-scrub vegetation today, making parts of it unsuitable even for grazing, a pattern perhaps related to this history of land use. Unlike every other reservoir in the Daroji Valley, VMS-1019 maintained its importance through time and even underwent one or more large-scale expansions, completely avoiding the major collapse of the Daroji Valley reservoir system after the fall of the city. The Daroji reservoir still waters a substantial expanse of fields, many under water-loving rice and vegetables. In the mid-twentieth century, the extension of the Right Bank High Level Canal of the Tungabhadra project meant that canal water could be diverted into the reservoir. In fact, this supply line makes a minimal contribution to the Daroji *kere* – the canal is dry most of the year in this area – but the fact that there has been an effort to both supply and maintain the reservoir points to its perceived significance.

In this light is worth noting that the major distribution channel of the Daroji reservoir, a channel which continues to be called the Nari Halla below the reservoir as it flows back down toward the river, is littered with a string of abandoned villages. These villages, Hanahalli, Mavinahalli, Sankalapuram, and Hosa Nalludi, have all, with the exception of Sankalapuram which is completely abandoned, been reestablished a short way away from their earlier location. Hanahalli and Mavinahalli have moved a little further away from the Nari Halla and, perhaps not coincidently, closer to a recently-built distributary channel. Hosa Nalludi has moved the least, shifting to a location less than 500 meters to the north but a location that is closer to a paved road. What this illustrates is one the one hand, something of the fluidity of south Indian rural settlements – a stable, named "place" is in almost all cases a complex series of actually-occupied places, half-finished and half-abandoned structures, of claims and rights to structures, fields, and building plots differentially used or held in reserve. Doravati was the name of a fort, a settlement, a region, a reservoir, and an administrative division. As both Doravati and Daroji, its physical locus shifted several times, incorporated Somalapuram for a time, released it, and finally split into old and new. This fluidity is not something much remarked on; some of it is in fact invisible to text-based scholarship as long-term use of the same place name may obscure the fact that the named place is actually in motion, albeit over a limited spatial range.

I have already remarked on the fact that during the Middle periods, south Indians were very much on the move. Historians have documented significant large-scale population movements, movements that fed, for example, the urban population of the city of Vijayanagara. In later centuries, documentary sources are relatively more complete and one can trace large-scale mobility during, for example, famine periods. At the same time (and on the other hand), we also see patterns of long-term stability in local geographic identities, stability illustrated by the case of Doravati/Daroji. All of this, of course, brings to mind the question of what such a contradictory pattern – constant movement of people and physical places and yet incredible continuity in the use of specific places in the landscape – might mean. How do particular local attachments, pattern of movement, use of places, get remembered, memorialized, and knowledge about them passed on? Why do places so often retain the same name even as they physically move or become filled with newcomers? It is difficult to answer these question in any simple way, but it is worth pointing out that what this continuity does *not* signify is an absence of change. Scholarly and popular notions about the stifling continuity, the timeless tradition, of south Indian rural life see only the name – Doravati, Dharmasagara – and its long-term salience, ignoring locational shifts, episodes of construction and reconstruction, economic restructuring, and changes in political context.

NOTES

1. "Field No. 36.—about the centre and slightly towards the north, is a mound about a hundred feet square, said to be the site of some ruined village where nothing but a kind of light stone resembling lava is to be found. There is also another small mound with the same kind of light stone towards the west of field No. 30." (Archaeological Survey of India 1904: 79)
2. This example was black on one side and red on the other; this sort of "Black and Red Ware" differs from the two-color variety where black and red slips are found on the same side of the vessel and, I have found, is also found in apparently Neolithic deposits at Brahmagiri.
3. The probability of late chipped-stone technology is discussed by Lycett and Morrison (1989) and Morrison (2006b). Blade technology does seem to become much less common in this area by the BC/AD boundary.
4. This Anglo-Indian term refers to fine gravel.
5. Leaving aside the Maski edict to the north, which is also not far away. The two Koppal edicts are located at Gavi Math and Palkigunda.
6. To clarify, from the northern edge of the Daroji Valley to the Tungabhadra River, the landscape alternates between long ridges of rocky outcrops and narrow colluvial valleys; this is the setting of the city of Vijayanagara. In contrast, the eastern Bellary plain is flat, tilting slightly down to the northeast, the monotonous black surface broken only by isolated granitic hills, solitary features rather than members of larger ridge complexes.
7. Recall that Pampa is a river-goddess and the early name for Hampi.
8. In 1871, the village had only 614 acres, of which 163 was held on *inam* tenure and the rest by individual farmers or farming households (*ryotwari*). The land revenue of this small, mostly dry-farmed place was less than 2 rupees, significantly less than the abandoned settlement of Pemmanahalli which, however, yielded in 1871 no income from *ryotwari* land.
9. Both this and the one-room shrine seem to have been built between about 1905 and 1970.

10. Maheshvara is a name for Shiva. Pampa, as noted above, is the Goddess associated with the original river-crossing and the germ of the Virupaksha temple in Hampi.
11. False not because the inscription is not genuine, but because it seems to claim construction credit for an older temple.
12. The Archaeological Survey (1904: 78) described it as follows, "Field No. 159 – The site of Kurikuppi village. – (1) A very ancient Ishwara temple, with a small *gopuram* built of brick and chunum. It contains a lingam, an image of Parvati about 2 feet high and a bull of about 3 feet long. On either side of the wall, statues of Virabhadrasvami and Ganesha each about 2 feet high stand in niches. The temple is in the Jain style, with some finely sculpted massive pillars, on two of which are old Telugu and Kanarese inscriptions. This temple is about the centre of the village and surrounded by four bastions."
13. The north side of the badly-damaged porch is graced by two carved elephants.
14. Some forts were adapted by the British for their own use, most notably the Bellary fort, formerly a stronghold of Tipu Sultan. Although the British did establish a sanatorium at Sandur, as far as I can tell they never modified or made any significant use of the forts around the Vijayanagara region.
15. Near the village of Somalapuram, northeast of Daroji and sharing the same low outcrop, the Archaeological Survey also reported an "ancient ruined village known as 'Narayanasvami Bagadai'" with a large Hanuman scuplture (1904: 80).
16. Of course, there is no evidence whatsoever for any Early Middle period reservoirs here.
17. *Vrittis* or *vrtti* are variously defined by Sircar (1966: 381) as "means; livelihood, occupation; grant of land for one's livelihood . . . land granted for service . . . [and] share; share in a village granted to a Brahmana as a free gift." In this context it could either refer to land or produce shares.
18. *Mahajanas* are members of a village assembly. Their social positions may vary as the term seems to variously refer to groups of merchants, Brahmins, or all (land-controlling, male, and presumably adult) members of a village. Early Middle Period inscriptions (cf. Nilakanta Sastri 1966: 166; Stein 1980:146) mostly refer to *mahajanas* as Brahmins, while by the seventeenth century, this term was securely associated with merchants (Subrahmanyam 1998; and see Sircar 1966: 177). In this case, the *mahajanas* are probably Brahmins.
19. "North of field No. 48 and west of No. 46 is a small temple on the slope of the hill, known as "*Nura-ondu* Linga Gudi (*Nura* = Kanarese for 100 and *ondu* Kanarese for 1) meaning a temple consisting of one hundred and one *lingams.* Those are of different sizes. There is also a small statue of a Ganeśa. Outside the temple, and in front of it, is an ancient statue of a bull." (Survey of India 1904: 80).
20. Kotinganahallu was occupied in 1871. At that time it was listed as having 1610 acres of land, 53 houses and a population of 257 people (Government of India 1874). In its 1904 report, the Archaeological Survey of India noted that, with the possible exception of a Hanuman shrine, there were no antiquities in the village.
21. This is supported by the Archaeological Survey of India notice of this shrine (1904: 79), "An ancient Nanjundeśvara temple with a *lingam,* on the slopes of a hill and statues of a bull, and a Ganesa. An overhanging rock forms the roof of this temple. Outside are a few *nagakals,* and a slab about a foot high with the image of Hanumar sculptured on it."
22. Bungalows could be attached to various departments and were for the purpose of accommodating visiting officials. It is not clear what sort of bungalow Gadiganur had, but the fact that this small place had any facility at all points to the importance of the route through the Daroji Valley at this time.
23. This is a very recent kind of ceramic, the graphite being added to give the ceramic vessel something of the sheen of a metal container (Sinopoli, personal communication).
24. Construction crews are sometimes lodged in temporary camps as they were, for example, during the Tungabhadra project. Specialized encampments are far from rare and include army camps, colonial-period famine-relief public work camps (cf. Morrison 2000), construction camps, temporary habitations of mobile pastoralists or other occupational groups, and so on.
25. Buvanahalli, although without precolonial architectural remains, was occupied at the time of the 1871 census, when it (Buvanahalli) is listed as having 732 acres of land, 53 houses, and 297 inhabitants (1874).
26. In the 1871 census, Pemmanhalli, in Gadiganuru Sammat, had no houses and no

population, but 1,307 acres of land. Of the latter, the majority (984 acres) was listed as unoccupied and the minority (294 acres) as held on private or non-government (*inam*) tenure. This land yielded a modest land revenue of just over 33 rupees (1874).

27. "Field No. 74—The site of the ruined village of Pemmanahalli. On the north-east side, is a platform wheron is a slab with the image of Hanumar 6 feet by 3 feet sculptured thereon. About a hundred feet east of this, lies a slab with an image of Hanumar, 6 feet by 3 feet, sculptured thereon. There is a well here, and many mounds are to be found in this field." (Archaeological Survey of India 1904: 79.)
28. The 1871 census lists only one Daroji, a village associated with almost 9,000 acres of land and a population of 2,397 in 612 houses (1874: 26-7). By 1928, both Darojis appear on Survey of India maps.
29. As noted, this form of quarry mark is associated with Vijayanagara-period structures and is quite distinct from twentieth-century quarry marks. However, given the shortage of well-dated structures from the seventeenth through nineteenth centuries (ones with visibly quarry-marked masonry), there is no reason to think that this style of quarrying was not also carried out later, perhaps as late as the mid-nineteenth century.
30. See also discussion by Eaton (2000) and Wagoner (1996) on the engagement of Vijayanagara kings and other elites with models of kingship, royal style, and deportment derived from Islamic rulers and traditions, including those of the nearby Deccani sultanates.
31. A calingula or calingulah is a waste weir or *kodi.* This Anglo-Indian term was derived from the Tamil word *kalingal* (Yule 1903: 148). This inscription suggests the presence of a waste weir near the middle of the reservoir, a facility destroyed in the flood and subsequently, one presumes, replaced by a new section of masonry. This also suggests, then, that the northern waste weir was also built or renovated following the flood.

    Also according to Yule (1903: 559), ". . . in Madras Presidency the word [maramut] had formerly a very specialised sense as the recognised title of that branch of the Executive which included the conservation of irrigation tanks and the like, and which was worked under the District Civil Officers, there being then no separate department of the State in charge of Civil Public Works."
32. There is a small, recent shrine atop this outcrop.
33. Cf. Kotraiah (1978). Boundary stones are often carved with small reclining Nandi sculptures though they may also be unadorned. Some are inscribed. Field and village boundaries were scrupulously maintained and recorded; inscriptions referring to grants of land generally provide land boundaries in some detail, mostly by reference to landmarks (rivers, canals, other people's fields, etc.).

Chapter Eight

THE AVINAMODUGU VALLEY

> The country is exceedingly bare, and the population scanty. All the houses are collected in villages; and the smallest village, of five or six houses, is fortified. The defense of such a village consists of a round stone wall, perhaps forty feet in diameter, and six feet high. On top of this is a parapet of mud, with a door in it, to which the only access is by ladder. In case of a plundering party coming to the village, the people ascend into this tower, with their families, and most valuable effects, and having drawn up the ladder defend themselves with stones, which even the women throw with great force and dexterity. Larger villages have square forts, with round towers at the angles. (Buchanan 1807: 32)

The mouth of the Avinamodugu Valley (Figure 159) joins the Daroji Valley near the latter's eastern end. Oriented primarily to the south/southeast, this large valley is a rather out-of-the way place defined by the Sandur Hills on the west and south and a long granitic spur of the Hampi-Daroji Hills on the east, separating it from the Bellary Plains. The Avinamodugu Valley is sparsely occupied today, a pattern congruent with its lack of any major transportation through-route. The primary path through the eastern hills that bound both the Daroji and Avinamodugu Valleys is now, and perhaps always was, the pass at Kudatini where the large Neolithic ashmound (and its later Iron Age burial) is located, a pass located just to the north of the Avinamodugu Valley. This pass was well-fortified by a series of heavily-built walls constructed during the Vijayanagara period; it appears to have been the primary access route into the valley from the east at that time. Depending on the exact chronology of the construction of the northern end of the Daroji *kere*, up until about the seventeenth century there may have been a second way into the valley north of the Daroji reservoir, right below the Daroji Fort.

Within the Avinamodugu Valley there is also one well-defined route up into the Sandur Hills, a route littered with material remains from many periods and still in active use today. Other roads and paths up into the hills are more recent and relate to the expansion of mining in this area in the latter part of the twentieth century. The valley floor itself is not continuous, being broken up by numerous outcropping hills. Only the southern part of the valley, the area now dominated by the Avinamodugu *kere* and the associated villages of Avinamodugu and Vittalapur, has much level land. Settlement in the valley clusters around the two primary seasonal water courses, the Nari Halla on the west and the Hire Halla on the east.

The Sandur Hills have figured in my account thus far as a boundary, a watershed, an island of more mesic vegetation in a sea of xeric plant taxa, and as a the source of iron ores, reddish soil and metamorphic rock. They thus served both as barrier – there are only a few ways up into them – and as resource. The landscape history of these hills reflects that dual identity. As a place for hill-forts, temple centers, palaces, a sanatorium, and finally, mining camps, human use of these hills has reflected both their topographic situation, resources, and their changing positions in regional cultural and political geographies. Although the Sandur Hills define the entire southern edge of the Daroji Valley, they are ascended most easily on their western and eastern ends, with the primary paved road up into the hills now beginning on the west, near Hospet.

The Avinamodugu Valley has not been

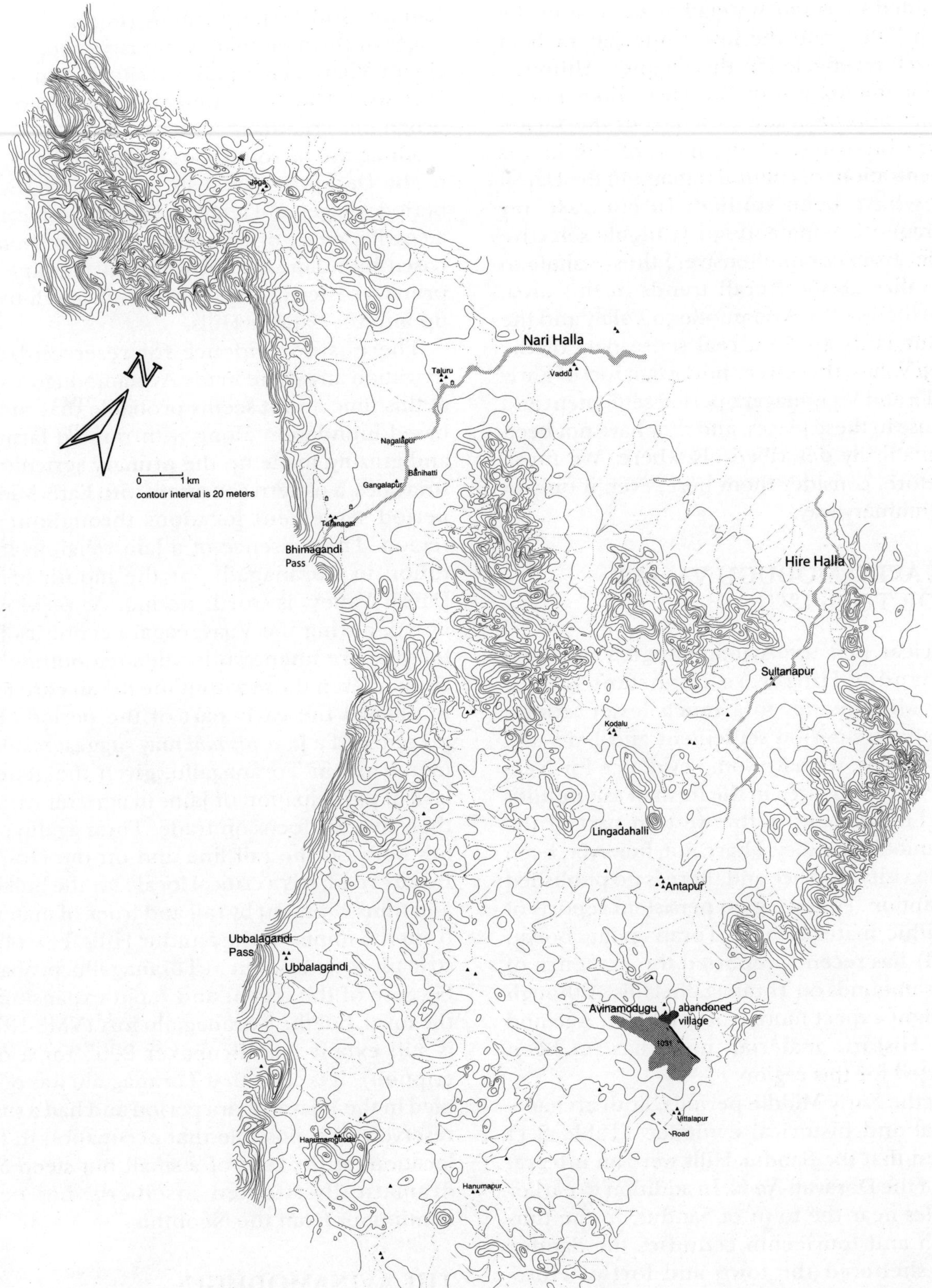

Figure 159. Avinamodugu Valley, overview.

examined in as much detail as the rest of the Daroji Valley and the lower intensity of field research is reflected in this chapter. Although my documentation of the latter does not in any way approach the closeness of the Vijayanagara intensive survey, most of the larger concentrations of cultural remains in the Daroji Valley have been studied. In contrast, my coverage of Avinamodugu is highly selective and far from comprehensive. I thus hesitate to generalize about overall trends in this area. Nevertheless, the Avinamodugu Valley and the Sandur Hills are in a real sense part of the Daroji Valley; there were important foci of Early Middle and Vijayanagara-period settlement and land use in these places, and they have not been systematically described elsewhere. We must, therefore, consider them here, even if only in a preliminary way.

THE AVINAMODUGU VALLEY PRIOR TO AD 1300

It is clear that the Avinamodugu Valley and the Sandur Hills were important loci of Early Middle and, to a much lesser extent, Vijayanagara-period settlement and land use. Prior to this, we have some evidence for Neolithic use of this area in the form of ashmounds near Lingadahalli in the western part of the Avinamodugu Valley. I have not, however, been able to visit this place and there is no published description. Following on persistent reports of Neolithic material near Toranagallu, Boivin (2004) has recently reported the existence of two ashmounds on Toranagallu Hills. Although we might expect more scattered Iron Age and Early Historic material, none has yet been reported for this region.

By the Early Middle periods, both archaeological and historical evidence (Table 8.1) suggest that the Sandur Hills were an integral part of the Doravati *Nadu*. In addition to earlier temples near the town of Sandur, in the thirteenth and fourteenth centuries the Sandur Hills sheltered the town and fort of Hosemaledurga (present-day Ramgad), associated with Kampila Raya (Patil 1996a). All of the major Kampila Raya fortified settlements, Kummata Durga, Doravati, Hosemaledurga, Kampli, and Haneya, then, ring around the edges of the area that would later support the city of Vijayanagara; all are situated in places that would became peripheral parts of the urban hinterland.

Along the seasonal Nari Halla, later a feeder to the Daroji *kere*, lie a string of Early Middle period villages and temples that not only reflect an earlier mode of agricultural land use (*nullah*-based inundation), but which also define the primary eastern route – the Bhimagandi pass – up into the Sandur Hills.

There is no evidence for reservoir-based irrigation anywhere in the Avinamodugu Valley at this time and it seems probable that *nullah*-based inundation along with rainfed farming and grazing made up the primary agricultural strategies, a pattern consistent with Early Middle period settlement locations throughout the region. The presence of a Jain religious institution in Toranagallu, at the mouth of the Daroji Valley, is worth noting. As previously noted, during the Vijayanagara centuries Jain temples are unknown in the area outside the city and even those within the urban core tend to date to the early part of the period. The presence of a Jain *nisadhi* may suggest resident merchants in Toranagallu, given the general lack of participation of Jains in agriculture and their historic focus on trade. Toranagallu now lies both on the rail line and on the Hospet-Bellary road; it is a critical locale for the bulking and transshipment by rail and truck of material from the mines of the Sandur Hills. Few older structures are evident in Toranagallu, probably because of the recent and rapid expansion of the town, but the Toranagallu fort (VMS-1077) is still extant (see Brubaker 2003 for a description). It is clear that Toranagallu was occupied in the Vijayanagara period and had a small reservoir; it is possible that occupation in this location, at the foot of a small but steep and dramatically situated inselberg, has been continuous from the Neolithic.

THE AVINAMODUGU VALLEY AFTER AD 1300

Although further from the city than the Daroji Valley, there is good reason to believe that

Table 8.1: Early Middle period inscriptions, Avinamodugu Valley[1]

Location	*Context*	*Date & King*	*Summary*	*References*
Toranagallu	on a rock called Tangammana-gundu on the Sankaradevara-gudda hill near the village	none, none	refers to the *nisidhi* of Bayichi-setti, a disciple of Akalankadeva (a Jain ascetic)	Patil and Patil 1997, no. 546; *ARSIE* 1922-3, no. 729 of 1922.
Taluru	on a column of a *mandapa* in a temple on the bank of the Narihalla	AD 1218, Sunday, 4 June (Hoysala) Vira-Ballala II.	*Mahanalprabhu* Bomma-Gavuda of Yavguvatti made a gift of land to Bommoja for constructing the Ishvara temple at Talara.	Patil and Patil 1997, no. 540; *ARSIE* 1922-3, no. 743 of 1922; *SII* IX I, no. 335.
Taranagara	copper plates discovered by bulldozers	AD 1047, Tuesday, 24 December Trailokyamalla-deva (Somesvara I) (Chalukyas of Kalyan)	Royal grant of 300 *nivarttanas* of land in the village Ganjiyapala in Ponnumumda-30 to the Grihamatya Muddimarya. The grant was made on Makara-Samkranti and was for the renovation of and worship and offerings in the Traipurusha temple in Vehura in Ponnumumda-30, in the Vilvola-*vishaya*. It was also to be used for feeding 200 students and 5 teachers of various Sastras in that temple.	Patil and Patil 1997, no. 541; *ARIE* 1974-5, no. A 3.
Taranagara	copper plates discovered as above	AD 1224, 22 December Vira-Narasimha-deva (Hoysala)	After agreeing to remit taxes in the amount of 20 *gadyanas*, Pesala-Hanuma, also known as Amitayya-Dandanayaka, received the *agrahara* Sripura in Kalkani-nadu as *kattu-guttage-pindadana* from the Hoysala king Vira Ballala. He built a *trikuta* temple in the center of that village in which the deities Amritesvara, Vamesvara and Lakshmi-Narayana were installed. Through the hand of the king and in the presence of the deities Vajreshvara and Somanatha, he made a grant of the village Komduka-Sivura for the services in and repairs of the temple	Patil and Patil 1997, no. 542; *ARIE* 1974-5, no. A 4.
Tarangara	copper plates discovered in the same temple	characters of *c.* 13th c. Krishna Kanharadeva (Rashtrakuta)	Spurious. Said to have been issued from Kamdharapura and to record the grant of some land in Karadikallu-30.	Patil and Patil 1997, no. 543; *ARIE* 1974-5, no. A 5.
Nagalapura	on a slab set up under a tree in the village	no year.	Records a grant of land at Nagala-pura made by Jillela Gopayadeva-Mahaarasu to the god Aubhalisvara-deva of Kanuve.	Patil and Patil 1997, no. 516; *ARSIE* 1922-3, no. 738 of 1922.

during the Vijayanagara period the Avinamodugu Valley was also considered part of the urban hinterland. Together with the Daroji Valley and the area included in the intensive survey, the Avinamodugu Valley was fortified by a semi-continuous string of walls, part of a larger complex of walls, forts, and occupied places that ringed the greater Vijayanagara region. In general, the many kilometers of fortification walls ringing the valley were informally, if solidly constructed, most consisting of two faces of locally-available unmodified cobbles and small boulders. Up to 8 meters wide, these discontinuous walls run along the tops of ridges and, especially, shore up passes through the rounded hills that form the eastern edge of both the Daroji and Avinamodugu Valleys. Walls are often wider and taller in these low-lying areas, but none of them employ the formal masonry and quarried blocks found in valley-floor portions of VMS-1085, the massive wall which divides the main Daroji Valley. Many of these fortifications have internal ledges or parapets, suggesting that they were manned by soldiers who must have maintained a lookout over these outer defensive works, the first line of the city's protection. Interestingly, some of these walls contain isolated segments with finished ends, perhaps small guide segments built along the proposed course of a wall by fortification planners, the spaces between these segments later completed by others.[2]

Although occupation clearly continued in the Nari Halla settlements, several locations along the Hire Halla were also settled during the Vijayanagara centuries. Within the valley as a whole, the town of Avinamodugu was the largest occupied settlement, with a large, reliable reservoir able to water wet crops such as rice and vegetables in most seasons. However, as discussed below, Avinamodugu also experienced a kind of boom and bust growth and decline not apparently matched by older, smaller settlements nearby. Avinamodugu and other Vijayanagara-period places in the valley clustered along the Hire Halla, a large seasonal stream running down from the Sandur Hills. In contrast to earlier (and continuing) occupation along the Nari Halla, Vijayanagara-era settlements along the Hire Halla relied on reservoir-supported agriculture, a strategy which, in the long run, turned out to be less sustainable. In general, the Avinamodugu valley has always been lightly settled and, in contrast to the Daroji Valley, reservoir-supported cultivation was never the primary form of agricultural production. Note, nevertheless, the existence of an Avinamodugu (Avinamaduvu) *Sime* as indicated in an inscription from Antapura (Table 8.2), indicating not only that this region was significant enough to have its own territorial identity, but also that Avinamodugu was at least nominally the center of that region, notwithstanding the importance of the Mallikarjuna temple at Antapura in the historical record. Note that donations of land under the Avinamodugu reservoir were made on the same day of 1551 by two people, possibly father and son, both associated with the title *mahamandalesvara.*

Inscriptional, historical, and architectural evidence (Patil 1992) suggests that most of the Early Middle period towns along the Hire Halla and in the Sandur Hills continued to be occupied throughout the Vijayanagara period and beyond; however, more research on occupational histories needs to be conducted in this area. My own work in this area is more limited, being focused primarily on cultural features along the Hire Halla. Here a series of smaller streams from the Sandur Hills converge near what is now the Avinamodugu reservoir, a large facility, still in use though much reduced in capacity, that served both Avinamodugu and Vittalapur. There are a number of modest-sized villages along the upper reaches of these small drainages, but no archaeological work has been conducted in this area.

The first recorded feature at the upstream end of the Hire Halla is a small containment reservoir, the embankment of which extends into a cobble wall incorporating an opening which allowed traffic to pass through (VMS-1029). Soils around and in this small, informally constructed facility about 500 meters south of Vitthalapura are very sandy and the vegetation is a degraded thorn scrub. Dry agriculture is still occasionally practiced in the area and a

Table 8.2. Vijayanagara-period inscriptions, Avinamodugu Valley

Location	*Context*	*Date & King*	*Summary*	*References*
Antapura	on a stone set in front of a ruined temples west of the village	AD 1553, 18 October	Records a gift of tolls for a perpetual lamp to the god Mallikarjunadeva for the merit of Sadasivaraya, Ramaraja, and Tirumalaraja	Patil and Patil 1997, no. 491; *ARSIE*, 1924-5, no. 291 of 1925.
Antapura	another slab near same temple	AD 1547, 5 July Sadasivaraya	With the consent of the headman (*gauda*), the *senabova* (an officer), and the people of the village, Harapanna restored the dilapidated Mallikarjuna temple at Antapura in the Avinamodugu *Sime*.	Patil and Patil 1997, no. 492; *ARSIE*, 1922-3, no. 733 of 1922.
Antapura	another slab near same temple	AD 1551, 15 June Sadasivaraya	Records Timmaraja, son of *Mahamandalesvara* Ramaraja Tirumalarja's gift of a garden under the reservoir at Avinamodugu to the god Mallikarjuna of Hireya-Antapura.	Patil and Patil 1997, no. 493; *ARSIE*, 1922-3, no. 734 of 1922.
Avinamodugu	on a boulder below the reservoir	AD 1551, 15 June, Sadasivaraya	Records Vitharadeva-mahaarasu, son of *Mahamandalesvara* Ramaraja Timmaraja's gift of land under the reservoir at Avinamodugu to the god Mallikarjuna at Antapura.	Patil and Patil 1997 no. 494
Kodalu	on a broken slab set into the enclosure wall of the Hanumantaraya temple	AD 1552, Saturday 12 November	Damaged. Records a gift made for the merit of king Sadasivaraya.	Patil and Patil 1997, no. 512; *ARSIE*, 1922-3, no. 737 of 1922.
Bannihatti	on a stone set up in front of the Hanuman temple	AD 1572	Mutilated and incomplete.	Patil and Patil 1997, no. 495; *ARSIE*, 1944-5, no. B 79.
Taranagara	on a stone lying in a field known as Muddappana-bilu.	AD 1536, 24 July Achyutaraya	Fragmentary and incomplete.	Patil and Patil 1997, no. 544; *ARIE* 1944-5, no. B 87.
Taranagara	on a stone lying near the Buddekallu	16th century	Mutilated.	Patil and Patil 1997, no. 545; *ARIE* 1944-5, no. B 88.
Nagalapura	on a slab set up under a tree in the village	no year.	Records a grant of land at Nagalapura made by Jillela Gopayadeva-Mahaarasu to the god Aubhalisvaradeva of Kanuve.	Patil and Patil 1997, no. 516; *ARSIE* 1922-3, no. 738 of 1922.

recent building and tomb indicate continued use of this place.

Further downstream is VMS-1031, the Avinamodugu reservoir and village. The village of Antapur, not far away, was clearly also associated with the reservoir. The latter (Figure 160), the largest irrigation facility in the valley and still the focus of agricultural production for the nearby village, appears to have been built during the early part of the sixteenth century, at the height of Vijayanagara urban expansion. Although the reservoir has lost the larger part of its capacity due to accumulated sediment, it still waters a large area planted largely in vegetables and rice. Note that few reservoirs have the capacity to support rice; it may be significant that one of the inscriptions from Antapur refers to land under the reservoir as garden land, a category usually reserved for high-value irrigated plots.

At the eastern end of this large reservoir is the small and now very remote occupied village of Avinamodugu, somewhat displaced from the abandoned remains of a more substantial Vijayanagara-period settlement of the same name.[3] The latter (Figure 161) consists of tightly-spaced, masonry-walled structures, now almost entirely collapsed. The village appears to have been walled and fortified with round bastions. Ceramic densities are high and household debris such as charcoal and ash are abundant; sculpted images lie among the rubble. The occupational history of this place after the sixteenth century is not entirely clear; the reservoir, as noted, has lost most of its capacity and thus could perhaps no longer support a settlement of this size. Evidence for multiple repairs to the reservoir as well as census data from 1871 (Government of India 1874: 3), when "Havinahala" is listed as containing 151 houses, 797 people, and 4,553 acres of land, both wet and dry, suggest a more or less continuous occupational history though it is clear that population levels as well as productive capacity have diminished significantly.[4]

The Avinamodugu reservoir is located near the eastern edge of the valley, well away from the Sandur Hills and its dangerously fast-moving streams which must flow all the way across the valley floor before entering the reservoir pool. Among the feeders to the reservoir is a stream emerging from the Sandur Hills at Ubbalagandi. Although there is a steep mining road up into the hills here, guarded at its base by the village of Ubbalagandi, it is not clear what the antiquity of this route might be.[5] Ubbalagandi is associated with a small (undocumented) reservoir, a facility positioned upstream from the Avinamodugu reservoir and thus part of the loosely connected group of system reservoirs in this valley. In addition to the medium-sized Ubbalagandi reservoir, there are five small reservoirs upstream from the Avinamodugu *kere* that may be integrated with it. Of these, I have visited only one, the Vitthalapur *kere* which, although marked on the Survey of India topographic maps, is no longer in existence (if indeed it ever was). Thus, although the Avinamodugu reservoir seems to have been part of an extensive and only loosely-connected reservoir system, I treat it here as if it were isolated.

The sediment in this reservoir, derived from the Sandur Hills, is remarkable for its redness and high clay content. This material forms deep cracks in the dry season when the reservoir becomes almost completely dry. Water does pool up in the rainy season and is conveyed through the one working tunnel into fields below. In spite of the accumulation of sediment and the consequent loss of at least half of the reservoir's capacity, the Avinamodugu *kere* is still very large and does water some wet crops. The embankment is long (*c.* 1,150 meters), wide (40 to 55 meters) and high (7 meters), relatively straight in plan, probably built in a single episode.

A road runs along the top of the *bund*, connecting the village of Avinamodugu with the unpaved road to Vitthalapur. At the western end of the embankment, near the village, the embankment has been raised a meter above the original masonry, clearly an attempt to increase capacity in response to siltation. Nearer the center of the *bund* there are two episodes of repair indicating both breaching and reconstruction; a history of destruction and renewal that may track the record of cultivation and occupation.

Figure 160. VMS-1031, Avinamodugu reservoir, overview.

Figure 161. Old Avinamodugu village.

Two of the three sluices are almost entirely buried in silt. The sluice on the west (Figures 162 and 163), is a double sluice with a carved Gajalakshmi, only its lintel visible above the sediment. The central sluice is also deeply silted in, but more of it is visible, suggesting that sedimentation has been more of a problem on the western side of the facility. Hydrological factors are critical here; runoff from the Sandur Hills enters this reservoir on the west while the eastern feeders run down from the rounded metamorphic hills making up the eastern edge of the Avinamodugu Valley. The central sluice (Figure 164) is similar to the western one but has a single set of uprights. Here the lower *makara torana* medallions flank a rectangle with two conch shell designs.[6] The easternmost sluice (Figure 165), still functioning, is similar to the others except for the carved Ganesha (or perhaps simply an elephant, it is difficult to say) flanked by elephants between the *makara torana* medallions, a striking contrast to the more common Gajalakshmi. This sluice is 3.58 meters high; if the others are of similar height, this would indicate more than 3 meters of sedimentation accumulation in VMS-1031.[7]

Atop the embankment near the eastern sluice is a small, south-facing, two-room Hanuman temple with lamp column and *mandapa*. The shrine is in worship and is built partly on the *bund* and partly on a large platform extending north from the embankment. Around the temple a large depression has been partly walled, creating an enclosing tank for the temple. As noted, this pattern of a small pavilion inside a walled water-holding enclosure is typical of temple-associated tanks. Although much of the structure is recent, it incorporates many older, reworked architectural elements as well as the Vijayanagara-period Hanuman. Also on the embankment a tree platform of unknown age has been built on a foundation of heavily weathered granite slabs.[8] This low platform is sheltered by a large acacia tree and supports a recently-built shrine containing a granite pestle and broken stone "cannon ball". This object of veneration, whatever its origins, may relate to local traditions that deify Kumararama, son of Kampila Raya (P. Bilimale, personal communication), thus linking the Avinamodugu Valley with ongoing local memories of Doravati and its rulers.

North of Avinamodugu village among dry-farmed fields is a small but well-built Shiva temple complex, VMS-1037. This fifteenth-century complex consists of an east-facing, three-room temple, associated *mandapa*, and platform. The temple is still in worship and is heavily plastered. The door to the antechamber, which contains a sculpted Virabhadra image, is guarded by Shaivite door guardians with clubs. The door to the sanctuary is similarly flanked by carved figures, devotees rather than *dvarapalas.* The image in the sanctuary is recent and in worship; the complex lies within a recent enclosure wall.

Closer to (old) Avinamodugu itself is a Vijayanagara-period shrine with two nearby step wells, VMS-1039. The two-room, east-facing shrine is built on sheetrock on the western edge of the settlement. This structure, too, shows a complex construction history with several reworkings of its basal platform. A Vijayanagara-period Nandi inside the antechamber faces a *lingam* in the sanctuary; the door to the latter is flanked by miniature columns which emerge out of large *purna kalasha.* Approximately 25 meters from the shrine is a square step well, clearly constructed at the same time as the temple. The second well is circular, and seems to have been built later.

Downstream from the large Avinamodugu reservoir there are a few small settlements along the Hire Halla which leads eventually into the Daroji reservoir. Antapur, as indicated in Table 8.2, has several inscriptions from the middle of the sixteenth century – unfortunately little archaeological work has been conducted here though I noted the presence of a Vijayanagara-period step well and Nandi. Downstream from the village is a large (8 meter high) breached reservoir (not recorded). Antapur does not appear in the 1871 census, but by 1901 it is listed as having 633 residents. After this, Antapur occurs consistently on maps and in census rolls, suggesting continuous occupation from the early twentieth century following what may have been a major gap in its occupational history.

Further downstream is Sultanpur (Suntana-

Figure 162. VMS-1031, western sluice, buried in silt.

Figure 163. VMS-1031, western sluice, detail.

Figure 164. VMS-1031, central sluice, partially buried.

Figure 165. VMS-1031, eastern sluice, in use.

Figure 166. VMS-1041, idgah near Sultanpur.

pur), another settlement missing from nineteenth-century census lists, perhaps because of a name change rather than a more recent establishment. The name suggests either a predominantly Muslim population or points to a specific patron, perhaps a nod to the rule of the Bijapur state or to seventeenth-century rulers Haider Ali or Tipu Sultan. Although this region was not studied in detail, we have recorded an *idgah* (open-air mosque), VMS-1041, similar in style to Deccani Islamicate structures (Figure 166). The *idgah* lies some distance from the village, about 750 meters upstream.

The town of Toranagallu and its small[9] containment reservoir, VMS-1034, do not lie right on the Hire Halla but instead huddle at the base of an isolated and very high granitic outcrop.[10] This reservoir is similar to the Vitthalapur facility in that is small and incorporates a masonry wall associated with a road as well as an earth and masonry embankment. This entire area is grazed and dry farmed, with long fallow periods between plantings. Atop the reservoir embankment is a small, low platform in front of a naturally-occurring boulder with a carved Nandi facing a *lingam* carved on a separate rock.

Away from the Nari Halla and Hire Halla, occupied places in the Avinamodugu Valley are rare. One of the few is the village of Lingadahalli (VMS-1062), which lies in the rocky western portion of the Avinamodugu valley and is situated in a narrow pass between rocky hills. There is little level agricultural land in this part of the valley and, consequently, this region is very sparsely settled even now. The present-day village is small; it is served by a paved road that leads from the Nari Halla settlements to Ubbalagandi. Inside the village is an isolated bastion of unknown date (Figure 168); it may have been built any time between the fifteenth and nineteenth centuries. The circular bastion sits atop a flat-topped hill and is now in use as a shrine.[11] Village houses are built on the hill all around the bastion, suggesting some defensive concerns on the part of this isolated village. Wall traces around the bastion suggest that it may have been part of a larger fortified complex. A small containment reservoir lies at the foot of the hill; it may have been used for water storage for humans and animals rather then for agriculture.

DISCUSSION: THE AVINAMODUGU VALLEY

The occupational history of the Avinamodugu Valley differs in many important respects from that of the Daroji Valley, though like the Daroji Valley, it was contained within the enclosing defensive walls of the city of Vijayanagara (Figure 167). Unlike the latter, there was significant Early Middle period occupation along the Nari Halla, small towns with both Shaivite and Jain residents practicing inundation agriculture, dry farming, and herding along this seasonal stream.[12] Kurekuppa in the Daroji Valley is the lowest of this string of settlements and contains a well-made temple, indicating the prosperity of its patrons. Unlike the Daroji Valley, where there was a major sixteenth-century extension of reservoir irrigation and an expansion of settlement, this pattern is seen in only a few settlements along the Hire Halla/Kanigana Halla, chief among them Avinamodugu itself. The Avinamodugu reservoir itself shows a complex history of construction, destruction, repair, and decline; the present-day village and reservoir are greatly reduced versions of their sixteenth-century counterparts but both the economic and ritual importance of the reservoir have endured in spite of this. Most of the rest of the reservoirs in the Avinamodugu Valley are smaller containment facilities, features more useful for watering animals and simply storing runoff than for large-scale agriculture.

After the fall of the city in the late sixteenth century and the consequent southward shift of the limits of the Vijayanagara polity, the political history of the Sandur Hills and a part of the Avinamodugu Valley diverged from that of the surrounding region, becoming part of the tiny princely state of Sandur. Today the Avinamodugu Valley is a transport dead-end, a remote place rarely visited by outsiders. With the exception of a small area under the Avinamodugu reservoir, most of the valley is used for grazing, plant collecting, and a limited

Figure 167. Fortification wall, VMS-1066, across the Sultanpur Gap.

Figure 168. VMS-1062, Lingadahalli bastion.

amount of dry farming. Some possible reasons for this divergent history are discussed in the following chapter.

NOTES

1. Notes from the table: (1) alternately spelled *nisadhi*, the tomb of a Jain monk; (2) *Mahanalprabhu* is the title of an official, probably a village official, though the term *Mahaprabhu* is also recorded as being used for subordinate rulers or merchants (Sircar 1966: 183, 210-11, 253). The exact meaning of this term is uncertain; it may have to do with control or oversight over cultivated land; (3) Makara Samkranti (Sankranti) is a major Shaivite religious festival falling in the winter.
2. Many of these differ slightly in construction from neighboring sections of wall. See Brubaker (2003) for more detail; the notion of "guide segments" comes from his descriptions.
3. Roads into the Avinamodugu Valley are generally poor and bus service is minimal.
4. In 1901, census data (Government of India 1901: 24) indicate 483 residents in 84 houses at "Avinamadugu", significantly fewer than in 1871.
5. Note that the pass down the south side of the Sandur Hills runs through the Ubbalagandi gorge (though there is no settlement there).
6. The conch is associated with Vishnu.
7. And because double sluices tend to be extremely tall, sluice 1 may actually be taller than sluice 3, so this 3 meter estimate is somewhat conservative.
8. There is also a small well beneath the embankment near the central sluice. It appears to be contemporaneous with the reservoir, unlike many wells in the Daroji Valley that were clearly constructed later than the reservoir they are paired with.
9. The embankment is 65 meters long and 5.9 meters wide. It is faced on both sides by masonry; water collects seasonally on the east side where up to nine cobble courses rise to a height of 1.7 meters above the basin.
10. North of the Kudatini pass, the Hire Halla is known as the Kanigana Halla.
11. The bastion is built of unmodified cobbles and has a solid earth fill. It is 5.8 meters high and *c.* 11 meters in diameter at the base. The top is ringed by a stone parapet, now incomplete. There is no evidence of stairs.
12. It is clear that residents of these towns also included merchants and craftspeople. Residents were evidently part of larger social, religious, and economic networks at this time, a pattern that contrasts with their relatively isolated positions today.

Chapter Nine

MAKING PLACES: A LONG-TERM VIEW

> India abounds with objects of interest. It presents every imaginable variety of scenery, from the loftiest and most sublime mountain ranges, to the gentle undulations and velvet swards of an English park. Its natural products are equal, if not superior, to those of any region in the world, and would furnish endless materials for the pen of the describer. It is rich in historical associations, and there is scarce a hill which is not crowned with the picturesque ruins of some old fortress, little known or altogether unvisited by Europeans, but bound up in the native mind with many a strange tale and legend. In Europe the small remains of some ruined cloister, or the mouldering walls of a solitary castle, are sought out with eager interest; but India is a land of ruined cities, and in one of these the antiquities of a whole European province might be collected. (Eastwick 1859: 129)

In this volume I have tracked the changing landscapes of the Daroji Valley over the last several thousand years, tracing both the physical remnants of past activity as well as looking for clues to the varied interpretations of specific structures and locales provided by their appearance both temporally *in situ* and "out of time". In these years the valley alternated between being a locus of human activity and, more often, constituting something of a backwater to more densely settled locations. Across this long history, specific, culturally-defined places emerged in the landscape – some of these had extraordinary staying power as evident, for example in the reoccupation of VMS-110 near Ingaligi more than a thousand years after it was abandoned as a residential locale. The use of the Kudatini ashmound as a receptacle for an Iron Age sarcophagus burial as indeed the contemporary mining of Neolithic ashmounds for lime indicate the continuing force of features and structures originally built centuries or even millennia ago. Numerous Vijayanagara-era temples, shrines, and even sluice gates are still in worship long after their initial construction; often in ways the original builders never intended.

The physical features of the Daroji Valley – its granitic northern boundary with numerous locations favorable for runoff harvesting, the higher Sandur Hills with their rich iron and manganese ores, (once) dense forests, its sandy soils – all constituted a dynamic force in this long history. Millennia of human occupation shaped and re-shaped these features. The Sandur forests were denuded by the early sixteenth century, only to regenerate and, once again, be virtually destroyed. The valley floor has been carpeted with colluvial inwash, a process that led to the abandonment of many, perhaps most, of the reservoirs in this area. Most recently, industrial production of steel has created huge open scars on the landscape, increased erosion, and expansion of population, roads, and rail traffic. From the Neolithic onward, the low and erratic rainfall regime has shaped agricultural strategies and crop possibilities. It has only been possible to grow water-intensive crops in this area since the advent of deep bore wells and electric pumps; prior to this only a narrow strip along the Tungabhadra River could support such produce.

Landscape history builds on, as well as modifies, these natural features, from forms of marking and memorializing, to routes of movement, locations of settlement, to forms and rhythms of production. The long-term patterns and tempos of human land use cannot be understood outside these parameters, but at the same time, this history is very much a cultural one. As I have discussed, the valley has been pulled into larger cultural projects at different points in its history. During the Early Historic, it served as a locus for the large-scale smelting of iron to serve the string of villages and towns along the river. In the Early Middle period, it saw the establishment of a few small villages with links to the Pampa *tirtha*; by the sixteenth century, the entire valley had been converted to a satellite of the city of Vijayanagara, part of the extensive agricultural supply line of this massive city. After the fall of the city, the rôle of the valley changed – fortifications shrank to the scale of individual villages, wells were dug beneath reduced reservoirs, and the few official signs of Vijayanagara authority such as Vaishnavite temples and well-built walls began to crumble.

LANDSCAPE HISTORIES: TIME IN PLACE

Even for those interested in the past, landscapes are experienced in terms of their arrangement in contemporary space. We touch and see features, structures, plants, soil, and other landscape elements as situated entities which, despite their differential histories, jostle together in space. Time, as for example in estimates of construction dates, is always an inferential dimension of such experience. I have suggested that this place-based perspective, a view of an integrated landscape where, for example, Vijayanagara reservoirs are "actors" in contemporary practices and perceptions, is both vital and necessary, despite its invisibility in standard archaeological and historical discourse. At the same time, we are properly interested in constructing temporal trajectories and only the dissection of this unity using tools such as typology and chronology will be able to accomplish this. Temporal distinctions allow us not only to construct narratives about past and present, but also to see some of the interesting disjunctions between expectations based on these narratives and the material record. For example, without the methodological tools of archaeology we might never be aware of the ways in which Neolithic ashmounds were re-used and reimagined for the thousands of years following their construction.

In Chapter 2, I discussed the methodological challenges that the accretional nature of the archaeological record poses, suggesting that efforts at landscape history will need to recognize the integral nature of places and the contemporary nature of "past" construction. On the other hand, it is clear that the secondary partitioning of landscapes in terms of (reconstructed) time is also a necessary component of landscape history. Strategies used to diagnose time from texts and objects compel us to make decisions about, and thus begin to reconstruct, process of construction and composition, reuse and retelling, abandonment and erasure. These *dual narratives* of place and time are always in tension, as is evident in the organization of this volume. While foregrounding the specifics of place, I was also forced to use temporal periodizations to make the analysis more legible.

Although landscape histories may not directly represent indigenous perspectives, structured as they are by our own tools of classification, they may provide important clues to cultural practice not apparent in the textual record. The complex adaptations of structures and features over time speak to the efforts of large groups of people, most of whom never appear in documentary history. Even when texts speak to aspects of landscape history, for example conventionalized urban descriptions which highlight irrigated areas and greenery, these are often idealized or proscriptive. Some of these silent (or silenced) voices are of contemporary people who have, for example, converted Middle period reservoir sluice gates to shrines, embankments to paddy fields, and Vaishnavite temples to Shaivite and Goddess temples. Megaliths may be explained in terms of the *Mahabharata*, ashmounds in terms of the *Ramayana*, an historical mode which, although different from academic history and archaeology, *also* makes temporal distinctions between structures and features co-occurring in place. Such "indigenous archaeologies" are constantly under construction as new configurations of place emerge from the possibilities posed by the material and conceptual record of the past.

In the sections below, I summarize what we have learned about the long-term landscape history of the Daroji Valley, a history marked by both remarkable continuity and disjuncture. A locus of activity in the Neolithic, the valley has remarkably little trace of the Iron Age and Early Historic periods. At the same time, particular Neolithic-era places were clearly remembered and, in some cases, re-used over the next millennium. The eastern end of the valley emerged as Doravati/Daroji by the Early Middle period, a distinction with exceptional long-term salience. While Early Middle period towns and villages clustered near the eastern end of the main valley with only sparse occupation of the rest of the area, by the Late Vijayanagara period the valley had emerged as an important bread-basket for the city, albeit one in which highly valued crops such as rice could generally not be grown. This fact, conditioned by valley topography and soils as well as hydrology, is of critical importance in assessing the changing power relations embedded in Daroji's history. In some sense, then, the history of the Daroji Valley is best seen in contrast with other regions (below and see Morrison 2006a) such as the canal-irrigated zones around the city to the north, home to many of the decision-makers who significantly affected the lives of valley residents. These disparate zones of production, structured by millennia of human action, were associated with different forms of agricultural production, compelling residents of each place to interact differently with past political-economic orders, often in ways they could not fully control. The contrast between the ecological, economic, social and ritual possibilities of dry farming versus permanent irrigated agriculture is especially salient here, as are the human consequences of agricultural expansion and intensification in both urban and rural areas.

THE DAROJI VALLEY

The Western Valley

The western valley contains a relatively small number of loosely-integrated reservoirs, most of which appear to be associated with specific settlements. Although VMS-1004 is not contiguous with any Vijayanagara-period habitation debris, VMS-1002 and 1003 undoubtedly belong to the walled town of Ingaligi. That these two reservoirs with their somewhat unusual sluice gates are contemporaneous seems very likely. Their date is more difficult to fix, but if I am correct that they represent a kind of deliberate archaism in detail while following sixteenth-century trends in size and proportion, then they may be assigned to the sixteenth century. The long reservoir VMS-1023 seems to serve the fort and settlement, VMS-6, which also lies along an important route to the north and to the walled town of Mallapannagudi. The terminus of the western valley consists simply of gently rising hills, but the location of Hospet, a major sixteenth-century settlement up on these hills, is surely significant.

The western valley also provides us with information on the longer-term land use history of this area. At least as early as the Early Neolithic, this section of the valley saw both intermittent and intensive use, a pattern which seems to change by around 2000 BC. After that, and before the Early Historic, we have little evidence of either occupation or use of the western valley, though it seems likely that there was some continuing exploitation of resources in this area, including iron ores and the flora and fauna of the Sandur Hills. In any case, the western valley did not see permanent, relatively obtrusive settlements again until the third century BC. The Early Historic inhabitants were, at least in part, occupational specialists, smelting iron for larger distribution. Not until the Early Middle period, with the village underneath VMS-1003, do we see something that looks like a rural settlement that involves both agricultural and craft production. Interestingly, Early Middle period material is scarce throughout the Vijayanagara region – there is more evidence for Early Middle period villages in the Daroji Valley than there is in the intensively-surveyed area around the city of Vijayanagara. Within the Daroji Valley itself, most of the Early Middle settlement is concentrated at the eastern end of the main valley, in and around Daroji/Doravati, Kurekuppa, and Gonahala. Further up into the

Avinamodugu Valley, there is a string of villages occupied at this time, all located along the Nari Halla. Although these villages and towns might be expected to be dependent on or subject to the larger center of Kurugodu, both Gonahala and Kurekuppa were clearly connected with the Hampi area and with Pampa/Virupaksha more specifically. Although Early Middle period reservoirs are known from inscriptions, there is scant evidence for any reservoir irrigation in the valley during these centuries. The only reservoir that might have been built at this time is VMS-1018, a badly-damaged facility almost 1 kilometer from Kurekuppa. All of the villages known to have been occupied during the Early Middle period (including that under VMS-1003) are, in fact, located near seasonal streams, suggesting that seasonal inundation may have been an important productive strategy, supplementing dry farming and herding.

Although, as noted, there was a dramatic Vijayanagara expansion into the western valley during the early sixteenth century, this area also seems to have been under active (re)construction in the seventeenth century. Both the fortified village of Ingaligi and the fort and settlement VMS-6 may date in part to the seventeenth or even eighteenth centuries, a pattern consonant with the unsettled politics of the time and the dangers of raids and warfare. That Ingaligi was occupied in the mid-nineteenth century is clear; local people indicate that the village has a long and to them, unbroken history of occupation. VMS-6 was, however, abandoned, as regional populations contracted in these centuries. In the post-Vijayanagara years, agriculture continued to be a mainstay of the economy. Both VMS-1003 and 1002 continued in use, though both eventually became something like glorified check-dams, not holding standing water but at least creating an area of damp soil in the erstwhile reservoir bed. VMS-1023 and 1004 were completely abandoned, probably after the fall of the city and the loss of urban markets and population. Since the advent of rural electrification in the mid-twentieth century, the use of machine-drilled bore wells fitted with electric pumps has transformed the western valley and the western part of the main valley. Rich irrigated fields of cash-cropped vegetables form green islands in the dusty brown landscape otherwise covered by dry fields, fallow more often than not. The western end of this area has been entirely transformed, having become a transshipment spot for the loading of crushed iron and manganese ores onto railway cars. The town of Kariganuru at the western end of the valley, apparently a twentieth-century phenomenon, is stained red by the huge piles of material waiting to be loaded. The streets of the town, the soil, even the pigs and dogs have a reddish tinge. The center of gravity has definitely shifted toward Hospet, which has grown rapidly since the completion of the Tungabhadra Dam in the early 1950s. Hospet is fast becoming an industrial center, supporting both mining companies in the Sandur Hills and the large new Vijayanagara steel plant. The Vijayanagara steel plant, inaugurated by then-prime minister Indira Gandhi but opening only some thirty years later, obviously invokes an imperial past, but we might also look further, to the iron workers of VMS-110 and beyond, to see both continuity and change in the western valley's agricultural and industrial history.

The Main Valley

Although the only direct evidence for pre-Vijayanagara use of the western valley are some fragments of a Neolithic ashmound near Kakuballu and a few Early Middle period hero stones, the evidence of Vijayanagara occupation and use is both abundant and complex. I have dissected the remains of the main valley into discrete clusters of features; the Bayaluvaddigeri cluster (earlier, further east) and the Papinayakanahalli cluster (later, further west). These clusters certainly, however, overlap in both time and space and I have allowed some of that ambiguity into the text by following the contemporary landscape of the valley rather than a reconstructed sequence of change.

Reservoirs in the Main Valley

The central system of Daroji reservoirs consists of at least 13 reservoirs, all but one linked and flowing to the east-southeast.[1] Not all of these were in use at the same time, however, and it is possible to identify at least three major trans-valley reservoirs and at least two settlement-associated reservoir clusters. Compared to the western valley, which appears to largely represent a later, sixteenth-century expansion of reservoir irrigation and settlement, the main valley has a long and complex Middle period history beginning as early as the tenth century. This history translates into a material record of reservoir construction, maintenance, repair, and abandonment that spans several hundred years and which, of course, like the western valley, is also of contemporary relevance.

Because the descriptions of the valley landscape presented above follow a kind of watery spatial logic, tracing human modifications by watershed, in this discussion I invert the order of objects in space to consider instead the temporal trajectory of agriculture in the main valley. Building on an earlier pattern of stream-side irrigation, reservoirs began to be constructed in the main valley sometime in the Early or Middle Vijayanagara period. Although none of the earlier reservoirs are very well-dated, it is clear that VMS-1012 and 1013, both associated with Bayaluvaddigeri, were built in either the fourteenth or fifteenth century, a conclusion strengthened by the presence of a fifteenth-century inscription in Bayaluvaddigeri itself. Interestingly, these two facilities, as well as the village, seem to have been continuously maintained and used. VMS-1012 and 1014 have an estimated 1 and 2 meters of silt accumulation, respectively, a modest amount in the overall context of this colluvial valley. Bayaluvaddigeri lies right along the main road through the valley and, judging from the remnant road VMS-1084 and the location of the northern gate in the trans-valley wall VMS-1085, it was also right on the sixteenth-century road through the valley. Neither of the Bayaluvaddigeri reservoirs is very large, however, and the amount of land they irrigate is not sufficient to suggest production geared primarily toward food export.

A second pre-sixteenth century cluster of features relates to the twinned trans-valley reservoirs, VMS-1016 and 1021, along with their small settlement, VMS-109. All of these remains are in such poor condition that it is very difficult to determine their age, though all can be confidently assigned to the Vijayanagara period. It seems most probable that 1016 and 1021 were constructed during the fourteenth or fifteenth century. They are both fully silted in – the probable reason for their abandonment – and, had they been functioning at the beginning of the sixteenth century when the later trans-valley reservoir, VMS-1015, was massively expanded, the latter would not have much land below it to irrigate. There are no sixteenth or seventeenth century remains in the vicinity of VMS-1016/1021/109 and it is most probable that this location had been completely abandoned, used only for activities such as grazing and firewood collection. Kotinganahallu, to the east, was founded later, sometime before 1871. This set of early trans-valley facilities apparently did not support a large local population: VMS-109 is very small and both Bayaluvaddigeri and Gonahala, contemporaneous settlements, are small and rather distant. Thus, even considering both the continuity and success of the Bayaluvaddigeri reservoirs and the abandonment and spectacular failure of VMS-1016 and 1021, it must be noted that the Early and Middle Vijayanagara-period reservoirs seem to have been geared more toward local production than production for urban markets, though it is almost certain that some produce did make its way north to the city at this time, at least in terms of the fulfillment of 'traditional' obligations (taxes, etc.).

In the early sixteenth century, the main valley saw a massive increase in both its resident population and its productive capacity. We also have some hints of new connections to the capital city and "imperial" interest in the defense and control of the valley itself, including the construction of a massive north-south fortification wall that spanned the entire valley. This wall, VMS-1085, seems to be associated with the early sixteenth-century expansion of the second trans-valley reservoir, VMS-1015, and is associated with the only Vaishnavite shrine in the entire valley. VMS-1015 itself grew from a small reservoir near the northern end of the valley to a huge facility with two additional (double) sluices and a curving breakwater.

Land under this "ocean of *dharma*" seems to have been controlled, in part, by a local *nayaka* but the sixteenth-century land grant inscription built into the embankment was commissioned by a group of merchants, a powerful reinforcement to the interpretation that by the sixteenth-century, agricultural production was increasingly geared toward the sustenance of the rapidly-growing capital city. Although we have not done the kind of research in the valley which would indicate what crops were being grown where, it is probable that sixteenth-century agricultural expansion also involved some production of cash crops (cotton, pulses, millets, and certain vegetables are all possibilities) and perhaps an expansion of grazing and animal husbandry (for milk products, meat, and manure), necessary to help meet the growing demand on dry farmers, herders, and others for cash.

The history of large reservoirs in the main valley is not one of unalloyed success (Figure 169). The initial trans-valley reservoirs, VMS-1016/1021, silted in and became completely unreclaimable, the area around them eventually degrading to a tangled thorn scrub. VMS-1015 is not deeply silted, except around its older northern sluice – its use life is in fact somewhat more spectacular, the reservoir having breached several times. The insecurity of the embankment and the danger to the village of Dharmasagara downstream, eventually led to its abandonment and replacement with rainfed farming and irrigation by wells and later, wells with electric pumps. Maintaining a large reservoir takes resources and organization; it may be that after the fall of the city and the loss of urban markets, such effort and perhaps even the resources and political structure required were either no longer available or no longer worth the trouble. The Daroji reservoir might seem to be an exception to this pattern unless we consider its troubled history of breaching and flooding. The Daroji *kafiayat* (a colonial-era document recording local history) mentions at least four episodes, one of which (during the Vijayanagara period) is said to have destroyed the village; this list seems not to include the breach and flood of 1851.

Although there is an interesting Early Vijayanagara temple (VMS-1037) south of Papinayakanahalli, both the maximal extent of the town and most of the cluster of reservoirs around Papinayakanahalli probably also date to the sixteenth century. Papinayakanahalli has a large and impressive sixteenth-century goddess temple and sits along a key route to Vijayanagara city. These reservoirs are in various states of maintenance though all have lost some capacity and none is well-maintained. Clearly, Papinayakanahalli has declined somewhat in importance; this decline is matched by the reduced productive capacity of its reservoir-watered land. Like other parts of the valley, Papinayakanahalli residents have now switched to well irrigation.

As impressive as the two trans-valley reservoirs are, however, they are dwarfed by the massive Daroji reservoir, which is still in use. The Daroji embankment is nearly 4 kilometers long and 12 meters high, damming up a large expanse of water year-round. Although substantial post-Vijayanagara construction and maintenance of the reservoir is evident, the larger part of the embankment as well as its three matching double sluices, seem to have been built in the early sixteenth century.[2] Settlement in and around Doravati/Daroji clearly extends from the Early Historic period (and certainly earlier, though the continuity of this occupation is yet unclear) to the present and it is certain that the Daroji *kere* has had a major impact on this region for, thus far, the last four hundred years.

In a real sense, the Daroji reservoir is the culmination of both the main and the Avinamodugu Valley reservoir systems. Not only is it the largest and most elaborate of all the valley reservoirs, but it is also the physical endpoint of the system, collecting overflow from all the reservoirs upstream in the main valley as well as from reservoirs in the Avinamodugu Valley and from three seasonal streams originating in the Sandur Hills. All of these large drainages carried runoff that was either too swift to be contained in a smaller reservoir and/or ran over substrates and through topography unsuitable for the construction of reservoirs. Thus, it is to these three major drainages that the Daroji reservoir owes both its persistence and its year-round supply of water, in an area where other reservoirs are only seasonally supplied or where they dry up in years of low rainfall.

What, then, are the difference between the western valley system and the main valley system? For one, the latter is much looser while the main valley reservoirs are packed relatively tightly together. This pattern is somewhat mitigated by the longer history of reservoir use in the main valley and the consequent abandonment and replacement of some facilities. The main valley has several isolable clusters of facilities, with the pre-sixteenth century reservoirs tending to be smaller and (now) more deeply silted in (Figure 169). The history of reservoirs in the western valley is almost solely a sixteenth-century history, but the existence of earlier facilities in the main valley should not obscure the phenomenal record of sixteenth century reservoir expansion there. Both the Dharmasagara reservoir (VMS-1015) and the Daroji reservoir (VMS-1019) were built at this time, two "oceans" which radically reshaped the valley, including water flow, water tables, vegetation, transport routes, sediment flows, agricultural potential, and appearance. In general, all sixteenth-century reservoirs are larger than earlier ones; the largest of these are concentrated in the main valley, ambitious features which tapped flow from the Sandur Hills.

Settlement History: The Vijayanagara Period

The entire main valley has very little evidence for Early Vijayanagara use. There are some Early Middle period places which appear again in the Late Vijayanagara period – in inscriptions or materially, though the construction of temples, reservoirs, or other features – and thus one might assume a continuous occupation. There is a small Early Vijayanagara temple (VMS-1037) south of Papinayakanahalli. The settlement covered over by the southern end of reservoir VMS-1003 might date to this period though it could also be Early Middle period. The best case is Doravati/Daroji itself which has strong evidence for continuous occupation through the centuries of Vijayanagara rule. Notably, Gonahala (eleventh through early twentieth centuries) had a long-standing association with the Pampa *tirtha* and later, with the god Virupaksha, a direct link to what would become the nucleus of the Early Vijayanagara city. Kurekuppa, too, appears to have a connection to the Virupaksha temple. With such sketchy evidence, it is difficult to say much about the organization of the valley in the fourteenth century. It does seem clear that the valley was sparsely settled, that reservoir irrigation had not yet taken hold in this area, and that while clearly connected with the outside world, valley residents were not orienting their production primarily toward that world.

Bayaluvaddigeri and its associated reservoirs seems to have been built in the fifteenth century, or Middle Vijayanagara period and it may be that VMS-109, associated with the initial pair of trans-valley reservoirs, VMS-1016 and 1021, was also occupied at this time. A major shift in focus followed on the siltation and abandonment of reservoirs VMS-1016 and 1021; this loss of capacity apparently precipitated the abandonment of the small settlement VMS-109 and perhaps also aided in the decline of Bayaluvaddigeri relative to the newer settlements of Papinayakanahalli and Dharmasagara, the former taking up Bayaluvaddigeri's position as a transport node sitting on an intersection between the east-west route running through the main valley and a road leading north to the city of Vijayanagara. Dharmasagara, positioned below the newer sixteenth-century trans-valley reservoir, VMS-1015, would have benefitted from its irrigation capacity in much the same way that VMS-109 had from the earlier trans-valley reservoir, VMS-1016, in its day.

The sixteenth century saw a massive expansion of reservoir irrigation into the valley and an increased spatial scale of individual facilities, a pattern consonant with that of the region as a whole. This expansion was mirrored by changes in population size and density; new villages filled in some of the interstices on the valley, other villages probably grew in size. Significantly, production seems to have been increasingly geared for sale outside the valley and we have indications of direct action in the valley by *nayakas* and merchant groups as well as less specific but no less direct evidence for

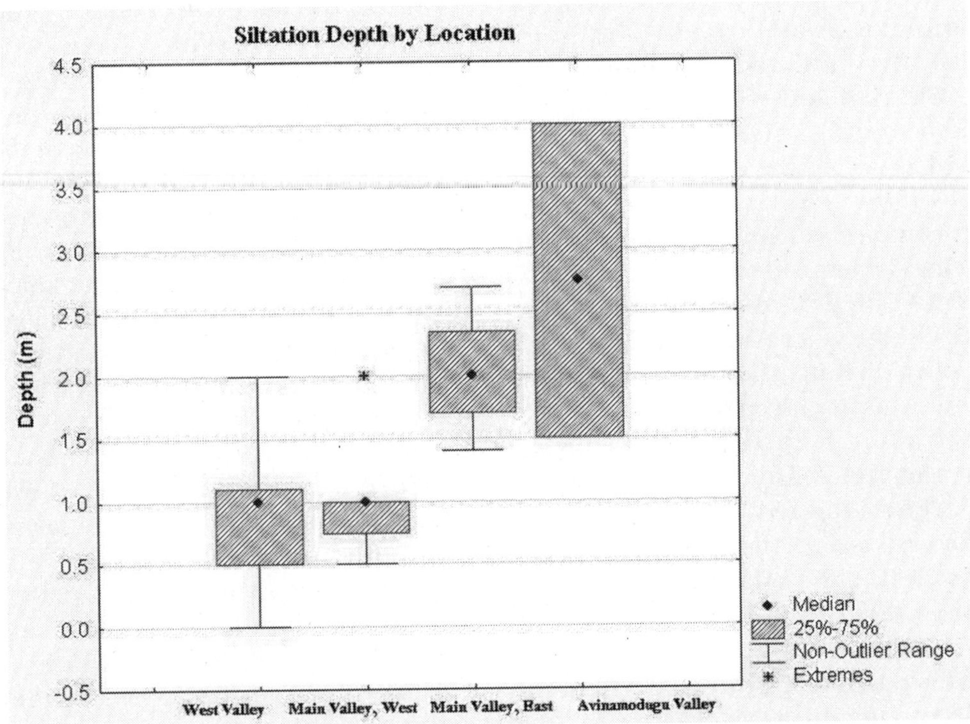

Figure 169. Daroji Valley, box plots of estimated siltation depths, by location.

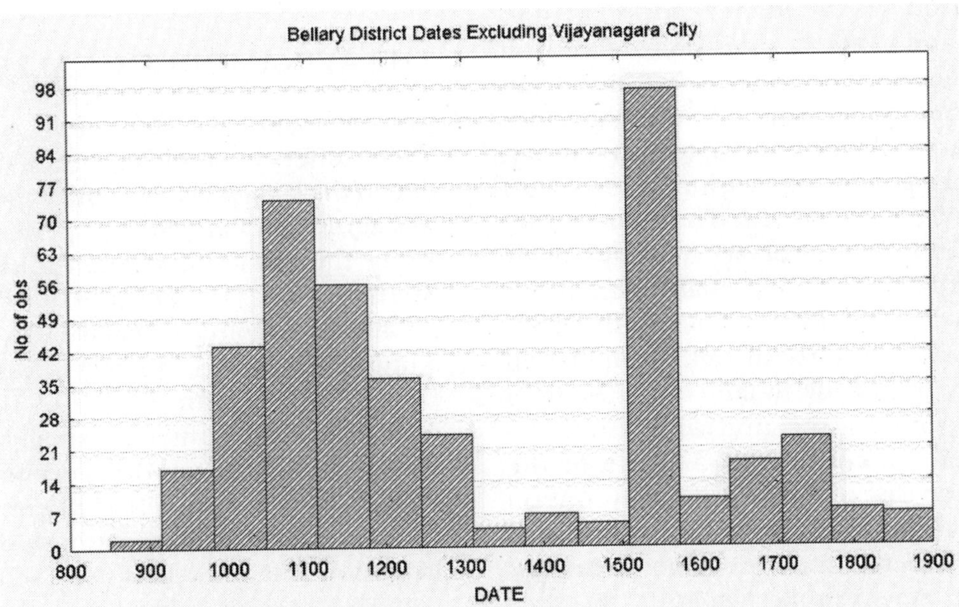

Figure 170. Numbers of inscriptions from Bellary District, excluding Vijayanagara city.

elite action in form of the construction of temple complexes, walls, roads, and gates (Figure 170). By the sixteenth century, too, changes to the regional vegetation that had been initiated much earlier intensified – the pollen record as well as the evidence for large-scale erosion off the granitic Hampi-Daroji hills tells of deforestation and degradation of the vegetation cover. Even aside from its ecological consequences – silted-in reservoirs, aggrading valley floors, enhanced erosion and slope wash – deforestation meant greater pressure on firewood and other fuel sources such as dung, pressure that would have removed fertilizing dung from the fields and thus further exacerbated trends toward soil exhaustion. Reduced browse would have affected goat foddering as well, although sheep and cattle may have been less affected, able to graze off the stubble of fallow fields.

Beyond the particular shift of settlement from the Bayaluvaddigeri cluster to the Papinayakanahalli cluster and other changes within the main valley, there is a larger pattern of change in the focal area of settlement and to a certain extent, in land use intensity, a shift generally from east to west, of which the main valley is but one example. Starting in the Early Middle period, we can identify a focal area to the east of and in and around Doravati/Daroji itself, a place which continued to be of importance even as the Daroji Valley filled with reservoirs and villages in the sixteenth century. Although Hospet, the large town at the western edge of the Daroji Valley, itself had a sixteenth-century foundation, its presence as the major town in the region was well-established by the nineteenth century. By this time, both Daroji and the Daroji Valley had shrunk in population and, more significantly, in land use intensity, a change certainly associated with the abandonment of the city of Vijayanagara to the north. To the east of the Daroji Valley, out on the Bellary plains, the town of Bellary followed a somewhat different trajectory. Already a major focus of settlement in the Neolithic, this area appears to have been continuously settled until the Iron Age or perhaps Early Historic. Although there is little Early Middle period architecture, the Bellary fort was established during the sixteenth century, and from then on the fort formed the locus of the town and its chief attraction, becoming a defensive outpost for Tipu Sultan in the eighteenth century and, by the beginning of the nineteenth century, for the British. Established by the British as the district headquarters in 1800, Bellary is still the largest town in the region today, though perhaps soon to be surpassed by Hospet. In all this, the main valley saw only a brief, sixteenth-century period of rapid growth, when it was in some sense central to regional-scale efforts at agrarian expansion and production for the city of Vijayanagara. Both before and after this time, the main valley, home to small populations of farmers, herders, and others, served the larger world primarily as a corridor of movement, a place with a major road, a rest house (in the colonial period), and a string of small fortified villages. In addition to its role as an east-west corridor, the valley also served as part of the watershed of the monumental Daroji reservoir, a vast facility that has, apparently, provided water to irrigated crops for the past 400 years, thus providing both sustenance and largesse, food and tax revenues, on a scale approximately equal to that of the entire main valley.[3]

THE AVINAMODUGU VALLEY

The occupational history of the Avinamodugu Valley differs in many important respects from that of the Daroji Valley. Unlike the latter, there was significant Early Middle period occupation along the Nari Halla, small towns with both Shaivite and Jain residents practicing inundation agriculture, dry farming, and herding along this seasonal stream.[4] Kurekuppa in the Daroji Valley is the lowest of this string of settlements and contains a small but well-built temple, indicating the prosperity of its patrons. Unlike the Daroji Valley, where there was a major sixteenth century extension of reservoir irrigation and an expansion of settlement, this pattern is seen in only a few settlements along the Hire Halla/Kanigana Halla, chief among them Avinamodugu itself. The Avinamodugu reservoir bears the legacy of a complex history of construction, destruction, repair, and decline;

the present-day village and reservoir are greatly reduced versions of their sixteenth-century counterparts but both the economic and ritual importance of the reservoir have endured in spite of this. Most of the rest of the reservoirs in the Avinamodugu Valley are smaller containment facilities, more useful for watering animals than for large-scale agriculture.

After the fall of the city in the late sixteenth century and the consequent southward shift of the limits of the Vijayanagara polity, the political history of the Sandur Hills and a part of the Avinamodugu Valley diverged from that of the surrounding region, enduring British rule only indirectly as part of the Princely State of Sandur. With the exception of a small area under the Avinamodugu reservoir, most of the valley is used for grazing, plant collecting, and limited dry farming.

Why was the land use history of the Avinamodugu Valley so different from that of neighboring Daroji? First, residents of the pre-existing string of Nari Halla settlements, apparently prosperous places with small but well-built temples, must have already had some claim to rights in land in and near their villages. Villages lands typically included areas, often jointly held, intended for grazing, collecting, and other land-extensive activities – the later reclassification of such lands as "waste", especially "cultivable waste" by the British led to serious problems, from outright appropriation to loss of effective control over such apparently "unused" places. I have already commented in the continued salience, in tax rolls, of abandoned villages, where land might continued to be farmed, owned, or otherwise used and controlled even though the named settlement it "belongs" to had long since turned to ruin. Previous land use, too, may have affected patterns of erosion and stream flow, making a major reorganization toward reservoirs more difficult. Thus, the prior existence of settled places in the Avinamodugu Valley and their paucity in the Daroji Valley must have powerfully influenced later land use trajectories.

Second, both the topography of the Avinamodugu Valley and its distance from the city undoubtedly played a factor. Further from the city, the valley is surrounded on three sides by hills and although these hills clearly played a major role in regional defense, the valley itself is a dead-end rather than a major route of movement as the Daroji Valley was (and is). Most significant, perhaps, is the uneven nature of the valley floor which limits the number and size of runoff-fed reservoirs it could support. Areas even more distant from the city such as that southwest of Hospet near Dhanayakanakere were developed for reservoir irrigation much as Daroji was. It may be the Avinamodugu Valley's limited productive potential away from its two major streams that ultimately limited agrarian expansion in the sixteenth century. This limit was also, certainly, influenced by the presence of the nearby Sandur Hills. As noted, reservoirs, temples, settlements, and other landscape features in the Daroji Valley tend to cluster along its northern edge, away from the dangerous runoff of the Sandur Hills, runoff worsened in recent centuries by mining and deforestation, the latter only now beginning to approach the scale of sixteenth century forest destruction. The sedimentation of the Avinamodugu *kere* is a clear example of this danger to irrigation works and the current low population density of the valley is a testament to the continued salience of these local factors.

During the Vijayanagara period and especially during the early sixteenth century, both the Daroji Valley and other outlying areas such as the Dhanayakanakere area south-west of Hospet saw a massive expansion of agriculture and settlement organized primarily around chains of runoff-fed reservoirs. These marginal dry areas were brought under production at a level of intensity not seen before or since. In contrast, the Avinamodugu Valley saw a continued focus on inundation agriculture along the banks of the Nari Halla and a very limited expansion along the Hire Halla, primarily around the large Avinamodugu reservoir. While both the Daroji and Avinamodugu Valleys were clearly fortified at this time, it is less clear what the defensive infrastructure of the Dhanayakanakere area was like.[5] The Sandur Hills, too, saw a continuation of older patterns of settlement and continued use of older forts and temples. Far to the east and west of our region, along the Hageri and Chikka Hageri rivers, centers of Early Middle period settlement apparently continued to be occupied although we know very little about the specific histories of these places. This pattern clearly reflects the reverberations, at some distance from the city itself, of the large-scale expansions of population and the consequent intensification and expansion of agricultural production that took place in the fourteenth and sixteenth centuries.

The abandonment, too, of a large part of these reservoir systems corresponds with population decline and political unrest in the late sixteenth and seventeenth centuries. This history – and even more so, the longer-term histories evident from the physical landscape – differ in many ways from that of the area in and around the city itself and indeed from larger regional patterns of change These patterns are discussed elsewhere (Morrison 2006a); here I simply note that existing data from inscriptional, architectural, and archaeological studies suggest that with the founding of the city of Vijayanagara and its rapid expansion in the early fourteenth century, elite attention shifted to the city itself and away from outlying settlements (Figure 12). These places mostly continued to be occupied but their wealth and power may have dimmed. The attraction of the city of Vijayanagara for capital investment, elite acts of piety, and attempts at garnering political and social legitimacy continued throughout the fourteenth and fifteenth century. By the early sixteenth century, however, as we have so clearly seen in the case of the Daroji Valley, the phenomenal growth of the urban population and the significant increase in the tempo and scale of building, donating, feeding, endowing, memorializing, and other activities involving inscriptions exploded into the countryside, a transformation also clearly visible in the natural and anthropogenic landscape. The occupational history of the city exerted an overwhelming force on the surrounding countryside, first attracting people, money, and power inward, and then, in the early sixteenth century, expanding back out into surrounding areas, pulling them in to the orbit of the city, its markets, its taxes, and its complex social and political networks (Morrison 1995, 2001).[6]

BEYOND THE VALLEY: IRRIGATION, POWER, AND RISK

The history of the Middle period Daroji Valley contrasts quite sharply with some of the other areas around the city. Like the Dhanayakankere area to the west of Hospet, the valley was densely settled in the sixteenth century in response to the greatly-increased demand for food production to supply the rapidly-growing capital city. Both of these areas relied on runoff to fill reservoirs and rainfall to water fields of hardy crops such as millets; after the fall of the city, both areas saw large-scale abandonment of reservoirs and contraction of cultivated land. While linked to temples and urban elites, neither area was in any sense a power center after the fourteenth century, a peripheral status closely linked to productive potential.

In contrast, the narrow alluvial strip along the Tungabhadra where perennial irrigation from river canals was possible served as the locus of power throughout the occupation of the city. The initial success of the city was made possible, in fact, by an early focus on the construction of perennial irrigation facilities (Morrison 1995a). At the same time, foods associated with auspiciousness and fertility such as rice, and with power and authority such as betel leaves and areca nuts, all required irrigation to grow in this semi-arid environment. The canal-irrigated zone along the river supported, at least in pockets, the lush green landscape extolled in contemporary texts, a landscape iconic of a successful ruler.

Well-watered areas were (and are) also extremely productive. Long-lived crops such as trees and sugar cane can be grown where sufficient water is available as can multiple crops of water-loving rice or vegetables. It is not surprising, then, that canal-irrigated zones continued to be farmed even after the abandonment of the city of Vijayanagara. In these areas we see a virtually continuous occupational history from the initial construction of the canals; in some places along the river, humans have lived and worked from the

Paleolithic to the present with only minimal interruption.

It is thus not surprising that all of the very large temple complexes of the Vijayanagara period are located within the irrigated zones, with most right along the river, Fritz, Michell and Nagaraja Rao's (1985) "Sacred Center". The few exceptions to this pattern include temples and temple complexes located along major roadways, such as the Goddess temple at Papinayakanahalli. While it is clear that produce from the Daroji Valley moved to the city, some of it destined for riverside temple complexes such as the Virupaksha temple built over the old Pampa *tirtha*, the connections between agrarian investment in the valley and temples is not as close as previous historical research has suggested. While temples controlled extensive holdings around the city, these appear to have been disproportionally concentrated in irrigated areas, leaving the somewhat riskier dry-farmed and reservoir-irrigated areas to small-scale farmers, entrepreneurs, and local leaders for development.

Reservoirs and Canals in the Landscape

Both canals and reservoirs require large investments in labor, time, and resources. Canals, despite their significantly larger costs, are ultimately less risky enterprises, producing more and more highly-valued forms of produce. Analysis of actual use-lives makes it clear that canals are more stable in the long term than reservoirs, though this stability needs to be contextualized in light of the cultural value placed on rice and other wet crops – such consideration cannot be dissociated from the functional and ecological constraints of each form. There is no doubt that canal construction and extension required significant resources and specialist labor; the services of specialist engineers as well as laborers were required. It is not, however, clear that engineers were routinely engaged for reservoir construction although specialist reservoir "diggers" were certainly in existence. Further, canal construction is locationally constrained in powerful ways and canal zones inevitably small in this environment.

In contrast to canals, reservoirs are a somewhat dubious economic investment. Although they may allow for limited wet cultivation or make dry farming more secure and productive, reservoirs silt in, breach – sometime with disastrous consequences as when the village of Daroji was swept away – and in this semi-arid environment, in some years they fail to collect any water at all. In some historically-recorded famines (Morrison 2000), reservoir-irrigated areas actually fared worse than dry farmed fields because of the rapid evaporation of water needing to flow some distance before reaching fields below; in this instance rainfed fields actually failed less disastrously.[7] Reservoirs create only isolated patches of irrigated ground, unlike the continuous distribution of canal-irrigated lands, and the very dispersal of such patches increases transportation costs.

On the other hand, reservoirs encode considerable cultural value of their own, particularly through their close association with temples, lotuses, fertility, and the eternal ocean; constructing a reservoir was a highly valorized act – more so even than canal construction if the inscriptional record is any guide. Reservoirs, like temples, sons, treasures, and literary works, were also seen to endure. They constituted one of the "sevenfold progeny", links between the present and the future. If modernist architecture can be seen as a "defense against the terror of time" (Harvey 1990: 206), a striving for eternity against a universe of flux, south Indian progeny might be seen in an analogous light. Here there is a focus on extension and longevity, but one that adopts a procreative rather than solely creative stance. To "give birth" to a reservoir, temple, son, other progeny is an ironic, if apt, metaphor in this male-dominated society where the actual work of reproduction is often elided.[8] The donor, as the text asserts, "causes the structure to be built", but in texts the actual labor of building, plowing, growing, and so on takes place invisibly; transparent work that nevertheless leaves enduring remains.[9] Further, as the archaeological data make clear, reservoirs vary tremendously in size so that the ambition of building or rebuilding a reservoir was much more possible for most people than the excavation of a canal. Inasmuch as patronage of irrigation was linked to political legitimacy and as political ambition was widespread and far-reaching in this decentralized empire, the plurality of power-holders alone makes the proliferation of reservoirs somewhat less surprising.[10]

Here, too, landscape histories matter. Reservoirs can be placed in areas where canals could never reach and thus are suited to the rocky, dissected landscape of northern Karnataka, with its seasonal rainfall. Places with long histories of cultivation, too, may be hemmed in with pre-existing rights and restrictions on the use of land. The construction of a new facility inevitably disrupts these social arrangements as well as existing physical patterns of water flow and transport. Canals must, of necessity, follow a carefully-laid path to maintain an appropriate gradient and such a path may well burst through existing features and lands already under cultivation. Reservoirs, on the other hand, are more modular and new facilities, within limits, can be placed in the interstices of older ones. Political clout, as well as resources, then, necessarily paves the way for major changes in irrigation regimes.[11]

Canals, no less than reservoirs, require constant maintenance and in this the two kinds of facilities make similar demands for seasonal labor. In both cases, water-borne silt constitutes something of a mixed blessing. Silt may block sluices and reduce capacity, as we have seen clearly in the case of the Daroji system, but silt also carries with it nutrients of great importance to the crop. The nature of these nutrients depends, critically, not only on the source of suspended sediment particles but also on the substrate through which runoff flows – in the case of many runoff-fed reservoirs, millennia of farming, grazing, and erosion have leached soil nutrients, reducing the benefit of dissolved and suspended material in rainwater. Canals, whose flow derives from river water, itself originating in the distant Western Ghats, carry more nutrient-rich water.[12] Rice paddies, especially, depend on the nutrients carried in water (Grist 1954) since paddy soils, which form a hardpan beneath the plow zone, contribute very little to the nutrient store of the growing plant. Although canal irrigation can promote both salinity and waterlogging, we have no evidence of this from our region and know of no significant break in use aside from occasional cleaning. In almost all places where a canal *could be* built, a canal *was* built, at least by the sixteenth century. Certainly, the costs of canal construction as well as of the transport of produce limited their expansion – the sixteenth-century construction of the massive aqueduct bringing water from the Anegondi channel to the large island in the river just north of the city is, in some sense, surprisingly late given the proximity of this island to the city.

In spite of evidence for investment by kings and other high-ranking elites, there is little indication of centralized control over canal water. There clearly existed special officers involved in water distribution, but many of these office holders seem to have operated at the local, village level. Even today, the Vijayanagara channels are famous as an example of farmer-managed irrigation as opposed to the more conflict-ridden government-administered Tungabhadra canals associated with the twentieth-century reservoir (Sivamohan 1991).

DISCUSSION

Power relations and life possibilities in southern India have always been tied to, though not necessarily determined by, productive potential. Such potential is constituted both through the conditions of the natural environment as well as a result of human action over millennia. Together, these agents create landscapes, inhabited and imagined places that both shape human experience and are themselves made, at least in part, by those experiences. Historical analysis tends to dissect places, with their complex, accretional histories, into neat time-slices such as periods, dynasties, and eras, as a result often ignoring the ways in which "older" parts of the landscape continue to operate "out of time" as meaningful places. This afterlife of structures and even natural elements is rendered invisible by standard archaeological practices of periodization; only formal architecture is routinely studied in terms of its refashioning and reuse. Nevertheless, the long centuries between, for example, the Southern Neolithic and the Early Historic periods were, somewhat unexpectedly, knitted together by continuing memories of specific locations and land use practices that kept even abandoned sites active in local imaginations. Little-noted, too, are the ways in which contemporary residents interact with places that ostensibly belong to earlier periods; across the study area, Vaishnavite shrines have been converted to Shaivite and Goddess shrines on a large scale, reservoir sluices, pestles, cannonballs, and trees are made into shrines, and megaliths and ashmounds dismantled for building material.

This volume has focused on a rural landscape, one linked with but generally peripheral to seats of political and economic power in the region. Although farmers of the Daroji Valley from the Neolithic onward (if indeed, there was any farming in the valley at this time) have always relied to a great extent on millets and other drought-resistant crops, they have also consistently made efforts to grow a larger range of produce, including rice and orchard crops. Such efforts have met with mixed success although electric pumps and deep bore wells, for now, have made this goal possible in limited areas. Although the exigencies of plant growth have clearly been of great importance in structuring local landscape history, these are not sufficient for understanding its trajectory. Agrarian landscapes consist of much more than simply bald equations of soil, water, and slope – they are also meaningful places where reservoirs could be monuments, eternal oceans, and even temples, as well as technological devices and physical manifestations of elite power, influence, just rule, and right action. These are places where histories are actively made and re-made, remembered and forgotten. Thus, while the specific fashionings of landscape and place, as well as the culturally defined and historically created meanings and relationships which structured the valley's history belong to it alone, the processes by which this took place are much more widespread, if not universal. In this regard, the Daroji Valley could be anywhere and the strategies of this study deployed further afield.

NOTES

1. And probably 14, considering the "missing" reservoir east of Dharmasagara. This figure does not include VMS-1006, which flows toward the west and which should be considered an isolated facility or perhaps part of the much more loosely integrated western valley system.
2. This date seems most likely on archaeological and stylistic grounds; the large double sluices of the Daroji reservoir are not unlike those of VMS-1015 and recall contemporaneous architecture of the Vijayanagara courtly style. Oral traditions which place the reservoir "before" the reign of Krishnadeva Raya can be accommodated within this chronology. This tradition is interesting inasmuch as Krishnadeva Raya probably gets too much credit as a great builder in other local oral traditions; the key to this difference must be the association of Doravati/Daroji with Kampila Raya and thus with an even older history.
3. This is an approximation, based on the reported 1871 tax revenues (all categories) for Daroji as compared to the other settlements in the valley.
4. It is clear that residents of these towns also included merchants and craftspeople; residents were evidently part of larger social, religious, and economic networks at this time, a pattern that contrasts with their relatively isolated positions today.
5. There are, however, numerous (unstudied) forts in the area which may have been built around this time. The fortification walls around the Daroji Valley were not indicated on any map and were first located by my fieldwork there; thus it is possible many similar walls exist to the west of Hospet.
6. Or, one could also say, the city itself exploded into more distant locations such as the Daroji valley, in so doing coming to terms with longer-term local landscape histories.
7. Some interesting examples of the reliability and productivity of land under reservoirs come from nineteenth-century British agricultural experiments with new crops and crop varieties. In an experiment with *Zea mays* (corn) cultivation in Bellary District, grain yields on "dry" land (which was, however, watered from two to twelve times a month) ranged from 100-875 lb./acre; on dry land under a well 200; on "dry garden land" watered once every four days 800; and on wet land under the Tungabhadra a whopping 3,520 bushels/acre. The "wet land

under a tank" yielded 250 lb./acre though the agent noted "the tank having dried up previous to the maturation of the crop, the crop withered away almost entirely" (Stokes 1884: 29). An experiment with paddy varieties under the Mylapore reservoir was problematic because "the tank was not filled until late in the season, and became empty before the paddy crops were fully matured" (Stokes 1884: 52); still the yields of "Goondoo Sumba" and "Madagascar Paddy" were as high as 1,331 and 2,258 pounds of grain per acre. Timing of rainfall was thus was critical and the rewards of cultivation as high as the risk.

8. Gender relations were certainly marked by a high degree of class/caste differentiation. Considering here only inscriptionally-documented patronage, unlike the Early Historic, when women constituted a large part of the donor pool, by the Early Middle period, women as donors occur in much smaller numbers and these are limited primarily to royal and elite women.
9. It may go without saying that it is not the donor who supplies this labor. The work of lower-status men and women is the foundation for the merit (*punya*) accrued to the donor, just as the reproductive labor of the wife, invisible labor in these texts, is the foundation for the son.
10. As should be clear from the thrust of this volume, I am not arguing that reservoirs are simply objects of "empty" political display. They are clearly also productive facilities of great consequence and their expansion must be viewed in light of *both* their functionality for food production and their cultural and political significance.
11. Thus, the relatively greater social rank of canal endowers (as compared to donors of reservoirs) makes sense both in terms of their presumably greater ability to mobilize the resources for such a costly undertaking as well as their apparent ability to break through, sometimes literally, existing arrangements of land and water use.
12. Particularly before the construction of the Tungabhadra Dam, when the river flooded annually. This regime did constitute more of a danger to canal headworks, but the dam now blocks a large portion of suspended silt which has reduced its capacity significantly.

REFERENCES CITED

Achaya, K.T. 1998. *Indian Food: A Historical Companion,* Oxford University Press, Delhi.

Allchin, F.R. 1960. *Piklihal Excavations,* Andhra Pradesh Government Publications, Archaeological Series No. 1, Hyderabad.

———, 1961. *Utnoor Excavations,* Andhra Pradesh Government Publications, Archaeological Series No. 5, Hyderabad.

———, 1963. *Neolithic Cattle-Keepers of South India,* Cambridge University Press, Cambridge.

Alcock, S. 2001. "The Reconfiguration of Memory in the Eastern Roman Empire", in *Empires: Perspectives from Archaeology and History,* ed. S. Alcock, T.N.D'Altroy, K.D. Morrison and C.M. Sinopoli, pp. 323-50, Cambridge University Press, Cambridge.

Ansari, Z.D. and M.S. Nagaraja Rao. 1969. *Excavation at Sangankallu, 1964-65 (Early Neolithic House at Bellary),* Deccan College Building and Centenary and Silver Jubilee Series 64, Deccan College Postgraduate and Research Institute, Poona.

Appadurai, A. 1978. "Kings, Sects, and Temples in South India, 1350-1800 AD", in *South Indian Temples: An Analytical Reconsideration,* ed. B. Stein, pp. 47-73, Vikas, New Delhi.

———, 1981. "The Past as a Scarce Resource", *Man, n.s.,* 16: 201-19.

Appadurai, A. and C.A. Breckenridge. 1976. "The South Indian Temple: Authority, Honour, and Redistribution", *Contributions to Indian Sociology,* 10: 187-211.

Archaeological Survey of India, 1904. *Annual Progress Report of the Archaeological Survey of Madras and Coorg for the Year 1903 and 1904,* Government Press, Madras.

Baker, C. 1984. *An Indian Rural Economy: 1880-1955,* Oxford University Press, New Delhi.

Balasubrahmanya, 1991. "Jambukesvara Temple, Hospet", in *Vijayanagara: Progress of Research 1987-1988,* ed. D.V. Devaraj and C.S. Patil, pp. 168-78, Directorate of Archaeology and Museums, Mysore.

Barrett, J.C. 1994. *Fragments from Antiquity: An Archaeology of Social Life in Britain, 2900-1200 BC,* Blackwell, Oxford.

Basu, K.K. 2000. "The Battle of Talikota – Before and After", in *Vijayangara: History and Legacy,* ed. S. Krishnaswami Aiyangar et al., Aryan Books International, New Delhi.

Binford, L.R. 1982. "The Archaeology of Place", *Journal of Anthropological Archaeology,* 1(1): 5-31.

———, 1983. *In Pursuit of the Past: Decoding the Archaeological Record,* Thames and Hudson, New York.

Boivin, N, 2004. "Landscape and Cosmology in the Southern Indian Neolithic: New Perspectives on the Deccan Ashmounds", *Cambridge Archaeological Journal,* 14(2): 235-57.

Bonny, A.P. 1976. "Recruitment of Pollen to the Seston and Sediment of Some Lake District Lakes". *Journal of Ecology* 64: 859-88.

Bradley, R. 1987. "Time Regained: The Creation of Continuity". *Journal of the British Archaeological Association* 140: 1-17.

———, 2000. *The Archaeology of Natural Places.* Routledge, London.

Breckenridge, C.A. 1985. "Social Storage and the Extension of Agriculture in South India 1350 to 1750", in *Vijayanagara: City and Empire,* ed. A.L. Dallapiccola, pp. 41-72, Franz Steiner Verlag, Wiesbaden.

Brittlebank, K.L. 1997. *Tipu Sultan's Search for Legitimacy: Islam and Kingship in a Hindu Domain,* Oxford University Press, Delhi.

Brohier, R.L. 1934. *Ancient Irrigation Works in Ceylon,* Ceylon Government Press, Colombo.

Brubaker, R. 2003. "Cornerstones of Control: The Infrastructure of Imperial Security at Vijayanagara, South India", unpublished Ph.D. dissertation, Department of Anthropology, University of Michigan.

Buchanan, F.H. 1988 [1807]. *A Journey from Madras through the countries of Mysore, Canara, and Malabar, performed under the orders of the most noble the Marquis of Wellesley, governor general of India, for the express purpose of investigating the state of agriculture, arts, and commerce; the religion, manners, and customs; the history natural and civil, and antiquities, in the dominions of the Raja of Mysore, and the countries acquired by the Honorable East India Company*, T. Cadwell and W. Davies, London.

Bryson, R.A. and A.M. Swain. 1981. "Holocene Variations of Monsoon Rainfall in Rajasthan", *Quaternary Research*, 16: 417-24.

Caratini, C., M. Fontugne, J.P. Pascal, C. Tissot, and I. Bentaleb. 1991. "A Major Change at *ca.* 3500 years BP in the Vegetation of the Western Ghats in North Kanara, Karnataka", *Current Science*, 61 (9 &10): 699-72.

Caratini, C., I. Bentaleb, M. Fontugne, M.T. Morzadec-Kerfourn, J.P. Pascal, and C. Tissot. 1994. "A Less Humid Climate since 3500 years BP from Marine Cores off Karwar, Western India", *Paleography, Paleoclimatology, Paleoecology*, 109: 371-84.

Chakrabarti, D.K. 1992. *The Early Use of Iron in India*, Munshiram Manoharlal, New Delhi.

Champakalakshmi, R. 1981. "Peasant State and Society in Medieval South India: A Review Article", *Indian Economic and Social History Review*, 18: 411-26.

———, 1996. *Trade, Ideology, and Urbanization: South India 300 BC to AD 1300.* Oxford University Press, Delhi.

Charlesworth, N. 1985. *Peasants and Imperial Rule: Agriculture and Agrarian Society in the Bombay Presidency, 1850-1935*, Cambridge University Press, Cambridge.

Chidanandamurthi, M. 1982. "Two Masti Temples in Karnataka", in *Memorial Stones: A Study of Their Origin, Significance and Variety*, ed. S. Settar and G-D. Sontheimer, Institute of Indian Art History, Karnatak University and South Asia Institute, University of Heidelberg, Manipal, pp. 117-31.

Childe, N.G., "Megaliths", *Ancient India* 1947–48, No. 4, pp. 4–13.

Clark, J.S. 1988. "Particle Motion and the Theory of Charcoal Analysis: Source Area, Transport, Deposition, and Sampling", *Quaternary Research* 30: 67-800.

Cole, R. 1838. "Note on Certain Mounds of Scoriaceous Nature Found Near Belley", *Madras Journal of Literature and Science*, 7: 130-3.

Coomaraswamy, A.K. 1993. *Yaksas: Essays in the Water Cosmology*, New Edition, ed. P. Schroeder, Indira Gandhi National Centre for the Arts and Oxford University Press, New Delhi.

Dagens, B. (Translator). 1985. *Mayamata (an Indian Treatise on Housing, Architecture, and Iconography)*, Sitaram Bhartia Institute of Scientific Research, New Delhi.

Dallapiccola, A.L. 1994. "The City of Vijayanagara: Kiṣhkindha, The Monkey-Kingdom", in *The Legend of Rama: Artistic Visions*, ed. V. Dehejia, Marg Publications, Bombay.

Dallapiccola, A.L., J.M. Fritz, G. Michell, and S. Rajasekhara. 1992. *The Ramachandra Temple at Vijayanagara*, Manohar and American Institute of Indian Studies, Delhi.

Davis, R.H. 1993. "Indian Art Objects as Loot", *Journal of Asian Studies*, 52: 22-48.

———, 1997. *Lives of Indian Images.* Princeton University Press, Princeton.

Dehejia V. 1992. "Collective and Popular Bases of Early Buddhist Patronage: Sacred Monuments, 100 BC-AD 250", ed. B.S. Miller, *The Powers of Art: Patronage in Indian Culture.* Oxford University Press, Delhi.

Denniston, R.F., L.A. Gonzales, Y. Asmerom, R.H. Sharma, and M.K. Reagan. 2000. "Speleothem Evidence for Changes in Indian Summer Monsoon Precipitation over the last 2300 Years", *Quaternary Research*, 53: 196-202.

Devaraj, D.V. and H.T. Talwar. 1996, *Interim Report on the Excavations at Sannati, 1993-95*, Directorate of Archaeology and Museums, Mysore.

Devaraj, D.V., J. Shaffer, C.S. Patil, and Balasubrahmanya. 1995. "The Watgal Excavations: An Interim Report", *Man and Environment*, 20(2): 57-74.

Dhaky, M.A. 1996. *Encylopedia of Indian Temple Architecture, South India, Upper Dravidesa, Later Phase, AD 973-1326*, AIIS and Indira Gandhi National Centre for the Arts, Delhi.

Dikshit, G.S. 1964. *Local Self-Government in Medieval Karnataka*, Karntak University, Dharwar.

Duncan, J.S. 1990. *The City as Text: The Politics of Landscape Interpretation in the Kanyan Kingdom*, Cambridge University Press, Cambridge.

Eastwick, E. 1859. *Murray's Handbook for India, Part I – Madras*, London, John Murray.

Eaton, R.M. 2000. *Essays on Islam and Indian History*, Oxford University Press, Delhi.

Eck, D. 1981, *Darshan: Seeing the Divine Image in India*, Anima, Chambersburg.

Enzel, Y., L.L. Ely, S. Mishra, R. Ramesh, R. Amit, B. Lazar, S.N. Rajguru, V.R. Baker, and A. Sandler. 1999. "High-Resolution Holocene Environmental Changes in the Thar Desert, Northwestern India", *Science*. 284(5411): 125-8.

Faegri, K., P.E. Kaland, and K. Krzywinski. 1989. *Textbook of Pollen Analysis, IV Edition*. John Wiley and Sons, Chichester.

Feldhaus, A. 1995. *Water and Womanhood: Religious Meaning of Rivers in Maharashtra*, Oxford University Press, New York.

Filliozat, V. 1999, *Vijayanagara as Seen by Domingo Paes and Fernao Nuniz*, National Book Trust, Delhi.

Filliozat, P.S. and V. Filliozat. 1988. *Hampi-Vijayanagar: The Temple of Vithala*. Sitaram Bhartia Institute of Scientific Research, New Delhi.

Flood, G. 1996. *An Introduction to Hinduism*. Cambridge, Cambridge University Press.

Foote, R.B. 1914. *Indian Prehistoric and Protohistoric Antiquities: Catalogue Raisonne*. Madras Government Museum, Madras.

———, 1916. *Indian Prehistoric and Protohistoric Antiquities: Notes on Their Ages and Distributions*. Madras Government Museum, Madras.

———, 1887a. "Notes on Some Recent Neolithic and Palaeolithic Finds in South India", *Journal of the Royal Asiatic Society of Bengal*, 56: 259-82.

———, 1887b. "Notes on Prehistoric Finds in India", *Journal of the Anthropological Institute of Great Britain and Ireland*, 16: 70-5.

Fritz, J.M., G. Michell and M.S. Nagaraja Rao. 1985. *Where Kings and Gods Meet: The Royal Centre at Vijayanagara*, University of Arizona Press, Tucson.

Fritz, J.M., R.P. Brubaker and T.P. Raczek, eds. 2006. *Vijayanagara: Archaeological Exploration, 1990-2000: Papers in Memory of Channabasappa S. Patil*, 2 vols., Manohar and American Institute of Indian Studies, New Delhi.

Fuller, C.J. 1992. *The Camphor Flame: Popular Hinduism and Society in India*, Princeton University Press, Princeton.

Fuller, D.Q. 2003. "An Agricultural Perspective on Dravidian Historical Linguistics: Archaeological Crop Packages, Livestock, and Dravidian Crop Vocabulary", in *Language and Farming Dispersals*, ed. P. Bellwood and C. Renfrew, McDonald Institite for Archaeological Research, Cambridge.

Gaussen, H., P. Legris, L. Labroue, V.M. Meher-Homji and M. Viart. 1966. *Carte Inernationale Du Tapis Vegetal, Notice de la Feuille: Mysore*. Extrait des Travaux de la Section Scientifique et Technique de L'Institut Francais de Pondicherry, Hors Serie 7, Pondicherry.

Gogte, V.D. 1982. *Megalithic Iron Smelting at Naikund. In Naikund Excavations – 1978-80*, eds. S.B. Deo and A.P. Jamkhedkar, Department of Archaeology and Museums, Government of Maharashtra, Bombay.

———, 1997. "The Chandraketugarh-Tamluk Region of Bengal: Source of the Early Historic Rouletted Ware from India and Southeast Asia", *Man and Environment* 22(1) : 69-85.

Gopal, B.H. 1985a. *Vijayanagara Inscriptions*. Vol. 1, Directorate of Archaeology and Museums, Mysore.

———, 1985b. *Vijayanagara Inscriptions*. Vol. 2. Directorate of Archaeology and Museums, Mysore.

Gopinatha Rao, T.A. 1969. *Elements of Hindu Iconography*, Vol. I, parts I and II, 2nd edn., Motilal Banarsidass, Delhi. [Originally published 1914, Madras.]

Government of India. 1874. *Census Statement of Population of 1871 in Each Village of the Bellary District, Arranged According to Area, Caste, and Occupation*, Government Press, Madras.

———, 1887. *Annual Report on South Indian Epigraphy (ARSIE)*, Government Press, Madras.

———, 1901. *Census of 1901 Village Statistics. Bellary District, Madras Presidency*, Government Press, Madras.

Government of Mysore. 1969. *List of Villages in the Mysore State*. Director of Printing, Stationary and Publications at the Government Press, Mysore.

Govinda. 2000. "Bailuvaddiegriya Immadi Devaraya Sasana [Bayaluvaddigeri inscription of Devaraya II]", in *Vijayanagara Adhyayana*, vol. 5, *Articles Presented at the Hampi Utsava 1999*, ed. M.V. Krishnappa and C.S. Patil, pp. 70-1, Directorate of Archaeology and Museums, Mysore.

Grist, D.H. 1954. *Rice*. Longmans, London.

Guha, S. 1985. *The Agrarian Economy of the Bombay Deccan 1818-1941*, Oxford University Press, Delhi.

Gunawardana, R.A.L.H. 1979. *Robe and Plough: Monasticism and Economic Interest in Early Medieval Sri Lanka*, University of Arizona Press, Tucson.

Gupta, A. 1998. *Postcolonial Developments: Agriculture in the Making of Modern India*, Duke University Press, Durham.

Habib, I. 1963. *The Agrarian System of Mughal India 1556-1707*, Asia Publishing House, Bombay.

———, 1995. *Essays in Indian History: Towards a Marxist Perception*, Tulika, New Delhi.

Hardy, A. 1998. "Form, Transformation, and Meaning in Indian Temple Architecture", in *Paradigms of Indian Architecture; Space and Time in Respresentation and Design*, ed. G.H.R. Tillotson, pp. 107-35, Curzon Press, Collected Paper on South Asia No. 13, London.

Harvey, D. 1989. *The Condition of Postmodernity: An Enquiry into the Origins of Cultural Change*, Blackwell, New York.

Howell, J.R. 1995. *Excavations at Sannathi: 1986-89*, Memoirs of the Archaeological Survey of India No. 93, Archaeological Survey of India, New Delhi.

Hultzsch E., trans. 1991 [1969]. *The Inscriptions of Asoka*, Delhi: Indological Book House.

Inden, R.1990. *Imagining India.* Basil Blackwell, Oxford.

———, 2000. "Imperial Puranas: Kashmir as Vaisnava Center of the World", in *Querying the Medieval: Texts and the History of Practices in South Asia*, by R. Inden, J. Walters and D. Ali, Oxford University Press, New York.

Johansen, P.G. 2004. "Landscape, Monumental Architecture and Ritual: A Reconsideration of the South Indian Ashmounds", *Journal of Anthropological Archaeology* 23(3): 309-30.

Karashima, N. 1984. *South Indian History and Society: Studies from Inscriptions,* AD *850-1800*, Oxford University Press, Delhi.

———, 1992. *Toward a New Formation: South Indian Society Under Vijayanagar Rule*, Oxford and IBH, Delhi.

———, 1999. "Viajayanagar Nayakas in Tamil Nadu and the King", in *Kingship in Indian History*, ed. N. Karashima, pp. 143-62, Manohar, Japanese Studies in South Asia No. 2, Delhi.

Kelsall, J. 1872. *Manual of the Bellary District: Compiled under the orders of Government*, Lawrence Asylum Press, Madras.

Korisettar, R., P.C. Venkatasubbaiah and D.Q. Fuller. 2001. "Brahmagiri and Beyond: The Archaeology of the Southern Neolithic", in *Indian Archaeology in Retrospect*, vol. I, *Prehistory: Archaeology of South Asia*, ed. S. Settar and R. Korisettar, Manohar and Indian Council of Historical Research, Delhi.

Kotraiah, C.T.M. 1978. "Boundary Stones: A Short Study With Special Reference to Those Available in the Hampi Museum", *Journal of The Andhra Historical Society* 37: 129-46.

———, 1983. "Hampi Before Founding of Vijayanagara", in *Srinidhi: Perspectives in Indian Art and Archaeology*, ed. K.V. Raman, K.G. Krishnan, M.S. Ramaswami, N. Karashima and A.V. Narasimha Murty, pp. 381-8. New Era, Madras.

——— (tr.). 1994. Bharatesa Vaibha Sangha (Kannada Work), Composed by Ratnakaravavarni *c.* 1457 A.D., unpublished manuscript.

———, 1995a. *Irrigation Systems Under Vijayanagara Empire*, Directorate of Archaeology and Museums, Mysore.

——— (tr.). 1995b, Padmaraja Purana (Kannada Work), Composed by Padmanaka c. 1385 A.D., unpublished manuscript.

——— (tr.). 1995c. Sivatattvacintamani (Kannada Work), Composed by Lakkanadandesa, *c.* 1450 A.D., unpublished manuscript.

Kramrisch, S. 1976. *The Hindu Temple*, 2 vols., Motilal Banarsidass, New Delhi.

Krishnaswami, V.D. 1949. "Megalithic Types of South India", *Ancient India* (5): 35-45.

Krishnaswami Ayyangar, S. (ed.). 1919. *Sources of Vijayanagara History*, University of Madras, Madras.

Krisnamurthy, M. 1978. *Geology and Mineral Resources of the Bellary District, Karnataka (Mysore) State*, Memoirs of the Geological Survey of India 108, New Delhi.

Kulke, H. and D. Rothermund. 1986. *A History of India*, Dorsett Press, New York.

Kutzbach J.E. 1987. "The Changing Pulse of the Monsoon", in *Monsoon*, ed. J.S. Fein and P.L. Stephens, pp. 247–68. John Wiley, New York.

Lamb, H.H. 1977. *Climate: Past, Present, and Future*, vol. II. *Climate History and the Future*, Methuen, London.

Leach, E.R. 1971. *Pul Eliya, A Village in Ceylon: A Study in Land Tenure and Kinship*, Cambridge University Press, Cambridge.

———, 1985. "Conclusion: Further Remarks on the Realm of Folly", in *Text, Play, and Story: The Construction and Reconstruction of Self and Society*, ed. E.M. Bruner, pp. 356-64, American Ethnological Society, Washington, D.C.

Leshnik, L. 1974. *South Indian "Megalithic" Burials: The Pandukal Complex.* Franz Steiner Verlag, Wiesbaden.

Liceria, M. 1987. "The Migration of Brahmanas to Karnataka", in *Essays in Indian Art, Religion, and Society*, ed. K.M. Shrimali, pp. 212-16, Munshiram Manoharlal, Delhi.

Longhurst, A.H. 1916. *Annual Report of the Archaeological Survey of India 1912-13*, pp. 145-7, Archaeological Survey of India, Delhi.

Ludden, D. 1985, *Peasant History in South India*, Delhi, Oxford University Press.

Lycett, M.T. 1991. "Chipped Stone Tools of the Vijayanagara Metropolitan Region", in *Vijayanagara: Progress of Research 1987-1988*, ed. D.V. Devaraj and C.S. Patil, pp. 85-94, Directorate of Archaeology and Museums, Mysore.

———, 1994. "Searching for Patterns in Ambiguous Categories: Nonarchitectural Sites of the Vijayanagara Metropolitan Region", in *South Asian Archaeology 1993*, ed. A. Parpola and P. Koskikallio, pp. 413-23, Annales Academiae Scientiarum Fennicae, Series B, vol. 271, Suomalainen Tiedeakatemia, Helsinki..

———, 1995. "Archaeological Implications of European Contact: Demography, Settlement, and Land Use in the Middle Rio Grande Valley, New Mexico", Ph.D. dissertation, Department of Anthropology, University of New Mexico.

Lycett, M.T. and K.D. Morrison, 1989. "Persistent Lithics: Post Iron Age Lithic Technology in South India", Annual Conference on South Asia, Madison, Wisconsin, 3-5 November.

———, 1998. "Scales and Monumentalities: The Production of an Iron Age Landscape in North Interior Karnataka", paper presented at the 97th Annual Meeting of the American Anthropological Association, Philadelphia, 1-3 December.

MacDonald, G.M., C.P.S. Larsen, J.M. Szeicz and K.A. Moser. 1991. "The Reconstruction of Boreal Forest Fire History From Lake Sediments: A Comparison of Charcoal, Pollen, Sedimentological, and Geochemical Indices", *Quaternary Science Reviews* 10: 53-71.

Mahadevan, I. 2003. *Early Tamil Epigraphy: From the Earliest Times to the Sixth Century A.D.*, Harvard Oriental Series, vol. 62, Harvard University Press, Cambridge.

Mahalingam, T.V. 1951. *Economic Life in the Vijayanagar Empire.* University of Madras Press, Madras.

Majumdar, G.G. and S.N. Rajaguru. 1966. *Ashmound Excavations at Kupgal*, Deccan College Postgraduate and Research Institute, Building Centenary and Silver Jubilee Series No. 56, Poona.

Michell, G. 1985a. "Architectural Traditions at Vijayanagara, I. Temple Styles", in *Vijayanagara – City and Empire*, ed. A.L. Dallapiccola, pp. 274-81, Franz Steiner Verlag, Wiesbaden.

———, 1985b. "A Never Forgotten City", in *Vijayanagara – City and Empire*, ed. A. Dallapiccola, pp. 196-207, Franz Steiner Verlag, Wiesbaden.

———, 1990. *Architectural Inventory of Vijayanagara*, 2 vols., Directorate of Archaeology and Museums, Mysore.

———, 1992. *The Vijayanagara Courtly Style*, Manohar and American Institute of Indian Studies, New Delhi.

———, 1994. "Revivalism as the Imperial Mode: Religious Architecture During the Vijayanagara Period", in *Perceptions of South Asia's Visual Past*, ed. C.B. Asher and T.R. Metcalf, pp. 187-97, AIIS, Swadharma Swarjya Sangha, and Oxford and IBH Press, Delhi.

———, 1995. *Architecture and Art of Southern India: Vijayanagara and the Successor States*, The New Cambridge History of India, I: 6, Cambridge University Press, Cambridge.

———, 1997. *The Blue Guide: Southern India*, A & C Black, London.

Morrison, K.D. 1990. "Patterns of Urban Occupation: Surface Collections at Vijayanagara", in *South Asian Archaeology 1987*, ed. M. Taddei, pp. 1111-26, Instituto Italiano per il Medio ed Estremo Oriente, Rome.

———, 1991. "The Vijayanagara Metropolitan Survey: Preliminary Season", in *Vijayanagara: Progress of Research 1984-1987*, ed. D.V. Devaraj and C.S. Patil, pp. 136-41, Directorate of Archaeology and Museums, Mysore.

———, 1993. "Supplying the City: the Role of Reservoir Irrigation in an Indian Urban Landscape", *Asian Perspectives* 32: 133-51.

———, 1994. "Monitoring Regional Fire History Through Size-Specific Analysis of Microscopic Charcoal: The Last 600 Years in South India", *Journal of Archaeological Science*, 21: 675-85.

———, 1995a. *Fields of Victory: Vijayanagara and the Course of Intensification*, Contribution No. 53 of the Archaeological Research Facility, Berkeley.

———, 1995b. "Trade, Urbanism, and Agricultural Expansion: Buddhist Monastic Institutions and the State in the Early Historic Western Deccan", *World Archaeology*, 27: 203-21.

———, 1996. "Typological Schemes and Agricultural Change: Beyond Boserup in South India", *Current Anthropology*, 37(4): 583-608.

———, 1997a. "Commerce and Culture in South Asia: Perspectives from Archaeology and History", *Annual Review of Anthropology*, 26: 87-108.

———, 1997b. "Agriculture at the Edges: Archaeology and History in the Vijayanagara Hinterland", in *South Asian Archaeology 1995*, ed. B. Allchin, pp. 783-91, Oxford and IBH, New Delhi.

———, 1999. "South Asia: Prehistory", in *Cambridge Encyclopedia of Hunters and Gatherers*, ed. R.B. Lee and R. Daly, pp. 238-42, Cambridge University Press, Cambridge.

———, 2000. "Naturalizing Disaster: from Drought to Famine in South India", in *Environmental Disruptions and the Archaeology of Human Response*, ed. G. Bawden and R. Reycraft, pp. 21-33, Anthropology Papers of the Maxwell Museum of Anthropology, Albuquerque.

———, 2001. "Coercion, Resistance, and Hierarchy: Local Processes and Imperial Strategies in the Vijayanagara Empire", *Empires: Perspectives from Archaeology and History*, ed. S. Alcock, T. D'Altroy, K.D. Morrison and C.M. Sinopoli, pp. 252-78, Cambridge University Press, Cambridge.

———, 2005. "Brahmagiri Revisited: A Re-analysis of the South Indian Sequence", in *South Asian Archaeology 2001*, ed. C. Jarrige and V. Lefèvre, pp. 257-62, Editions Recherche sur les Civilisations-ADPF, Paris.

———, 2006a. "Intensification as Situated Process: Landscape History and the Causes and Consequences of Change", in *Agricultural Strategies*, ed. J. Marcus and C. Stanish, pp. 71-91, UCLA Cotsen Institute of Archaeology, Los Angeles.

———, 2006b. "Historicizing Foraging in South Asia: Power, History, and Ecology of Holocene Hunting and Gathering", in *Archaeology of Asia*, ed. M.T. Stark, pp. 279-302, Blackwell, Oxford.

———, 2007. "Making Places and Making States: Agriculture, Metallurgy, and the Wealth of Nature in South India", in *The Wealth of Nature: How Natural Resources Have Shaped Asian History, 1600-2000*, ed. G. Bankoff and P. Boomgaard, pp. 81-102, Palgrave MacMillan.

———, in press a. "Patterns of Transportation Outside the City of Vijayanagara: Some Archaeological Evidence of Roadways", in *Professor A.V. Narasimha Murthy Felicitation Volume*, ed. D.V. Devaraj, R. Gopal et al., Mysore.

———, in press b. *Oceans of* Dharma*: A Political Ecology of Farming and Food in South India*, University of Washington Press, Seattle.

Morrison, K.D. and M.T. Lycett. 1994. "Centralized Power, Centralized Authority? Ideological Claims and Archaeological Patterns", *Asian Perspectives*, 33(2): 312-53.

———, 1997. "Inscriptions as Artifacts: Precolonial South India and the Analysis of Texts", *Journal of Archaeological Method and Theory*, 3(3-4): 215-37.

Morrison, K.D. and C.M. Sinopoli. 1992. "Economic Diversity and Integration in a Pre-Colonial Indian Empire", *World Archaeology*, 23(3): 335-52.

———, in press. "Archaeological Survey in the Vijayanagara Metropolitan Region: 1990", in: *Vijayanagara: Progress of Research 1989-91*, ed. D.V. Devaraj and C.S. Patil, pp. 59-73, Directorate of Archaeology and Museums, Mysore.

Mosse, D. 1999. "Colonial and Contemporary Ideologies of 'Community Management': The case of Tank Irrigation Development in South India", *Modern Asian Studies*, 33(2): 303-38.

———, 2003. *The Rule of Water: Statecraft, Ecology and Collective Action in South India*, Oxford University Press, Delhi.

Mukherji, P.D. (tr. and ed.). 2001, *The Citrasutra of the Visnudharmottara Purana*, New Delhi, Indira Gandhi National Centre for the Arts and Motilal Banarsidass, Delhi.

Myrdal-Runebjer, E. 1994. "Vavala vava – Sigiri Mahavava Irrigation System: Preliminary Results from an Archaeological Case Study, in *South Asian Archaeology 1993*, pp. 551-62, ed. Asko Parpola and Petteri Koskikallio, Annales Academiae Scientiarum Fennicae, Series B, vol. 271, Suomalainen Tiedeakatemia, Helsinki.

Nagaraja Rao, M.S. 1983. "Nomenclature of a Royal Road of Vijayanagara", in *Vijayanagara: Progress of Research 1979-1983*, ed. M.S. Nagaraja Rao, pp. 57-60, Directorate of Archaeology and Museums, Mysore.

———, 1983. "Ahmed Khan's Dharamsala", in *Vijayanagara: Progress of Research 1979-1983*, ed. M.S. Nagaraja Rao, pp. 64-7, Directorate of Archaeology and Museums, Mysore.

Nagaraja Rao, M.S. and K.C. Malhotra, 1965. *The Stone Age Hill-Dwellers of Tekkalakota*, Deccan College Postgraduate and Research Institute, Poona.

Naidu, P.D. 1996. "Onset of an Arid Climate at 3.5 ka in the Tropics: Evidence from Monsoon Upwelling Record", *Current Science*, 71: 715-18.

Naqvi, S.M. and J.J.W. Rogers. 1987. *Precambrian Geology of India,* Oxford Monographs on Geology and Geophysics 6. Clarendon Press, New York.

Narayana Rao, V., D. Shulman, and S. Subrahmayam. 1992. *Symbols of Substance: Court and State in Nayaka Period Tamil Nadu,* Oxford University Press, Delhi.

Newbold. 1836. "Note on the Occurrence of Volcanic Scoria in the Southern Peninsula", *Journal of the Asiatic Society of Bengal,* 5: 670-1.

———, 1843. "On some Ancient Mounds of Scorious Ashes in Southern India", *Journal of the Royal Asiatic Society,* 7: 129-36.

Nelson, M.C., "Abandonment: Conceptualization, Representation, and Social Change", in *Social Theory in Archaeology,* ed. M.B. Schiffer, pp. 52-62, University of Utah Press, Salt Lake City.

Nilakanta Sastri, K.A. 1966. *A History of South India,* 3rd edn., Oxford University Press, London.

———, 1992 [1963], *Development of Religion in South India,* Munshiram Manoharlal, Delhi (originally 1963, Orient Longman, Madras).

Overpeck, J., D. Anderson, S. Trumbore, and W. Prell. 1996. "The Southwest Indian Monsoon over the last 18,000 years", *Climate Dynamics* 12(3): 213-25.

Paddayya, K. 1973. *Investigations into the Neolithic Culture of the Shorapur Doab, South India.* Brill, Leiden.

———, 1993a. "Ashmound Investigations at Budihal, Gulbarga District, Karnataka", *Man and Environment* 18(1): 57-88.

———, 1993b. "Further Field Investigations at Budihal", *Bulletin of the Deccan College Postgraduate and Research Institute,* 53: 277-322.

———, 1998. "Evidence of Neolithic Cattle-Penning at Budihal, Gulbarga District, Karnataka", *South Asian Studies,* 14: 141-53.

Paddayya, K., P.K. Thomas, and P.P. Joglekar. 1995. "A Neolithic Animal Butchering Floor from Budihal, Gulbarga District, Karnataka", *Man and Environment,* 29(2): 23-31.

Palat, R. 1987. "The Vijayanagara empire: Re-integration of the Agrarian Order of Medieval South India", in *Early State Dynamics,* ed. H.J.M. Claessen and P. van der Velde, pp. 170-86. E.J. Brill, Leiden.

Patil, C.S. and V.C. Patil. 1995. *Inscriptions at Vijayanagara (Hampi),* Directorate of Archaeology and Museums, Mysore.

———, 1997. *Inscriptions of Bellary District,* Directorate of Archaeology and Museums, Mysore.

Patil, C.S. 1991a. "Epigraphical Studies", in *Vijayanagara Progress of Research 1987-88,* ed. D.V. Devaraj and C.S. Patil, pp. 15-34, Directorate of Archaeology and Museums, Mysore.

———, 1991b. "Mummadi Singa, Kampila and Kumara Rama", in *Vijayanagara Progress of Research 1987-88,* ed. D.V. Devaraj and C.S. Patil, pp. 179-98, Directorate of Archaeology and Museums, Mysore.

———, 1991c. "Kummata", in *Vijayanagara Progress of Research 1987-88,* ed. D.V. Devaraj and C.S. Patil, pp. 199-216, Directorate of Archaeology and Museums, Mysore.

———, 1992. *Temples of Raichur and Bellary Districts, Karnataka, 1000-1325 AD,* Directorate of Archaeology and Museums, Mysore.

———, 1996a. "Hosemaledurga", in *Vijayanagara: Progress of Research 1988-91,* ed. D.V. Devaraj and C.S. Patil, pp. 236-42, Directorate of Archaeology and Museums, Mysore.

———, 1996b. "Doravati", *Vijayanagara: Progress of Research 1988-91,* ed. D.V. Devaraj and C.S. Patil, pp. 243-7. Directorate of Archaeology and Museums, Mysore.

Patterson, W.A., K.J. Edwards, and D.J. Maguire. 1987. "Microscopic Charcoal as a Fossil Indicator of Fire", *Quaternary Science Reviews* 6: 3-23.

Phadtare, N.R. 2000, "Sharp Decrease in Summer Monsoon Strength 4000-3500 cal. Yr BP in the Central Himalaya Based on Pollen Evidence from Alpine Peat", *Quaternary Research* 53(1): 122-29.

Possehl, G.L. and P.C. Rissman. 1992. "The chronology of Prehistoric India: From Earliest Times to the Iron Age", in *Chronologies in Old World Archaeology,* vol. I, pp. 465-90, vol. II, pp. 447-74, University of Chicago Press, Chicago.

Prell W.L. and J.E. Kutzbach. 1992, "Sensitivity of the Indian Monsoon to Forcing Parameters and Implications for its Evolution", *Nature* 360: 647-52.

Raheja, G.G. 1998. *The Poison in the Gift: Ritual, Prestation, and the Dominant Caste in a North Indian Village,* University of Chicago Press, Chicago.

Randhawa, M.S. 1980. *A History of Agriculture in India,* Indian Council of Agricultural Research, New Delhi.

Ray, H.P. 1986. *Monastery and Guild: Commerce Under the Satavahanas,* Oxford University Press, Delhi.

———, 1994. *The Winds of Change: Buddhism and the Maritime Links of Early South Asia,* Oxford University Press, Delhi.

Richman Paula (ed.). 1991. *Many Ramayanas: The Diversity of a Narrative Tradition in South Asia,* Oxford University Press, Delhi.

———, 2000. *Questioning Ramayanas: A South Asian Tradition,* Oxford University Press, Delhi.

Robert, B.L. 1983. "Economic Change and Agrarian organization in 'Dry' South India 1890-1940: A Reinterpretation", *Modern Asian Studies,* 17(1): 59-78.

Saletore, B.A. 1934. *Social and Political Life in the Vijayanagara Empire (A.D. 1346-A.D. 1646)*, Paul and Company, Madras.

Sankar, P. 1982. "The Hero in Medieval and Modern Kannada Literature and Folk-Songs – A Glimpse", in *Memorial Stones: A Study of Their Origin, Significance and Variety,* ed. S. Settar and G.-D. Sontheimer, pp. 37-46, Institute of Indian Art History, Karnatak University and South Asia Institute, University of Heidelberg, Manipal.

Schroeder, P. 1993. "Editorial Introduction", in *Yaksas: Essays in the Water Cosmology,* ed. P. Schroeder, Indira Gandhi National Centre for the Arts and Oxford University Press, New Delhi.

Seneviratna, A. 1989. *The Springs of Sinhala Civilization: An Illustrated Survey of Ancient Irrigation Systems of Sri Lanka,* Navrang, New Delhi.

Settar, S. and G.-D. Sontheimer (eds.). 1982. *Memorial Stones: A Study of Their Origin, Significance and Variety,* Institute of Indian Art History, Karnatak University and South Asia Institute, University of Heidelberg, Manipal.

Settar, S. and H.B. Sunkad, 1982. "Vijayanagara Artists of Memorial Stones", in *Memorial Stones: A Study of Their Origin, Significance and Variety,* ed. S. Settar and G.-D. Sontheimer, pp. 339-346, Institute of Indian Art History, Karnatak University and South Asia Institute, University of Heidelberg, Manipal.

Sewell R. 1900. *A Forgotten Empire (Vijayanagar): A Contribution to the History of India,* Sonnenschein, London.

Sharma, R.K. and T.K. Sharma. 1990. *Textbook of Irrigation Engineering,* vol. I: *Irrigation and Drainage,* Oxford and IBH Publishing Co. Pvt. Ltd., New Delhi.

Shulman, D.D. 1985. *The King and the Clown in South Indian Myth and Poetry,* Princeton University Press, Princeton.

Singh. G., R.D. Joshi, S.K. Chopra and A.B. Singh. 1974. "Late Quaternary History of Vegetation and Climate in the Rajasthan Desert, India", *Philosophical Transactions of the Royal Society of London,* 267: 467-501.

Singh, G., R.J. Wasson and D.P. Agrawal. 1990. "Vegetational and Seasonal Climatic Changes since the Last Full Glacial in the Thar Desert, Northwestern India", *Review of Palaeobotany and Palynology,* 65: 351-8.

Singh, N.P. 1988. *The Flora of Eastern Karnataka,* Mittal, New Delhi.

Sinopoli, C.M. 1986. "The Organization of Craft Production at Vijayanagara, South India", *American Anthropologist* 90: 580-97.

———, 1993. *Pots and Palaces: The Earthenware Ceramics of the Noblemen's Quarter of Vijayanagara,* Manohar and American Institute of Indian Studies, New Delhi.

———, 2001. "On the Edge of Empire: Form and Substance in the Satavahana Dynasty", in *Empires: Perspectives from Archaeology and History,* pp. 155-78, ed. S. Alcock, T.N. D'Altroy, K.D. Morrison and C.M. Sinopoli, Cambridge University Press, Cambridge.

———, 2003. *The Political Economy of Craft Production: Crafting Empire in South India, c. 1350-1650,* Cambridge University Press, Cambridge.

Sinopoli, C.M. and K.D. Morrison. 1995. "Dimensions of Imperial Control: The Vijayanagara Capitol", *American Anthropologist,* 97: 83-96.

———, 2006a. "Land Use and Settlement in the Vijayanagara Metropolitan Region: Results of the Vijayanagara Metropolitan Survey", in *Recent Advances in Vijayanagara Studies: An Anthology,* ed. P. Shanmugam and S. Srinivasan, pp. 91-109, New Era, Madras.

———, 2006b. "The Vijayanagara Metropolitan Survey: Overview of the 1992 Season", in *Vijayanagara, Archaeological Exploration, 1990-2000: Papers in Memory of Channabasappa S. Patil,* ed. J.M. Fritz, T. Raczek and R. Brubaker, pp. 437-58, Manohar and AIIS, Delhi

———, in press. "The Regional Landscapes of the Imperial City of Vijayanagara: Report on the Vijayanagara Metropolitan Survey Project", in *South Asian Archaeology 1999,* ed. K.R. van Kooij and Ellen Raven, Egbert Forsten Publishing, Groningen.

Sircar, D.C. 1966. *Indian Epigraphical Glossary,* Motilal Banarsidass, Delhi.

Sirocko, F., M. Sarnthein, H. Erlenkeuser, M. Arnold and J.C. Duplessy. 1993. "Century-Scale Events in Monsoonal Climate over the Past 24,000 Years", *Nature* 364: 322-4.

Sivamohan, M.V.K. 1991. "Vijayanagar Channels: A Traditional Agricultural System in Transition", in *Farmers in the Management of Irrigation Systems,* ed. K.K. Singh, pp. 53-72, Sterling, New Delhi.

Soundara Rajan, K.V. 1994. *Kaveripattinam Excavations 1963-73 (A Port City on the Tamil Nadu Coast),* Memoirs of the Archaeological Survey of India No. 90, Archaeological Survey of India, New Delhi.

Stein, B. 1978. "Temples in Tamil Country, 1350-1750 A.D.", in *South Indian Temples,* ed. B. Stein, pp. 11-45, Vikas, New Delhi.

———, 1980. *Peasant State and Society in Medieval South India.* Oxford University Press, Delhi.

———, 1989a. *Vijayanagara,* The New Cambridge History of India, vol. 1, part 2. Cambridge University Press, Cambridge.

———, 1989b. *Thomas Munro: The Origins of the Colonial State and his Vision of Empire,* Delhi, Oxford University Press.

Stokes, Eric. 1978. *The Peasant and the Raj: Studies in Agrarian Society and Peasant Rebellion in Colonial India,* Cambridge University Press, Cambridge.

Subrahmanyam, R. 1975. *Nagarjunakonda (1954-60),* Memoirs of the Archaeological Survey of India No. 75, Archaeological Survey of India, New Delhi.

Subrahmanyam, S. 1998. "Introduction", in *Money and the Market in India 1100-1700,* ed. S. Subrahmanyam, pp. 1-56, Oxford University Press, Delhi.

Sugandhi, N. 2003. "Context, Content, and Composition: Questions of Intended Meaning and the Asokan Edicts", *Asian Perspectives,* 42(2): 224-46.

Sukumar, R., R. Ramesh, R.K. Pant and G. Rajagopalan. 1993. "A ^{13}C Record of Late Quaternary Change from tropical Peats in Southern India", *Nature,* 364: 703-5.

Sundara, A. 2001. "Menhirs in Karnataka and Andhra Pradesh", in *Sri Subrahmanya Smrti: Essays on Indian Pre-History, Proto-History, Archaeology, Iconography, Art, Architecture, Epigraphy, Numismatics, Crafts and Conservation (Dr. Raviprolu Subrahmanyam Commemoration Volume),* ed. I.K. Sarma and B. Vidyadhara Rao, Sundeep Prakashan, New Delhi.

Sutherland, G.H. 1991. *The Disguises of the Demon: The Development of the Yaksa in Hinduism and Buddhism,* State University of New York Press, Albany.

Thapar, R. 1997. *Asoka and the Decline of the Mauryas,* revd. edn. Oxford University Press, Delhi.

Tillotson, G.H.R. 1998. "Painting and Understanding Mughal Architecture", in *Paradigms of Indian Architecture: Space and Time in Representation and Design,* ed. G.H.R. Tillotson, pp. 59-79, Curzon Press, Collected Paper on South Asia No. 13, London.

Trigger, B.G. 1989. *A History of Archaeological Thought,* Cambridge University Press, Cambridge.

Van Campo, E. and F. Gasse. 1993. "Pollen and Diatom-inferred Climatic and Hydrological Changes in Sumxi Co Basin (Western Tibet) Since 13,000 Yr. B.P.", *Quaternary Research,* 39: 300-13.

Venkata Ramanayya, N. 1929. *Kampli and Vijayanagar,* Christian Literature Society, Madras.

———, 1990 [1933]. *Vijayanagara: Origin of the City and the Empire,* Asian Educational Services, New Delhi.

Verghese, A. 1995. *Religious Traditions at Vijayanagara, as Revealed Through its Monuments,* Vijayanagara Research Project Monograph Series Volume 4, Manohar and American Institute of Indian Studies, Delhi.

———, 2000. *Archaeology, Art, and Religion: New Perspectives on Vijayanagara,* Oxford University Press, Delhi.

Wagoner, P.B. 1991. "Architecture and Mythic Space at Hemakuta Hill: A Preliminary Report", in *Vijayanagara Progress of Research 1984-1987,* ed. D.V. Devaraj and C.S. Patil, pp. 142-8, Directorate of Archaeology and Museums, Mysore.

———, 1993. *Tidings of the King: A Translation and Ethnohistorical Analysis of the Rayavacakamu,* University of Hawaii Press, Honolulu.

———, 1995. "Modal Marking of Temple Types in Kakatiya Andhra: Toward a Theory of Decorum for Indian Temple Architecture", in *Syllables of Sky: Studies in South Indian Civilization in honor of Velcheru Narayana Rao,* ed. D. Shulman, pp. 431-72, Oxford University Press, Delhi.

———, 1996. "Sultan Among Hindu Kings: Dress, Titles, and the Islamicization of Hindu Culture at Vijayanagara", *Journal of Asian Studies,* 55(4): 851-80.

Washbrook, D. 1994. "The Commercialization of Agriculture in Colonial India: Production, Subsistence and Reproduction in the 'Dry South', c. 1870-1930", *Modern Asian Studies,* 28(1): 129-64.

Wheeler R.E.M. 1947. "Brahmagiri and Chandravalli 1947: Megalithic and Other Cultures in the Chitaldurg District, Mysore State", *Ancient India,* 4: 181-309.

———, 1954. *Archaeology from the Earth,* Penguin, Baltimore.

Willis, J.D. 1992. "Female Patronage in Indian Buddhism", in *The Powers of Art: Patronage in Indian Culture,* ed. B.S. Miller, pp. 46-53, Oxford University Press, Delhi.

Wilson, W. 1884. *Annual Report of the Department of Revenue Settlement and Agriculture for 1882-83,* Government Press, Madras.

Yule, H. 1903. *Hobson-Jobson: A Glossary of Colloquial Anglo-Indian Words and Phrases, and of Kindred Terms, Etymological, Historical, Geographical and Discursive,* new edn., ed. William Crooke, B.A. London: J. Murray.

Zagarell, A. 2002. "Gender and Social Organization in the Reliefs of the Nilgiri Hills", in *Forager-Traders in South and Southeast Asia: Long-Term Histories,* ed. K.D. Morrison and L.L. Junker, pp. 77-104, Cambridge University Press, Cambridge.

Zeuner, F.E. 1959. "On the Origin of the Cinder Mounds of the Bellary District", *Bulletin of the Institute of Archaeology,* 1: 37-44.

Zimmer, H. 1974. *Myths and Symbols in Indian Art and Civilization,* ed. J. Campbell, Bollingen Series VI, Princeton University Press, Princeton.